CAPTIVE

— TO —

THE WORD OF

GOD

A PARTICULAR BAPTIST PERSPECTIVE
ON REFORMED AND COVENANT THEOLOGY

By

Stuart L. Brogden

2016

PUBLISHED *by* PARABLES
Earthly Stories with a Heavenly Meaning

As we live in times of enormous dysfunction, disagreement, and even disunion in local gatherings professing to have faith in Jesus Christ, Stuart Brogden's voice rises in the wilderness as a servant and workman of Christ who, by God's grace and in His providence, has been made manifest among us. Although his message is couched in a Particular Baptist perspective, the underlying theme of his treatise is found in the main title of his book: *Captive to the Word of God*. A thorough and thoughtful passion for God's Word has always been needed by the Christian believer, and today, more than ever. Too many, these days, are departing from their First Love, Jesus Christ, because they have divorced who He is and what He has done from what has been written of Him from Genesis to Revelation. Whether you identify with Baptists or not, Stuart Brogden provokes us to love God's Word unto loving Christ... and loving Christ and His holy Word as much as a sinner saved by grace is able, by God's grace.

— Jon J. Cardwell, pastor of Sovereign Grace Baptist Church, Anniston, Alabama and author of *Christ and Him Crucified*

Stuart Brogden's excellent work, subtitled, *A Particular Baptist Perspective on Reformed and Covenant Theology*, is not only rich in church history, but also in theological substance. Mr. Brogden details the Baptist view of Reformed and Covenant Theology in a scholarly and authoritative manner. Without a doubt, this work should be considered a necessary addition to any serious theological student's study library, as well as a wonderful resource for any pastor, teacher, or professor.

— Rev. Jeff Canfield, D. Min., Pastor at Word of Life Church, Sullivan, Indiana and author of *A Call to Honor* and *When Church and Government Collide*

Eliza Spurgeon told her son: "I have often prayed for your conversion, but I never thought you would become a Baptist." With his quick wit, the young Charles responded: "Mother, that shows you that God has not only answered your prayers, but has done exceeding abundantly above all you asked or thought." Like Charles Spurgeon, I am joyful to be a Baptist but concerned we have lost sight of what it means to be a Baptist. With confessions of faith being stored in the attic as archaic relics of the past, it is no wonder that the labels defining denominational distinctives are being dropped from churches' names. To recover the Baptist name, it is vital that we recover the historic Baptist distinctives. For this reason I cannot recommend *Captive to the Word of God* enough. Stuart Brogden covers all the major components of the Baptist faith and traces every doctrinal tenant back to the Scriptures. Above everything else, Brogden explains why Baptists are called "people of the book." In my opinion, this helpful work needs to be required reading for all

Baptist seminary students. In fact, everyone who wants to know what it means to be a Baptist should read this book. Since I love the historic Baptist faith, I love this book.

—Jeffrey D. Johnson, pastor at Grace Baptist Church, Conway, Arkansas and author of *The Fatal Flaw of the Theology Behind Infant Baptism*

Captive to the Word of God

A Particular Baptist Perspective on Reformed and Covenant Theology

Appendix 1: Guidance for Deacon Ministry. Suggested guidance for the proper utilization of those called to serve as deacons in the local church.

Appendix 2: A Comparison Between Arminianism and Calvinism. A side-by-side comparison of the Arminian remonstrance and the ruling of the Council of Dort.

Appendix 3: The Forgotten Confession. The First London Baptist Confession, with Benjamin Cox's appendix incorporated.

Appendix 4: The Impact of Unexamined Presuppositions. An Examination of Richard Barcellos' Defense of the paedobaptist view of 1 Timothy 1:8-11.

Appendix 5: Salvation is of the Lord! Scripture that demonstrate the biblical truths of election and predestination.

Appendix 6: Comparison of Old and New Covenants. A tabular comparison detailing the many differences between these covenants, eliminating the idea that they are one.

Acknowledgments

It has long been recognized as truth, that no man is an island. Certainly in the realm of accumulated knowledge every one of us has benefited from the countless men and women with whom we've come in contact with, even if by nothing more personal than the printed page. As good as our minds are at adopting ideas, each of us arrives at a given point in life having learned from many people that we no longer recall nor connect to what we have learned. Of all the books I have read and the people I have met that have been used of God to sanctify and equip me, no doubt I am forgetful of many of them. The older I get the more I realize this: that I can claim no idea as mine, for there truly is *nothing new under the sun*, just as the ancient preacher declared.

But there are some men and books that *do* stand out as having made a big impression; and it is our duty as saints to thank God in all circumstances; knowing that even what we think is bad, God means it for our good and His glory. And so right off the bat, I must thank our Lord for Rick Warren. From the first I heard of this man and his work, I was amazed at the influence he had; not just in Baptist circles but in ever-enlarging arenas around the world. As I read his books and saw the impact his work was having in Houston churches, including the one I belonged to, I wept with sorrow as I recognized the Pelagian pragmatism that pervaded virtually everything he put his hand to. Each of Warren's *Purpose-Driven* books opens with a good statement ("It's not about you", and "Only God can build a church") and each book then fills 400-odd pages teaching how Warren's god is "you-focused," describing how Warren's church was built by a man who blamed God for his efforts. Why am I thankful for this? YHWH used Warren to shake me awake from a near-sleep and renew in me a desire to know Him through the study and application of His Word, recognizing that everything man does has sin in it and must be tested in light of Scripture (this book included). One friend and defender of Rick Warren condescendingly told me I would better understand Warren's perspective if I were to study church history. Ah, how sweet this has turned out to be: to see how the Lord God of Heaven has preserved His remnant in each and every generation, as His redeemed saints cling to His Word imperfectly and refuse to bow to whichever false religion was ruling the day, demanding the worship of the people.

Rather than bringing me to embrace Rick Warren, the study of Scripture and church history have shown me more and more how great the Creator of all things is and how desperately we as sinful creatures need Him for life and godliness. This study also impressed on me the underlying truth of the importance of being Baptist, in the historical sense; those who were called "people of the Book" by others. If Christians are not people of the Book, we must be willing to repent and turn our affections and attentions back to the Lord's Scriptures. We must be disciples of Christ, not merely disciples of any mere man.

So I am thankful to God and acknowledge His hand of providence in my life as He has brought myriad men and books to my attention, even those I disagreed with and came to see as warnings more than instruction. As I was introduced to the doctrines of grace and realized how wonderful it was to see the redemptive story played out in the Old and New Testaments, I realized the Scriptures had a far deeper meaning than casual reading of the sacred texts could reveal. My need for other godly men to help me grasp the timeless truths became more and more clear. Some men invited me to study with and serve under them as they taught about right worship, preaching, and home life. The elders of Grace family Baptist Church (GfBC) in Spring, Texas will always have a special place in my heart, as they were used by God to deepen my faith and see the Lord more clearly. The time I spent as Man Friday to Voddie Baucham was a year of wonder as I saw the Lord at work in people across this country, Canada, Romania, Denmark, and Sweden. I saw how our King was using this man I was blessed to have as my pastor counsel people and preach to those who hate reformed theology, but loved hearing it from this big, congenial, black preacher. I saw how the gospel would draw some people to faith in Christ while repelling others. I experienced the love of God in Christ in every church we went to, as His people were drawn together to hear deep truths presented well.

Others demonstrated a love for God's Word more than their love for men, willing to step out in faith with a desire to preach the Word and shepherd God's flock. Louis Lyons has demonstrated that pastor's heart and been a great encourager and teacher to me as he deliberately sought out his calling to preach and serve, putting more flesh on the image painted in the biblical portraits of those called to serve in that capacity.

And the books! After joining GfBC I was immersed into the world of Reformed Theology, with much of the view of covenants being informed and founded upon the basic view espoused by the Westminster Confession of Faith. I read, studied and taught the 1689 London Baptist Confession and saw it had much the same view of the Mosaic Covenant as taught by the WCF; and I wondered how this could be. Then I found a book that shook me with some simple explanations from Scripture on the covenants. Jeff Johnson's *The Fatal Flaw of the Theology of Infant Baptism* exposed the flawed foundation of paedobaptism, but more importantly, it explained the dichotomist nature of the covenant given unto Abraham as clearly presented by the Apostle Paul in Galatians 4. This whetted my appetite for more Baptist writings on the covenants, which is part of the impetus behind my collecting and publishing (via the Internet and DVD and flash drive distribution) a digital library of mostly Baptist books and articles; my effort to equip and build up my Baptist brothers and sisters. While our Presbyterian brothers have written far more books, there is no shortage of solid, well written books by Baptists, explaining our view on covenants and other doctrines. Books and commentaries by John Gill, John Bunyan, John Spilsbery, Benjamin Keach, Nehemiah Coxe, Thomas Patient, and others too numerous to name here have been eye-opening and Christ-exalting; all showing that Baptists have a rich heritage of being used by God to proclaim His glories to a watching world.

Some men have been good friends who have encouraged me and claim to have learned from me. That the Lord of Heaven would use such a wretch as me continues to astound and humble me. I will cherish the friendship of Andy Wolfskill, Ron Barth, Randy Spear, and others because of the time we've spent together searching out deeper truths from God's Word. There are few things in this age more dear to the Christian than having close friends with whom all matters of life and faith can be vigorously discussed, with the aim of reforming to the Word of God.

And what a wreck I would be without the dear woman our Lord gave me as my wife when I was a young man, so long ago. I could write a book describing the countless ways she has been used of God to encourage me, pray for me, rebuke me, stand with me when I deserved anger, and more. Joan didn't want to be a pastor's wife but she supported me when I was called to that office. And when free-will deacons ran me out, she encouraged me to put my efforts into writing a book, since I was no longer preparing sermons. And she has given us two wonderful children, now grown and walking with the Lord. A man has no greater joy than to see his children walk in grace! Our daughter Carole is married to wonderful young man, Grant, for whom we very thankful; our son, Brad, has been faithful to the church plant he joined more than a decade earlier and recently married to Leah, a dear young Christian lady he met at that church, both giving us grandchildren. We have more to give thank for than we can wrap our minds around.

I am, from what I can see, the most indebted man alive. So many have given so much. And I am no more worthy of their love than I am for that lavished upon me by the Shepherd of my soul, without Whom none of this would matter. For by Him and through Him and for Him were all things created and in Him all things are held together. Who are we, *who am I*, to say I have anything other than what He has given to us, to me? To God alone be all glory and honor and power and dominion, now and forever!

Introduction

April 18th, 1521. Martin Luther was on trial for believing the Scriptures were the ultimate authority for the Christian, rather than dogma developed by men. He is quoted as having said, "My conscience is captive to the Word of God" when asked to recant his writings. I've taken part of Luther's statement as my title because while I am thankful to God for myriad men in the Reformed Baptist world that have taught me much, I cannot claim full allegiance to a document written in the 17th century; it being *mostly* right. The Word of God – alone! – demands and warrants our full allegiance. While we have disagreements, let Holy Writ be our foundation and wisdom as we *test all things and hold to that which is good.*

For most of the time since the Reformation, terms and theology connected with reformed theology have been largely defined by Presbyterians. Early Baptists who held to the battle cry of the Reformation were known as particular Baptists, to differentiate them from Baptists who held to general atonement. Baptists were not seeking commonality with the Presbyterians until late in the 17th century when they sought a way to make peace with the state church and government in England, weary of being persecuted. There has been much activity in the last few decades by Baptists who have claimed "reformed" as a legitimate label. With this renewed and much welcomed interest in reformed theology by Baptists there came a growing consumption of reformed writings, and Baptists were influenced by varying degrees by the theology and presuppositions of our Presbyterian brothers, as their works on theology were far more abundant and available than what Baptists had written. This illustrates why we must recognize that every man, including you and me and each of those Baptists who came before us, is "trapped" in his own context of culture, custom, and language. This is why those who were closest in time to the escape from Rome clung to practices learned from Rome more than those who came later. This should remind us to humbly examine what others have written and use the same hermeneutic principles we use in studying Scripture as we read theology. Otherwise, we are apt to be misled, as man is so naturally inclined.

Why anyone would pick up a book about being Baptist and reformed by an unknown man with little experience as a pastor and none as an author? It is true that, even in Christian circles, human authors are often revered too much. Dare this unknown man raise the question of whether the status of the author being well loved by many is the most important aspect of a book? Far too many Christians have become disciples of their favorite author, many of whom suffer from the pressure of expectations to write something new every few months or years, which helps explain the plethora of Christian books; most of which are best left unread. The fact remains: everything man puts his hands to is twisted a bit by the sin in the man. Any good in any work a man does, be it a ditch or a book, is good only because the Spirit of God abides in him and prompts him and enables him to do good. So this book does not come to you on the reputation of the man whose name it bears. If there be anything good herein, know that it comes from the Lord of all and will align with the Scriptures He has condescended to give us. Whatever error lies in these pages is mine alone.

This book is a labor of love that has been stirred up in my soul by the Lord of all as I have read and studied many volumes on each of the main topics discussed herein and experienced much of them. And this book would have been left unwritten if my dear wife of more than three decades had not suggested I write a book. She has been an encouragement and sister in Christ who reminds me of what is important and loves me biblically.

There have been a great many books written over the years on theology, Baptist distinctives, and the use of confessions (see bibliography for complete list of books referenced herein). I am thankful to God for bringing a few exceptional books to my attention that have been of great help to me in working through these issues. I highly recommend these few books to anyone seeking a more biblical and historically accurate understanding of reformed theology and Baptist distinctives:

> *The Fatal Flaw of the Theology Behind Infant Baptism* – Jeffery D. Johnson
> *The Church, Why Bother?* – Jeffrey D. Johnson
> *The Distinctiveness of Baptist Covenant Theology* – Pascal Denault
> *The The Sabbath Complete: And the Ascendency of First-Day Worship* – Terrence D. O'Hare
> *The Rickety Bridge and the Broken Mirror* – Hal Brunson
> *Tablets of Stone* – John G. Reisinger
> *The Priesthood of All Believers* – David H.J. Gay

None of these books, or any others, would be of any use to the student of theology if they were not based on solid exegesis of Scripture and understanding of historical context. Each of these books provides keen insight into one or more topics that are covered in this one. While I will attempt to annotate each quote I use, know that many thoughts I put down were formed and informed by these books, and others, as the Lord deepened my understanding of His Word and awe of His person.

This book is not intended to be a complete apologetic or theological argument for any of the positions advocated. It is my intention to provide a concise summary on each topic, based on my study of the Scriptures and the work of those who have gone before me. It is focused on the theology and history of Particular Baptists, not the entire Baptist world. After most chapters I have listed a short reading list to point the reader to a few books that will go deeper into the subject presented. In each reading list and the main bibliography, books that are available in digital format in a Baptist library I maintain are indicated with an asterisk. That library is available online at http://reformedbaptistlibrary.tk/ and I will send a copy of the latest version to most anyone who asks.

May all who name the name of Jesus never be content with what he knows at a given time, but remember the words of our Lord through the Apostle Peter: *make every effort to supplement our faith with virtue, and virtue with knowledge, and knowledge with self-control, and self-control with steadfastness, and steadfastness with godliness, and godliness with brotherly affection, and brotherly affection with love.* Grace and knowledge go hand in hand, as Peter went on to say, **But grow in the grace and knowledge of our Lord and Savior Jesus Christ. To him be the glory both now and to the day of eternity. Amen.**

My goal in writing this is to examine my own beliefs, strengthen my fellow Baptists, provoke fellow Christians to think biblically, and be a faithful steward of all the Lord has given me. My goal in life is to serve our God for the glory of His name and the good of His people, and to be remembered by my family and our God. May all who have benefited from anything I have said or done forget my name; may it be the name of the Lord Jesus that is remembered. A more excellent way to sum this up was written by an 18th century pastor, William Mason in his booklet, *The Believer's Pocket Companion*:

> *The design of my writings is to stir up and quicken the Lord's children in the way of . . .*
> *greater trust in Christ,*
> *more intense looking to Christ,*
> *greater dependence upon Him,*
> *and more consistent abiding in Him*
> *-   so that they may . . .*
> *enjoy more sweet fellowship with Him,*
> *find more of the His inestimable preciousness,*
> *and experience more of His wonderful love, which surpasses knowledge.*

Amen and amen!

Part 1: The Baptists

As we examine distinctives that mark people as Baptists, we must bear in mind that the label "Baptist" is secondary. Being true to biblical principles and precepts is essential. The label "Baptist" *reflects* who we are, it does not *determine* who we are. There are several doctrinal teachings Baptists have historically held that mark us as Baptist. Some divide these up into as many as eight points, but the essential Baptist distinctives can be summed up in the four categories examined below: Ordinances, The Nature of the Local Church, Liberty of Conscience, and View of Scripture. It is my experience that, other than baptism, we are not well informed as to what it means to be Baptist. And even with baptism, I believe we will see there is more to it than most of us have considered. First, we will look at the name and how we got it.

Chapter 1 - The Name: When Were We First Called "Baptists"?

In the 1500s and 1600s, *Anabaptist* was widely used as a label for all sorts of religious groups that did not submit to the state churches, both in England and on the European continent. This label means "re-baptizing" and was first used to describe those varied groups who properly realized that infant baptism is no baptism at all and required professing Christians to be baptized even if they had been sprinkled as infants. Those called Anabaptist included groups that eventually gave birth to such as Mennonites and Unitarians. Far from being a homogeneous group of people, the folk called Anabaptist were varied in their theology, ecclesiology, and doctrine. Sam Storms categorizes Anabaptists into three theological groups:

> (1) Revolutionary Anabaptists, who worked to establish an OT theocracy. These, of course, would be the more radical Anabaptists who gathered at Munster. (2) Contemplative Anabaptists, who emphasized the inner word and tended toward mysticism. John Denck, an anti-Trinitarian, was chief among their leaders. (3) Evangelical Anabaptists, among whom were Hubmaier, Grebel and Blaurock, who stressed simplicity of life, strict adherence to the ethical teachings of Jesus, pacifism, and rigid separation from the world.[1]

These theological differences evidenced themselves in various forms of worship, church structure, and relationship with others. This is easy to imagine if one meditates for even a short time on terms such as "revolutionary", "pacifism", "inner word", "rigid separation;" terms now long associated with Quakers, Mennonites, and others on the theological fringe. These theological categories are largely true, but not comprehensive. There were some Anabaptists who held to what were later identified as Baptist distinctives, not easily classified into any of the three groups Storms identified. To further complicate the neat classification of these people, one historian observed, "The great majority of them were peaceable folk, law-abiding people, asking nothing but that they might be permitted to worship and serve God in their own way, and wishing no harm to those who held to different ways."[2] That author, Henry Clay Vedder, goes on to explain that Anabaptists, in general, had a view of the body of Christ that was biblical and at odds with the state church. They saw the church as being comprised only of those who have been raised from spiritual death to new life in Christ. They held to a line of separation between church and state, maintaining that civil magistrates had nothing to do with matters of religion but had responsibility for law and order.[3] Vedder also points out that Anabaptists agreed on "the supremacy of the Scriptures as a rule of faith and practice."[4] Some of the criticisms of "inner light" or "inner word" mysticism are due to the failure of historians to recognize the biblical truth that every Christian has the Spirit of God indwelling him, illuminating Scripture for him. Vedder explains, "Though we may trace some likeness here between their teaching and the doctrines of the earlier Montanists and the later Friends, we miss altogether that exaggerated notion of an inner light of the Spirit which is superior in authority to the external word. This inner light, according to the Anabaptist, is bestowed not to supersede the written word, but to make it possible for the humblest believer to understand and follow that word."[5] That idea, that every Christian is indwelt by the Spirit of God Who illuminates our understanding of the Scriptures is a truth fundamental to the Christian faith. No historian, including Vedder, claims the Anabaptists were without theological errors. Storms' criticism of the Anabaptists is based on a narrow set of historical facts. There were some, a minority, who, as Vedder admits, "were seditious, turbulent, fomenters of social revolution, and therefore dangerous subjects, potential rebels even when not in actual rebellion."[6] As is true in our day, a few radicals can easily be used to broadly paint a larger group, giving a false but compelling picture.

Another point is brought to mind: history, unlike math, is comprised of the subjective opinions and observations of sinful men; all of whom, like you and I, have error in what we say and do. This is why it is vital for Christians to read widely, and not stay in a rut of reading only what aligns with one's beliefs. To *grow in grace and knowledge*, as the Word commands us, requires each of us to resist the temptation to seek only confirmation of our beliefs. We are to test everything, including our personal presuppositions, to see if they align with Scripture. We must let go of any doctrine or theological belief if clear teaching from the Bible shows it to be error.

As harassment and persecution from state churches on each side of the English Channel waxed and waned, people called Anabaptists traveled between the continent and the island seeking relief and fellowship with like-minded Christians. Several groups emerged, some known as General Baptists, others as Particular Baptists.[7] Each of these groups was influenced to some degree by those who were known as Anabaptists and were looking for like-minded brothers. These factors, documented in various history books such as *Bye-paths in Baptist history*, by Joseph Jackson Goadby; *The Baptists*, by Henry Clay Vedder; and *Persecution for Religion Judged and Condemned*, by John Murton, mean that we must admit that English Particular Baptists cannot be proven to have a pure line descending from the Puritans, as some claim. Nor do Baptists have a pure Anabaptist heritage as other claim. History is not so neatly summarized. These people continued to influence one another, as the distinctions between the two groups of Baptists were clarified and each declared their own beliefs as truth and pronounced the other group as heretics. There is striking evidence that implies a direct influence of the Anabaptists on the early Particular Baptists. Menno Simons' *Foundation-Book* was widely available in Europe, having been published multiple times from 1539 – 1616. This book's emphasis on discipleship, repentance, faith, baptism, the Lord's Supper, and other doctrines are very much aligned with Particular Baptist views. In comparing Simon's book to the 1644 London Baptist Confession, Stassen says, "The section on baptism is even more striking in its similarity to the core of the Baptist pattern. The emphases are almost identical. The order of their presentation is almost identical. The Scripture passages which are mentioned are almost identical. ... Each aspect of the Baptist pattern appears, and the sequence is identical: The ordinance of the Lord, hearing, believing, professing faith, discipleship, death, burial, and resurrection with Christ. The Scripture Menno quotes is the same Scripture which the Baptists quote."[8] While a causal relationship between the Anabaptists and the early Particular Baptists cannot be proved, no reasonable person would rule out all influence of one group on the other.

Both groups of Baptists took measures to describe themselves to the state in order to distance themselves from the factions that posed a threat to the state and its church (this will be explored in some detail in Part 2 of this book). This was complicated by the participation of some Baptists in the reactionary 5th Monarchy movement of the mid-17th century. This was a group that wished to install a "Christian government" over all England, and had some brief success with Cromwell. These few caused problems for the majority of Baptists, making their denial of being a threat to the state suspect. This emboldened those who wanted to eliminate credo-baptists for theological reasons. "The Baptists argued that the Church of God should be a community of godly men; that faith is the gift of God, and not to be compelled by force of arms; that only those rites sanctioned or commanded by Christ and His Apostles are binding upon His people; and that the only Lawgiver of the Church is Christ Himself. Each party [Roman Catholics, Anglicans, and Presbyterians] had, therefore, its own reason for hating the Baptists; and as each had yet to learn the true nature of religious freedom, each oppressed and persecuted in turn."[9] Baptists protested that they were not Anabaptists, because they did not see baptizing believers who had been sprinkled as infants as re-baptizing and because they did not want the radical, anti-state label hung on them as earned by some Anabaptist and 5th Monarchy activists. It appears that after some time of such protests, in answer to the inevitable question, "If you're not Anabaptists, what are you?"[10] the name "Baptist" emerged.

The manner and meaning of baptism has been, from the earliest times, a distinctive doctrine and practice that has divided people. We are called Baptists because we see the importance of practicing believer's baptism, by immersion; the only baptism found in Scripture. This alludes to the long-time description of Baptists as "people of the Book." We have most always been a people who know the importance of clinging to the truths God has revealed to us in holy writ. To depart from His special revelation, the Bible, means we rely on our wisdom; and of that we find no approval in God's Holy Scriptures.

There are some who hold to various views of successionism, which claims that Baptists have existed since the time of Jesus, often pointing to John the Baptist as our "father." History does not bear this out, John's label notwithstanding. He had that label because of his main mission as the last prophet, baptizing for repentance and faith in the Lamb of God who takes away the sin of the world (Luke 3:3-9 and John 1:29). There is no evidence he started a denomination. It has been observed that Baptists who try to prove an unbroken lineage with John the Baptist have something in common with Roman Catholics who insist on an unbroken lineage with Peter as the first pope. Both groups lose sight of the only man who matters in history; the God-Man, Jesus Christ. In their vain efforts to put stock in their fleshly connections with men from ancient time they are much like the first century Jews who clung to their status of being Abraham's natural offspring. What *is* true is that we find in Scripture and in history credible accounts of people who held to certain distinctive doctrines that, when Baptists emerged from the chaos of the Reformation, were true of Baptists. But until the early 1600s, history knows nothing about a people calling themselves Baptists. When we see historical records of Christians holding to a few key doctrines, we see brothers and sisters struggling against the spirit of the age to be true to the Scriptures – to be people of the Book.

> Baptist growth has always been in proportion to the staunchness with which Baptist principles have been upheld and practised. So it ever has been with all religious bodies. Nothing is gained by smoothing off the edges of truth and toning down its colors, so that its contrast with error may be as slight as possible. On the contrary, let the edges remain a bit rough, let the colors be heightened, so that the world cannot possibly mistake the one for the other, and the prospect of the truth gaining acceptance, is greatly increased. The history of every religious denomination teaches the same lesson: progress depends on loyalty to truth. Compromise always means decay.[11]

True success for the local church will be gained by holding tight to the Word of God, not toning down its colors, not smoothing off the edges of truth, so the world cannot mistake a false gospel for the "real thing." *This* is how Baptists earned the label as "people of the Book", and *that's* why being Baptist matters.

Recommended reading on this topic:
*Baptist - Why and Why Not** – James Frost
*Balthasar Hübmaier: the Leader of the Anabaptists** – Henry Clay Vedder
*Bye-paths in Baptist History** – Joseph Goadby
*A Short History of the Baptists** – Henry Clay Vedder
*The Baptists** – Henry Clay Vedder
*The Political Activities of the Baptists and Fifth Monarchy men in England during the Interregnum** – Louise Fargo Brown
*Baptists, The Only Thorough Reformers** – John Quincy Adams
*Facts for Baptist Churches** – Andrew T. Foss
Baptists and the Bible – L. Russ Bush

Chapter 2 – Ordinances: The Gospel Displayed.

Called sacraments by some, ordinances are those acts of worship that have special significance to life in the church. Baptists see in Scripture two ordinances, baptism and the Lord's Supper, both of which are considered by many to be "ordinary means of grace" given to by God, Who is the God over ends and means. By this, we mean that He determines the results as well as the methods of gaining the results. This may be most graphic in the life of Joseph in the book of Genesis. All the trouble that Joseph experienced was providentially provided by God for His glory and the good of His people. God provided the means through which the end He desired, the preservation of the promised seed, would be delivered. All of creation primarily exists to glorify the Creator (Psalms 16:1). This is the motivation, and the priority, for *everything* that happens in time and eternity. Joseph learned this the hard way; we can learn it from God's Word, through the illumination of His Spirit. This puts the term, means of grace, into context. He has given us things – prayer, worship, Bible reading, and ordinances, etc. – all designed to bring glory to His name and do good to His people. They are important because of Who has given them to us and why He has done so. We are never to get the Giver confused with the gifts and end up worshiping the gifts.

Baptism: the History, Mode, Candidates, and Significance. Baptism is the best-known Baptist distinctive, although *why* it is significant is often not well understood. We will quickly look at three aspects of baptism, which will demonstrate why people have misunderstood and fought about it and why it is significant. Books have written about each of these points; this will be a brief summary.

1. The History. The overwhelming majority of religious groups that claim the name of Christ "baptize" babies, including Roman Catholics, Eastern and Oriental Orthodox, Anglicans, Lutherans, Presbyterians, Methodists, some Nazarenes, the United Church of Christ (UCC), Moravian Church, Wesleyans, and Episcopalians. There are those who believe baptism is salvific: Church of Christ, Disciples of Christ, and those who hold to Federal Vision. We Baptists baptize believers, by submersion, as a testimony; we're in the minority.

For Baptists to rightly be called "people of the book", our claim to being among those who stand on the sure foundation of Scripture and under the authority of Scripture is crucial. May this be true of us, as many wise sounding arguments have been marshaled in support of the opposing view of baptism. I do not want to spend much time explaining why the paedobaptist view on baptism is wrong, I will appeal to a few of their finest theologians to tell us they are wrong.

> John Calvin: "John and Christ administered baptism *totins corpore submersione*, by the submission of the whole body[1] ... The very word 'baptize' ... signifies to immerse entirely, and it is certain that immersion was the practice of the ancient church.[2]" ([1]Calvin's commentary on Matthew 3:12-13, [2] *Institutes of the Christian Religion*, V 2, 491)

Martin Luther: "The Greek word baptizo means 'immerse' or 'plunge', and the word baptisma means immersion." (*Martin Luther: Selection From His Writings*. "Babylonian Captivity of the Church," edited by John Dillenberger, Anchor Books, 1962, pp. 298, 302)

Ulrich Zwingli: "Immersion of the whole body was used from the beginning, which expresses the force of the word 'baptize', whence John baptized in the river. It was afterward changed into sprinkling, though it is uncertain when or by whom." (*panstrat. Cathol., tom.* Iv, l. v, chii, 6))

And the great B.B.Warfield: "It is true that there is no express command to baptize infants in the New Testament, no express record of the baptism of infants, and no passages so stringently implying it that we must infer from them that infants were baptized." (*Studies in Theology*, 399) [1]

There are other paedobaptists who agree with them, but these four giants of the Reformation and the development of Presbyterian theology unabashedly tell us their position is not based on the Scriptures. These and others whose doctrines are not found in Scripture are what I call "white space theologians." We should humbly examine doctrines we tightly cling to, to seek honestly whether or not we comply with God's Holy Word.

If believer's baptism is what the Bible teaches, why and when did people start "baptizing" babies? In the 3rd century some became convinced that baptism was meritorious and had a magical power to help save the soul. At first, people only baptized (by immersion) infants who were sick, as an insurance policy. Soon thereafter, all infants were baptized for their spiritual health; and sprinkling was soon adopted for their physical health. Church men began to argue over when the infant should be "baptized;" right away, or on the 8th day, or delayed as long as possible so that more sins would be covered.[2] Lack of knowledge and trust in the Word of God leads men astray, to trust in the imaginations of men.

When Christianity was legalized, the church, already suffering from an unhealthy view of "holy clergy," saw infant baptism as an effective way to number the people so they could be taxed and controlled.[3] And to convince the ignorant masses, these compromised churchmen played up the false notion that baptism plays a part in saving one's soul. This is called Sacerdotalism, using a sacrament (a religious rite) as a means of conveying God's favor to the people. When the Reformation broke out, some were called Magisterial Reformers; they maintained the close connection between church and state magistrates. One of these, Zwingli, was stuck between his belief that the Bible commends believer's baptism and his practice of infant baptism. He is said to have feared the loss of influence if he abandoned infant baptism, so he persecuted those who did not practice what the state commanded.

Such is the power of our presuppositions and the influence of the culture and traditions that pull at each of us and has ruined many a man.

In the early 17th century, the Puritans fled Europe in search of religious liberty. They had been persecuted because they believed in salvation by grace alone, through faith alone in Christ alone while the state church held to a sacerdotal view. Yet they, like Zwingli, failed to escape the trap they fled – they brought it with them, just like Lot did when he fled Zoar (Genesis 19:30-38). Baptists, who also fled to the New World to escape religious persecution, found it in the new country. The Puritans had established state churches in the colonies and they persecuted those who did not agree with their religious views; just like the Church of England which persecuted them. Our theology affects how we think and live, just as it did these Puritans and these Baptists.

In his book, *Baptists, the Only Thorough Reformers*, John Quincy Adams (not the President) noted these circumstances:

> In Virginia, where the first permanent colony in America was established, the charter bearing date 1606, fourteen years before the Pilgrims landed at Plymouth, Baptists were bitterly persecuted. By law, a fine of two thousand pounds of tobacco was imposed on "those who neglected to have their infants baptized." Baptist ministers were arrested and imprisoned as vagrants; some were pulled down from the stand as they were preaching, insulted and whipped, and many were imprisoned for preaching the Gospel. Elders John Waller, Lewis Craig, and James Childs were seized at a meeting, June 4, 1768, dragged before the magistrate, and imprisoned for forty-three days in Fredericksburg. Mr. Wofford was severely scourged, and carried the scars to his grave.
>
> Dr. Hawks, historian of the Episcopal Church of Virginia, says: "No dissenters in Virginia experienced harsher treatment than did the Baptists. They were beaten and imprisoned, and cruelty taxed its ingenuity to devise new modes of punishment and annoyance."[4]

Many books and papers have been written on this topic of the meaning and consequences of one's view of baptism, from such as John Gill, Isaac Watts, and John Splisbery. I highly recommend Jeff Johnson's *The Fatal Flaw of the Theology Behind Infant Baptism* to anyone who wants a clear and biblically sound explanation of this topic from a theological basis. This is theological issue, not merely an ecclesiastical one. We need to have theology that leads us to speak and act like these Baptists of old, as did the Apostles and disciples; and not hold to faulty theology that leads us to persecute those with whom we disagree.

2. The Mode. How is baptism administered? It ought not to be contested as the only mode found in Scripture is immersion. All we see, beginning with the baptism of our Lord Jesus (Matthew 3:13-17), is clearly the manner of immersion: being dipped or plunged beneath the water. There is not an exception to this mode and there are many examples of it. Consider the eunuch with Philip (Acts 8:34-39), they went down into the water and came back up. If sprinkling was the mode, there was undoubtedly drinking water in the chariot that would have been plenty. They stopped at a river and went down into the water.

Here's how the Particular Baptists described the manner of baptism in the First London Baptist Confession of 1644, article 39 (see Appendix 3 for the complete confession):

> That the way and manner of the dispensing this ordinance, is dipping or plunging the body under water; it being a sign, must answer the things signified, which is, that interest the Saints have in the death, burial, and resurrection of Christ: And that as certainly as the body is buried under water, & risen again, so certainly shall the bodies of the Saints be raised by the power of Christ, in the day of the resurrection to reign with Christ.
>
> Matt. 26:16; Mark 15:9, reads [into Jordan] in Greek John 3:23; Acts 8:38; Rev. 1:5; & 7:14; with Hebrews 10:22; Rom. 6:3, 4, 5, 6; I Cor. 15:28, 29;
>
> The word Baptism signifies to dip or plunge, yet so as convenient Garments be both upon the Administrator and subject with all modesty, which is also our practice, as many eye witnesses can testify.

That last comment about garments being used, "subject with all modesty", was added because myriad paedobaptists accused Baptists of being naked during the performance of the baptism ordinance in attempts to smear them.

John Clark observed, in his short essay, "Defense of Credo-Baptism:"

> That this appointment of Christ is by way of dipping, and not sprinkling, appears in that for the resemblance and likeness hereunto. The Israelites passing under the cloud and through the Sea where the Egyptians that were their lords and commanders, their pursuers and enemies, that sought their destruction were drowned, left behind and seen no more, is by the Holy Spirit called a baptism (1 Cor 10:1,2) They were baptized in the cloud etc. Observe, it is not here rendered with the cloud and with the Sea, as in the other place (Mar 1:8) with water, because it suits with sprinkling although the word be the same, but in the cloud and in the Sea which suits with dipping or overwhelming. So, with the appointment of Christ, they passing through the midst of the red or bloody Sea on dry land which stood on both sides as a wall, and

being under the Cloud, were as men, in a carnal eye, overwhelmed and drowned and yet truly saved and safe from their enemies.[5]

The very word baptism comes from a Greek word that primarily refers to a ship that has sunk.

> There is one root term used in the New Testament for baptism: bathos, which denotes depth. From this derived the common Greek noun bathys, "deep, depth," and the verb, "to make deep."[8] This root has entered the English language in terms that derive from "bath," e.g., "bathyscaph" and "bathysphere," vehicles for deep–sea exploration. From this root derive two words: baptō, a verb which denotes "to dip," "plunge," "immerse," or "wash by dipping." The noun form is baptisma, or "baptism."[9] Had the inspired writers of the New Testament desired to convey the idea of sprinkling, they would have used the common term in the New Testament for sprinkling, rhantizō.[6]

The words and examples used in Scripture both proclaim, in word pictures and in specific expression that the mode of baptism is to immerse the candidate under the water and bring him back up. The significance of this act will be discussed later, and makes the argument in favor of believer's baptism all the more compelling. As people of the Book, we dunk people under the water because that's what the Book shows.

3. The Candidates. Who is eligible to be baptized? The great commission is often a source of debate on this question, specifically verses 19 and 20, which read: *Go therefore and make disciples of all nations, baptizing them in the name of the Father and of the Son and of the Holy Spirit, teaching them to observe all that I have commanded you. And behold, I am with you always, to the end of the age."* (Matthew 28:19-20) Who are those that are be baptized according to this passage? Some paedobaptists argue that the making disciples of all nations refers to the general sanctifying effect the church should have on the culture, pointing out that baptism comes before the *"teaching them to observe"* all the commands of Christ. Therefore, they argue, infants are to be baptized and then taught. While it is clear in Scripture (John 6:60-69, for example) that many who are called disciples are not among the redeemed, nowhere do we find a command or example that we are to *make* disciples of any but those who have been redeemed. The Lord preached some very hard truths about who was fit to be His disciple in Luke 14:26-33. These descriptions of disciples use common Jewish hyperbole to demonstrate to the crowds that one cannot serve self and be His disciple. Such is the teaching we are to take to the world: surrender to Christ, abandon hope of being found good enough for God's approval, repent and be baptized for the remission of sin! The sequence is consistent: repent and believe on Christ; *then* be baptized. Teach as many as you can about their sin and the hope found only in Christ. Those who believe are to be baptized as a testimony of their new, clear (or good) conscience toward God (1Peter 3:18-22). Peter uses baptism in this passage as the believer's pledge that he has been born from above

(John 3:5-8); nowhere in Scripture do we find baptism described as a pledge that one will be, sometime in the future, born again. Yet that is what those who sprinkle infants claim to be doing, in actions if not words.

Nearly everyone who sprinkles babies agrees that believers are to be baptized as adults if not "baptized" as a child. Since babies cannot be examined to see if they believe, all sorts of alternatives to confirm the faith of the candidate are presented by those who sprinkle infants. Jeff Johnson reviews eight arguments that have been used to defend paedobaptism over the years since its early adoption:

1. *Fides Aliena*: The church supplies the *faith* necessary for infant baptism.
2. *Fides Infusa*: Baptism infuses *faith* into the infant.
3. *Fides Infantium*: An infants' own *faith* is present in baptism.
4. *Sacramental Symbolism*: The legitimacy of infant baptism is independent of *faith*.
5. *Pre-credobaptism*: Baptism precedes *faith* in the infant, but does not guarantee it.
6. *Presumptive Regeneration*: The church assumes its baptized infants have *faith* until proven otherwise.
7. *Baptismal Regeneration*: Baptism imparts *faith* to all infants (including the non-elect).
8. *Paedofaith*: Infants have *faith* prior to their baptism.[7]

Advocates of baby sprinkling read between the lines of lines in Scripture and imagine babies being baptized in a few passages. To support this view, they must then imagine the rationale for it. But there is no support or rationale for the sprinkling of infants nor for calling this baptism. Recall what the learned advocates of this practice admitted. There is no mention of small children being baptized in God's Word. Small children are held up as metaphors of those who belong to the kingdom of God, in contrast to those who are jaded by and conformed to the world. This does not warrant is to consider them "covenant children." 'Tis far more straightforward and biblical to require the individual wanting to be baptized to declare his faith and belief in Christ; to be examined by parents and pastor to see if there is evidence of a new creature. Another man's faith will not serve well on Judgment Day when we each stand before the Lord.

4. The Significance. What does baptism mean? This is the reason we cannot compromise on the previous points, demands the most from our attention, and requires a redeemed mind to properly comprehend. The main reason baptism is given in Scripture is to point to the death and resurrection of Jesus. He said of His baptism *I have a baptism to be baptized with, and how great is my distress until it is accomplished!* (Luke 12:50) By this, Jesus was not referring to John's baptism of Him in the Jordan, though that is a type and shadow of the spiritual truth of what Jesus speaks of in Luke 12. The Lord's true baptism was His punishment on the tree for our sins. This baptism is what caused the Lord of glory to be in great distress. Thinking forward to His punishment on the cross, suffering the spiritual punishment due us for our sins; this is what caused the King of kings to sweat drops of blood in the garden. No mortal man can stand where Jesus did, cursed by God for the sins of others. He laid His life down for us, knowing He would pick it back up again. Death could not contain Him, for Jesus, unlike the priests of Moses' time, had no sin of His own. He saw beyond the cross to His glorification, knowing His Father was faithful and would vindicate His death by raising Him up to a glory surpassing that which He had from eternity past. His resurrection is what gives us the hope to not grow weary in well doing (1 Cor 15:20-28). When we baptize believers, we read from Romans 6:4, *We were buried therefore with him by baptism into death, in order that, just as Christ was raised from the dead by the glory of the Father, we too might walk in newness of life.* This gives us a picture of what has been done (spiritually) to us, that as the Lord Jesus was put to death and raised up, so were we - spiritually. This is an important truth that we must never forget.

But I hope to open our eyes to the greater meaning of this simple ordinance and pray that we see together what a glorious picture has been given to us by our great and gracious Lord. The Lord's life, death, and resurrection are the keystones of our faith.

Much support and insight for what follows was drawn from a small book by Baptist Pastor Hal Brunson, titled *The Rickety Bridge and the Broken Mirror*, a book of parables about baptism.

The baptism in Romans 6:4 gives us the active or present reality of the meaning of Christ's death, and refers directly to the reality of the first resurrection, when we die to sin and are raised to new life in Christ. But this verse and the act of baptism also point back historically to His death and prophetically forward to the physical resurrection of all the saints when Christ returns to judge all flesh. Baptism is a multifaceted word picture that ought to remind us of far more than the glorious change wrought in the life of the redeemed sinner. One aspect of baptism that baby sprinklers cannot lay claim to is baptism as a picture of submersion into great waters, portraying the great waters of Divine judgment. We do see in Scripture several passages where great waters are graphic symbols of God's judgment and wrath against sin – which Christ took upon His body as the Lamb sacrificed for our sin. He was submersed into the ocean of God's wrath on our account, and raised up on the third day. We will look to God's Word to learn more about this rich teaching on this simple ordinance, graphically presented in four word pictures:

1. The flood of Noah.
2. The sorrows of David, described as "great waters".
3. Jonah being cast into the sea.
4. Jesus' understanding of His death.

First, the flood as a picture of the death of Christ is portrayed in baptism. The Apostle Peter points to this great flood of the entire earth as a vivid picture of the believer's baptism as well as a figure or type pointing to the suffering of Christ. In proclaiming (1 Peter 3:18) that Christ also suffered once for sins, the righteous for the unrighteous, that he might bring us to God, being put to death in the flesh but made alive in the spirit, Peter then alludes to the flood and how only eight persons were saved in the ark, brought through the great waters of God's judgment against sin. And Peter goes on in his first letter (3:21) to tell us that baptism corresponds to this – the flood of Noah, the outpouring of God's wrath in judgment and the only refuge being in the ark which is Christ. Both the great flood and our baptism are types which point to the death of our Lord and His provision for our safety. In 2 Peter 2:6, the flood is listed with another well-known symbol of God's wrath against sin: Sodom and Gomorrah. God's wrath against sin is real, it is certain, it is final. We need a Savior, One Who can bear up under this wrath, One Who has no sin of His own to atone for. Not only did Christ provide refuge for the redeemed from God's wrath, He was buried in God's judgment as payment for sin – our sin. He is worthy of our praise.

The messianic prophet Isaiah, who told of the suffering servant who *was crushed for our iniquities,* brings us back to the flood in describing the covenant of peace the Messiah, *the Holy One of Israel is your Redeemer* (Isaiah 54:8) will bring.. This is the promise to all who are called, not a promise to the nation-state of Israel. Jesus, the Holy One of Israel, saves all who have been appointed unto eternal life, from every nation, tribe, and tongue. This redemption is *as the waters of Noah to me,* says the Lord of Hosts (vs 9). Brunson says:

> this points backwards, not merely to the language and theology of the slaughtered and speechless Lamb, but even to the very moment at which God would impute the transgressions of His people to their Savior and His righteousness to them. *"This"*, God says, *"is as the waters of Noah to me"* - *"this"* - His being *"despised and rejected of men"*; "this is as the waters of Noah – His identity as *"a man of sorrows, and acquainted with grief"*; His *"bearing our griefs and carrying our sorrows"*; the Savior *"stricken, smitten of God, and afflicted … wounded for our transgressions, bruised for our iniquities, chastised for our peace, and striped for our healing"* - *"This is as the waters of Noah to me"* - His oppression, His affliction, His slaughtering, His substitutionary imprisonment within the iron bars of injustice, His burial with the wicked in the grave of hell's billows: *"This"*, says the Almighty, *"is as the waters of Noah to me.*[8]

And who is Noah other than a type for all who have found refuge in Christ? What is the ark other than a type of the everlasting covenant of redemption whereby God's people rise above the waters of judgment? The flood of Noah is God's judgment against sin. It portrays the suffering of Christ in payment for sin, securing the redemption of those chosen by God the Father. None but those so chosen and called could enter in the ark; God Himself shut the door to secure Noah and his family in and to keep all others out. None but those chosen were shielded from the wrath of God. The flood of Noah shows us how great the price our redemption, how great the Father's wrath on sin; how helpless we are to secure that safety.

Briefly, let us talk about the ark, made of earthy things: wood and pitch. Christ, the second person of the Godhead came to us wrapped in earthy things: flesh and blood. The ark and the cross, both made of wood. Both signs of judgment and redemption. The ark covered with pitch, to waterproof it, just as in the day when baby Moses, like Noah, would ride upon dangerous waters in a vessel covered with pitch. This pitch was flammable and used as fuel, used by Isaiah as a metaphor for God's judgment: *For the LORD has a day of vengeance, a year of recompense for the cause of Zion. And the streams of Edom shall be turned into pitch, and her soil into sulfur; her land shall become burning pitch* (Isaiah 34:8-9). The Hebrew term for pitch, *kaphar*, is usually translated not as pitch but is overwhelmingly interpreted as to atone, to purge, to reconcile, to forgive, to cover, and to propitiate. Can you see the glorious scene of how grand the picture is painted by the baptism of a child of God? Again, from Brunson: "The captain of our salvation may have gone to the depths for the salvation of His people, but the old ship of Zion rides the waves with linen sails unfurled, impervious to raging winds and roaring waves, speeding safely upon the scarlet billows of judgment to the soul's desired haven."[9] We get a glimpse of what the Lord Jesus meant when He told the disciples that Moses and the prophets had written about Himself, and how glorious is this glimpse!

That is but a portion of what the great flood of Noah teaches us about baptism, but we must press on and look at what we are taught by the sorrows of David. This man after God's own heart knew of his own sin and the despair of trusting in any mortal man for reconciliation with Holy God. David and other Psalmists described their deep sorrows as a kind of burial beneath the billows and waves of the Almighty. In Psalm 42:5 & 7 we read, *Why are you cast down, O my soul, and why are you in turmoil within me?* In this sorrowful lament with his soul, he describes his afflictions in terms that point to baptism - *Deep calls to deep at the roar of your waterfalls; all your breakers and your waves have gone over me.* Three images of water: waterfalls, breakers, and waves; all communicate the idea of a cascading waterfall pummeling the poet, with the brutal breakers and waves of an angry ocean violently washing over his head. These terrifying metaphors of his torment and anguish wash over him, drowning him in his sorrows. Carried along by the Spirit of God to write these things, perhaps the Psalmist knew not that he prophesied of the promised Messiah, but his words were given to him by God's Spirit and anticipate the predestined sufferings and death of Christ as a kind of baptism. The word for deep in the psalm is used as a synonym for sheol, connecting to the death of Christ as a submersion into the deepest waters of the place of the dead. And the water metaphors in this psalm undoubtedly describe the suffering servant of God - *As with a deadly wound in my bones, my adversaries taunt me, while they say to me all the day long, "Where is your God?"* (Psalm 42:10) This is widely recognized as prophecy of the Lord's sword-pierced side and the cruel mockery of those who blasphemed while He hung on the cross.

David's description of his soul's suffering in deep water takes us more deeply into the sufferings of Jesus. "Like the high priest of Israel, we pass through the first veil, the holy place of Christ's impeccable flesh, and gaze upon the physical sufferings of Christ; and then through the second veil into the holy of holies, to the very heart of Christ, where we gaze upon the innermost secrets of the Savior's suffering soul"[10] as He was put under the rod of God's wrath. In Psalm 18 David wrote about his persecution at the hand of Saul; but the eternal message of redemption contained throughout Scripture portrays here the Savior's passion, not merely David's sorrow; death and hell as the persecutor of Christ, not merely Saul's pursuit of David. The king of Israel describes his trials which have human and divine causes, in terms of sorrow, death, and hell; stark images of his soul's baptism into the lesser sea of man's wrath and the greater ocean of God's wrath. David is immersed in human wrath; Saul's rage is real. David's words tell of God's judgment on sin and care for His people:

> Then the earth reeled and rocked; the foundations also of the mountains trembled and quaked, because he was angry. Smoke went up from his nostrils, and devouring fire from his mouth; glowing coals flamed forth from him. He bowed the heavens and came down; thick darkness was under his feet. He rode on a cherub and flew; he came swiftly on the wings of the wind. He made darkness his covering, his canopy around him, thick clouds dark with water. Out of the brightness before him hailstones and coals of fire broke through his clouds. The LORD also thundered in the heavens, and the Most High uttered his voice, hailstones and coals of fire. And he sent out his arrows and scattered them; he flashed forth lightnings and routed them. Then the channels of the sea were seen, and the foundations of the world were laid bare at your rebuke, O LORD, at the blast of the breath of your nostrils. He sent from on high, he took me; he drew me out of many waters. He rescued me from my strong enemy and from those who hated me, for they were too mighty for me. (Psalm 18:7-17)

Like the pitch on Noah's ark, God's judgment here invokes images of fire and water. But as God did not leave David's soul in torment, neither would He suffer His Holy One to see corruption. Christ was not left buried beneath the sea of God's wrath and the ocean of His judgment. As David cried out in his distress and called upon the Lord from beneath the deep waters of his sufferings, so also the Savior, as it were, from beneath the burning waters of the cross, *Jesus cried out with a loud voice, saying, "Eli, Eli, lema sabachthani?" that is, "My God, my God, why have you forsaken me?"* (Matthew 27:46) As deep calls to deep, the Almighty heard the voices of David and David's seed, and thus He bowed the heavens and came down, riding on a cherub and flying on the wings of the wind; God answered the cry of His Son and sent from above and drew Him out of many waters.

The sorrows of David and other psalmists resonate with all who suffer, but they ultimately point us to the One Who suffered what we deserve, to bring many sons and daughters to glory. The love of God for His elect caused the Son of God, David's promised seed, to submit to the baptism of His Father's wrath, so we who are called by His name would be reconciled to our Father and not left to our just deserts.

Let us now look at what we are taught by the casting of Jonah into the sea. This one is specifically called out by the Lord Himself as a type pointing to His death. *Then some of the scribes and Pharisees answered him, saying, "Teacher, we wish to see a sign from you." But he answered them, "An evil and adulterous generation seeks for a sign, but no sign will be given to it except the sign of the prophet Jonah."* (Matthew 12:38-39) Two symbols of Jonah's experience point to the death of Christ, and to baptism. The terrifying great fish and the deep waters – both of which swallowed up Jonah, and both of which point to baptism by immersion as the proper sign of Christ's death, burial, and resurrection. Consider what the prophet said from the belly of the fish: *Then Jonah prayed to the LORD his God from the belly of the fish,* [quoting the 18th Psalm] *saying, "I called out to the LORD, out of my distress, and he answered me; out of the belly of Sheol I cried, and you heard my voice. For you cast me into the deep, into the heart of the seas, and the flood surrounded me; all your waves and your billows passed over me. Then I said, 'I am driven away from your sight; yet I shall again look upon your holy temple.' The waters closed in over me to take my life; the deep surrounded me; weeds were wrapped about my head at the roots of the mountains. I went down to the land whose bars closed upon me forever; yet you brought up my life from the pit, O LORD my God."* (Jonah 2:1-6) Like David, Jonah testifies not only to his personal experience; he also prophesies of the death of Christ as a kind of submersion into deep waters. Like Jonah, our Lord was swallowed up by the jaws of death, buried in the heart of the earth, at the bottom of death's sea. As by the decree of God the great fish could not hold Jonah, it was not possible that death should hold the Son of God. So baptism is not only of immersion but also of emersion – a coming out from the deep waters. Thus Jonah and the Son of God were not only submerged into the belly of the fish and the deep waters of death, they also emerged from leviathan's jaws and the ocean's depths. *How can the sprinkling of a baby rightly convey this message?* When the child of God is baptized by immersion, the testimony is not only the vicarious submersion with Christ into His death, but also our emersion from death by virtue of His resurrection.

Finally, we look to what the Lord Jesus understood about His death as an apocalyptic baptism, interpreting Scripture with Scripture. No tradition or imagination of man can bring us the light and truth that God has given us in His Word.

In the short gospel penned by Mark, we have this response from the Lord Jesus to the request from James and John to sit on either side of Him in glory. *Jesus said to them, "You do not know what you are asking. Are you able to drink the cup that I drink, or to be baptized with the baptism with which I am baptized?" And they said to him, "We are able." And Jesus said to them, "The cup that I drink you will drink, and with the baptism with which I am baptized, you will be baptized."* (Mark 10:38-39). Other than the ten being indignant at these two, what might they have thought about the cup and the baptism? They would soon learn that this cup the Lord spoke of was not the cup of communion nor a water baptism. Jesus had spoken in terms that left his disciples uncertain, but we know from the record of Scripture that what He was speaking about was the cup of wrath and the baptism of death that awaited Him; of which He lamented: *I have a baptism to be baptized with, and how great is my distress until it is accomplished!* (Luke 12:50) The disciples would be able to drink of His cup and be baptized with His baptism vicariously through Him. No mortal man can stand where Jesus did: cursed by God for the sins of others and lay His life down knowing He would pick it back up again. When we take communion, we are not drinking His cup, but we drink in remembrance of what He did – to cut the New Covenant in His blood to reconcile sinners to Holy God. When we are baptized, it is not merely following His example when John baptized Him in the Jordan. Paul asks, *Do you not know that all of us who have been baptized into Christ Jesus were baptized into his death?* (Romans 6:3) And further he tells us, (1 Corinthians 12:13) *For in one Spirit we were all baptized into one body—Jews or Greeks, slaves or free—and all were made to drink of one Spirit.* We were baptized into Christ's death, the death He died for us, to break down what separates us from God and one another, to make one people that will bring honor and glory to His name.

Oh, the Savior's love for His Father and all those He chose to redeem in Christ! Baptism: it's an ordinance which shows how spiritually dead people have been raised to new life in Christ. But, oh my dear brothers and sisters, it is much, much more than that. I pray you have glimpsed a better, if incomplete, picture of the grand and glorious sacrifice of our Lord and Savior as prophesied and portrayed in various ways as a baptism into God the Father's judgment. The price He paid and the suffering He took as He drank the cup of wrath due us, summed up the submersion and emersion as one is plunged beneath the waters of baptism and raised up from the deep as was our Savior. Let us never see baptism as the *mere* sprinkling of water over a little one who knows nothing and fears not the wrath of God, nor see it as *only* the celebration of a new-born brother in Christ. Let us always remember the One Who was baptized in a way you and I could never survive. Christ paid the price we could not pay. He drank the cup and underwent the baptism that we could not. Every time we see this ordinance, let us think on His sacrifice, His obedience, His submission. And let us be thankful we have a faithful God Who did not allow His Holy One to see corruption – that we would have the firm hope of life eternal. *We were buried therefore with him by baptism into death, in order that, just as Christ was raised from the dead by the glory of the Father, we too might walk in newness of life* (Romans 6:4). Water baptism is a glorious picture of our Redeemer and a reminder of the spiritual baptism mentioned here, when we were raised up to walk in Christ!

The Lord's Supper – the Elements, Participants, the Frequency, the Purpose, the Significance. Just as baptism represents much more than the new birth of a believer, so it is with the Lord's Supper. He drank the cup, filled up with the wrath of Holy God, to purchase those lost sheep chosen before time. His death, in the deepest sense, and His victory over that enemy are the main theme of both ordinances. By His sinless life and atoning death, He redeemed His bride.

This reflects the main over-arching story God's Word brings to us – the redemption of God's elect by the work of Jesus Christ.

Every time we are given the blessed opportunity to be nourished spiritually with this ordinance, we should ponder how it represents the broken body and shed blood of Christ, which cut the New Covenant and in which we have our adoption as sons of the Living God. This description is right and it is a main point we are supposed to gain from observing this ordinance. We will examine these truths; but there is another aspect that I think will add a deeper appreciation and greater holy awe of our Lord and Savior. While people often read from 1 Corinthians 11, the establishment of this ordinance is found in Matthew 26, Mark 14, and Luke 22. This is an important means of grace God has given us, so we must diligently inquire of His Word as to its meaning and how we are to practice it.

In the gospel accounts, Jesus tells His disciples that He will not partake of the Passover again *until it is fulfilled in the kingdom of God.* John Gill explains that this does not mean that Jesus will take the Passover in the consummated kingdom of God, for the Passover was to be fulfilled very shortly in the inaugurated kingdom. Jesus had been telling people *The kingdom of God is among you* (Luke 17:21) as the gospel was being spread and the kingdom became more real, closer to its culmination after Christ was resurrected and people from all nations were added unto it. The Apostle Paul tells us that Jesus was our Passover (1 Corinthians 5:7), showing us the Passover is not a continuing observance, but a ceremonial shadow or type that pointed God's people to the promised seed who would save His people from their sin. The Lord's Supper has connections to the Passover, but is itself the sign of a better covenant (Luke 22:20 & Hebrews 8:6). As the infant Hebrew nation was saved by the blood of the Passover lamb being shed only once, so the New Covenant was ratified and made effective for the salvation of all the elect by the one-time sacrifice of the Lamb of God, the Lord Jesus. The Passover was a type of the Lord's Supper, something temporal pointing to something eternal.

The Roman Catholics portray the table as an altar, upon which their Jesus is sacrificed (a so-called "bloodless sacrifice") every time they partake in their blasphemous version of this ordinance:

> On the subject of the Mass the whole of the Catholic teaching, as a matter of fact, has been set forth by the Council of Trent in three chapters and five canons, which may be summed up as follows:
>
> 1. There is in the Church a Sacrifice instituted by Christ, the Sacrifice of His Body and Blood, under the appearances of bread and wine.
>
> 2. That Sacrifice is in some sense one with the Cross: the same Victim, the same Priest: only a different manner of offering bloodstained on the Cross, bloodless on our altars.

3. It is a Sacrifice of atonement for our sins and the sins of those for whose sake it is offered, be they living or dead—but dead in Christ.

4. Its worth and efficacy is derived from the Sacrifice of the Cross, the benefit of which it applies to us.

5. Although offered up to God, and to God only, yet it may be celebrated out of devotion for the Saints, as a manner of honouring their memory, in *honorem et memoriam.*

6. The institution of that Sacrifice goes back to the Supper, when Christ, who was about to deliver Himself up for us on the Cross, wishing moreover to endow His Church with a Sacrifice commemorative of His own, in His capacity of High Priest according to the order of Melchisedech, first, offered up His Body and Blood under the appearances of bread and wine, and next, appointed His apostles (and likewise their successors for ever) to renew the same offering after Him.[11]

What sayeth the Scripture on this question? *For Christ has entered, not into holy places made with hands, which are copies of the true things, but into heaven itself, now to appear in the presence of God on our behalf.* **Nor was it to offer himself repeatedly**, *as the high priest enters the holy places every year with blood not his own, for then he would have had to suffer repeatedly since the foundation of the world. But as it is,* **he has appeared once for all at the end of the ages to put away sin by the sacrifice of himself** (Hebrews 9:24-26). Christ paid the price once, for all who place their trust in Him; and this ordinance is to teach us more about who He is and what He has done for us. Just as with baptism, the Lord's Supper is primarily about the Lord Jesus – and we benefit greatly from what He has done and continues, as our great High Priest, to do for us. Look closely in God's Word and see if there be any mention of an altar in the New Covenant church; why do so many retain the perspective of Rome, which claims an altar, with blasphemous theology behind their use of that term.

J.H. Merle D'Aubigne reported that Ulrich Zwingle wrestled with the text to determine if the Roman Catholic view of this ordinance was proper. Martin Luther was unable to do this successfully, his mind numbed to the meaning of the text, *this is my body* (Luke 22:19), by what he had been taught and the influence of his native language. During a public discussion in Zurich, in 1525, "Zwingle observed that ἐστί (*is*) is the proper word in the Greek language to express *signifies*, and he quoted several instances in which this word is employed in a figurative sense." The discussion occupied Zwingle's mind for hours after the meeting and that night he had a dream in which he was disputing with the Swiss under-secretary of state, Joachim Am-Grütt. In that dream, "a figure stood before him and said: "Why do you not quote the 11th verse of the 12th chapter of Exodus: *Ye shall eat it* (the lamb) *in haste: it is the Lord's passover?*" Zwingle awoke, sprung out of bed, took up the Septuagint translation, and there found the same word ἐστί (*is*), which all are agreed is synonymous with *signifies* in this passage. Here then, in the institution of the paschal feast under the old covenant, is the very meaning that Zwingle defends. How can he avoid concluding that the two passages are parallel?"[12] Just as the Passover meal signified the passing-over of the angel of death, so the Lord's Supper signifies the passing through death of our Savior.

This ordinance belongs exclusively to the gospel age, being typified in several Old Testament passages, such as when Melchizedek brought wine and bread to refresh Abram and his warriors who had just defeated several pagan kings (Genesis 14:17-20). Even so, we who are born again by the will of God are immediately at war with our flesh, the system of the world and its present ruler. Christ gives us spiritual nourishment with this simple symbol, the bread and wine of the Lord's Supper, of His victory over sin and death and hell and Satan. 'Tis a far, far better respite than what Melchizedek gave Abram. We see another reference to this church ordinance in Proverbs 9:1-5, as lady wisdom bids God's people come to the table she has set, bread and wine, for refreshment and refuge from lure of the culture which wars against our souls.

And read the prophet Isaiah on this topic: *On this mountain the LORD of hosts will make for all peoples* **a feast of rich food, a feast of well-aged wine, of rich food full of marrow, of aged wine well refined.** *And he will swallow up on this mountain the covering that is cast over all peoples, the veil that is spread over all nations.* **He will swallow up death forever;** *and the Lord GOD will wipe away tears from all faces, and* **the reproach of his people he will take away from all the earth, for the LORD has spoken.** *It will be said on that day, "Behold, this is our God; we have waited for him, that he might save us. This is the LORD; we have waited for him; let us be glad and rejoice in his salvation."* (Isaiah 25:6-9)

This is the message of the Lord's Table: **"Behold, this is our God; we have waited for him, that he might save us. This is the LORD; we have waited for him; let us be glad and rejoice in his salvation."**

From Pastor Brunson:

> But deep as this glorious truth (that of the Lord's Supper) may be, it is not the bottom of the cup. Our vicarious burial into Christ's death is deeper still, plunging us ever deeper and deeper into the Savior's precious wounds. Our vicarious participation in Christ's death, our drinking of His cup, is no mere abstract and distant imputation of our sins to Him at the cross. Do we not believe that the cup which Jesus drank, and which we by grace drink with Him, is a cup filled with *"wine of the wrath of God, which is poured out without mixture into the cup of his indignation"* against our sins? Do we not believe in that eye for eye, tooth for tooth, stripe for stripe, and blood for blood, God perfectly measured His unbearable wrath with exactitude, precisely meted out hell's fury against us, and poured the full measure of His indignation into the cup of our

Savior's suffering? Do we not believe that the sufferings of Christ transcend His mere physical sufferings in Pilate's hall or upon Golgotha's hill? Do we not believe that in the hour and power of darkness, when the moon turned to blood and the sun to blackness as sackcloth of hair, that there beneath the ebony sun and crimson moon, a great transaction between the Godhead, a holy transaction too terrible for human eyes to gaze upon, and too wonderful for the minds of men and angels to comprehend? And it is in this moment of Christ's submersion into the dark and scarlet billows of Divine wrath that we see deeply, not only to the bottom of the cup, but also into the deepest meaning of immersion as the only accurate symbolic representation of Christ's horrific burial in the sea of God's wrath.[13]

This brief review shows another aspect of the continuity of the redemptive message of God's Word. The unchanging God does not come up with plans in response to what His creatures do. Jesus becoming man and giving Himself to purchase a people was the plan from the beginning (Acts 2:22-24). This is His ordinance; let us make sure we understand the Elements, Participants, the Frequency, the Purpose, and the Significance of it.

1. The Elements. The Gospel accounts of the institution of the Lord's Supper show that Jesus and His disciples were observing the Feast of Unleavened Bread (Ex 12:14-20), taking the Passover meal when He instituted this ordinance. The elements of the Passover were wine, unleavened bread and a dipping sauce called charoseth, "made of figs, nuts, almonds, and other fruits; to which they added apples; all which they bruised in a mortar, and mixed with vinegar; and put spices into it, calamus and cinnamon, in the form of small long threads, in remembrance of the straw; and it was necessary it should be: thick, in memory of the clay."[14] This was a further reminder of their slavery and the conditions thereof while they were in Egypt.

Heinrich August Wilhelm Meyer explains the structure of the Jewish Passover in his New Testament Commentary. Below is a short extract of this complex tradition from Meyer's work (slightly modified to simplify and shorten it):

> According to the Rabbis, the order of the Passover meal was as follows. (1) It began with drinking wine, preceded by the head of the family offering thanks for the wine and the return of that sacred day. (2) Then bitter herbs (intended to represent the bitter life of their forefathers in Egypt) were put upon the table, some being dipped in a sour liquid, were eaten amid thanksgivings. (3) The unleavened bread, the broth charoset, the lamb and the flesh of the chagiga [a feast offering] were now presented. (4) The head of the family, after a blessing, took as much of the bitter herbs as might be equal to the size of an olive, dipped it in the broth charoset, and then ate it, the others following his example. (5) The second cup

of wine was now mixed, and at this stage the father was expected to explain to his son the peculiarities of this meal. (6) This did not take place till the Passover viands had been put a second time upon the table; then came the singing of the first part of the Hallel (Psalms 113, 114), another short thanksgiving by the father, and the drinking of the second cup. (7) The father then washed his hands, took two pieces of bread, broke one of them, laid the broken pieces upon that which remained whole, repeated the blessing, rolled a piece of the broken bread in bitter herbs, dipped this into the broth charoset, and ate, after having given thanks; he then took some of the chagiga, after another thanksgiving, and so also with regard to the lamb. (8) The feast was now continued by the guests partaking as they felt inclined, concluding, however, with the father eating the last bit of the lamb, which was not to be less than an olive in size, after which no one was at liberty to eat anything more. The father now washed his hands, and, praise having been offered, the third cup was drunk. Then came the singing of the second part of the Hallel (Psalms 115-118) and the drinking of the fourth cup, which was, in some instances, followed by a fifth, with the final singing of Psalms 120-137.[15]

The questions we must ask are these: How much of the Passover ritual is passed on and is to be observed in the Lord's Supper? Are the rules for religious ritual in the shadow applicable to ordinances of worship in the light? Certainly the actual 8 step ritual described above is *not* part of this ordinance; we see no mention of it anywhere in Scripture. Since unleavened bread and wine were commanded to be used in the type, are they required in the antitype? One brother, Peter Ditzel, has written a very provocative article, "The Elements of the Lord's Supper; What Kind of Bread and Fruit of the Vine Are We to Use?"[16] examining the elements of this ordinance. He tweaks Baptists as being very detail focused and particular about Baptism (the mode, the participants) but not so much on this ordinance. Ditzel argues the strong connection between Passover and the Lord's Supper, in conjunction with a plain reading of the gospel accounts relating its institution, unleavened bread and wine, not crackers and juice, are the only options open to Christians. The unleavened bread is used to represent the body of Christ, and since His flesh had no sin of its own, unleavened the bread it will be. Leaven is used frequently in Scripture as a metaphor for sin. As for the wine, there is nothing in Scripture declaring wine to be sinful, only the excessive use thereof. The alcohol content of the wine used in biblical times was not far different from normal wines of our time, between 8% and 20%. Ditzel claims opposition to the use of wine in this ordinance was brought to a head during the temperance movement of the 19th century, with movement advocate Thomas Bramwell Welch developing the first commercially pasteurized grape juice for use in the communion services of his Methodist church; not, he says, adequate rationale for departing from the Bible.

Ditzel implies the use of elements other than unleavened bread and wine is sinful: "If someone is so lacking in faith that he cannot take a tiny amount of wine that symbolizes the blood of His Savior who died to give him the precious gifts of forgiveness and eternal life, that person ought not take the Lord's Supper at all." One Baptist elder I hold dear has observed that the elements of the Lord's Supper have no efficacy in themselves, but in the faithful presentation of the meaning of the supper. This ordinance is a means of grace not because one uses wine and unleavened bread, but because the Bible tells us they symbolize the body and blood of our Lord and Savior. Our spiritual eyes need to be opened, drawn away from the physical to the spiritual truth of this ordinance. This dear friend sums up the issue thusly: "Though wine and unleavened bread is a better translation (such as the NASB is to the NIV) of the purity of Christ, crackers and juice (like the NIV) is still sufficient in symbolizing and communicating Christ's death to us."[17] Another dear friend and Baptist elder has observed that if we were to be as scrupulous with the specific elements as Ditzel exhorts, we need to find out what recipe was used for unleavened bread and also quit calling our Lord and King "Jesus", as His name is either "Joshua" or "Yeshua." He agrees unleavened bread and wine are to be preferred, but disagrees that objecting to its use is a sin or lack of faith that should keep one from participating in this ordinance. Assuming agreement on the elements, this friend says he fears "getting into discussions about how much fermentation is enough. If we do so, then we end up straining out a gnat only to swallow the camel of religious pride (Matthew 23:23-24). Scripture does not give us a recipe for what type of bread to use, simply that it be unleavened. Nor does Scripture give us a recipe for what degree of fermentation we should use simply that it be fruit of the vine. If those are available then I say, "use them." If they are not available then I say, "use what you have" because the weightier matters of religion are "justice, mercy and faithfulness." I don't think that God is upset that we are using grape juice instead of wine. I think that he's more interested in the heart of the taker and not the amount of fermentation in the drink."[18]

With baptism, the mode is vital because it is a visual reminder of the death, burial, and resurrection of our Lord. But we do not insist on a river, much less the Jordan River, just because that is where Jesus was baptized. The circumstantial details of baptism are not the important aspect of that ordinance; rightly portraying the death and resurrection of our Lord is. With the Lord's Supper, the important thing is also the message; not the specifics of the elements. Since the elements are *not* the body and blood of Jesus, but merely symbols or types, the faithfulness to the antitype is what is vital. How the elements are handled is more important than what the elements are comprised of. Withholding the cup, as the Roman Catholic Church often does, for fear of the common man dribbling some of their "savior's blood" onto the floor, or being so casual with the administration that nobody is warned (1 Corinthians 11:27 & 28) or there is no sober reminder of the purpose (1 Corinthians 11:26) are signs of something seriously wrong. Much more so than if a church handles the ordinance rightly and uses juice and crackers.

2. The Participants. Who can take the table of communion? John Gill, a Baptist elder from the 17th century, gave 5 categories to describe these boundaries;[19] I have combined the last two into one, giving four categories:

a. Infants in the literal and natural sense should not take the table. God's guidance on this is found in 1 Corinthians 11:27 & 28. This instruction for each person to examine himself before taking the bread and the cup rules out all who are unable or unwilling to humble himself. There can be no argument as to whether infants are capable of this. Spiritually they are not able to benefit from the body and blood of Christ, not able to examine themselves nor remember His death, much less comprehending the meaning of it. In the third century, some folks began giving communion to infants, to which they have as much right, Gill said, as they to the ordinance of baptism, which is say they have no right. Yet infants were admitted to communion in the same century as they began to be baptized. Very few paedobaptists today allow their "covenant infants" to take communion.

b. People who are scandalous and shameful in their lives and conversations, are by no means to be participants of this ordinance; 1 Corinthians 5:11 *But now I am writing to you not to associate with anyone who bears the name of brother if he is guilty of sexual immorality or greed, or is an idolater, reviler, drunkard, or swindler—not even to eat with such a one.* That is, Gill says, at the Lord's table; I would add the dinner table.

c. "Ignorant persons are unfit for this ordinance. Such who partake of it, ought to know themselves, the sinfulness of their state by nature, and the guilt of sin; that they may see their need of, and be affected with the grace of God in the remission of their sins, through the sufferings, death, and bloodshed of Christ." This is grounded in the same instructions given in 1 Corinthians 11:27 & 28. They ought to have knowledge of God as their covenant God, whose covenant, testament, and will, is ratified and confirmed by the blood of Christ. And they ought to be acquainted with the various doctrines of the gospel, which this ordinance shines forth; as justification, pardon of sin, reconciliation, atonement. But none of this can be true of them unless God Himself opens their eyes and grants them life and faith. One whose spiritual eyes have not been opened by God is, by definition, ignorant, and should not take this ordinance.

d. People who are able to reason, know what they are doing, and are penitent believers are to be allowed to partake of this ordinance; for only such can look to Christ whom they have pierced, and mourn, and exercise godly sorrow and evangelical repentance. Only these people have spiritual life in them, able to humble and examine themselves, are capable of receiving spiritual food, and can discern spiritual things (the Lord's body). Only these "have their taste changed, and can relish divine things; only these hunger and thirst after Christ, and can be satisfied with feeding on him by faith, and be nourished thereby". These are the children of God who are welcomed to this table, in anticipation of the great feast to come in the next age!

We should hear similar counsel every time we gather for this ordinance; a fence, as it were, set where we see it in Scripture. It is an ordinance for the redeemed and it is an ordinance which was given to the church, not individuals. So each church ought to welcome obedient brothers and sisters from other churches who are not under discipline and who are penitent and humble before God the Father. As we will see, this ordinance has deep significance and it is unthinkable that it would be handled in a cavalier manner by those administering it or partaking of it.

3. The Frequency. One of the most striking differences among churches is the meaning they pour into the practice of this ordinance. The frequency, purpose, efficacy, and protocol of this ordinance reveal what the people of each local church believe about it. Many churches observe this ordinance 4 times a year, often on Sunday evenings so as not to disturb the "normal" worship service; a few observe it only annually, some with weeks of preparation. It's as if the Bible has nothing to say about this topic. While the Bible does not explicitly command us on the frequency, we do see a narrative showing it was an important part of their weekly gatherings, some 30 to 40 years after Pentecost. *Now on the first day of the week, when the disciples came together to break bread, Paul, ready to depart the next day, spoke to them and continued his message until midnight* (Acts 20:7). O'Hare observes: "Most commentators agree that this was a Sunday evening meeting, at a recurring gathering of Christians on the first day of the week following their normal activities and work. [Note: this was before Christianity was legal and before Sunday was a regular day off for workers.] They came together in order to break bread. This does not mean that preaching was secondary, but when they came together, they purposed to commune in the symbolism of the covenant meal as the Lord had commended and as the apostles has established by tradition. ... Christ promised, with a view to congregational worship, that when the saints gather together, they can count on His mystical presence (Matthew 20:18). The Lord's Supper uses symbols of His presence: the bread of His life and the wine of His blood." [24]

Scripture does command us to take it, revealing that it is nourishing to our souls, that it enhances our fellowship. This puts a new light on this question about frequency; perhaps the question for some should be, why don't we take this ordinance more frequently? The commonly discussed down-side to observing this ordinance regularly is that it can (they often mean *will*) become routine, dull, meaningless. That was my first thought when I served in a church that took the Lord's Table weekly. It had always been "something special", typically on a Sunday night, when the crowd is smaller, less likely to have people who don't "get it". My time at that church showed me that, properly handled, the weekly observance of this ordinance is *not* routine, dull, or meaningless. If Christ be rightly presented, if we are put in our place of coming to Him with gratitude, in humility, aware of our not-yet status of being conformed to Him, then this simple ordinance is what God intended it to be, bringing glory to the Father through the Son and building up His people spiritually.

The beloved Baptist preacher, Charles Spurgeon, declared, "Shame on the Christian Church that she should put it off to once a month, and mar the first day of the week by depriving it of its glory in the meeting together for fellowship and breaking of bread, and showing forth the death of Christ til He comes." [25] Throughout the history of the church, weekly observance of the Lord's Supper has been the traditional practice, ably supported by the Word of God. The question is open to those who desire an infrequent observance of this ordinance: "What is your biblical basis for your Practice?" To my ongoing sorrow, deacons in one church I briefly belonged to told me they relegated this ordinance to Sunday evenings every fifth Sunday because there were people in the Sunday morning service who would not come if the Lord's Supper was observed in the Sunday morning service. This is a sad commentary about those who profess Christ and care to neglect rather than take part in this sign of the New Covenant.

We are to never stop growing in knowledge and grace of the Lord Jesus (2 Peter 3:18), for there is no end to Him. The eternal God, one God in three persons, cannot be comprehended completely by a mere creature! We cannot truly know our spouse, though the Lord may grant us decades of life together in close quarters. How pitiful a view of God is it to relegate this ordinance to "special occasions"; He commanded us, all Christians, to keep it, until He comes again! God has given this to us for His glory and our good. May it never be that we regard it lightly or accept its practice only on "special occasions." We need more of God, not less. We need a more frequent reminder of the grace poured out to us in Christ, not less. The Lord's Supper is another ordinary means of grace our Lord has given His people.

4. The Purpose. The reason this ordinance was given to the church is to declare the death of Christ; that He did die for the sins of His people; to demonstrate the manner of His death, by crucifixion; "by his being pierced, wounded, bruised, and broken; and to express the blessings and benefits of his death, and the faith of his people"[20] in Him, and thankfulness for His obedience. Again, we look to John Gill, who set forth five reasons for this ordinance; the first given above. The other four reasons (Gill's points, slightly modified, with Scripture references added) are[21]:

b. "To commemorate the sacrifice of Christ; Christ was once offered, and needs not to be offered up again". He has by one offering made perfect atonement for sin (Hebrews 10:12-14). Because Christ was sacrificed for us, we should keep this ordinance (1 Corinthians 11:26) as a memorial of that (1 Corinthians 11:25), and through it look to Christ, the Lamb of God, who takes away the sins of men (John 1:29).

c. "To remember the love of Christ in dying for us (1 John 3:1). He directed his disciples both to eat the bread and drink the wine in remembrance of Him, of His body being broken and His blood being shed for them to remember His love to them, which He expressed" in this ordinance given to us. I would add that higher than His love for His church is the love Jesus has for His Father (Matthew 26:39-42). There is no other person to whom the Lord Jesus would submit Himself. As much as He loves those He died to save, I think the Scripture shows us a higher order of love that exists amongst the god-head. God's love for Himself, in any and all of the three persons of the Holy Trinity, surpasses the unspeakable love He has for the church. God alone can love without sin. He desires glory be unto His name. When sinners are redeemed, there is joy in heaven (Luke 15:7 & 10). But nothing has been done in conjunction with sinners being redeemed that compares to the honor and glory heaped upon each member of the god-head by the other.

d. "To show our love to Christ, and thankfulness to Him, for the blessings of His grace", by participating in this ordinance. We should call upon our souls, and all that is within us, to bless His name, and remember His benefits, especially the great benefit of the redemption of our lives from destruction, by His blood, sufferings, and death. We must be careful not to think we are capable of mustering up from within ourselves this total devotion Gill speaks of. We *are* to make every effort to obey the Lord and honor Him; yet we know doing this is beyond our human ability. Who of us does *anything* with all that is within us? We love God, and one another, because He first loved us. As Jesus told the Jews, *If God were your Father, you would love me, for I came from God and I am here. I came not of my own accord, but he sent me* (John 8:42). Any good in us or through us is from the Father of lights, in Whom there is no shadow or change.

e. "To maintain love and unity with each other; for by joining together in holy fellowship in this ordinance, we keep the unity of the spirit in the bond of peace." For this reason, it is important that people be rightly warned about taking the supper in an unworthy manner as it is an offense to Him. It brings judgment from God for two reasons: because it presumes upon His grace and because it makes for division rather than unity in His church. How does this cause division, you ask? Consider, unworthy persons taking communion give a public witness that they are in right standing with God. Children of God who are walking in humility have an openness in fellowship with one another that cannot exist with one who is in secret rebellion against God. The inevitable conflict that arises in such circumstances brings division, which the Lord hates. We are to love one another (see John 13:34 & 35 and John 15:12-17), for this honors God when we keep His commandments; and this ordinance is one of them. When we allow false sons to bring dishonor to our Lord, we join in his sin by turning a blind eye towards them and their sinful behavior. This is the message of 1 Corinthians 5: the one who bears the name of a brother is to be shunned and purged from the fellowship that he may yet repent. This is the love of God.

5. The Significance. Lastly, we will examine what the broken body and shed blood of Christ mean, beyond the act of redemption. When we consider the cracker as a symbol of Christ's broken body, we must consider why His body being broken is significant, why it is sufficient. By His active obedience to the entire construct of law in Moses and the prophets, Jesus earned the right to offer Himself as the Lamb of God. Because His body was unblemished by sin, He could lay down His life for you and me and all the elect of every nation, tribe, and tongue.

As with baptism, this ordinance has much good and rich meaning for each and every blood-bought child of the living God. I mentioned in the introduction that all of creation exists to bring glory to God and to do good to His people, in that order. It is easy to focus on the good done to us and give less honor than we ought to the One Who does this good. So it is with this last point, the significance of communion that I hope to shine the light on the person and work of Christ Jesus, as He sought to honor His, and our, Father.

The fact that Christ instituted the Lord's Supper on the night He was betrayed reveals the great love Christ the Redeemer has for the church, which is the reflection of His great love for the Father. There He sat, knowing what lay ahead, taking care to show again how unworthy sinners were reclaimed and yet cared for by the Shepherd of their souls. *I am the good shepherd. I know my own and my own know me, just as the Father knows me and I know the Father; and* **I lay down my life for the sheep.** *And I have other sheep that are not of this fold. I must bring them also, and they will listen to my voice. So there will be* **one flock, one shepherd.** *For this reason the Father loves me, because I lay down my life that I may take it up again. No one takes it from me, but I lay it down of my own accord. I have authority to lay it down, and I have authority to take it up again. This charge I have received from my Father* (John 10:14-18). This tells us the great authority Christ has as the second person of the Holy Trinity, God in the form of man. While any man can lay down his life, no mortal has ability or authority to take it back up again. Jesus is God: very God and very man. His status as man is key to His having earned the right to lay down His life as the sacrificial Lamb of God. His status as God is key to His having picked it up again, defeating death.

He was the promised seed of Abraham, Isaac, Jacob, and David. As with all national Israel during the time of Moses and the prophets, Jesus came as a man born of woman, born of flesh, and under the law. Galatians 4:4-5: *But when the fullness of time had come, God sent forth his Son, born of woman, born under the law, to redeem those who were under the law, so that we might receive adoption as sons.*

We know from Hebrews chapter 12 that saints of old, born in the time of Moses and his covenant, were saved by faith in the promised seed yet to come. In this, they had much in common with us: we have faith in the promised seed delivered, but our life is hidden in Him and yet to be revealed fully (Colossians 3:3 & 4). Saints of all ages live in the tension of the already but not yet, ongoing fulfillment of the kingdom of heaven and of God.

> *For all who rely on works of the law are under a curse; for it is written, "Cursed be everyone who does not abide by all things written in the Book of the Law, and do them." Now it is evident that no one is justified before God by the law, for "The righteous shall live by faith." But the law is not of faith, rather "The one who does them shall live by them." Christ redeemed us from the curse of the law by becoming a curse for us—for it is written, "Cursed is everyone who is hanged on a tree"— so that in Christ Jesus the blessing of Abraham might come to the Gentiles, so that we might receive the promised Spirit through faith.* (Galatians 3:10-14)

These Galatian passages show us plainly that Jesus was, from birth, under the law, just as every Jew was. What did this entail, for this Jew to grow and learn obedience to his earthly parents, to keep from all sin in thought, word, and deed? His food was to do His Father's will; this is the focus we need, being infected with sin and easily led astray. He was the law giver who became the law keeper that He might save us law breakers. What did it mean for anyone to keep the law and the prophets without any violation in word, thought, or deed?

You shall love the LORD your God with all your heart and with all your soul and with all your might (Deuteronomy 6:5). This one verse is a command to all of God's people, cited by Jesus as the first and greatest command. God's law requires, it demands, perfection; which no man can even *attempt* to do apart from the indwelling of the Holy Spirit. Even no redeemed mortal does consistently or completely. I have never read any testimony of any man who could credibly claim to have kept this command – it is comprehensive, affecting every thought, word, and deed; that which is committed and that which is omitted. Not too long before he died, the well-known preacher Adrian Rogers was on a radio talk show wherein he mentioned that even if he believed all the good things people said about him and even if he thought he had not committed any volitional sin, he was horrified of what was written in James 4:16-17: *As it is, you boast in your arrogance. All such boasting is evil. So* **whoever knows the right thing to do and fails to do it, for him it is sin.** For to love the Lord our God with your whole heart, soul, and mind is to do everything He has commanded and to not leave anything undone you know to be right in His sight. None of us are free from the effects of the Fall, the sin that so easily entangles our flesh; none of us are so consistent and diligent and focused to be able to claim full obedience for 5 minutes.

All of this is to show the perfection of Christ, He who had no sin, being made sin, so that in Him we might become the righteousness of God (2 Corinthians 5:21). His perfection, unmatched and unmatchable by any creature, perfectly reflects God's holiness and the humanly unreachable standard of the Old Covenant law (Romans 3:19; Galatians 2:16; James 2:10).

This is most significant, for under the Law, it took man-flesh to atone for sins against man or God. *Whoever strikes a man so that he dies shall be put to death. But if he did not lie in wait for him, but God let him fall into his hand, then I will appoint for you a place to which he may flee. But if a man willfully attacks another to kill him by cunning, you shall take him from my altar, that he may die* (Exodus 21:12-14). We know sins against God bring death from the record of Genesis 2:15-17, which warns: *in the day that you eat of it you shall surely die.* We know this death spoke of by God was immediate spiritual death, followed by physical death, for Adam and Eve lived long lives after being thrown from the garden. Transgressions against God are spiritual transgressions and must be paid for spiritually. The sin in the garden by Adam infected the soul and the flesh of man and brought physical death to creation (Genesis 3:17 & 18; Romans 8:20-22). There is no hope for sinners unless someone with perfect flesh and spirit is willing to die to pay the price that we are unable to do. It was the work of Christ to obey Moses and the prophets so that He would be perfect, and therefore, able to shed His blood for us.

There are some who teach His primary purpose in living as a man was to leave us an example. Yes, He did leave us an example; but His life has a higher purpose. The primary reason He lived as a man before He died as a man was to earn standing as the Lamb of God. *In the days of his flesh, Jesus offered up prayers and supplications, with loud cries and tears, to him who was able to save him from death, and he was heard because of his reverence. Although he was a son,* **he learned obedience through what he suffered. And being made perfect, he became the source of eternal salvation to all who obey him,** *being designated by God a high priest after the order of Melchizedek* (Hebrews 5:7-10). Hebrews 8 tells us the priests of the Old Covenant and the sacrifices thereof were copies and shadows of the heavenly things. Because He was the obedient son, the faithful witness, the righteousness of God, He was qualified to appear *as a high priest of the good things that have come, then through the greater and more perfect tent (not made with hands, that is, not of this creation) he entered once for all into the holy places, not by means of the blood of goats and calves but by means of his own blood, thus securing an eternal redemption. For if the blood of goats and bulls, and the sprinkling of defiled persons with the ashes of a heifer, sanctify for the purification of the flesh, how much more will the blood of Christ, who through the eternal Spirit offered himself without blemish to God, purify our conscience from dead works to serve the living God.* (Hebrews 9:11-14)

John Gill helps us understand the significance of the bread:

> *The bread which we break, is it not the communion of the body of Christ?* (1 Corinthians 10:16) not his mystical body, the church, but his natural body, which was formed in the womb of the Virgin by the Holy Spirit, and which Christ took into union with his divine Person, and which he offered up upon the cross. And the bread in the supper is a symbol of this body, not as living either on earth or in heaven, but as dead, the life of it being laid down by Christ, and given for the life of his people.[22]

"The phrase, *This is my body,* (Mark 14:22; found in the synoptic gospels) is to be understood in a figurative sense; the bread is a figure, symbol, and representation of the body of Christ." The Lord made this statement while holding bread and offering the bread to His disciples – is there any hint they thought He meant His actual flesh? They made no effort to bite Him (not trying to be sacrilegious, but merely pointing out the obvious.) Further, many scriptural phrases are word pictures, symbols, or metaphors; "as when Joseph said to Pharaoh, *The seven good kine are seven years, and the seven good ears are seven years.* Seven kine (oxen or cattle) and ears signified, or were symbols of, seven years of plenty; and the lean kine and thin ears were symbols of so many years of famine (Genesis 41:26, 27 KJV). Again, in the parable of the sower, the seed and tares, signified various persons, and were emblems of them." Also, as 1 Corinthians 10:1-4 (HCSB) reports, the Hebrews *were baptized into Moses in the cloud and the sea. They all ate the same spiritual food and they all drank the same spiritual drink. For they drank from a spiritual rock that followed them, and that rock was Christ.* This speaks of the physical manna and physical water that serve their primary purpose of being figures and representations of him (see Exodus 17:5 & 6; Numbers 20:7-13; John 4:13 & 14; 6:30-35). The bread is the body of Christ, a figure, sign, and symbol of it just as the water is. Christ compares himself to a kernel of wheat falling into the ground; dying, and reviving and bringing forth fruit, expressive of his sufferings and death, and of the blessed consequences thereof (John 12:24). "Bread corn (Isaiah 28:24, KJV) is a figure of Christ, as prepared for food, which is beaten out, winnowed, ground, kneaded, and baked, before it becomes proper food for men; so Christ, by his various sufferings, being bruised, broken, crucified, and sacrificed for us (Isaiah 54:3-5), becomes proper food for faith; and as such is he represented, viewed, and received in the ordinance of the supper." Bread has historically been the main provision for the sustenance of men, and is called the staff of life which is the principal means of maintaining and preserving life. All of this reference points to the crucified Christ, both in the preaching of the gospel and in the administration of this ordinance, for He refers to Himself as the bread of life (John 6:32-35; 48-51). Bread is not merely food for the belly; it is a picture of the blessed spiritual life Christ gave His people.[23]

What is the significance of the cup? *Jesus answered, "You do not know what you are asking. Are you able to drink the cup that I am to drink?" They said to him, "We are able."* (Matthew 20:22) And in Matthew 26:36-39: *Then Jesus went with them to a place called Gethsemane, and he said to his disciples, "Sit here, while I go over there and pray." And taking with him Peter and the two sons of Zebedee, he began to be sorrowful and troubled. Then he said to them, "My soul is very sorrowful, even to death; remain here, and watch with me." And going a little farther he fell on his face and prayed, saying, "My Father, if it be possible, let this cup pass from me; nevertheless, not as I will, but as you will."*

Some teach this cup was the agony of the garden, triumphing over this supposedly last and greatest temptation, not succumbing to rebellion against His Father, but proceeding to His humiliating death on the cross. Yet the testimony of John, taking place after the Lord's time in the garden, shows the drinking of the cup to yet be future: John 18:11 - *So Jesus said to Peter, "Put your sword into its sheath; shall I not drink the cup that the Father has given me?"* This makes clear that the cup Christ has been talking about is not His temptation in the garden. This cup was the cup of God's wrath on sin. All of the curses from the Law of Moses (Deuteronomy 28:15-68), all of the vengeance due sinners (Romans 1:18), the full weight of the judgment of Almighty God the Father (Revelation 14:10; 16:19) poured out on Christ Jesus as He hung on the cross. *This* is the cup He was talking about.

In talking about the Lord's Supper, we must make sure we know what that cup signifies; if not the same as the cup of judgment Christ drank on behalf of the elect, what is it? Christ had offered a cup to the disciples during the Last Supper, calling it the cup of the New Covenant, that covenant of redeeming grace He cut with His blood. The cup of communion is a sign of the peace we have with God the Father by the blood of Christ, a far, far different cup than the cup of God's wrath that Christ took for us. That which brought us peace will be poured out on all who are not invited to take the cup of the New Covenant. And yet we see **The cup of blessing that we bless, is it not a participation in the blood of Christ?**

The bread that we break, is it not a participation in the body of Christ? (1 Corinthians 10:16)

When we take the cup of the Lord's Supper, we should remember the cup of wrath He took on our behalf. The cup we hold is a symbol of the glorious benefit of being redeemed by His sacrifice, so we thank our God for His grace while we also soberly remember the price that was paid. No small price; He drank the cup of wrath and shed His blood to secure our redemption. As we drink the cup of His peace, the New Covenant, we do drink vicariously the cup of wrath. When we eat the bread or cracker, which is broken in remembrance of His atoning death, we participate vicariously in the death He died. This is why Paul said Galatians 2:19-20: *For through the law I died to the law, so that I might live to God. I have been crucified with Christ. It is no longer I who live, but Christ who lives in me. And the life I now live in the flesh I live by faith in the Son of God, who loved me and gave himself for me.* This is what is real – our spiritual life. It is what is eternal. All the things of this present world are being prepared to be burned up in the final judgment of God when Christ comes again (2 Peter 3:10; Revelation 8:7), not to deal with sin but to save those who anxiously await Him. This is why Scripture tells us to put on the Lord Jesus and make no provision for the flesh, to gratify its desires (Romans 13:14) and to seek after Christ and think on things above (Philippians 4:8).

Conclusion. We've covered five topics concerning this second ordinance God has given to the church. We examined the elements, who can take it, how often should we take it, what is its purpose, and its significance. The death of Christ, portrayed in baptism and the Lord's Supper, was the crime of eternity, took place according to the counsel of the God-head before time began (Acts 2:23), as the eternal covenant of redemption (Hebrews 13:20) was laid out. His death we proclaim (1 Corinthians 11:26); see how this is presented within Luke 24:25 – 35:

> *And he said to them, "O foolish ones, and slow of heart to believe all that the prophets have spoken! Was it not necessary that the Christ should suffer these things and enter into his glory?" And beginning with Moses and all the Prophets, he interpreted to them in all the Scriptures the things concerning himself. … When he was at table with them,* **he took the bread and blessed and broke it and gave it to them. And their eyes were opened, and they recognized him.** *… And they rose that same hour and returned to Jerusalem. And they found the eleven and those who were with them gathered together, saying, "The Lord has risen indeed, and has appeared to Simon!" Then* **they told what had happened on the road, and how he was known to them in the breaking of the bread.**

This is, I believe, what Paul had in mind when he wrote that *we proclaim the Lord's death* by taking part in this ordinance. It helps open our eyes to beauty and truth of Who Christ is and what He's done. We proclaim His death until He comes again; and this He will do (John 14:3) and not until then will He eat the Passover Meal (Luke 22:16). The Passover is over, until He comes again; because He fulfilled the Passover (1 Corinthians 5:7) just as He fulfilled Moses and the Prophets

(Matthew 5:17). Every promise of God finds its answer and fulfillment in Christ (1 Corinthians 1:20).

As He was glorious before He came in the likeness of man, He was glorious as a man, perfect in His obedience to the Father. And having fulfilled the law, He was glorious in His death, He was glorious in His resurrection (John 17:1-4), and He is glorious in His reign as the King and kings and Lord of lords (Revelation 11:15; 17:14). He is coming to judge the quick and the dead. Are you ready? Is your lamp-wick trimmed? Have you been reconciled to the Creator and sovereign ruler of all things? Can you, by faith in Christ, call God your Father? If you have peace with God, His Word gives great comfort. Be reconciled to God through faith in Jesus, for He alone is able to reconcile us to God. *Now may the God of peace who brought again from the dead our Lord Jesus, the great shepherd of the sheep, by the blood of the eternal covenant, equip you with everything good that you may do his will, working in us that which is pleasing in his sight, through Jesus Christ, to whom be glory forever and ever. Amen.* (Hebrews 13:20-21)

Recommended reading on this topic:
*Ill News from New England** – John Clark
*God's Ordnance, the Saint's Privilege** – John Spilsbery
*Defense of Credo-Baptism** – John Clark
*A Body of Practical Divinity** – John Gill
*Doctrine of Baptism and the Distinctiveness of the Covenants** – Thomas Patient
*Concerning the Administration and Receiving of the Lord's Supper** – Benjamin Cox
The Rickety Bridge and the Broken Mirror – Hal Brunson
The Sabbath Complete – Terrence D. O'Hare
The Fatal Flaw of the Theology Behind Infant Baptism – Jeffrey D. Johnson

Chapter 3 - The Nature of the Local Church: its Purpose, Local Autonomy, Offices, Membership, Relation to Civil Government, Liberty of Conscience, and the Gospel.

In each of the following characteristics of the local church, we will have our bedrock of reasoning in the Word of God. One has no basis for considering himself a Baptist if his view of the Bible does not demand that as his foundation for his view of his person or the person of Christ. Since the church is the body of Christ, how we view it reveals how we view the Lord.

a.) Purpose. There are three forms of government given to man by our Creator. In chronological order, God gave us: a) The family, which teaches children the things of God (Genesis 2:18-24; Ephesians 6:4; Genesis 18:19; Deuteronomy 4:9; 6:7; 11:19; Psalms 78:4; Proverbs 19:18; 29:17; 2 Timothy 3:15) and is the smallest government of all. b) The civil government, needed as mankind grew in number, to reward those who do good and punish evil-doers (Genesis 4:17-21; 1 Kings 3:5-9; Romans 13:1-7; Titus 3:1; 1 Peter 2:13); handling disputes involving citizens of the world (1 Corinthians 6:1-8). And third, c) the church, which is the *pillar and buttress of the truth* (1 Timothy 3:15), representing the kingdom of God in this age (Acts 11:25 & 26; 14:21-23; 20:28; Hebrews 13:7, 17 & 18; Ephesians 4:7-13; 1 Timothy 3:1-7; Titus 2:1 & 15; James 5:14); handling disputes amongst the saints (Matthew 18:17; 1 Corinthians 1:10-17; chapter 5; 6:1-8; 11:17-22; Titus 3:1 & 2, 8-11). It is here in the local church that families and individuals gather for worship, instruction, prayer, and fellowship. It is here, primarily, that God meets with His people, having given the church *shepherds and teachers to equip the saints for the work of ministry, for building up the body of Christ, until we all attain to the unity of the faith and of the knowledge of the Son of God, to mature manhood, to the measure of the stature of the fullness of Christ, so that we may no longer be children, tossed to and fro by the waves and carried about by every wind of doctrine, by human cunning, by craftiness in deceitful schemes* (Ephesians 4:12-14). The church, both its local form and the universal form, represent the bride of our Lord; one a mixture of wheat and chaff (Matthew 13:24-30), the other pure and clothed in the righteousness of Christ (Revelation 7:9-17). Paul expounds on this Ephesians 5 and it is beyond even his inspired mind to represent it completely. The local church has its role or function to perform, just as the family and civil governments do. And since the church represents the bride of Christ, we should take extra care to understand what God has told us about the structure and function of the church.

With that background, we will take a look at four aspects of the local church. I won't spend time on the universal church, because the life we live out takes place in the local church and that's where our challenges lie.

b.) Local autonomy. This is another area in which the vast majority of Christian churches differ with Baptists. Contrary to the long-standing hierarchal structures of other groups, Baptists have no formal authorities higher than the local church (although many calling themselves Baptist do support various structures beyond the local church). We see in Scripture local churches in various towns had relationships with other local churches, but not subject to men outside any given church after the apostolic era. This may be most clear in the opening chapters of John's Apocalypse, as letters were addressed to individual churches along a normal mail route. Why would the Lord command John to write a separate letter to each church if there had been a regional authority over them? Early in the life of the church, each Apostle had God-given authority over the churches he had planted. Yet we see, as the church matured, the last and least Apostle appointed elders in each church to shepherd the flock God gathered at each. The Council of Jerusalem, found in Acts 15, shows how the Apostles and elders handled a contentious issue that affected many of the new churches. It was a one-time event, handled gently, with the desire that Christians stand before God with a clean conscience and not be a stumbling block for other believers. Matthew 18:15-18 describes the local church as the highest spiritual authority on earth, answering to the Lord alone. This pattern was the practice of the early church, according to a wide range of respected church historians (see the works of Gibbon, Mosheim, Neander, Coleman, Whately, Burton, Barrow, Schaff, etc.) The church is repeatedly declared in the New Testament to be the body of Christ (Romans 12:5; 1 Corinthians 6:15; 10:17; 12:27; Ephesians 1:23; 4:12; 5:23,30; Colossians 1:18,24; 2:17); the only Head of this body is Christ, who guides and controls and preserves the her, His body. The office of Apostle does not continue, as the foundation of any structure is laid once with no need or ability to lay it again; so it is with the church (Ephesians 2:20). And we see nothing in God's Word about popes, presbyteries, or other denominational hierarchies that populate the professing Christian world and hold local churches under the thumb of elevated religious offices. While some men are called to serve in one of two positions in the local church (elders and deacons), Scripture shows no division of Christians as many have been taught, consisting of clergy and laymen. This was developed by post-apostolic church leaders and institutionalized by the Roman Catholic Church as it grew in influence and sought to establish its clergy as a permanent class of rulers, as Schaff recounts.

> After the gradual abatement of the extraordinary spiritual elevation of the apostolic age, which anticipated in its way the ideal condition of the church, the distinction of a regular class of teachers from the laity became more fixed and prominent. This appears first in Ignatius, who, in his high episcopalian spirit, considers the clergy the necessary medium of access for the people to God. "Whoever is within the sanctuary (or altar), is pure; but he who is outside of the sanctuary is not pure; that is, he who does anything without bishop and presbytery and deacon, is not pure in conscience." Yet he nowhere represents the ministry as a sacerdotal office. The Didache calls "the prophets" high-priests, but probably in a spiritual sense. Clement of Rome, in writing to the congregation at Corinth, draws a significant and fruitful parallel between the Christian presiding office and the Levitical priesthood, and uses the expression "layman" (λαϊκὸς ἄνθρωπος) as antithetic to high-priest,

priests, and Levites. This parallel contains the germ of the whole system of sacerdotalism. But it is at best only an argument by analogy. Tertullian was the first who expressly and directly asserts sacerdotal claims on behalf of the Christian ministry, and calls it "sacerdotium," although he also strongly affirms the universal priesthood of all believers.[1]

The local church was founded by Jesus and each one answers to Him. These other religious institutions were dreamed up by man. Each church stands before the Lord, and her elders will give an account to God for how they have served Him and them (Hebrews 13:17). This is why no man or man-made group can insert himself or itself as lord over a local church; each pastor answers to Christ for his service and needs the love and support from the people the Lord has gathered there.

c.) Offices. The Scriptures are clear in describing two distinct offices (by this I mean positions with defined responsibilities) within the local church: elder/overseer/pastor and deacon are identified and qualified in 1 Timothy 3. The men who serve in these offices are co-laborers, with distinctly different roles within the church. The Apostles, forerunner of church elders, were to devote themselves to prayer and the preaching of the Word; deacons are to tend to the physical needs of the dynamic and diverse body of Christ. In Acts 6 the people did not vote for who would serve as deacons; they nominated seven godly men to the Apostles, who appointed the men to serve. This passage does not show a democracy in action as many Baptists falsely believe. It shows the active participation of the members, recognizing the rule of those God had appointed to lead them. As the church matured, the Scripture shows us that elders/pastors had oversight on all the church did and deacons provided much more service than "waiting tables." As there are spiritual issues behind every temporal matter a deacon might be called upon to help with, these men must be qualified and there must be a good rapport between the deacons and pastors, so the body of Christ gets the best care possible.

i. Deacon. Who can serve as a deacon in the church is a hotly contested issue. This issue exists because the use of the Greek (*diaconos*) and English words refer both to one who serves the local church in this capacity as well as those who are simply known for being servants to the body of Christ. Deacons *are not* required to be spiritual guides, feeders of the flock, or teachers; they *are* required as to be trustworthy and of moral character as they deal with matters of temporal importance and the related spiritual foundations. The ambiguity of the term gives some men permission to enlarge the office to include women. That is a position which *can* be argued from God's Word, but there is *no* support for those who label "under-elders" or elders in training as "deacons." The health of the church depends on deacons functioning well, which requires the cooperation of the elders and the people. As we consider the various ways local churches deploy the office of deacon, it is painfully apparent that many of us have lost sight of the completeness of the wisdom our Lord has provided us and the reason for it. How we serve Him and one another is be to the glory of His name and the good of His people.

Robert Boyt C. Howell laments "much confusion and division of sentiment regarding the nature of the office"; and he points out how so many church groups miss the Scriptural teachings that describe the role of those who hold the office of deacon.

> Nearly all the churches have made them ministers of the gospel. In the Roman Catholic church he is an inferior ecclesiastic, the second in the sacred order, who, with the permission of the bishop, has authority to preach and baptize. In the English church the Deacons are clergymen, but of the lowest grade; who can perform all the offices of priests, except the consecration of the sacred elements and the pronouncing of the absolution. In the German Protestant churches, when more ministers than one in the same congregation are necessary, the second, or assistant minister, is called the Deacon; and if there are two assistants the first is called the Arch-Deacon. In the Presbyterian church, the office is commonly merged with that of ruling elder, and, therefore, mostly disused. Where it is still retained, it embraces, as among Congregationalists and others, merely the distribution of alms. The Methodist and Episcopal churches in this country adopt, substantially, the practice of the English church, of which they are descendants. In the Baptist churches, the Deacons are not ministers who preach, on the one hand, nor mere distributors of alms on the other, but serve in a different capacity. They are a board of directors, and have charge of all the secular affairs in the kingdom of Christ.[2]

It is not unusual for Baptist deacons to have hire & fire authority over the elders (a corollary error in this circumstance is the absence of a plurality of elders). In the end, nobody escapes unscathed! And this all-too-common Baptist practice is blatantly taken from the modern business world, and puts the lower office of deacon as overseers of those called of God to be overseers, turning Scripture on its head.

We need to ask, is the Bible *so* unclear on the nature and duties of the office of deacon? Brothers, this is not the case! It is sin that keeps God's people from seeing clearly, not a lack of clarity in God's Holy Word; for we still see through the glass darkly. This background is necessary, if we are to rightly see the biblical case for actual role of the deacon and how we, as reforming Baptists, should employ the men who serve in this office. We must abide by what the Book reveals, and guard against traditions not found therein. *Sola Scriptura!* applies here, not only in the deeper waters of soteriology.

Let's look at the text, 1 Timothy 3:8-13: *Deacons likewise must be dignified, not double-tongued, not addicted to much wine, not greedy for dishonest gain. They must hold the mystery of the faith with a clear conscience. And let them also be tested first; then let them serve as deacons if they prove themselves blameless. Their wives likewise must be dignified, not slanderers, but sober-minded, faithful in all things. Let deacons each be the husband of one wife, managing their children and their own households well. For those who serve well as deacons gain a good standing for themselves and also great confidence in the faith that is in Christ Jesus.*

The qualifications of deacons differ from those of elders on the single requirement of elders, but not deacons, being able to teach the Word of God. Deacons are to be men of good reputation, full of the Holy Spirit, holding the mystery of the faith with a clear conscience. I have seen these bedrock character traits often neglected when selecting deacons, as churches focus on the man's record of financial giving, business acumen, and abstinence from alcohol. While those traits can be easily measured, they cannot be found in the Bible as qualification for this office. The three traits found in Scripture are not so easily quantified. It takes serious thought and hard work to determine if a man has a good reputation among his neighbors and work colleagues. It takes time and discernment to see if there be evidence of the Holy Spirit in a man. And who wants to put a man on the spot and see if he holds the mystery of the faith with a clear conscience? Can you even explain this requirement, much less investigate it? Installing men to serve the local church as deacons is sober work, not to be taken lightly or without serious prayer and reflection. We are talking about service to God and His people, not planning a men's night out.

The requirement that deacons be tested first gives us a hint that we should invest the time and energy in examining would-be deacons; and not merely assuming these traits be theirs. This testing also provides the opportunity to see if his wife is sober minded and faithful, if his children are "managed well". We must exercise the full measure of the biblical text to prove the men who would serve as deacons; they are care-takers of God's sheep and co-laborers with His under-shepherds. This is a high calling (those who serve well gain a good standing) and we cannot allow our lazy human minds to rest on our own wisdom, or the taking of shortcuts or reliance on the traditions handed to us by other men. Finding men who tithe and do not frequent bars is wrong-headed and too low a bar for the office our Lord established for the temporal care of His redeemed.

The Scripture tells us much more about what is required of elders in the performance of their shepherding duties than it tells us about what temporal care responsibilities are required of deacons. Deacon care is broad and left largely to the church to define; the City of Man is temporal, the City of God is eternal. Yet this does not give us permission to be unhinged from Scripture in defining the role of deacon service in our churches. For example, one must seek to understand what Paul meant in describing "the role" within a church to which only "widows indeed" were to be enrolled in order to serve well in this office (1 Timothy 5:3). As in all aspects of life, lack of diligence in handling manna within the church can have serious consequences; this role demands maturity and love for God and His people.

The job of deacon gets more complicated when one rightly recognizes that there is a spiritual, or theological concern tied to every temporal issue, as was the case with the situation recorded in Acts chapter 6, where we see selfishness (idolatry of self) on display. Elders and deacons in each church must have solid fellowship and open lines of communication; elders refer people to deacons rather than resolving "table issues" themselves and deacons address some spiritual/theological issues as they work on temporal matters. Elders need to devote themselves to prayer and the Word of God; deacons cannot carry an elder in their pockets when the theological aspect of a temporal matter is addressed. Deacons need wisdom to know when an elder is needed; elders and deacons must trust one another. They must know one another well to develop this trust. This calls for maturity and is one of the main reasons the Word of God lays out pretty much identical qualifications for each office.

A good approach is to work according to a framework for how elders shepherd the flock and assign duties to the deacons. This "shepherding matrix"[3] recognizes that these ministries must be biblical, not merely busy. They must be systematic, not left to whimsy; comprehensive, not focused on whiners and needy people; and they must be relational, not merely programmatic. These three rules provide the foundation for this matrix:

> Systematic + Relational without Comprehensive = Exclusional (some are left out)
> Systematic + Comprehensive without Relational = Institutional (impersonal)
> Comprehensive + Relational without Systematic = Recreational (lack of focus)

Shepherds are to know the sheep God has gathered in the local church. They should visit the homes of their families periodically and call each home more frequently. Deacons should take attendance, call and visit those who are absent, and review that with the elders; as one of the first signs of a sick sheep is inconsistent attendance.

At one church I served in, we had far more deacons per member than any other churches I have served in or heard of: 10 deacons with a membership of approximately 260. Each deacon was responsible for staying in touch with an assigned group of families (5 to 7 families per deacon), at least a monthly phone with each, and visits when possible and when needed. These visits were for fellowship, providing requested assistance, and for checking up on a family. Do they appear in their home to be the same family that shows up for church on Sunday? Does the father exhibit those Christian characteristics we read in 1 Timothy 3? Negligence of a father to properly lead and teach his family would be a matter of prayer and reproof, with intervention by the assigned elder when appropriate.

As we desire our men to provide for their families, spiritually as well as physically, our deacons are to help families in each arena, with boundaries in both. Neither the church nor either office therein can unreasonably meddle with a family. God has established three spheres in this age, with specific roles and limits. It's been said that to the state God gave the sword, to the church He gave the keys to the kingdom, and to the family He gave the rod of correction. We should not cross these boundaries without a clear biblical basis. Wisdom and care is needed if we are to tend to God's people without ruling over them as "Gentiles" tend to do.

When a deacon assists a family in managing its money, for example, the goal is for the family to learn to live within its means and see those means as a gift from God to be properly stewarded. To provide both deacons and members a clear picture of responsibilities for each, the local church should provide a simple document describing how the benevolence program works and what its limits are (see Appendix 1 for an example). Properly managed by deacons and overseen by elders, the benevolence ministry can be a large percentage of the church's annual budget; knowing that we must be ready to help members when extraordinary circumstances arise. Participation in this benevolence program carries certain responsibilities for the family as well as for the church. The simple document should explain this and provide a means to escalate authority to the elders if certain limits (money and membership) are exceeded. This not only guides all concerned, it provides accountability on the entire ministry and those who administer it. We are, after all, to avoid all appearance of evil and covetousness.

Healthy church members let their deacons know ahead of time when they will miss, and explain why. They will be more inclined to assemble with another local body while away if they properly understand church membership. This exercise of membership responsibilities is representative of any number of other earthly matters that deacons are likely to get involved with, each of which most often reflects the spiritual condition of the person. Lack of attendance and interest in church life, neglecting to worship in giving money, and many other concerns can be prompted by earthly things: illness, loss of work, death in the family, etc. In order to be wise stewards of the office, deacons must not presume to know the cause without investigating it, learning from Job who investigated the cause of what he did not know (Job 29:16). This keeps us from the sin of presumption and all that tends to follow closely behind.

As we examine men who would and do serve in our churches as deacons; as we consider how we determine the role of the office and how we select these men, let us humbly petition our God for wisdom and grace to do what is right in His sight. Let our aim be to glorify our God and Savior and do good for His people, who are His body, the bride of the resurrected and soon coming Lord Jesus, the Christ of our God!

ii. Elder. This role can only be fulfilled by a qualified man who is called and equipped by God for this service (John 15:16). There is no possible interpretation that allows self-identified or lost men, or women to serve in this capacity; and yet many churches do just this. This latter error is always the first big step to total apostasy for a church, preferring fallen man's view of order over creator God's declared view.

In our English Bibles we see the words Elder/Presbyter, Overseer/Bishop, Shepherd/Pastor. Each pair of these words comes from one Greek word; Elder/Presbyter is from *presbyteros*; Overseer/Bishop from *episkope*; and Shepherd/Pastor from *poimen*. They are used interchangeably and they all refer to a single office in the church which has several important functions, each of which is designed by the Lord to insure the health of each local church. The terms elder and presbyter refer to a man's experience; in the Word and in the church. Overseer and bishop convey the act of being a spiritual guardian or protector, while pastor and shepherd refer to the spiritual care and feeding of God's flock. We see overlap among these three functions in 1 Peter 5:1-5, where elders are exhorted by the Apostle Peter to shepherd God's people with the right motive and attitude, serving as examples for the less mature Christians. In Acts 20:28, elders are instructed by the Apostle Paul to *pay careful attention* to themselves and the flock of God, *in which the Holy Spirit made you overseers, to care for the church*. One aspect of being a faithful elder that is implicit in these passages is that of being among the saints, knowing them as a shepherd knows his flock and being known as the shepherd is by the sheep. A man who does not live among his church members, who lives at a higher station of life, who spends all his time with other preachers is not faithful to his call. The elder must be an able teacher of the Word (1 Timothy 3:2, Titus 3:1-8) and a diligent servant of God's people (1 Timothy 5:17 & 18). He must also be able and willing to rebuke those who contradict the Word of God within the local church (Titus 1:7-9), and he must be about training others to work alongside him as under-shepherds of Christ (2 Timothy 2:1-3). One who would hold this office must lead the church, serving as a proper example (2 Thessalonians 2:11 & 12; 2 Timothy 2:15), and the saints are commanded to submit to them, not being burdensome for them (Hebrews 13:17). Elders were given to the church, by God, to equip the saints for the work of the church, bringing them to maturity and the fullness of Christ so they would not be vulnerable to the deceptive schemes of the enemy (Ephesians 4:11-14). This means the biblical elder must feed God's sheep the whole counsel of His Word, not trusting his opinion or theirs as to what is true nor picking some Scriptures from which to teach and ignoring others. His teaching is to be tested in light of Scripture; not accepted nor rejected by personal whimsy or blind friendship. All of these responsibilities of elders are beyond any man's abilities, so the Bible reminds us that elders, like the Apostles who preceded them, must be men of prayer (Acts 6:4). The Lord Jesus spent time in prayer while He walked among men, knowing He needed close communion with His Father. How misguided is the man who thinks he can lead and serve God's people without spending much time in prayer for them and himself!

There is another requirement of the man who would serve as an elder. While in centuries past this might not have seemed like a serious concern; but increasingly in our day, the notion of what marriage is has come under intense fire from the prince of the air. While some read 1 Timothy 3:2 to mean a single man cannot serve as an elder, the view most compatible with Scripture is that an elder who *is* married must be in a biblical marriage and work at keeping it. While homosexual activity has been around for a long time, it is only recently that shame has been cast aside and Christians have been coerced into making clear pronouncements as to what God ordained as marriage. We should learn from this not to wait until the enemies of our Lord attack us to present a defense, an apologetic, for what He has given us as truth. Elders must be one-woman men, and they must lead their churches to defend marriage in the face of reprobates. 1 Timothy 3 goes on to say the elder must be sober minded and not quarrelsome; all the more so in defending God's people from unrighteous men, who by their unrighteousness suppress the truth (Romans 1:18).

Being God's spokesman is no job for a new convert, one who is unsure of God's Word, unwilling to proclaim God's Word, unable to rebuke those who contradict God's Word, or unworthy of being followed as God's servant. The times in which we live are treacherous, with many professing Christians embracing abominable sin in order to be well thought of by those outside the camp of Christ. Christians are never to compromise God's truth for the applause of men (Galatians 1:10) and elders must be held to a high standard so that the Lord's name not be disgraced among the pagans and the local church not be led astray.

Thabiti Anyabwile preached a sermon on the role of elders in the local church at a conference I attended[4]. His message was taken from Ezekiel 33 & 34 where the watchman appointed by God had certain responsibilities to warn, guard, and care for the people of God. In these two chapters we see a contrast of the watchman with the shepherd: the watchman warns, the shepherd tends. In each passage, unfaithful watchmen and shepherds are contrasted with those who are faithful. Ezekiel 34:1-10 describes the failures of the leaders of Israel, showing what shepherds are supposed to fulfill. Shepherds are supposed to *care* for the flock. These men were *feeding* on the sheep; fleecing the sheep. These men had all the appearance of shepherds, but they were wolves. Pastoral ministry is hard work, not glamorous. Those who pose as celebrities, living the high life, are not pastors. Pastors should smell like sheep, walking in the mud and mess, scarred by the teeth of biting sheep. This is difficult but rewarding work. Every man should aspire to be a commendable man who leads his family as a shepherd leads the flock. He must diagnose and treat appropriately – you don't strengthen the stray, you strengthen the weak; you don't bind up the lost – you search for the lost. Each spiritual condition requires the pastor to apply the correct spiritual remedy. The pastor must know illnesses and the people, else he cannot properly treat the sheep. Verse 10 in Ezekiel 34 shows the omnipotent hand of God rescuing His sheep from the teeth of the wolves. A true pastor will watch the flock like a man who must give an account to the God who has purchased the sheep with the blood of His own son. Because that is what God's Word tells us the truth about those who would call themselves "pastor" (Hebrews 13:17).

Even with the best of intentions, we can go far afield from the narrow path of eternal truth. Over time, man has developed unbiblical structures, imagining that

Bishop is more honorific and must carry more responsibility (by which they mean fame). Most men who preach call themselves "pastor" regardless of whether they shepherd the flock God has gathered there or not. One who preaches but does not work to know and care for the saints the Lord has put under his watch cannot rightly call himself pastor; he is merely a preacher. These words are not titles by which the men who serve are to be called, but descriptions of service they provide within the local church. And though these words are not meant to be used as titles, we find it convenient to put labels on functions and people. So one church will call these men elders, another, pastors. As long as the men serving in those offices are not being exalted, there's really no harm. Yet because God has given these terms to describe the roles of men He calls to the office, we must be careful to use them correctly.

d.) Membership. Local church membership is important for two over-arching reasons: it reminds the members that we are not of the world, but aliens and sojourners; and it tells the world that we do not belong to them, but serve a different King. Membership is, for most churches, closely related to baptism. For the vast majority of churches which sprinkle babies and call that baptism, this means the infants are declared "covenant children" in some form or fashion. When pressed for a description of the covenant these unregenerate infants supposedly belong to, most who hold this view are at a loss. They want to believe their little children are in the New Covenant, but they admit that only believers in Christ are members of the New Covenant. Membership in this covenant is a prerequisite for membership in a local church, which God's Word makes abundantly clear, *To the church of God that is in Corinth, to those sanctified in Christ Jesus, called to be saints together with all those who in every place call upon the name of our Lord Jesus Christ* (1 Corinthians 1:2). The local church is to be comprised of people who are sanctified in Christ No matter how our emotions run, a sober examination of the biblical record on this topic clearly communicates that belonging to the body of Christ in the expression we call the local church represents the eternal community to which we belong by virtue of having been born again.

As we examine the Word of God we see that the Bible does not talk directly about church membership; we learn about it by seeing it in practice in various contexts. These include Christians being gathered together, being family, being a body, being equipped by God; in disciplining of those who rebel against God and in seeing how the world acts towards the church. We will look at each of these, examining what the Scriptures tell us about them and what the implications are for us today.

In more places than we can refer to, Scripture reveals the Lord gathering His people; to Himself and together as His children, often contrasting one thing with another in order to see both more clearly. Scripture tells us there are children of wrath and the devil (Ephesians 2:3; John 8:48) and there are children of God (Matthew 5:9; John 1:12 & 13; 11:52; Romans 8:16, 21; 9:8; Ephesians 5:1; Philippians 2:15; 1 John 3:1 and much, much more). What is the import of this relationship? If God is emphatic that the redeemed are His children, we must be diligent in seeking proper understanding of what this means for us. Ephesians 2:3

informs us that we are *by nature* children of wrath. This is the part of the contrast that most shrink back from as it is uncomfortable to recon a loved one as such; yet it is who we were until God's Spirit raised us as He described in John 1 and 3. There is no "demilitarized zone" in the spiritual realm; only two categories and two spiritual fathers of all people. Some run to Acts 17:29 to claim that all men are children of God, denying the impact of the Fall. In this passage, Paul is summing up his argument to the pagans in Athens. In verse 18, he quoted one of the Greek's poets, Aratus, who penned *For we are indeed his offspring.* In verse 19, he asserts this as he exhorts these pagans to see God rightly. The Apostle is not claiming all men are God's children; this would contradict what he wrote in Ephesians 2 and other places. It seems clear that Paul is merely acknowledging mankind's common standing as creatures made by God who are responsible to Him. If we are all God's children, then there would be no need of the Spiritual birth that Jesus told Nicodemus was necessary: you must be born again! *The wind blows where it wishes, and you hear its sound, but you do not know where it comes from or where it goes. So it is with everyone who is born of the Spirit* (John 3:8). Jesus is saying that, as no man controls where the wind blows – it seems as it blows where it wishes – no man can control where the Spirit of God goes and upon whom He bestows the new birth. John had established this early in his gospel that those who become children of God *were born, not of blood nor of the will of the flesh nor of the will of man, but of God* (John 1:13). This is the consistent record of Scripture: salvation is of the Lord, not of man; and not of a natural condition.

Another way Scripture tells us that those who have been redeemed are children of God is by use of adoption as a means of describing our new identity. The Apostle who had trusted in his genealogy wrote much of this change in identity that Christians have. *For all who are led by the Spirit of God are sons of God. For you did not receive the spirit of slavery to fall back into fear, but you have received the Spirit of adoption as sons, by whom we cry, "Abba! Father!"* (Romans 8:14-15) Those who are led by the Spirit of God, not those who are left to their sinful desires, are children of God; adopted by the Lord and King of all. The same point is made in Galatians 4:3-5: *In the same way we also, when we were children, were enslaved to the elementary principles of the world. But when the fullness of time had come, God sent forth his Son, born of woman, born under the law, to redeem those who were under the law, so that we might receive adoption as sons.* Here the Apostle describes how we move from being "children", those who are enslaved to the base aspects of the world, to being "sons," redeemed by the Son of God who was born in the same status as those He came to save. In the introduction of Paul's letter to the Ephesian church, one reads a glorious hymn of praise to God in Christ, who chose us before He created the world to partake in the adoption of sons.

Yes, the Scripture talks about God's great love for His children and we certainly need to try to comprehend this and joyfully gives thanks to Him for loving us; if He did not, we would not love Him (1 John 4:19). Yet Paul's letter to the Ephesians also tells us of another, higher reason that motivated God's redemptive work in fallen mankind: God's will coming to completion, sinners being raised to life and made holy and blameless, *to the praise of His glorious grace.* Since YHWH alone is, by nature, without sin and unable to sin, He alone can be "self-absorbed" and desire all to glorify Him. When Jesus told the parable of the lost coin (Luke 15:8-10), He said the angels rejoice over one sinner who repents. We can be certain much of this joy is due the sinner himself, who is now a child of God. But I submit the primary reason there is joy is because God's name is glorified when He is faithful to His own promises. God declared that Abraham would be the father of many nations; this news was revealed slowly over the sad history of disobedience that characterized the Hebrews. The Lord of Heaven called to Himself unlikely people, many who were remarkable for their sin; none who could claim their own righteousness. We see in many places in Scripture how God moved for man's benefit so that His name would not be profaned among the nations. In Exodus 32:7-14 He relents from destroying Israel so the Egyptians would not be able to say evil things about Him. Numerous times in the writings of Old Testaments prophets we read of the Lord acting for the sake of His name. In Ezekiel 20, for example, we see this four times, in verses 9, 14, 22, and 26. Psalms 106 recounts Israel's disobedience and their rescue by God who *saved them for his name's sake, that he might make known his mighty power*. This shows up in the New Testament as Christians are given ethical instructions so our lives will not cause pagans to profane His name; see Ezekiel 36:22, Ephesians 5:15, Colossians 4:5, and with particular application in 1 Timothy 3:7 as elders/pastors are required to *have a good reputation among outsiders* for his own sake, and for the sake of the church and the One Who gave Himself for her (Ephesians 5:25-27). In our day, when the impact of Charles Finney's focus on man is so prevalent, when those charged with preaching the Word spend themselves on influencing man to "accept Jesus", we need to be called back to the notion that God alone saves and to Him alone is all honor and glory due. Let the words from the Apostle Paul humble us and draw us to the one true God.

> *Oh, the depth of the riches both of the wisdom and the knowledge of God! How unsearchable His judgments and untraceable His ways! For who has known the mind of the Lord? Or who has been His counselor? Or who has ever first given to Him, and has to be repaid? For from Him and through Him and to Him are all things. To Him be the glory forever. Amen.* (Romans 11:33-36)

And yet, there is still more to life in the local church that we learn from God's holy Word. Acts 4:32-37 describes life in the early church; one to which social-gospel folk love to run as it shows what they call "communal living." What's important for proper understanding of this passage, showing Christians being a "gathered people," is to see what took place immediately before this, as recorded in Acts 2:37-41, when the Lord added some 3,000 souls to His church. As any new-born child of God tends to be excited about their spiritual resurrection, these new saints *devoted themselves to the apostles' teaching and fellowship, to the breaking of bread and to prayer* (Acts 2:42). In this community, they gave to one another as each had need; just as family members ought to act. This passage does not show each person was given what they wanted or demanded, but they *distributed to all* (those within the church, with no respect of persons) *as any had need*. (This changed rather quickly, as the scene in Acts 6 reveals.) In our day of plenty, by any historical standard, it is difficult to rightly comprehend needs. In the day of the apostles, people depended on production from local farms in a hand-to-mouth relationship from which we are far removed, with our refrigerated trucks and low cost fruits and vegetables available year-round. History records frequent, often severe periods of lack due to insects and/or drought. Family members were known to provide food and clothes to their kin who were in prison (the Roman government did not provide "3 hots and a cot" to its prisoners in the first century); hence Christians were known to provide for those in their spiritual families (Matthew 25:31-40).

This is further illustrated as the church grew and matured, as Paul addressed the church in Galatia. The first ten verses of Galatians 6 show much of the dynamic of family life in the local church. A brother caught up in sin is gently restored; saints bear one another's burdens; walk in humility and work to feed his own. The instruction continues, as Christians are encouraged to share with teachers; stay focused on the eternal; persist in good works; and, *as we have opportunity, let us do good to everyone, and* **especially** *to those who are of the household of faith.* These passages showing the care we are to have for one another within the local church is fleshed out in the Scriptures by use of family and body language, such as rebuking a man who does not provide for his family (1 Timothy 5:8), to the reminder that we have been brought from one kingdom to another (Ephesians 2:19), to a lengthy instruction that being a member of God's household affects how disputes are handled (1 Corinthians 6:1-8).

We see several dynamics at work as the Lord used Paul to describe life in the church, showing the tight relationships therein and the tension between the church and the temporal family. In Romans 12 we have the famous description of various sinners made clean by the blood of Christ being identified as the body of Christ, with each person being given different functions with different gifts. *For as in one body we have many members, and the members do not all have the same function, so we, though many, are one body in Christ, and individually members one of another* (verses 4 & 5). This is amplified in 1 Corinthians 12:12-31 as the Apostle takes great pains to show how arrogant we are when we think we are worth more to the Lord than someone else, or worth less. And all because we are ungrateful sorts who think we know better than our Creator and Redeemer how to gift and use each one of us. Let us be careful to learn from what was written, so we do not stumble in the same way as the Hebrews of old as they grumbled day-by-day against YHWH's provision. Tension between spiritual family and temporal family is shown in several well-known passages as we are told we must "hate" father and mother, sister and brother if we are to be considered worthy of being disciples of Jesus (Luke 14:26). We see in 1 Timothy 5:16 that this "hatred" does not relieve us of the duty temporal families have of taking care of their own so they won't be a burden on others within the church: *If any believing woman has relatives who are widows, let her care for them. Let the church not be burdened, so that it may care for those who are truly widows.*

We have reviewed the function of the officers within the local church, but here as we consider membership let us examine how the Lord has equipped the local church and see what that means regarding one's belonging to a local church. We see in several places that it is God who equips the local church, not man. Man is no more fit to decide the structure or function of the local church than Aaron's sons were fit to determine what kind of fire was to be used to worship God (Leviticus 10:1 & 2). When the early church had growing pains (Acts 6), and people with selfish desires and legitimate needs rubbed one another the wrong way, the Lord worked through men He had called to service to work out a plan to handle these inevitable conflicts; providing us much needed guidance as we face very similar circumstances with people who are no different from those who have gone before us. When the Corinthian church had disputes centered around personal rivalries and petty human fleshly desires (1 Corinthians 12:1-27), the Apostle was moved by the Holy Spirit to remind those disgruntled, selfish Corinthians that God had given the church various leaders and gifts (verses 28-31) with clear teaching that while all Christians are equal in value, we are not identical in gifts or function. As the Lord Jesus desired that the world would know we are His disciples by our love for one another (John 13:35), the Apostle was used to put all these desires for gifts and position in the proper light by reminding the Corinthians, and us, that Christian love is the bottom line of who we are as those have been bought at a high price (1 Corinthians 6:20 and 7:23). To insure proper teaching and solid doctrine be taught His people, it pleased God to put elders/pastors and deacons in the local church (see Ephesians 4:11-16, James 5:14, Titus 1:5-9).

Two other topics taught in Scripture show us the nature of the local church, with the clear implication that those in fellowship have joined with one another in what is more than a casual meeting of convenience. Church discipline is irrelevant if membership is not a reality. Read carefully the last paragraph in 1 Corinthians 5:

> *I wrote to you in my letter not to associate with sexually immoral people— not at all meaning the sexually immoral of this world, or the greedy and swindlers, or idolaters, since then you would need to go out of the world. But now I am writing to you not to associate with anyone who bears the name of brother if he is guilty of sexual immorality or greed, or is an idolater, reviler, drunkard, or swindler—not even to eat with such a one. For what have I to do with judging outsiders? Is it not those inside the church whom you are to judge? God judges those outside. "Purge the evil person from among you."* (1 Corinthians 5:9-13)

The main point I want to make here is not so much the process of church discipline (this will be addressed in chapter 11), though that *is* the main point of this chapter in the Bible. What I want you to see is the contrast between the local church at Corinth (and the local church in every town) and the world. We see the oft-told tale of two categories of people: those who have been made alive in Christ and those who are dead in their sins and trespasses, at home in the world where they are having their best life now. The Apostle is not preaching against sin in the world; he expects the world to be sinful! He protests against the church that allows one who calls himself "brother" and lives like the world. The unrepentant sinner is thrown out of the local church. How can this be if he had not joined himself to the local church? How can he be thrown out of a local church unless he belongs to the local church?

We see this point further applied in 1 Timothy 5:19 & 20 as the elder who persists in sin is rebuked in front of the local church. And this is done, in part, so that all the people in the local church would *stand in fear*. This scene conveys the autonomy of the local church: the elder who sins and will not repent is brought before the church, not to a bishop or presbyter of religious authorities from another place. The church stands before her Shepherd, not a religious hierarchy of men. This is why the sinning elder ought to cause a church to *stand in fear;* because everything is done in the open, fully seen by God. Christians ought to fear God at all times, but we must understand what it means for us to fear Him. A dear friend and pastor (Louis Lyons) remarked in a sermon one time that a Christian ought to fear offending God. This is a wonderful way to put it, in stark contrast to the phobia-like fear those under His wrath will have when their deeds are judged. The local church that rightly fears God will not turn a blind eye to an elder who has gone astray, just as they will not allow a brother to continue in public sin. The local church stands before God and has been given His authority to *purge the evil person*, so the church might not bring shame to the name of her Savior. Scripture on church discipline shows us the "back side" of church membership. See also 1 Corinthians 1:10-13a, Titus 3:1-11, and Matthew 18:15-20. These passages show the importance of unity within the local church (which Jesus prayed would be true of all the saints, John 17:20 & 21) and the role of elders in leading the flock so that God's people would bring honor and glory to His name and not be brought down by their sin.

This is an important aspect of Christian life, individually and as part of a local church, for the unholy trinity of our sinful flesh, the system of the world, and Satan is aligned against us; seeking to cause us harm and bring shame and disgrace on name of our Lord and those which Christ has bought. We see this war in the early days of the church, as the unconverted Saul ravaged the people of God (Acts 8:1-3 and 9:1-2) and as king Herod *laid violent hands on some,* killed James, and imprisoned Peter (Acts 12:1-5). People of the world hate God, because **we all** are, by nature, children of wrath (Ephesians 2:3); unloved (salvifically) by God and hating Him and His children. Christ warned us that the world hated Him and if we are hated by the world it is because they hate Him (John 15:18). John told us not to be surprised if the world hates us (1 John 3:13) and Peter tells us friends from our time in the flesh would rail against us as we walk in the light, wondering why we don't rejoin them in their celebration of sin (1 Peter 4:1-6). We see this played out (Acts 16:16-24) as Paul and Silas go about proclaiming the gospel and delivered a slave girl who was possessed by a demon, making her owners rich. When she was delivered from demonic slavery, she was of no more profit to her owners; and they had Paul and Silas hauled off to prison where they were beaten. Those preachers who tell you we must be like the world to win them to the Lord know not the gospel nor the world. The world and its prince are at war with God, knowing their time is short. Like a caged animal, Satan seeks to deceive and destroy as many as he can; through compromise and deception (*did God actually say … ?*).

We need one another, with the leaders God has called into His service, in order not to fall prey to the enemy. Righteous Lot (as Peter called him) ran from Zoar because it was as full of sin as Sodom. But rather than running to Uncle Abraham, he went to the other side of the valley where he would be alone with his daughters. And his sin went with him and found him out (Genesis 19:30-38). God gave us to one another for our own good. Pursuing membership in a biblical church and actively participating there is a crucial element of a healthy Christian life.

None of these scenarios or warnings make sense if small children and unregenerate people are considered members, as they cannot judge accusations in light of Scripture nor examine themselves to see if they be in the faith, nor reason with one another about sin and righteousness. Everything we *do* see in the Word of God around local church membership reveals that it is an active relationship where people have differences, conflicts, and share joy and sorrow together. Church membership *does* have a relationship with baptism: both require a credible profession of faith in Christ and a willingness to walk in obedience to Him. Infants can do neither. So we must do what we can to insure that every member of our church is, as best we can tell, a born-again believer in Jesus Christ. Submission to the command to be baptized is an evidence of personal, saving faith in Christ Jesus, and should not serve as presumptuous declaration that the child will prove himself to be a covenant child later in life. If churches do take seriously their commission from God to be *the pillar and foundation of the truth* (1 Timothy 3:15) then all sorts of traditions of men will find a home in our midst. God keep us from idols! (1 John 5:21)

e.) Relationship to civil government. In the apostolic record of the Bible, each local church existed as on outpost for Christians in a hostile world. Christianity was illegal in the Roman Empire because the church did not embrace the fable of the Caesar being a god. Until Constantine legalized Christianity, governments either persecuted Christian churches or barely tolerated them. When infant baptism was settled upon, initially for superstitious reasons, it was quickly seen as a wonderful tool for the newly crafted state church to know how many little tax payers lived within her boundaries. Even to this day, the state church in Scotland allocates geographical regions to each local church. If you live there, that's where you go to church; very much the way our government schools operate in these United States. This is an issue that shows one reason the state churches hated the Anabaptists. All the so-called radical reformers had one thing in common: they believed the local church answered to Christ Jesus directly and that polluting the church with politics works against God's people. Baptists developed this topic and embraced a healthy separation of church and state, a doctrine that recognizes the different spheres of responsibility God has given to each and recognizes that governments need counsel from churches so they can fulfill their roles, for how else will a pagan government know "good" and "evil"? And contrary to many of the Anabaptists, who thought it sinful for Christians to serve in government offices, Baptists think such service is one way God's church can influence civil governments to be better ministers according to Romans 13.

f.) Liberty of Conscience

In practice, liberty of conscience is a product of one's view of the nature of the local church and the individual believer. Firstly, each Christian is described as a priest (1 Peter 2:5 and Revelation 1:6), describing our "alien righteousness", given to each of us by the Lord Jesus, which allows us unveiled and unregulated access to our Father in Heaven. And Jesus is our great high priest (Hebrews 4:14-16) who intercedes for us and His Spirit helps us pray (Romans 8:26-27). This means we cannot be told by another man what to believe nor how to worship. We are informed by faithful men who have gone before us and serve alongside us, but God alone rules our conscience. Secondly, if the local church answers to none but Christ, to Him alone the elders/pastors answer and He alone rules the hearts of those in the church. If, however, the local church answers to a regional bishop, a pope, or a governor; that political/religious hierarchy inevitably asserts itself and demands obedience of the church and the individual.

Here's how this doctrine worked out in the 1500s, in striking parallel to the circumstances surrounding the birth of Christ. Just as the Roman network of roads and the wide scale influence of Greek language and culture were orchestrated by God to bring about the fullness of time for the Lord's first advent, in like manner He brought about the printing press and common language Bibles to a people who were awakening from the dark ages and beginning to see a great light. Men such John Wycliffe and William Tyndale were used of God to bring His Word to the common people in their own tongues. As time progressed and the Word of God was better understood, Puritans refused to submit to the Roman Catholic Church regarding salvation; they believed in salvation by grace alone. They were persecuted by the Roman Church, which had the power of the state in hand, and fled to the colonies. Baptists who had fled from England, where the Anglican Church used the power of the state to persecute them for not sprinkling babies, landed in the American colonies; and were persecuted by the Puritans for not submitting to their requirement that babies be sprinkled and churches submit to the colonial government. Men with power are prone to misuse it, and it is nowhere more damaging to good order than when the power of the state is wedded to a perceived religious authority. And when a few children of God desire to walk as they see fit in Scripture, the religious authorities inevitably take actions to stop it and try to bind the consciences of the "rebels." The danger of state churches is clearly demonstrated by history, as man cannot rule as God does. So having each local church be autonomous is the only acceptable way; and it has the benefit of aligning with Scripture. So the local church and each saint therein stands before God with, as Luther put it, a conscience bound only by the Word of God. This is what is meant by each Christian being part of the priesthood of believers: we each stand before God as individuals and our conscience can be bound by Him alone. Christians have minds that can comprehend spiritual truths but are still affected by inherited sin and active sin, keeping us from understanding Scripture perfectly. Hence, these tensions exist between Christians and the various views of secondary issues we hold to.

g.) Biblical Gospel. As important as the previous characteristics of a biblical church are, and they are crucial, they matter not if the church gets the gospel wrong. This is a vital topic which is directly affected by our view of Scripture, God, and man. What is more important to those made in God's image than being cleansed from the sin that stains and separates us from our Creator? Jesus said it's more important than the whole world! *And he said to all, "If anyone would come after me, let him deny himself and take up his cross daily and follow me. For whoever would save his life will lose it, but whoever loses his life for my sake will save it.* **For what does it profit a man if he gains the whole world and loses or forfeits himself?** *For whoever is ashamed of me and of my words, of him will the Son of Man be ashamed when he comes in his glory and the glory of the Father and of the holy angels* (Luke 9:23-26.) If we take God at His Word, we will want to get this part right. Proclaiming His message of reconciliation is the only role He has given us in His grand plan of redemption. We can't save anyone's soul, we can't know who God will save. All we can do, and it is a glorious privilege, is to be faithful with His Gospel, trusting Him to do what only He can do.

One should be able to take at face value that professing Christians should agree that there is salvation in none other than Jesus, the Christ. But this is, sadly, not the case. We must seek to gain a better understanding of the gospel of God so that we can see Him and ourselves more clearly.

First, the gospel is not an urgent call to obey the Law, based on and extracted from the Mosaic Covenant. The Law of God demands perfect obedience and the Scriptures remind us of what we know to be true, we cannot do it (Romans 3:9-18). The Law demands to be answered, but, as an old Baptist hymn reminds us, the lost man senses something is wrong and often runs to the wrong place:

> *I felt the arrows of distress*
> *And found I had no shield, no hiding place*
> *Holy justice stood in view*
> *To Sinai's fiery mount I flew*
> *But justice cried with frowning face*
> *"This mountain is no hiding place!"* [25]

If we cannot answer Mount Sinai's demand for justice, how can we face the Holy God who shakes the earth (Hebrews 12:18-29) with His demands? The holiness of God causes man to tremble (Isaiah 6) and that is what we hold up in the gospel. The Law may be useful to break the pride of some men, but the Law is not the gospel. Jesus Christ and Him crucified – the holy One of God sacrificed for sinners; that is the gospel!

God the judge provides the God-Man as the justifier; that is the mystery and the glory of God's gospel. 1 Corinthians 15:1-8 is considered by many to be the best summary of the gospel given to us in the Scriptures. This message proclaims the mighty work of redemption completed by the biblical Jesus; no pale, culturally relevant imitation will suffice. This biblical gospel is tied to a place in time and space, the hill and the grave-site near Jerusalem; where the Lamb of God was slain as a wrath-satisfying (propitiating) sacrifice to save sinners and make them presentable to God the Father. And, lastly, this God-Man was raised from the dead and seen by many people. The resurrection of Jesus is one of the most substantiated events of the ancient world, and it gives us the firm hope that He will raise us from our graves one day and make us like Himself and make His home among us (Revelation 21:3).

The biblical gospel recognizes that, as Jonah declared from the belly of the fish, *Salvation is of YHWH!* We are told that we can plant seed (which is the proclamation of the gospel – Mark 4:14), we can water (which is making disciples of those God has saved – Acts 18:27), but it is God Who gives the increase (which is the work of reclaiming ruined sinners, see 1 Timothy 1:15). People become the children of God, not according to blood, to the will of flesh or the will of man; but according to the will of God (John 1:10-13). Within the pale of those Christians who agree that there is no other name, there are those who mistakenly think man has something to do with securing reconciliation with God. Mostly, this is the result of poor teaching, which takes a verse here and there out of context and settles in one's mind as "gospel." Since Scripture cannot be broken, it will not contradict itself. Therefore, we must seek to understand the whole counsel of God's Word, not just a few "proof texts," to rightly comprehend this most important doctrine. If anything man does contributes to his justification, to being reconciled to Holy God, then that man's gospel is polluted, reducing the supreme work of redemption completed by Jesus to something that doesn't quite save anyone. If the work of Jesus is not enough, nothing we can do can close the rift. We must think carefully and deliberately to weed out any shred of self-confidence or self-will regarding this most important change, of being made a new creature (2 Corinthians 5:17). Salvation is a monergistic work of God; man plays no role in being raised from the dead any more than he did in being born physically (John 3:1-8). Man is by nature spiritually dead, following after the spiritual father of fallen humanity, this according to the Word of God. Paul's letter to the church, those who had been redeemed, at Ephesus provides an excellent summary of man's problem and God's redemptive answer (Ephesians 2:1-10):

> *And* **you were dead in the trespasses and sins** *in which you once walked, following the course of this world,* **following the prince of the power of the air,** *the* **spirit that is now at work in the sons of disobedience** *—* **among whom we all once lived** *in the passions of our flesh, carrying out the desires of the body and the mind, and* **were by nature children of wrath, like the rest of mankind.**

> **But God, being rich in mercy, because of the great love with which he loved us, even when we were dead in our trespasses, made us alive together with Christ — by grace you have been saved — and raised us up with him and seated us with him in the heavenly places in Christ Jesus,** *so that in the coming ages he might show the immeasurable riches of his grace in kindness toward us in Christ Jesus.*

*For by grace you have been saved through faith. And **this is not your own doing; it is the gift of God**, not a result of works, so that no one may boast. For **we are his workmanship, created in Christ Jesus for good works, which God prepared beforehand, that we should walk in them.***

This passage shows that there is no "demilitarized zone" in the spiritual realm; one is a child of Satan unless and until God gives new life and faith to the sinner, adopting him as His child. 1 Corinthians 15:1-8 is considered by many to be the best summary of the gospel given to us in the Scriptures.

> *Now I would remind you, brothers, of the gospel I preached to you, which you received, in which you stand, and by which you are being saved, if you hold fast to the word I preached to you—unless you believed in vain. For I delivered to you as of first importance what I also received: that Christ died for our sins in accordance with the Scriptures, that he was buried, that he was raised on the third day in accordance with the Scriptures, and that he appeared to Cephas, then to the twelve. Then he appeared to more than five hundred brothers at one time, most of whom are still alive, though some have fallen asleep. Then he appeared to James, then to all the apostles. Last of all, as to one untimely born, he appeared also to me.*

Christians were chosen in Christ before the foundation of the world (Ephesians 1:4), predestined for adoption as sons through Jesus Christ according to His will (Ephesians 1:5), and we were formed and predestined for good works (Ephesians 2:10). There is no biblical support for man choosing to save himself or for a saved man to continue in sin with no concern for being obedient to his Savior and Lord. Jerome Zanchius reminds us, "God efficaciously operates on the hearts of His elect, and is thereby the sole Author of all the good they do (see Ephesians 3:20; Philippians 2:13; 1 Thessalonians 2:13; Hebrews 13:21)."[5]

There are truths in God's Word that rub our flesh the wrong way; predestination is one of them. I refer the reader to Appendix 5 for a biblical defense of this doctrine. We must embrace the truth of Scripture, even if it goes against what we've learned from our favorite author or preacher. *For the word of God is living and active, sharper than any two-edged sword, piercing to the division of soul and of spirit, of joints and of marrow, and discerning the thoughts and intentions of the heart* (Hebrews 4:12). God's Word is sharp and, as wielded by the Holy Spirit, cuts like a scalpel, bringing healing to our broken souls. False teaching is seen as less threatening, like a butter knife. And it works the same way, tearing the flesh as it pierces, bringing destruction rather than healing. Good counsel presents the truth of Scripture; this is biblical love, even though our beloved traditions may have to be abandoned.

Many who disbelieve predestination run to John 3:16, as if this verse disproves it. Let us briefly examine this verse to see what its message truly is. Here's the verse, from the King James: *For God so loved the world, that he gave his only begotten Son, that whosoever believeth in him should not perish, but have everlasting life.* That settles it for many, who do not stop to see if the words may have had a different meaning when written 500 years ago than they do today; including Baptist preachers who ought to know better. But contrary to a popular hermeneutic which declares, "when the plain sense of Scripture makes common sense, seek no other sense," the plain sense of Scripture often contradicts the true meaning of Scripture and our common sense often makes no heavenly sense. The genre of the text we are reading will indicate how we are to read it: poetry and apocalyptic books cannot be taken literally, and even historical narratives are full of word pictures that must be interpreted rightly to get God's view of His Scriptures. The Jews of the first century had common sense and they took certain prophecies in the plain sense. This caused them to look for a king like David, a man of war, and miss the true meaning of their own Scripture.

In regards to John 3:16, let us examine a couple of key words upon which the meaning of this verse hang. In English, the word "so" can be either an adverb or an adjective. We see it in verse 14: *And as Moses lifted up the serpent in the wilderness, even so must the Son of man be lifted up* (KJV). Here, the word "so" is an adverb, meaning "in like manner" or "in the same way," describing the nature of something. Many people think the word "so" is an adjective in verse 16, describing the degree of the thing that follows: God loves the world *SO* much. The problem with this view is that the Greek word translated as "so" in English (*houtos* – Strong's #3779) is rarely used as an adjective. Strong's Greek and Hebrew dictionary defines it only as an adverb. *Houtos* shows up more than 200 places in the Greek New Testament. In only four occurrences it is definitely an adjective: Galatians 1:6; 3:3; Hebrews 12:21 (*houto*); and Revelation 16:18. In more than 97% of the uses the word *houtos* is an adverb.[6] Now looking back to John's gospel, let us read a little more for context:

> John 3:14-16 (KJV) *And as Moses lifted up the serpent in the wilderness, even so must the Son of man be lifted up: That whosoever believeth in him should not perish, but have eternal life. For God so loved the world, that he gave his only begotten Son, that whosoever believeth in him should not perish, but have everlasting life.*

Is there a compelling argument that John's use of *houtos* changes from the common adverb in verse 14 to the extremely rare adjective in verse16? If its use in verse 16 is as an adjective, the Bible tells us God loved the world to such a great degree that He sent Christ to die for the same world He said we are not to love (1 John 2:15). Since Jesus said *Scripture cannot be broken* (John 10:35) we must interpret Scripture with Scripture and *lean not on our own understanding* (Proverbs 3:5), even if the plain sense makes common sense to us. Our common sense is *our* understanding, not God's. I do not have space here to examine "the world" and how it is used; but since not everybody at all times in every nation, tribe, and tongue has been forgiven, it is reasonable and in keeping with Christ's high priestly prayer in John 17 that Jesus did not come to save the whole world in the comprehensive sense some assert. As noted in Ephesians 5:25, Jesus gave His life for the church, not everybody in the world. And since "the world" often means a region (Luke 2:1; John 12:19), or the system which lies under Satan's rule (John 15:19; 17:13; 1 Corinthians 2:12), we have no reason to assume this term means everyone everywhere as regards salvation, as the Lamb of God died for the redeemed, not the damned.

The argument is not whether or not the death of Christ is sufficient to save everyone; His death is more than sufficient for the entire human race. The question is, did Christ die for all men; is the atonement universal? One English Bible translates this phrase, "*in tasting death He should stand for us all;*" those for whom Christ stands are the redeemed. The word, man, is not in the Greek text, meaning the original phrase would be "*should taste death for the whole;*" the whole body, the church for whom Christ gave Himself. Jesus died for every son God brings to glory. God the Father chooses only some to be saved; election is not universal. God the Spirit regenerates only some to bring them to new life, He only seals those who are born again; the Spirit's work in saving and sealing is not universal. For Christ's death to be universal, it would mean that some of His blood, some of His trials and suffering under the wrath of God the Father, was for those who are spending eternity under God's wrath. Any blood or work done by Christ on their account would be wasted! And if the death of Christ was universal, it would put Him at odds with the Father and the Spirit, because their work in salvation is particular, not universal.

Here's this passage from John 3 in the Holman Christian Standard Bible:

> *Just as Moses lifted up the snake in the wilderness, so the Son of Man must be lifted up, so that everyone who believes in Him will have eternal life. "For God loved the world in this way: He gave His One and Only Son, so that everyone who believes in Him will not perish but have eternal life.*

This is more in line with the common use of the Greek and keeps consistency within the passage and with the whole teaching of the redemptive work of the Lord Jesus. The ESV has a note in the margin agreeing with the HCSB on verse 16a. If man was in charge of seeing to it that he was saved from the wrath to come, this might be his song:

> *All hail the power of my dead faith, let demons prostrate fall. Bring forth my free will trophy of works and hail me, lord of nil! Bring forth my free will trophy of works and hail me, lord of nil!*

But even the most ardent free will believer doesn't sing or pray in line with his professed beliefs. He prays for God to save, he thanks God for his salvation. And he claims to believe that God gave him the freedom to do so. But that is not how God gets things done.

If Christ died for all people, either hell is not a place of wrath poured out on sins (because people there had their sins paid for by the One Whose death satisfied the Father's wrath and wouldn't pay again) or the blood of Christ is not truly sufficient to save anyone or does not satisfy the Father's wrath (as not everyone gets saved). Both of these consequences of that perspective contradict clear teachings in Scripture. Therefore, we can strenuously teach and believe that when Jesus says He gave His life for His sheep (John 10:11) and He gave Himself for the church (Ephesians 5:25) He meant exactly that!

Another aspect of getting the gospel wrong shows up in a segment within Baptist circles which claims that one can be saved but have no evidence thereof, and professing Christians should not be held accountable for how they live. A youth pastor in Phoenix reported,

> I have one teenager in our group that has walked away from God over the past two years. He is the typical troubled teenager who has a horrible home life and is rebelling against everyone and everything. I called him into my office after I heard rumors of him having inappropriate relationships with some of the girls in the youth group. As I confronted him on these issues, he admitted to them and didn't really seem to care. I asked him what he thought God would think of his behavior. He went on to explain to me how he never really understood why the Bible says that you can't have sex before marriage. I knew this to be a lie, because we had talked about this issue many times over the three years he had been in our youth group. I explained that God did not want him to live this way, to which he replied, "It's not like I can lose going to Heaven! I am going to go with the flow and do what I want and maybe someday I will start living for God again." My Free Grace Theology had just been used against me. Everything inside of me wanted to tell this guy that since he was living in such rebellion to God, he might not have been truly saved in the first place. I wanted to scare him into obedience to God. And yet, I couldn't. He was right, he can't lose going to heaven. I ended up reassuring him that if he had trusted in Jesus for his eternal life that he was eternally secure.[7]

So allergic to works-based salvation are they, this Free Grace Alliance group denies any teaching that says a redeemed person *will* exhibit good fruit. Such a person *may* walk as child of God, but he should *not* have his position in Christ questioned if he at one time "trusted in Jesus for his eternal life;" even if he lives like the world and enjoys it. A rebel is eternally secure, his lifestyle notwithstanding, according to this view. *What shall we say then?* **Are we to continue in sin that grace may abound? By no means! How can we who died to sin still live in it?** *Do you not know that all of us who have been baptized into Christ Jesus were baptized into his death? We were buried therefore with him by baptism into death, in order that, just as Christ was raised from the dead by the glory of the Father, we too might walk in newness of life* (Romans 6:1-4). Clearly the Bible tells us Christians will learn to hate sin, not be accepting of it. And, as was shown in the section on church discipline, the Bible spells out consequences for those who claim the name of Christ but live like hell.

As an aid in help man see the biblical case for the awesome work God does when a sinner is redeemed, theologians have developed a systematic theology (a process of taking the whole counsel of God into account) of salvation.

Order of Salvation (Ordo Salutis)

Predestination – As it refers to the elect, God did, in eternity past, chose who He would save. By default, all not so chosen are left to their sinful desires and predestined to eternal torment. (Ephesians 1:3-14)

Effectual Calling (Regeneration) – While God's choosing of His elect took place before the foundation of the world, each of us was called and born again in time, as the Holy Spirit worked by the sowing of the Word. In Mark 3:13 we see the effective call of the apostles, Jesus called those whom He selected. How much more valuable is the call to salvation, and yet many declare man chooses. Only those with ears to hear, those whose names were written in the Lamb's book of life before the foundation of the world (Rev 13:8), hear and respond to the call – our nature being changed so we could hear and joyfully answer (Matthew 22:8-14; 2 Timothy 1:9). As Conrad Mbewe put it, making sure we get the sequence right: "We're born again in order for us to repent & believe; & not that we repent & believe in order to be born again. Regeneration comes first!"[8]

Faith/Repentance – The soil having been prepared, the seed having been sown, true growth – root and fruit – begin to emerge. As the Spirit of the living God gives ears to hear, so He gives faith & repentance to God's elect only; and without fail (Mark 4:10-20; Acts 20:17-21).

Justification (Legal Declaration) – Those whom God chose and called and brought to faith & repentance, He declares to be NOT GUILTY! No, that's not enough. He declares us to be RIGHTEOUS! Our legal system lets people off with the lower standard; God's justice demands perfection and the earned righteousness of Christ is credited to each of our accounts, irreversible. The calling of God is without repentance; no undoing what He has predetermined to do. His will is what history records (Romans 3:27 & 28; 8:29 & 30).

Adoption – Herein is the kindness of God towards those He has redeemed. Knowing we are weak minded and forgetful, creator God adopts us into His family! No longer strangers, we are sons and daughters, joint heirs with Christ Jesus (Romans 8:14 & 15; Galatians 4:3-7; Ephesians 1:3-6).

Definitive Sanctification – That fertile soil allows the seed to sprout and put down roots and begin "above ground" growth. There will be evidence of being made a new creature in Christ. We do not have a litmus test of tongues or other gifts, but we do expect to see some evidence, as no one born again by the Spirit of God can be unchanged (2 Corinthians 5:17; Mark 4:20).

Progressive Sanctification (Preservation of the Saints) – As we mature in Christ, our appetites change. Things that used to appeal to us and draw us into sin are less attractive; the Truth of Scripture that proclaims the glories of God and sinfulness of man nourish our souls, whereas they used to repel our flesh (Hebrews 12:1 & 2; 1 Thessalonians 5:23 & 24).

Glorification – At the end of all things, we will be made like our Savior, free from temptation and unable to sin (Philippians 3:17-21).

With each aspect of this Ordo Solutis, God is the one who either does it outright or enables us to cooperate with Him in the work. There is nothing we do outright; God is the source of all good and we have nothing that He has not given us (1 Corinthians 4:7).

> *For I delivered to you as of first importance what I also received: that Christ died for our sins in accordance with the Scriptures, that he was buried, that he was raised on the third day in accordance with the Scriptures.* (1 Corinthians 15:3-5)

The Biblical gospel – one of the marks of a biblical church; and that's what a Baptist church should be.

Recommended reading on this topic:

The Deaconship* - Robert Boyt C. Howell
The Glory of a True Church* – Benjamin Keach
Corrective Church Discipline* – Patrick H. Mell
The political activities of the Baptists and Fifth Monarchy men in England during the interregnum*, Louise Fargo Brown
Building Blocks of the Church – Anton Bosch
Finding Faithful Elders and Deacons – Thabiti M. Anyabwile
The Church – Why Not? - Jeffrey D. Johnson
Persecution for Religion Judged and Condemned* - John Murton
When Church and Government Collide - Jeff Canfield
Tracts on liberty of conscience and persecution* - Edward Bean Underhill
Ill News from New England* – John Clark
Religions Peace* – Leonard Busher
The Priesthood of All Believers: Slogan or Substance? – David H.J. Gay
The Pastor: Does He Exist? – David H.J. Gay
The Arminian Heresy of Universal Atonement* – Angus Stewart
Gospel - Repentance floweth from faith* – Francis Cornwell

Conclusion

I have endeavored to show the reader where the Baptist came from, what are distinctives are and why it matters that we are Baptists. Having that name is not the important thing; being true to the Scriptures is. Each of these points (Ordinances, the Nature of the Local Church, Liberty of Conscience, and one's view of Scripture) reminds us of Whom we serve and where our hope lies; not that our label is "Baptist". We live as citizens of God's kingdom; traveling through a world at war with Him, proclaiming His life-giving gospel and walking as children of the Light. Let us love one another in word and deed, spurring each other onto good works prepared for us before the foundation of the world, as people of the Book, to bring glory to the name of our Lord and Savior and do good to all in the household of God.

Part 2: A Baptist View of Reformed Theology

Reformed theology is a phrase that conveys various meanings depending on who is using it. This phrase has definite meaning and yet it is indefinite, due to the ambiguity that inevitably accompanies the efforts of man. At its core, to be reformed means to always be conforming to Scripture, as that is God's revelation of Christ, into Whose likeness we are ever being conformed. But it is helpful, we being of finite minds infected by sin, to drill down a bit to clarify what we mean. There are, sadly, many divergent views on several important doctrines, meaning clarity is all the more necessary. One friend of mine has summed up this one in an easy to remember, but, in my opinion, inaccurate way. He says to be Reformed is to be Confessional, Calvinistic, and Covenantal. These are true of reformed believers, but not in an absolute or unambiguous way as I hope to demonstrate.

First, what is meant by confessional? Does this mean that we must confess Christ before men or does it mean we hold to a confession of faith written by men? While the Bible is clear about the first (Matthew 10:32-33), I think it reasonable and fair to say that most reformers in our day mean the second, and endorse the idea that one must hold to a confession of faith (they have one of two or three specific documents in mind) to claim this label. But this is not expressed clearly in the phrase. And I think we do not need to be confined or conformed to the Westminster Confession and its "children," the Savoy Declaration and the 1689 London Baptist Confession (1689 LBC). These documents are good, imperfect expressions of myriad doctrines, reflecting what certain men believed in the 17th century. Yet adherence to any of these type documents cannot be exegeted from the Bible. We should have the grace to accept one another without insisting our favorite confession be the standard of *"sound doctrine"* (Titus 3:9). Holding to certain ancient creeds that were written to expose heresies and protect against them would seem to be a higher priority than 17th century confessions, which tend to cover a much broader area of doctrine in detail and tends to be very difficult for people to actually agree upon.

Secondly, as for being Calvinistic, some take this to mean holding to John Calvin's teaching in general, others (most people) understand this to be short-hand for the system of salvation (known as soteriology) endorsed by the Council of Dort in 1619. To be Reformed is clearly to be Calvinistic in one's view of soteriology; it is not required to agree with John Calvin's teaching in general. I think most Baptists calling themselves Calvinists have a different view of the Lord's Supper than what Calvin taught, for example.

Lastly, my friend claims reformed folk must be covenantal. This could mean we hold to covenant view of theology (this could include the Presbyterian view, the Baptist view, or the New Covenant view) or it could mean we have a membership covenant within the local church. In practice, holding to a covenant view of theology is what is meant, although Reformed churches are nearly universal in their adoption of membership covenants as well. Which view of the biblical covenants one must hold to then becomes the question. Most people claiming the label of Reformed and those holding to a New Covenant view do not consider New Covenant Theology (NCT) a covenant-based system. My research leads me to believe NCT men refute being called covenantal so as not to be confused with the Westminster covenant view. Most people conversant with reformed theology think "covenant theology" equals Presbyterian covenant theology, making it necessary for others who are covenantal in their theology to keep clarifying who they are; this echoes the circumstance of the 17th century! This topic of covenant theology will be addressed in part 3 of this book. In short, it is easy to see that short, easy to remember phrases are often vague and need to be clarified to be very helpful.

I would add that to be Reformed means one must deliberately pursue an examination of his theological views, always reforming to Scripture for the glory of God; for no man will come to a complete, comprehensive understanding of the whole of Scripture during this age. Without this last idea, we, as sinful humans, tend to get comfortable with what we believe and soon take it for granted; not stopping to think we might have been taught wrong or believed something that simply is not so. These presuppositions are rarely examined and ought to be, as they are they cause of much disagreement and hard feelings between Christians; and such things ought not to be.

As with any concept, the historical context is most helpful in coming to an accurate understanding. In chapter 1, I briefly reported how the reformation developed into two main streams. One group was called the Magisterial Reformers, consisting of those who continued to embrace the state-church concept and combined, to one degree or another, church leadership with the magistrates; governmental leaders. The Presbyterians (those who hold to the Westminster Confession of Faith) are the current day progeny of this group. Paedobaptism is the other key distinctive of this group, although (as mentioned in chapter 2) many other religious groups that are in no way reformed also hold to this practice. The other group of reformers was called the Radical Reformers, consisting of varied protesters who held to the baptism of believers and the autonomy of the local church. Among them were also folks who held to "inner light" mysticism and pacifism; all were called by the name of Anabaptist by the several state churches (see chapter 1 for more detail on this). Current day progeny of the Radicals include the Brethren, Mennonites, and many Baptists. Some Baptists hold to a successionist view, wherein they believe that Baptists have existed since Apostolic times, and have no part in the reformation. As previously discussed, wherein we saw the lines blurred between the confessional Baptists in England and the Anabaptists, history also reveals blurred lines between Baptists who protested against Rome in the 16th century (and all those that followed) and the alleged non-protestant Baptists who believe they predate the Reformation. What we learn from history and study of theology is that all who hold to a biblical view of Christianity protest the errors of Rome, and are rightly called Protestants.

We see a line of Christians whom God preserved in every generation, never submitting to Rome (in either its political form or its religious form), always clinging (imperfectly) to the Word of God. The name protestant came into use as a product of the Reformation, but Christians have been protesting against Rome in either of its forms since apostolic times.

The Magisterial group has been most prolific over the years writing countless books espousing their views and claiming that Reformed Theology consists primarily of holding to their Westminster Confession of Faith. The Westminster Theological Seminary defines it this way: "The best English expression of the Reformed faith is arguably contained in the Westminster Confession of Faith, the doctrinal standards of Westminster Theological Seminary. This statement, penned at Westminster Abbey in London in the mid-seventeenth century, has stood the test of time as a summary expression of the teaching of the Bible."[1]

As 20th and 21st century Baptists have been awakened to the importance of returning to our roots of being a biblical people, the books describing the doctrines of grace and sovereignty of God written by our Presbyterian brothers have been widely consumed. While these books have been of much value in providing clear teaching on several important doctrines, they carry with them the presuppositions of infant sprinkling and state-church ecclesiology and the resultant view of the covenants. Hence, the importance of gathering books and other documents written by Baptists over the years, which confirm the truth we share with saints but also reaffirms those distinctives which characterize us Baptists. With the advent of the Internet and so many old documents being available, Baptists have no excuse for being led astray by reading *only* the works by our Presbyterian brothers. We have some excellent resources that show us are not inventing something new; we are rediscovering something old; something that aligns with the Word of God.

Chapter 4 - The 5 Solas: The Basics of Reformation.
The hallmark cry of The Reformation centered on 5 Solas; five statements of core Christian doctrines that define the Christian faith from the Scriptures, providing a clear line of demarcation from Roman Catholic theology, which had been developing and controlling public religion in Europe for centuries.

Sola Scriptura
Sola Gratia
Sola Fide
Solo Christo
Soli Deo Gloria

Though these are familiar to countless brothers and sisters, we will take a look at each of these; all of them important, as I pray this chapter will demonstrate. I am of the opinion that *Sola Scriptura* is the most crucial of these doctrines, as the others are valuable only because they are based on Scripture. This doctrine is the key for Baptists, for without embracing it we cannot call ourselves, people of the book – and that is what all Christians must be.

Here is a brief overview of these five statements that define what it truly means to be reformed.

Sola Scriptura -The Scripture Alone is the Standard
The essence of *Sola Scriptura* is that we take the Word of God as sufficient for life and godliness, just as our Lord intended (2 Peter 1:3). But this requires deliberate thinking and actions than most folks realize. How do we apply the Scriptures to life to assure godliness? Certainly this is not something those not born again nor indwelt by the Holy Spirit can do. Certainly this is something those born again and indwelt by the Holy Spirit should *want* to do (Hebrews 10:24)! This is why William Tyndale was determined to put the Bible in the common tongue, so common folk could read and understand the Word of God and grow in grace. He cried, "I defy the Pope, and all his laws; and if God spare me I will one day make the boy that drives the plough in England to know more of Scripture than the Pope himself."[1]

God's people have long recognized His Word as different from the mere words of man. Theologians have summed this up in four characteristics about the Nature of Scripture: Authority, Clarity, Necessity, and Sufficiency. Without these attributes or characteristics being true, *Sola Scriptura* would be a call to deception, not to Truth.

As we take a look at the nature of Scripture, bear in mind it is the very Word of God and the enemies of YHWH seek to distract us from it. The Fall frames this up very nicely. *Now the serpent was more crafty than any other beast of the field that the Lord God had made. He said to the woman, 'Did God actually say, 'You shall not eat of any tree in the garden'?'* (Genesis 3:1) The first and primary point of attack of Satan and all his allies is to cause people, both God's redeemed and those who are lost, to doubt God; to doubt what He said, to doubt that He said anything; to doubt that He matters. Seeking to cloud what was clearly revealed by God to man is of utmost importance to the enemies of God. Often times, false teachers put false words in the mouth of God: *But the serpent said to the woman, "You will not surely die* [the lie]. *For God knows that when you eat of it your eyes will be opened, and you will be like God, knowing good and evil* [the truth]*"* (Genesis 3:4-5). Falling for the wiles of Satan or the siren call of our own sinful desires will lead us away from the Truth of God's Word, and displays a lack of contentment with what the Creator and Ruler of all things has decided was adequate to provide and reveal to us.

As if our nature was not enough of a reason for God's people to rightly respect the authority and clarity of God's Word, the first and most important reason comes from God; His Word is important to Him. It is a reflection of His holiness and rightful rule of all of His creation. Throughout the history of God's people, understanding His Word and being obedient to it have been tied to His creatures bringing glory to the name of God. When Christ was tempted in the desert, He pointed to what God the Father had said, in a way that implied it was possible to know and understand what had been said; and that what had been said was authoritative. If Scripture is not clear, how can it be authoritative, for who can respond to the call of an unclear trumpet? And if Scripture does not have the authority of Creator God, why try to understand it, why work at testing what we read and hear? If the Word of God is not authoritative and clear, it is up to us to determine the mind of God. And we go right back to the garden, wanting to put ourselves in His place.

Wayne Grudem says[2] that the Bible is necessary for a.) knowledge of the gospel (salvation), b.) maintaining spiritual life, and for c.) obtaining certain knowledge of God's will. He points out that the Bible is not necessary for knowing that God exists or for knowing something about God's character. The Bible *is* necessary for knowing how wretched man is in his natural state and how he might be reconciled to Holy God.

Scripture is sufficient to guide us to salvation and equip us for every good work, as proclaimed in Ephesians 2:10; *For we are his workmanship, created in Christ Jesus for good works, which God prepared beforehand, that we should walk in them.* Where does one go to discover God's will for his life? To whom does one turn to find out what good deeds are to be done? Can any man add to the wisdom of God? No! The Word of God is sufficient for what it is intended.

As redemptive history unfolded, we can be sure that almighty God gave enough light for the ancient saints to walk in. We wonder if we would have understood the promise given in Genesis 3:15; it was the first mention within man's hearing of the predetermined plan of God to rescue sinners. I dare say most of us didn't comprehend the totality of this verse when we first read it. What did Adam and Eve think? One thing not easily quantified is the effect that sin would have had on their thinking at this point in history. This was a couple that had communion with

God, untainted by sin; they knew intimacy with God that we cannot presently comprehend. How much did they realize about the promised seed that would crush the serpent's head? Enough for the day in which they lived.

Those not satisfied with the sufficiency of Scripture invent doctrines that will intrigue and enslave ignorant and superstitious people.[3 & 4]

If any of these four attributes (Authority, Clarity, Necessity, Sufficiency) were to be false, it would call into question the entire cannon of Scripture and any faith built thereon. We study these attributes because they are important reminders of the character of our God and because it will equip us to stand against the wily schemes of Satan and his countless minions.

But since these traits are true of Scripture alone, not of any other book, the call to revere it above all other authorities is necessary and wise. Properly understood, *Sola Scriptura* means that Scripture alone is esteemed as the Word of God. It is His special revelation to man, revealing Him as Creator and Judge of all flesh and us as fallen creatures who deserve His wrath. The Bible reveals to us the hope of redemption that is possible in Christ Jesus alone, and in Whom alone there is safety from the judgment of God against sinners.

Sola Scriptura also guides us as to how *not* to take the Bible. God's Word is not a math or science book, for example; nor do we accept it as a study on anatomy or surgery. We recognize that God gives men, even unredeemed men, wisdom and knowledge in these, and many other areas and skills; just as He did when the nation of Israel was wondering in their Exodus (Exodus 31:1-11). And while the Bible is not a science book, its Author is the author of science. This means no true science (the discovery of natural truth) will contradict the Bible, rightly understood. Of interest in our time is the notion that science supports Darwinian evolution as the origin of the species; the race of men. The scientific method (inquiry, hypothesis, test) cannot be used to prove historical facts; they must be accepted by faith, supported (but not provable) by evidence. There is no test that can prove Darwinian macro-evolution, there are no transitional artifacts (moths and bacteria hailed as evidence remain true to their kind, remaining as moths and bacteria) or living examples. Yet it is accepted by many as fact. There is "evidence that demands a verdict"[5] regarding the crucifixion and resurrection of Christ Jesus, but these facts of history must also be accepted by faith as they cannot be proven scientifically. We learn from this one example that faith is not generated by facts, though it may be strengthened by facts. Faith is given to man by God, by communication of the Gospel from His special revelation known as the Holy Bible. *Sola Scriptura* tells us that nothing of man can be held up to the same level, that there is no authority equal to, much less superior to, the Word of God. To His Word alone we submit our conscience and hold everything taught by man and man's institutions as subordinate.

The Roman Catholic Church decries this doctrine, claiming the authority of their church tradition and a few dozen confidants of the pope as necessary for understanding and supplementing the Scriptures. They claim to support traditions given by the apostles, buttressed by 2 Thessalonians 2:15. But, as has been noted by many who have read extensively on this topic, none of Rome's extensive apologetic material on their apostolic traditions documents which traditions were allegedly given by the apostles. And that verse talks about traditions that were, past tense, handed down; not continuing to be handed down. William Webster, in a short paper on *Sola Scriptura*, points out that as early as the 4th century there was a conflict over the date Easter should be celebrated. The Orthodox Church claimed an apostolic tradition of Easter on Passover; Rome claimed apostolic tradition of Easter on whatever Sunday they claimed lined up with the lunar calendar. If their "apostolic traditions" were actually apostolic traditions, one would think they would be easily defended and agreed to; even if subtle nuances in meaning and practice were cause for disputes.

Rome claims Protestants ignore tradition and lean on our own private interpretations of Scripture. Tradition mentioned in Scripture always refers to the teaching of the Scriptures by the Apostles, not doctrines and interpretations made up by men and turned into encyclopedias as time goes by. As for the proper use of extra-biblical traditions, we are well advised to learn from those who have gone before and be informed by what they've written; but not to be ruled by them. It has been wisely observed that if you have an interpretation or system of theology that has not been evident in the history of the church, you are very likely to be very wrong. This counsel helps guard us against new theories and should cause us to be very cautious with those novel systems others may promote; whether it began in 2015 or 1830. So said one ancient church father:

> Concerning the divine and sacred Mysteries of the Faith, we ought not to deliver even the most casual remark without the Holy Scriptures; nor be drawn aside by mere probabilities and the artifices of argument. Do not then believe me because I tell thee of these things, unless thou receive from the Holy Scriptures the proof of what is set forth: for this salvation, which is our faith, is not by ingenious reasonings, but by proof from the Holy Scriptures....In these articles we comprehend the whole doctrine of faith….For the articles of the Faith were not composed at the good pleasure of men, but the most important points chosen from all Scriptures, make up the one teaching of the Faith….This Faith, in a few words, hath enfolded in its bosom the whole knowledge of godliness contained both in the Old and New Testaments. Behold, therefore, brethren and hold the traditions (2 Thes. 2:15) which ye now receive, and write them on the table of your hearts....Now heed not any ingenious views of mine; else thou mayest be misled; but unless thou receive the witness of the prophets concerning each matter, believe not what is spoken; unless thou learn from Holy Scripture....receive not the witness of man.[6]

That is a tradition that is anchored on the Word of God and points back to the Word. That's a tradition we can hold onto!

Another side of this issue is our natural tendency to seek novelty. The pastor in Ecclesiastes chapter 1 noted that the ear never tires of hearing something new and the Apostle warned us (2 Timothy 4) that people will gather particular teachers to themselves because they have an itch to hear something new, turning away from truth to being entertained and misled by myths. *Sola Scriptura* tells us God's Word is sufficient, that we don't need something more in order to be pleasing to God or content in Him (2 Timothy 3:16 & 17). Read carefully the following quotes from Robert Martin to gain a better understanding of this doctrine.

> The Bible is inspired in such a way that its very words are inspired (i.e., 'verbal' inspiration); and that inspiration extends to all the words of Scripture (i.e., 'plenary' inspiration). ... The so-called 'dynamic' view of inspiration, on the other hand, argues that God inspired the thoughts of the biblical writers but left them to express those thoughts or ideas in their own words. ... Since most of the great doctrines of the faith, however, are not capable of visual expression (e.g., justification), one is left with the inescapable conclusion that these 'ideas' came to the minds of the inspired writers in verbal (word) form. ... An inspiration that extends to the divine choice of the words can only imply that God is concerned with much more than general ideas. It is clear that God intends that we understand Him exactly.[7]

> Unlike the modern newspaper, the Bible was never meant to yield the fullness of its message to those who are only willing to expend the absolute minimum of effort necessary.[8]

> Inaccurate and paraphrasic Bible translations cannot but contribute to the further erosion of theological precision in the decades to come.[9]

No reformer (or ancient Christian) that I know of discounts the value or importance of the early church councils or church history. These act as informants and guardrails against novel interpretations, though they do not serve as authoritative as they were written and acted out by sinful men who were not inspired by God for the purpose of recording His special revelation to man. Here's how Charles Hodge summed it up:

> Again, Protestants admit that as there has been an uninterrupted tradition of truth from the protevangelium to the close of the Apocalypse, so there has been a stream of traditionary teaching flowing through the Christian Church from the day of Pentecost to the present time. This tradition is so far a rule of faith that nothing contrary to it can be true. Christians do not stand isolated, each

holding his own creed. They constitute one body, having one common creed. Rejecting that creed, or any of its parts, is the rejection of the fellowship of Christians, incompatible with the communion of saints, or membership in the body of Christ. In other words, Protestants admit that there is a common faith of the Church, which no man is at liberty to reject, and which no man can reject and be a Christian.[10]

Commenting on another issues that Rome uses to accuse Christians of being an authority each to himself (charging that we embrace "private interpretations" not subject to church rule), Hodge provides clear thinking:

The Bible is a plain book. It is intelligible by the people. And they have the right, and are bound to read and interpret it for themselves; so that their faith may rest on the testimony of the Scriptures, and not on that of the Church. Such is the doctrine of Protestants on this subject.

It is not denied that the Scriptures contain many things hard to be understood; that they require diligent study; that all men need the guidance of the Holy Spirit in order to right knowledge and true faith. But it is maintained that in all things necessary to salvation they are sufficiently plain to be understood even by the unlearned.

It is not denied that the people, learned and unlearned, in order to the proper understanding of the Scriptures, should not only compare Scripture with Scripture, and avail themselves of all the means in their power to aid them in their search after the truth, but they should also pay the greatest deference to the faith of the Church. If the Scriptures be a plain book, and the Spirit performs the functions of a teacher to all the children of God, it follows inevitably that they must agree in all essential matters in their interpretation of the Bible. And from that fact it follows that for an individual Christian to dissent from the faith of the universal Church (*i.e.:* the body of true believers), is tantamount to dissenting from the Scriptures themselves.[11]

The Bible is a plain book regards the essentials of the faith: who is God, who is man, what is wrong in the world and in me, and how can it be made right. Other things (such as how free the will of man is) are less plain. What Protestants deny on this subject is that Christ has appointed any officer, or class of officers, in his Church to whose interpretation of the Scriptures the people are bound to submit as to a final authority. What we affirm is that our Lord has made it obligatory upon every man to search the Scriptures for himself, and determine on his own discretion what they require him to believe and to do. Once again, Hodge provide solid and concise counsel:

The arguments in support of the former of these positions have already been presented in the discussion concerning the infallibility of the Church. The most obvious reasons in support of the right of private judgment are,

1. That the obligations to faith and obedience are personal. Every man is responsible for his religious faith and his moral conduct. He cannot transfer that responsibility to others; nor can others assume it in his stead. He must answer for himself; and if he must answer for himself, he must judge for himself. It will not avail him in the day of judgment to say that his parents or his Church taught him wrong. He should have listened to God, and obeyed Him rather than men.

2. The Scriptures are everywhere addressed to the people, and not to the officers of the Church either exclusively, or specially. The prophets were sent to the people, and constantly said, "Hear, O Israel," "Hearken, O ye people." Thus, also, the discourses of Christ were addressed to the people, and the people heard him gladly. All the Epistles of the New Testament are addressed to the congregation, to the "called of Jesus Christ;" "to the beloved of God;" to those "called to be saints;" "to the sanctified in Christ Jesus;" "to all who call on the name of Jesus Christ our Lord;" "to the saints which are in (Ephesus), and to the faithful in Jesus Christ;" or "to the saints and faithful brethren which are in (Colosse);" and so in every instance. It is the people who are addressed. To them are directed these profound discussions of Christian doctrine, and these comprehensive expositions of Christian duty. They are everywhere assumed to be competent to understand what is written, and are everywhere required to believe and obey what thus came from the inspired messengers of Christ. They were not referred to any other authority from which they were to learn the true import of these inspired instructions. It is, therefore, not only to deprive the people of a divine right, to forbid the people to read and interpret the Scriptures for themselves; but it is also to interpose between them and God, and to prevent their hearing his voice, that they may listen to the words of men." [12]

Faith in Christ is personal, but it is to be lived out with others who have been translated from the kingdom of darkness into His glorious light (Colossians 1:13).

When one understands *Sola Scriptura*, the content of the local church worship service will come to mind. How does one determine what practices are right and proper to include in a service intended to be the worship of our Creator and Savior? The regulative principle is the idea that man's worship of holy God must be according to what He has revealed to us, not according to our alleged wisdom. This is a concept rejected by default by most Christians. While the long-time discussion used to be about the regulative vs normative (which declares man can worship God in all ways *except* as prohibited by His Word) principles, it now tends to be a neglected concept all together, as men posing as pastors give little or no thought to what the Word of God says about the worship of God. The result is a concept of worship that is entirely the product of man's "wisdom" and whimsy, resulting in practices designed to have the right influence on the creature; what my friend Voddie Baucham terms "affective worship," that which is built on influencing and relating to moods, feelings, and attitudes, to affect the crowd to get the desired response. The effect of this approach can be seen in countless churches across the US of A, in large cities and small towns, as men grow more careless about what God has said and more concerned about what sinful men desire. Infected by the cancer of Charles Finney, churches in every protestant denomination have developed patterns of worship that are designed to attract and please men. This was precisely the mind-set behind Finney's "new methods." Again, I refer to my former home town of Houston, where Kerry Shook has created a circus with motorcycle jumps, athletic showmanship, and life-size recreation of the Angry Birds game at various times, all on the stage of what he calls Woodlands Church (what I call *Cirque du Shook*). Look around and you cannot help but see the effects of the affective principle at work in more churches than can be counted. Sadly, I have seen this same perspective at work in small country churches as well as in the so-called mega-churches. I heard Paul Washer observe that such nonsense in local churches is God's judgment on the people that gather there, as 2 Timothy 4 tells us it is the people who gather up false teachers who will tickles their ears; it is not the false teachers who gather a following. Those who cannot accept God's Word as sufficient will seek out teachers who will tell them what they want to hear. That *is* God's judgment on the false sheep, on those who cannot accept His Holy Scriptures as such.

The dire consequence of following our heart's desire in worship should cause us to inquire seriously into the regulative principle. Simply put, the regulative principle restricts the gathered saints to worship God only as He has commanded or commended to us in the Scriptures. This principle affects the elements of worship, not the circumstances of worship. This means that what we do – singing, praying, preaching, giving, etc. - all should be clearly commanded or commended in the Bible. It also means that where we meet, what time of day, whether we have air conditioning, electric amplification, etc. are not governed by this principle. What is excluded, therefore, are practices and traditions developed by men; things as benign as announcements of church activities to things as wretched as having unregenerate people being featured for song performances.

Again, my friend Terrence O'Hare comes to our aid, describing the regulative principle as how worship that honors the Lord is to be approached and conducted.

> This emphasis of adhering to the word of God during worship is certainly understandable since it was especially important that a gathering of the saints was marked by a unity of faith (Eph 4:11 – 14) and peaceable relations (1 Cor 14:33). The orderly conduct of

worship services (1 Cor 14:40, Col 2:5) requires conformity in doctrine (1 Cor 15:1 & 2; Col 2:7) and uniformity in practice (1 Cor 14:26 – 39; Eph 4:3)."[13]

Does this not ring with truth and consistency with God's Word? I hope in Christ that all who call on His name as Lord would seek to worship Him in spirit and truth, as He has revealed those things to us in His holy writ. This is why the sufficiency of Scripture is important; it shows us God's Word just as superlatively adequate for instruction on life and godliness as Christ's redemptive work is for our eternal standing as sons of the most high.

On the other hand, there are those who go too far in restricting what is acceptable in corporate worship, effectively elevating certain traditions of men (formulated through "sound and necessary deduction") to the same level as God's precepts. Some claim believers are in sin if they don't participate in every activity the local church offers, such as Sunday and Wednesday evenings, or prohibit the use of musical instruments or any songs other than Psalms. For these, "the regulative principle is wielded as if it were the Eleventh Commandment."[14]

> David's use of the harp and psaltery was not ceremonially mandated by God, but was chosen by David because he was gifted by God with musical skills; they were instruments culturally available to him, and it added beauty and richness to his compositions for personal worship and pleasure. Though not specifically commanded, the divine approbation of David's opus has resonated in the hearts of the faithful, inspiring them to magnify the name of the Lord in concert (Ps 34:3). David praised the Lord with his whole heart (Ps 9:1), his lips (Ps 119:171), his mouth (Ps 51:15), and also in song (Ps 69:30), with the lute (Ps 71:22) and harp (Ps 33:2). The accompaniment of voice with instruments displays a unity and fullness of worship with which God is exceptionally pleased (2 Cor :12 – 14).[15]

An implicit aspect of O'Hare's perspective is the age-old rule of interpretation: narratives are not normative, which means we don't take a singular narrative passage (such an historical account) as the basis for rules of doctrine. Doctrine can be supported by narrative text, but must be founded on didactic or teaching texts.

The Word of God is an anchor that holds, it is the rock of Truth upon which we must base our lives. All men have error and those who are not content with God will intrigue and enslave foolish people with vain fables and worship of things created by their own hands and minds. Thomas Patient, a 17th century English Baptist, made this wonderfully insightful comment: "Now where Scripture has not a mouth to speak we must not have an ear to listen."[16]

Scripture alone is the word of God; it is authoritative. Scripture alone is the Word of God; its meaning is clear. Scripture alone is necessary because man needs to hear from God. Scripture alone is sufficient because it is true, all other revelation is from man or demons and will only lead us astray.

Elders are accountable to God for how they lead, what doctrine they teach, how the flock entrusted to their care is taught to worship Him. While God has called those men called to serve the local church as elders, He has not given them the freedom to bring cultural novelties, entertainment, and showmanship into the order of worship; nor to restrict worship to his personal view of what types of music is commended. These men must ensure worship is in alignment with God's Word; not man's wisdom. Scripture is sufficient for righteousness and godliness; that's *Sola Scriptura!*

Soli Deo Gloria! - For the Glory of God Alone

This principle of the Reformation calls us to do everything for the glory of God. This doctrine was introduced in chapter 3, as we examined membership in the local church. These five statements of the Reformation each echo the sufficiency of God and His Word and work by declaring "alone" after each. Creator God will not share His glory with anyone (Isaiah 42:8), so we are to do all we do for the glory of God, and to Him alone. This doctrine must follow the first, for how can sinful man know what honors and brings glory to God other than from His revealed Word? How do we determine what is for His glory verses what glorifies our sinful flesh? For the same reasons discussed above, man's wisdom cannot be relied upon to determine what this doctrine means. 1 Corinthians 10:23-33 gives guidance on not abusing the liberty with food and drink one has as a child of God to the detriment of unbelievers and weaker saints, summed up in verse 31: *So, whether you eat or drink, or whatever you do, do all to the glory of God.* If these small, mundane things of life are captured up in this command, how much more the larger issues that loom in our daily spiritual lives? In describing basics of the Christian life (Colossians 3:1-17), as new creatures made alive by the Spirit of God, this same Apostle is used of God to contrast our former lives with our new lives, resulting with the beautiful exhortation to **Let the word of Christ dwell in you richly**, *teaching and admonishing one another in all wisdom, singing psalms and hymns and spiritual songs, with thankfulness in your hearts to God. And* **whatever you do, in word or deed, do everything in the name of the Lord Jesus**, *giving thanks to God the Father through him.* To do something *in the name of the Lord Jesus* means that we do (in manner, mode, and motive) what is pleasing to Him. The Apostle tells us we have died to the law through the body of Christ, so we would belong to Him who was raised from the dead in order that we would bear fruit for God (Romans 7:4). To bear fruit for God is cited as the reason we have been raised from spiritual death to new life in Christ, to bear fruit for God means He would be glorified in us.

Paul also remarked that the reason for his apostleship, and the benchmark reason for all gospel ministry, is for the sake of His glory: *Paul, a servant of Christ Jesus, called to be an apostle,* **set apart for the gospel of God**, *... concerning his Son, who was descended from David according to the flesh and was declared to be the Son of God in power according to the Spirit of holiness by his resurrection from the dead, Jesus Christ our Lord, through whom we have received grace and apostleship to bring about the obedience of faith* **for the sake of his name** (Romans 1:1-5). Let no preacher think that his own reputation is what's at stake; it is the very name of our Lord Jesus that we are called to guard! Further, we see that the apostle was focused on praying for his spiritual children in this matter: *And* **it is my prayer** *that* **your love may abound more and more***, with* **knowledge and all discernment***, so that you may approve what is excellent, and so* **be pure and blameless** *for the day of Christ,* **filled with the fruit of righteousness** *that comes through Jesus Christ,* **to the glory and praise of God** (Philippians 1:9-11). All of life for the Christian is brought into view in this short passage, from our time now until Christ returns; and all of this to be **to the glory and praise of God.**

Peter reminded Christians who were being hounded to death for their faith that since Christ suffered in the flesh, so we ought to. For *whoever has suffered in the flesh has ceased from sin, so as to live for the rest of the time in the flesh* **no longer for human passions but for the will of God**. We are to cease living to please ourselves, to live for and in accordance with the will of God, just as Jesus did. Because we are slow of understanding, this apostle continues. *For the time that is past suffices for doing what the Gentiles want to do, living in sensuality, passions, drunkenness, orgies, drinking parties, and lawless idolatry.* This is what it means to live for self: sexually driven, drugs to dull the pain, a law unto one's self. For the child of God, that time is past! *For this is why the gospel was preached even to those who are dead, that though judged in the flesh the way people are, they might* **live in the spirit the way God does.** This paragraph (1 Peter 4:1-6) ends as it began, telling us the reason God gives us continued life on this earth, to bring glory to His name by living in the spirit the way He does. If anyone wonders, "how do I glorify God?" let him see clearly: we honor and glorify our Lord by living according to His will. Obedience is better than sacrifice. Prayers are heard when they align with His will. The consistent teaching of Scripture is clear.

The Lord Jesus Himself declared that while walking as a man, He did not speak on His own authority, but only what His Father told Him (John 12:49). In the garden, contemplating the cup of wrath He would drink on our account, our Messiah sought out His Father in prayer and asked, *Father, if you are willing, remove this cup from me. Nevertheless,* **not my will, but yours, be done** (Luke 22:42). Doing the Father's will, obedience to what He has told us, is what honors and brings glory to our Creator (1 Samuel 15:22). And we find this guidance only in His revealed Word, not in our vain imaginations or deceitful minds.

There is another Latin phrase used by many to describe this attitude of life: *Coram Deo*, which means "before the face of God." For the Christian, everything we do ought to be with the knowledge that *Nothing is covered up that will not be revealed, or hidden that will not be known. Therefore whatever you have said in the dark shall be heard in the light, and what you have whispered in private rooms shall be proclaimed on the housetops* (Luke 12:2-3.) Since the Lord knows all things, sees all things, and will judge all things, should we not be sober minded (1 Peter 1:13 & 5:8) and diligent in how we walk? And all the more, I dare say, when it comes to our corporate worship, when we, as the gathered saints of the living God congregate to declare His glory and our devotion to Him. And yet; in so many churches of all sizes, the corporate worship services appear to be organized with little thought as to the elements and whether they are given to us in His Scripture as means to worship Him. Small, innocuous things such as announcements and larger, questionable things such as having unregenerate children participate in various functions. In this latter case, we must ask the question: are those unsaved children worshiping God (remember how Cain's offering was rejected?) or are they entertaining their parents and others? Our culture is partly based on the notion that "everything is for the children!" (a ruse, I think, intended as part of the culture's plan on destroying the family unit), and it appears many Christians have swallowed that proposition without thinking it through. Consider the main goal of parenting is to raise up ADULTS, responsible people who know the law and the gospel (parents cannot save their children); the goal is NOT to have children that never grow up (no apologies to Peter Pan).

We who are *not* of Rome tend to cling to our traditions as tightly as do the Roman Catholics. How can we defend this while rightly decrying their practice? Oh how I wish that Baptists would see the danger of our own traditions that are not based on Scripture and cry out for repentance!

This is why we must engage our minds in the worship of God; love the Lord our God with our souls, our strength, and our minds (Matthew 22:37). If not, we *will* worship ourselves and allow our unexamined presuppositions to rule our lives and our worship. This highlights the importance of the call of our long dead brothers – *Soli Deo Gloria!* Let us do *all* for the glory of our Lord, and for Him alone. He alone is worthy of our worship, we should be sober minded and diligent to worship Him and live as He has shown us in His Word. As with every aspect of Christian living, we can succeed at nothing if our focus is not on the Lord Jesus, in Whom we are complete and have our life, and for whose glory we exist. The Christian life cannot be lived on auto-pilot; we must be deliberate and diligent in our pursuit of godliness, as individuals and as local churches. *If then you have been raised with Christ,* **seek the things that are above***, where Christ is, seated at the right hand of God.* **Set your minds on things that are above***, not on things that are on earth.* **For you have died, and your life is hidden with Christ in God.** *When Christ who is your life appears, then you also will appear with him in glory* (Colossians 3:1-4). Seek the things above, seek *first* the kingdom of God, that is the key to living life *Soli Deo Gloria!*

We now come to the last three Solas, which will be handled together as they give us the foundation for the gospel (chapter 3).

Sola Gratia - Salvation by Grace Alone
Sola Fide - Justification by Faith Alone
Solo Christo! - By Christ's Work Alone are We Saved

These statements were crafted to remind the people of God who had escaped or never submitted to Rome that, as Jonah declared from the belly of the fish (Jonah 2:9), *salvation is of the Lord!* Rome has taught for many years that salvation is partly from the Lord, partly from the sinner, and partly from the church of Rome. But the Scripture teaches salvation is by *grace alone* through *faith alone* in *Christ alone*. And that is the deep but simple truth of the biblical gospel. See how all three of these elements are described in Paul's letter to the brothers and sisters in Rome:

> But *now* **the righteousness of God has been manifested apart from the law**, *although the Law and the Prophets bear witness to it* — **the righteousness of God through faith in Jesus Christ** *for all who believe. For there is no distinction: for all have sinned and fall short of the glory of God, and are* **justified by his grace as a gift**, *through* **the redemption that is in Christ Jesus, whom God put forward as a propitiation by his blood, to be received by faith**. *This was to show God's righteousness, because in his divine forbearance he had passed over former sins. It was* **to show his righteousness** *at the present time, so that he might* **be just and the justifier of the one who has faith in Jesus.** (Romans 3:21-26)

This doctrine is pressed on us throughout the Bible, as the New Covenant was slowly unveiled as redemptive history was unfolded. In apostolic times, the Old Testament was the only Bible they had and from it Christ was preached (Acts 17:2)!

Perhaps the most clear, comprehensive illustration of the gospel in the Old Testament is portrayed in the story of the great flood. In the days of Noah, as in all eras of humanity, men were evil and there were few who knew and worshiped the One God. Noah found favor in the eyes of YHWH (Genesis 6:3). Noah alone, of all the men on earth at that time, found favor in God's sight. What does this mean? Abraham declared that he had found favor in God's sight (Exodus 33:12 & 13) and Moses, like Noah, is said by YHWH to have found favor in His eyes (Exodus 33:16 & 17). Each man was solitary in his standing as God's chosen vessel in the midst of a wicked and crooked generation, just as was the Christ to Whom each of these men pointed. These mortal men, however, had no righteousness of their own, as the types always fail to fully portray the antitype. They found favor in God's sight because, as we see in the tale of Joseph in Egypt (Genesis 39-50), God was with each of them and His favor was given to each of them. While each of the ancient patriarchs serve our purpose of showing how salvation has always been by grace given to sinners through faith given to sinners to believe God's message about the promised Savior, Noah is the one example we will focus on.

In Genesis 6:9 we read that Noah was righteous, blameless in his generation; because he walked with God. Noah's blamelessness means he was circumspect in his living and did not give his generation cause to blaspheme God, just as described in 1 Timothy 3:7, wherein the qualifications of elders are revealed. As our Lord kept Himself pure (John 17:4), using His walk with and prayer to His Father (Luke 22:39-46) to strengthen Him, so Noah was strengthened by walking with God; just as you and I are in our day. The earth was corrupt in God's sight, filled with violence (verse 11); note the contrast to Noah, who found favor in God's sight. As He will do at the end of the age, God the Righteous Judge declared His judgment upon the wicked world (verse 13) and told Noah how to save himself and his family (verses 14-17). Noah was told to make an ark and make many rooms in it, for the salvation of his family and all the animals God would shut up in the ark (Genesis 7:11-17). None but the people and animals that God called would be allowed in the ark, none but those effactually called by YHWH into His provision of refuge would be saved. The vast majority of the earth's population was consumed by God's wrath; there was no refuge for anyone other than being in the ark (verses 20-23).

Do you see how this story points us to Christ? He was the solitary Son who was pleasing to the Father, hated by the world (John 15:18 & 19) and the wicked and corrupt generation that was seeking after signs (Matthew 16:4). God pronounced His judgment that will cause the earth and its starry heavens to burn up and be consumed in His wrath (2 Pet 3:10), brought forth in resurrected glory as will His children be (1 Corinthians 15:35-49). Jesus went to prepare many rooms in His Father's house, promising to take us there (John 14:2 & 3). The house, the temple (Ephesians 2:21 & 22), the city in which our Lord will dwell with those He saves (Revelation 21:1-3); is built up of His elect, spiritual stones (1 Peter 2:4 & 5); firmly planted on the foundation laid the prophets and apostles (Ephesians 2:20) and by Jesus (1 Corinthians 3:11), our Chief Cornerstone (Acts 4:11). This foundation will never be shaken (Hebrews 12:28). None but those effectually called by God (John 17:1 & 2) will be allowed to enter in to the New Jerusalem that Christ is building by His blood and His righteousness (Hebrews 9:12; 1 Peter 1:18 & 19; 1 Corinthians 1:30).

If you recall the parable on baptism in chapter 2, you will also know that this ark is specifically called out by Peter as a type, with the flood representing Jesus' baptism in the wrath of God (1 Peter 3:21), the cup of which He drank to the fullest, all the dregs (Psalms 75:2-8; Christ stood in our place as the one condemned, Who is portrayed here), to save those He predestined for that glorious end.

This is why I think this bit of history from God's Holy Scriptures is one of the best for showing the comprehensive story of God's redemptive purposes shown throughout His Word, which is the main theme in all of Scripture. This is what the Captain of our salvation said to dull minded disciples shortly after His resurrection. *And he said to them, "O foolish ones, and slow of heart to believe all that the prophets have spoken! Was it not necessary that the Christ should suffer these things and enter into his glory?"* **And beginning with Moses and all the Prophets, he interpreted to them in all the Scriptures the things concerning himself** (Luke 24:25-27). This is further driven home by an earlier conversation Jesus had the Jews of His day, telling them, *I have come in my Father's name, and you do not receive me. If another comes in his own name, you will receive him. How can you believe, when you receive glory from one another and do not seek the glory that comes from the only God?* **Do not think that I will accuse you to the Father. There is one who accuses you: Moses, on whom you have set your hope. For if you believed Moses, you would believe me; for he wrote of me.** *But if you do not believe his writings, how will you believe my words?"* (John 5:43-47). Moses accuses the Jews for their unbelief in Christ; for by disbelieving in Jesus they demonstrate their disbelief in Moses. Jesus is *the* central theme in *all* of Scripture.

Since the main point of the entire Bible is to reveal the Savior to those in need of salvation, we should not find it odd that the doctrine of soteriology would be an important doctrine that would divide those not in agreement on it. The well-known 19th century Baptist, C.H. Spurgeon, referred to Calvinism as a nickname for the gospel, citing Jonah 2:9 (*Salvation is of the Lord!*):

> That is just an epitome of Calvinism — it is the sum and substance of it. If anyone should ask me what I mean by a Calvinist, I should reply, "He is one who says Salvation is of the Lord." I cannot find in Scripture any other doctrine than this. It is the essence of the Bible. "He only is my rock and my salvation." Tell me anything contrary to this truth and it will be a heresy. Tell me a heresy and I shall find its essence here, that it has departed from this great, this fundamental, this rock-truth, "God is my rock and my salvation."

> What is the heresy of Rome but the addition of something to the perfect merits of Jesus Christ — the bringing in of the works of the flesh to assist in our justification? And what is the heresy of Arminianism but the addition of something to the work of the Redeemer? Every heresy, if brought to the touchstone, will discover itself here. I have my own private opinion that there is no such thing as preaching Christ and Him crucified unless we preach what nowadays is called Calvinism. It is a nickname to call it Calvinism. Calvinism is the Gospel and nothing else.[17]

Our old Baptist brother was emphatic about the sovereignty of God in salvation of sinners! Not all who hold to this view are disciples of John Calvin; as Spurgeon aptly described it, Calvinism is a nickname for the biblical gospel. This view is monergistic salvation, depending on only YHWH, and often referred to as the doctrines of grace, known by the familiar Calvinistic acrostic:

Total Depravity (also known as Radical Depravity, Total Inability, and Original Sin)
Unconditional Election
Limited Atonement (also known as Particular Atonement)
Irresistible Grace
Perseverance of the Saints (not the same thing as easy-believism's Once Saved Always Saved)

We know that these five points were drawn up by the Synod of Dort in the early 17th century in response to a protest by activist disciples of Jacob Arminius. But this easy-to-remember acrostic was first recorded during a presentation before the Presbyterian Union in Newark, NJ in 1905 and popularized by Loraine Boettner's *The Reformed Doctrine of Predestination*, published in 1932. While the TULIP is relatively new, this dispute over how a sinner is reconciled to Holy God has been raging among men since Cain's offering was refused.

Here are the five articles contained in the Remonstrance that precipitated the Synod of Dort's response:

I. God elects or reproves on the basis of foreseen faith or unbelief.
II. Christ died for all men and for every man, although only believers are saved.
III. Man is so depraved that divine grace is necessary unto faith or any good deed.
IV. This grace may be resisted.
V. Whether all who are truly regenerate will certainly persevere in the faith is a point which needs further investigation.

(The full statements of both sides heard by the Council of Dort are compared in Appendix 2.)

I personally think the TULIP is an early example of church marketing and find these five points theologically solid, but not optimum for clearest communication of the doctrine. I am not alone in thinking this, as someone has come up an alternative acrostic:

Bad people
Already elected
Completely atoned for
Overwhelmingly called
Never falling away

Everybody knows BACON makes everything better, so this is a welcome alternative. But still not optimum, in my opinion. As discussed above, trying to fit theological essentials into cute acrostics or 3 alliterative points rarely present God's truth in the best light.

So provided below is a short review of these contested points to help us see the issue more clearly. One verse from Scripture easily under-girds this entire discussion and will be used to frame it up, in a slightly different order than TULIP: *No one can come to me unless the Father who sent me draws him. And I will raise him up on the last day* (John 6:44). Let us examine each aspect of this doctrine in light of this one verse.

No one can come to me … **Total** or **Radical Depravity** refers to original sin which infects every person, in every part of his being, resulting in **spiritual death for all men**. Think of it as complete inability to do good or be good in the sight of God. It doesn't mean that every person is as bad as he can be, but it's not hard to understand why some think so. People in their natural state are depraved (Genesis 6:5; Jeremiah 15:9; Psalm 51:5; Ephesians 2:1-3). Depravity is the rule of fleshly desires without the saving restraint of the Holy Spirit, which leaves people in their natural state being unable to want, will, or do anything good (Romans 3:9-18; Isaiah 64:7). Even the redeemed suffer the ongoing effects of the Fall, as the Apostle Paul said *I know that nothing good dwells in me, that is, in my flesh* (Romans 7:18). While we Christians have the Holy Spirit within us, our sinful flesh will not be redeemed; it will die and be resurrected as a glorious body fit for eternity with our Lord. Christians are not depraved; we are a work-in-process as the Spirit of God sanctifies us.

Unless the Father … This leads to **Unconditional Election**, which is the only sensible perspective. Election, being chosen by God to be redeemed, must be unconditional, **not based on anything in the creature**. Since we are, by nature, depraved, how could anything we do or think be instrumental in being reconciled to holy, omniscient God? God's foreknowledge is of persons, not their actions. Romans 8:29 says ***those whom*** he foreknew, Romans 11:2 confirms: *God has not rejected* **his people whom he foreknew**. 1 Peter is addressed *to* ***those who are elect*** exiles … *according to the foreknowledge of God.* I know of no place in the Scriptures where we find God's foreknowledge related to choices or actions of humans. Election is unconditional in that it is God's choice alone, based on His will (John 1:12); and not dependent in any measure on the will or blood of man (John 1:13). We see this in a temporal type of election that confirms the Reformed position. First example is found in 1 Kings 19:20ff as YHWH rebukes the king of Syria, telling him of the woes that He planned long ago: *Have you not heard? I designed it long ago; I planned it in days gone by. I have now brought it to pass.* Secondly, as Jesus called His Apostles, those men chosen to be foundation stones of His church, *He called to those whom He desired, and they came to Him* (Mark 3:13). If He called those whom He desired to be the foundation stones, why would He leave the determination of who would be the spiritual stones used to build the superstructure (1 Peter 2:5) on the foundation stones He chose, of which He is the chief cornerstone (Ephesians 2:20)? He is the builder of His temple, as Peter specified; He has chosen His materials. He has not revealed in His Holy Word the rationale for choosing one person and not another; merely that all things are by His choice and for His glory.

Who sent Me draws him … The third point, **Irresistible Grace**, repulses some people who think man's nature enables him to grasp hold of God's saving grace on one hand and to resist it on the other. For God to make someone believe, they say, is no way for a gracious, loving God to treat people. In truth, God is irresistible in His effectual, gracious call to His elect; they will come to Him. And God is impassible and resolute in making this way narrow and exclusive; nobody can be saved unless He calls them. These truths are clearly taught in Scripture and should not be cast aside because they do not align with our view of "fairness" or "love". Possibly meditating upon Isaiah 14:27, the Apostle Paul was led by God to ask the rhetorical question, *Who can resist His will?* (Romans 9:19; see also 2 Chronicles 20:6; Job 23:13, and Daniel 4:35). Clearly, the Apostle knew the answer was "No-one!" But, they say, Scripture tells us in Acts 7:51 that people *can* resist God! These people who were resisting the Spirit were not being called to new life. One can resist and even work against God (Romans 1). But no being called to new life can resist that call.

The Greek word in our text behind *draws* conveys the notion of dragging. The gracious act of the Holy Spirit giving life to that which was dead is overwhelming; it's irresistible, just as when Jesus commanded Lazarus, by name, to come out of the tomb. The man, who had been dead four days, responded to the call of Christ, and rose up and came out of the grave; alive again. No one can come to the Father of his personal volition; all are useless and dead in sin; bound up tightly in sin. No one can refuse the call of the Father; though he may seek refuge in the belly of a big fish. God's will *shall* be accomplished in this grand redemptive plan of His; Christ Jesus will have His full reward for the suffering He faced on their account.

Most reformed folk take pains to explain that God gives new life which brings about a change in nature, so the creature now wants to come to Christ and does so willingly. No argument from me; yet I see no reason to back away from what we see in Scripture, that God works against the natural bent of man to redeem him, giving him a new nature with new appetites.

> If man is free to resist, God is not free to act, for He is bound by man's freedom. If God is to be free to act, man must be bound by the will of God. ... But in a fallen world, God's grace must be irresistible or man's will can remain forever opposed to God, and the will of the creature overrides the will of the Creator.[18]

Once born again, we want to please Him, but we must be borne by the Spirit who, by definition, works against our natural condition (enemies of God, Romans 5:10; children of wrath, Ephesians 2:3) to bring us to Christ. All who are called by Him will be saved, none will be lost (John 10:25-30). All who are raised to new life in Christ will have a change in nature (1 Corinthians 5:17) and want to grow in grace and knowledge of the Savior (1 Peter 3:18). His saving grace *is* irresistible! We should seriously ponder our view of the sovereignty of God if we are inclined to think creatures can say no to the Creator in matter, as if the clay could refuse the potter! *The LORD of Hosts Himself has planned it; therefore, who can stand in its way? It is His hand that is outstretched, so who can turn it back?* (Isaiah 14:27, HCSB)

And I will raise him up ... **Limited Atonement or Particular Redemption** is the point that sticks in the craw of most people; even though *both sides* in this argument limit the atonement of Christ. Calvinists limit the *scope* of the atonement: it applies only to the elect. Others limit the *effect* of the atonement: it doesn't save unless man acts. One side has a narrow bridge that carries some sinners completely across the broad expanse between creatures and Creator. The other has a very wide bridge that carries all sinners to a point somewhere short of the other side of the chasm. Which view gives all glory to God and which gives some to the creature? The Calvinist view of the atonement is better termed *Particular Atonement*: the blood of Christ is intended and applied only to His elect. Christ gave His life for the church (Ephesians 5:25), not indiscriminately to the entire world. Those verses which appear to teach otherwise must be interpreted in light of the whole counsel of God on this topic. Jesus prayed to His Father only for the elect in John 17:

> *I have manifested your name to the people whom you gave me out of the world.*
> *... I am praying for them. I am not praying for the world but for those whom*
> *you have given me. ... I have guarded them ... I have given them your Word*
> *... They are not of the world, just as I am not of the world. ... I do not ask*
> *for these only, but also for those who will believe in me through their word. ...*
> *Father, I desire that they also, whom you have given me, may be with me where*
> *I am, to see my glory that you have given me because you loved me before the*
> *foundation of the world. O righteous Father, even though the world does not*
> *know you, I know you, and these know that you have sent me. I made known*
> *to them your name, and I will continue to make it known, that the love with*
> *which you have loved me may be in them, and I in them.*

The special love that is manifested in saving grace is meant only for those who will be saved, not for those who will spurn Him for eternity. His death saves sinners; He is called Jesus because He *will* save people from their sins (Matthew 1:21), not try to save them, not make salvation possible (I am thankful to God for Shai Linne putting that phrase in my mind). He *will* save them! He is the Messiah who will *save* His people. That should give us much more hope and trust in our God than the view of Him as one Who *wants* to save but depends on the creature to seal the deal. And it is the biblical Truth of Who He is, as sovereign Lord of all. Further, if the blood of Jesus was shed for those who are hell-bound, what punishment do they face? Does not His blood atone for sins? Certainly the sinful creature does not decide which sinner gets cleansed as if the blood of Christ washes over all mankind!

On the last day ... Lastly, the doctrine of **Perseverance of the Saints**. I prefer to call this the *Preservation* of the Saints, as our perseverance would fail if God did not preserve us. I think "perseverance" can be interpreted as to put too much emphasis on our performance. Jesus is the one *who works in you, both to will and to work for his good pleasure* (Philippians 2:13). I have come to the conclusion that while justification (salvation, redemption) is monergistic, sanctification (perseverance, preservation) is not. But it's not synergistic, either. That term conveys the notion that both elements or parties are required for the process to function. Even a casual read through the Bible will reveal the fact that God bids us to obey (Galatians 6:9) and enables to do so (Hebrews 13:20 & 21), He commands us to press on for the prize that will not tarnish and sustains us in the doing (Hebrews 12:1 & 2), and reminds us that apart from Him we do nothing (John 15:5). This is the essence of Augustine's famous prayer that ignited the controversy with Pelagius: "God, command what you will, grant what you command." The Christian will want to obey God and trust Him to bring it to completion. Yet He also works to conform us to His Son when we rebel and are not careful to walk as children of the light (1 Corinthians 5:9-13; Hebrews 12:3-11; James 1:2-4 & 12). Brothers, this should not be the case, we should not kick the goads; but it is comforting (and convicting) to embrace a God Who is not dependent on us! So I conclude that God can work to sanctify us without our active participation, yet we cannot work towards growing in likeness to Christ without His active participation (John 15:5). We take 100% responsibility for the sin in our lives, we give God 100% of the credit for the good thoughts, words, and deeds we do. His Spirit in us works so that we pray effectively (Romans 8:26), without Him we can do nothing. This is why a proper understanding of the doctrines of grace is helpful. Short, easy-to-remember methods of men are not always best at explaining key theological concepts to people.

But this one verse is from YHWH, not man, and is short, easy-to-remember and will serve you well: ***No one can come to me unless the Father who sent me draws him. And I will raise him up on the last day*** (John 6:44). Jesus said that only those chosen by God and drawn to Him by Him can come to Him. And only that man, the elect, would be raised up on the last day. This is the narrow gate, the eye of the needle through which no camel enters. It is impossible for man to save himself, but it is possible for God to do so. And He has made a way for some, not all, to be reconciled to Himself.

> Consider: if we are actually dead in our sins (radical depravity), then only God could choose us in Christ (unconditional election), only Christ could atone for our sins (particular redemption), and only the Spirit could draw us to Christ (efficacious grace) and preserve us in him (persevering faith). Therefore, all praise and glory belong to God alone: "For from him and through him and to him are all things. To him be the glory forever!" (Rom. 11:36).[19]

The bedrock of the Arminian objection to monergistic salvation is the shallow, man-centered notion that divine sovereignty is not compatible with human freedom and that man's limited ability limits his obligation to obey. This last point is complementary to the Pelagian view that God would never command man to do that which man was incapable of doing. However, in the Scriptures we find commands from God to the creature to do that which nobody but God can do (Matthew 5:48; 19:24-26; Luke 10:27; Acts 16:30); these commands are meant to drive self-righteousness from us and draw us to Christ, the only man who is able keep them. Arminians claim God gives every human the ability to believe on Jesus, and that God will never refuse anyone who exercises that ability and comes to Him in the faith that he summoned up from within himself, that God allegedly gave to everyone. But the Word of God says not all men have faith (2 Thessalonians 3:2). All men have faith in themselves, but this is not the gift of saving faith God gives to some, which will always result in the sinner being reconciled to Him.

Pelagianism argues that man doesn't need that "prevenient grace" which the Arminians invented; that every child was born without sin and had an absolutely or libertine free will, that which is not influenced by anything in whatsoever it chooses. I wonder if Pelagius had or ever spent time around small children. I have certainly never seen or heard of a small child that did not exhibit extreme self-centeredness from the earliest age. Are we supposed to think babies are born without sin and then condemn themselves at some unstated age and spiritually die? Or, as others claim, little children do not have their sin counted against them until they are competent to understand it. If either claim were the case, the worst form of child abuse would be to allow one's baby to live past the supposed "age of accountability" subjecting him to the possibility of never coming to faith and being damned to hell. This sort of thinking makes abortion an act of kindness by ensuring that every child goes to heaven. But that is not the case. Consider these three points:

> A. Christians acknowledge that a human being is formed at the time of conception.
>
> B. Scripture says humans are sinful upon conception (Psalms 51:5 & 58:3); by nature dead in sins and trespasses (Ephesians 2:1) and children of wrath (Ephesians 2:3); enemies of God (Romans 5:10).
>
> C. If A and B are true, a person is spiritually dead from conception; a child of wrath before his parents know of his existence; an enemy of God before his heart begins beating. And from the time he can think, he will add his own sin to that which he inherited.

All these things are true of every human from his time of conception and will grow worse unless God saves them. People are sinners by nature; that is why people sin. We do not have a neutral position until a mythical "age of accountability." What does the death of a child in the womb teach us, if not a reminder of the curse of death brought on by sin? A right understanding of human depravity explains all the evil in the world. The doctrines of grace explain how depraved human beings can be reconciled to Holy God.

Did David believe he would see his dead son again (2 Samuel 12:23)? Yes, he did. Does that establish a universal truth that all children who die before some mythical "age of accountability" inherit the kingdom? No, it does not. It might be that David's view of paradise was the Jewish view found in the parable of Lazarus and the rich man (Luke 16). Does it appear that John the Baptist knew the Lord Jesus before he was born (Luke 1:41)? Yes, it does. Does that establish a universal truth that all unborn children have this saving faith? No, it does not. If children are "saved" until some indeterminate time later, then the names of all people were written in the Lamb's Book of Life and many are rubbed out by sins during the lifetime of those who survive childhood. Does the Bible teach this anywhere? We see that those who are in Christ will NOT have their names blotted out; we do *not* see that those who end up rejecting the gospel have their names blotted out. Revelation 3:5 is an encouragement to the saints to persevere, not a threat that some will have their eternal status reversed. Every argument I have read or heard in favor of "all children go to heaven" has its foundation based on a sentimental view of God and His justice. We know that "infant baptism" was started because 3rd century Christians knew their infants were sinners in need of salvation. They thought water baptism was salvific and started baptizing sick infants to make sure they were not damned. Then they "baptized" all infants.

If they knew their infants deserved wrath, when did the view that they don't get started? Is it not presumptuous to declare that God saves all infants? How is it different than the Presbyterian idea of covenant children? They declare that all children born to Christian parents are in the covenant (one assumes they mean the New Covenant, but they typically don't name it). The presumption is these little ones are saved and unless they demonstrate at some later point that they are, in fact, unrepentant sinners, they are "confirmed" as Christians and members of that church. If they prove themselves reprobates, they are "covenant breakers" and no longer considered Christian or member. How does this, or the similar doctrine that all infants are heaven-bound, fit with the biblical doctrines of predestination and the security of the believers?

One example of little children being put to death to set the balance against the normal examples of little children being held up as our examples: the aftermath of the Battle of Jericho. The Israelites were told to destroy everything of Jericho (except Rahab and her household) and specifically told not to keep anything from the spoils or else destruction would follow them (Joshua 6:15-21). Chapter 7 starts with a common, but sad, report: some Israelites were unfaithful regarding the things that were to be destroyed. A man named Achan took some spoils for himself and YHWH was angry with the whole people. Joshua confronts him (verse 19) and Achan confesses (verse 21) and we read in the balance of this chapter how Achan and his wife and children, his animals and his tent; everything of his family was killed and destroyed. Covenant people who disregard YHWH's command; stoned to death. Temporal death is a shadow of spiritual death; note the references to Sodom and Gomorrah used in this fashion (2 Peter 2:6; Jude 1:7).

The bottom line is that one should not be dogmatic and erroneously claim all babies, or even all babies born to Christians, go to heaven. Neither should one be dogmatic and erroneously claim that no babies are heaven-bound. Since we cannot know from Scripture who is heaven-bound before we see the fruit of their salvation, our best course of action is to be obedient to teach our children their need for a savior and point to the biblical Jesus. We should take comfort in the thought that God gives children to Christian parents, knowing the instructions we should be giving those charges. But no one should presume upon Holy God and claim to know this or that one *will* be saved. If God is not the One who decided, past tense, who He would save and be faithful to do it, then man is the one who decides, in time, who God will save. Then man commands God to save him. That is the bare essential of the humanistic, sentimental view espoused by so many. And it is flat out heretical nonsense.

To sum up, the five solas of the Reformation are five short statements that have deep meaning; drawing the line between biblical Christianity and all false religion. It is my prayer you will dig deeper into the doctrines taught by these statements and that you will embrace the Word of God for all it is worth. For Scripture alone tells us who God is (the Creator and Judge of all things), who we are (by nature, sinners who love the darkness and are children of wrath), how we are reconciled to God (by grace alone, through faith alone, in Christ alone), and what will eternity be (for some, eternal punishment; for God's elect, eternal bliss). For the liberating knowledge of this, and for life and godliness, we need the revelation from God found only in the closed canon of Scripture.

Sola Scriptura
Soli Deo Gloria!
Sola Gratia
Sola Fide
Solo Christus!

Truth that not only sets us apart from Rome; properly understood it is truth that sets us free indeed.

Recommended reading on this topic:
Solo Scriptura - What a Difference a Vowel Makes! * - Keith A. Mathison
*Sola Scriptura** – William R. Downing
*The Five Solas of the Reformation** – James M. Boice
*The Works of the English Reformers** - William Tyndale and John Frith
The History of Protestantism, three volumes* – James Wylie
*Baptist View of the Reformation** – A.H. Newman
Baptists and the Bible – L. Russ Bush
Scripture Alone – James R. White
The Doctrines of Grace – James M. Boice & Philip G. Ryken

Chapter 5 - Confessions: Their Purpose and Proper Use.

To remind us of these biblical truths and provide a clear understanding of what those within a local church have in common faith, Reformed Churches are confessional, they hold to a written confession which explains how key Scriptures are interpreted and applied to life. While confessions, as such, are relatively new (dating to the late 16th century), they have an ancient foundation in the creeds of the early church. The Apostles' Creed was written between 200 and 400 AD, in part to refute Marcionism, a gnostic-like view that taught the God of the Old Testament was a demon. The Creed of Nicaea, written in 325 AD, was mainly to refute Arianism; the teaching that Jesus was not eternal, but created. The doctrine of the Holy Trinity was at the heart of the Creed of Nicaea. The First Council of Constantinople, 381 AD, modified the Creed of Nicaea by adding a phrase that added support to the eternality and deity of Christ; refuting Apollinarism, which taught that Jesus had but one nature. There are other creeds, but these are the earliest and they show us a common basis for their existence: to make clear certain doctrines of core Christian belief and expose particular heresies with very specific language that would not allow vague statements or those contrary to accepted and proven Christian theology to stand. The earliest confessions (which tend to be much longer than the early creeds, espousing a far broader range of topics) appear to have much in common with the historic creeds of the faith. They were concerned with core doctrines and identifying those who embraced them as orthodox Christians, rather than politically active radicals seeking to overthrow the state.

The 17th century was a busy time for the publication of confessions, and we can see the political and religious history of England as a complex tapestry that explains why so many Christian groups felt the need to publically declare their beliefs. In the early days of the Reformation, more than two dozen confessions and catechisms were published, as those who fled Rome for the freedom of unfettered grace sought to define what they believed; in large part to help teach people biblical truths to keep them from retreating to the known evil of the Roman Church. This list included Ulrich Zwingli's Sixty Seven Articles (1523), Martin Luther's Short Catechism (1529), the Augsburg Confession (1530), Lausanne Articles (1536), and the Heidelberg Catechism (1563). The most enduring and well known confessions were written in the 17th century, in the middle of persecution by state churches on both sides of the English Channel.

Before we look at those documents and their historical context, let's read about how some confessional churches in our day use confessions. Here's what the Association of Reformed Baptist Churches says in its constitution about the 1689 LBC:

> Confessional subscription employs three main terms in its nomenclature: absolute, strict/full, and loose. ARBCA has adopted the middle position. According to Dr. Morton H. Smith, "strict or full subscription takes at face value" the terminology used in adopting a confession of faith.

We declare that our primary rule of faith and practice is the inerrant Word of God, and adopt as our subordinate standards the excellent document commonly known as the London Baptist Confession of 1689, and the Constitution of this Association.

"We accept the London Confession of Faith of 1689 as an accurate and reliable expression of what the Scriptures teach and the faith we confess." In each case, the member churches commit themselves to the Confession as a whole. We maintain the primacy of the Scriptures, and "embrace and adopt" the Confession as a truthful expression of our convictions with regard to the details of Scripture.

In addition, as Dr. Smith says so well, "full subscription does not require the adoption of every word of the Confession or Catechisms, but positively believes that we are adopting every doctrine or teaching of the Confession or Catechisms."

Full subscription honestly adopts all of the doctrines expressed in the confessional formulation. In the case of the Association of Reformed Baptist Churches of America, this means that by subscribing to the document commonly known as the London Baptist Confession of 1689, we receive all of the doctrines contained in it as true, founded on the Word of God.[1]

On their frequently asked questions page the first question asks: "How do I become a pastor of a Reformed Baptist Church in your Association?" The first answer: "A suitable candidate for an ARBCA pastorate must fully subscribe the 1689 Second London Baptist Confession of faith. Click here to see the ARBCA Constitution and the definition of full subscription as an appendix to the ARBCA Constitution."[2] Of interest to Baptists, I hope: Dr. Morton H. Smith, whose definition of full subscription ARBCA embraces, is a life-long Presbyterian. Their view of confessions has influenced Baptists as much as their view of covenants has.

Another brief example from a web page promoting a 2016 conference on end times: "Good Shepherd OPC, Westside Reformed Church, and Redeemer Community Church are congregations that are **devoted to the Bible as it is understood within the Reformed and Presbyterian tradition**. We believe that this teaching is not only true but also helpful to the Christian life."[3] (emphasis mine)

These brief statements reveal deliberate use of a confession as the primary document (no matter their written protests to the contrary) that defines the doctrine and identity of the association and the churches that belong to it. The confession is "excellent" and becomes the "sum of sound doctrine" for them (as one elder in a 1689 LBC church put it to me), "founded on the Word of God", and, in some cases, displacing it as the first line of defense and doctrine. This sad condition is well known among churches that hold to the Westminster Confession and some that hold to the 1689 LBC; and it shows up in their ecclesiology, how they function as a church, such as requiring "strict or full subscription" for serving as an elder while failing to take into account what is laid out in 1 Timothy 3 or Titus 3[4]

Is this the intended purpose of these aged confessions?

In discussing Martin Luther's focus on learning Scripture, author D'Aubigne reflects, "Such are the principles of Christianity and of the reformation … we should not consult the Fathers to throw light upon Scripture, but Scripture to explain the Fathers."[5] I would add that this same principle applies to our use of confessions: we should not consult the confessions to throw light upon the Scriptures, but Scripture to explain the confessions.

The famous Baptist preacher, Charles Hadden Spurgeon, published the 1689 LBC for his congregation, instructing them in the preface that the confession "is not issued as an authoritative rule, or code of faith, whereby you are to be fettered, but as an assistance to you in controversy, a confirmation in faith, and a means of edification in righteousness."[6] This harkens back to the intended purpose and use of the early creeds – to refute heresy and build up the saints. Joseph Jackson Goadby provides support for Spurgeon's view in the following observation:

> The Confessions published by the Baptists in the Seventeenth Century were neither creeds written to secure uniformity of belief, nor articles to which subscription was demanded. They were rather expressions of their opinions, issued in this particular form, as being most convenient. They were defences, or Apologies (in the original senses of that term), wrung from them by the shameless calumnies and bitter misrepresentations of their enemies.[7]

In his short article, *Confessing the Faith in 1644 and 1689*, James M. Renihan agrees with many other historians in seeing myriad issues behind the sudden rush to publish confessions of faith in the 17th century. One of the main motivations for Baptists was their desire to escape or reduce the persecution of the state church of England. Renihan also provides a concise summary of the political/religious environment of England in the 17th century:

> In the space of a few short years, their numbers [the Baptists] had grown, and people were beginning to take notice of their presence in London. But it was often not a friendly notice. In 1642, an anonymous pamphlet entitled *A Warning for England, especially for London; in the famous History of the frantick Anabaptists, their wild Preachings and Practices in Germany* was published. It is an amazing piece of work. The author, in 9 double sized pages, described the

sad events of Munster, Germany. Rebellion, sedition, theft, murder are all charged to the "anabaptists." Throughout, there is no mention of anything but these events from another time and place—until the very last sentence of the pamphlet which stated "So, let all the factious and seditious enemies of the church and state perish; but, upon the head of king Charles, let the crown flourish! Amen." The warning was in one sense subtle, but in another brilliantly powerful: beware! What was done in Germany by the anabaptists may well happen again in London, if these people are allowed to spread their doctrines.[8]

He later makes the following comment in his paper, agreeing with Goadby's observation that the main reason confessions were written in this era was to tell others what the confessors thought, not to bind the confessors to an in-house creed:

> As the Baptists faced these circumstances, they decided that they needed to take action to relieve the fears and misinformation spreading. God had blessed their efforts thus far, and they did not want to see those efforts frustrated by the rumor and innuendo of their enemies. *So they adopted a practice frequently used by others in the last 150 years*—**they issued a confession of faith so that anyone interested in them might be able to obtain an accurate understanding of their beliefs and practices**.
>
> **One of the primary purposes in publishing their Confession of Faith in 1644 was to disavow any ties with the Continental Anabaptists.**[9] (emphasis mine)

You may recall from chapter 1 that *Anabaptist* was a label the state church placed on virtually any religious group that did not submit to their view on any of several issues, baptism being the most common, but not the only one. This label was used in England to brand religious groups that refused to bow to the state church as rebels against the national government. We know, from the accounts of the 5th Monarchy Movement (chapter 1), that these allegations were not all together without merit. Hence it was a most important and delicate matter for Baptists to identify themselves to the state in a way that would show they did not mean to over-throw it. Renihan continues:

> The Baptists were concerned to demonstrate to all that their doctrinal convictions had been, from the very start, orthodox and **too a large degree identical with the convictions of the Puritans around them**. In order to do this, **they looked for the best available means by which to prove that their views were indeed closely in line with the convictions of the other churches around them.** They did this by issuing a Confession of faith. This First London Confession of 1644, published prior to the

Westminster Confession of Faith, was heavily dependent on older, well-known documents. It was their purpose to prove that they did not hold wild new ideas, but rather shared the same basic theological perspectives of the best churches and ministers around them.

This is how we must understand the appearance of the First London Confession in 1644. **It was an apologetic tool to say "Hey, we really are like you in almost every way. We are not like the anabaptists of Munster.** We are like you. Give us a break. Accept us for what we are. Don't reject us just because someone else, at another time and in another place, did some really bad things. We repudiate them. We are not anabaptists. We are reformed Christians." This action had two important facets. First, by publication they desired to make their views, held commonly and unanimously, known to a wide audience of readers. Secondly, by subscribing their names as representatives of the churches, they were publicly asserting that these doctrines were a true representation of the theological views held among them. **Much was at stake, especially their on-going freedom in the face of rising Presbyterian anti-toleration political power.** Remember Milton's famous words: "New Presbyter is but old priest writ large." Few of the Presbyterians were for religious toleration, desiring to replace the episcopalian state church with a presbyterian state church. Subscription was not a nicety, it was a sober, serious and public proclamation that they were orthodox Christians.[10] (emphasis mine)

He goes on to describe how the First London Baptist Confession was modified a couple of years later, in part, to mollify a high-profile Presbyterian, Daniel Featley: "In article 38, they dropped the language against state support of ministers. They even slightly altered their language on baptism to head off some of his carping."[11]

The same cultural pressures were at work 30 years later, when the Second London Baptist Confession was written. Goadby reveals a story about the state persecution of non-conforming churches (lots of Baptists therein) in which this scene is recorded, having taken place in England in 1662, shortly after the Clarendon Code was adopted to crush all dissent from the official religion of the state:

Baptists were being spied out by paid informers, including bishops in the state church. One bishop, Dr. Peter Gunning, marched at the head of the posse of constables, to disperse the assemblies of the schismatics. If he found the doors closed, he gave orders that they should be broken open with sledge hammers. On seeing this done, one wag in the crowd (that had gathered) exclaimed, "What! Has Peter lost his keys?"[12]

While humorous its view of Rome, this scene brings to light the sad state of affairs in 17th century England for those who cherished the Word of God more than comfort and convenience. Subterfuge, surveillance, and harassment were the common tools of the state church in England during this time. Recall that John Bunyan spent most of twelve years, from 1660 to 1672 and again for a short time in 1675-76 (which is when he began writing *The Pilgrim's Progress*) in England's prison. Baptists did not have peace with the authorities for most of the 16th and 17th centuries. The ongoing conflict and persecution was wearing on them and they were looking for relief, while seeking to remain faithful to God.

The 1689 LBC was initially published in 1677, anonymously, as if the authors were testing the waters, as even those non-conformists who openly refuted the Anabaptist label were still being spied on, hunted down, and persecuted for their simple faith in the God revealed in Holy Writ. It was published openly with the signatures of pastors from seven area churches in September of 1689, four months after the Toleration Act, which granted freedom of worship to non-conformists such Baptists. The authors made clear their intent of conforming to the Westminster and Savoy confessions as much as possible, with ecclesiological issues being the clearest area of difference. The Presbyterians and Congregationalists had established relative peace with the state by confessing their beliefs and the Baptists of the late 17th century looked to them for examples as they sought relief from persecution. Renihan and others comment at length on this, mostly making the case that theological agreement was the main basis for the 1689 LBC being so similar to the WCF, with some things in common with the First LBC. I would agree whole-heartedly that the essential doctrine of soteriology (how is one saved) is addressed biblically in the WCF and the 1689 LBC, but that does not mean one should turn a blind eye to error that may lurk any document written by man. In a short book addressing primitive Baptists in Wales, Baptist pastor Michael N. Ivey addresses the question of why the 1689 LBC is so similar to the WCF. He quotes Pope A. Duncan, a long-time student and teacher of church history who taught at Southeastern Baptist Seminary for 10 years in the 1950s and 60s:

> Baptists in the seventeenth century stood squarely in the Protestant tradition insofar as the great majority of their doctrines were concerned. What they had to say about most of the classic tenets of the faith differed almost none at all from those of the other Protestant churches of England. **Indeed, the widely used "Second London Confession" purposely used the order and often the very words of the Westminster Confession in order to demonstrate the agreement of Baptists with classical Protestantism.** Thus, with regard to such articles as those dealing with the holy Scripture, the Trinity, Christ, the Holy Spirit, faith, justification, sanctification, the resurrection of the dead, and the judgment, one could note no significant differences between Baptist thought and that of other Protestant Christians of England. In fact, there was essential agreement on most doctrines.[13]

(emphasis mine)

Ivey follows this quote with a summary of the historical context, explaining a bit of the political posturing that took place among church groups.

> The Baptists, yet suffering terribly at the hand of the Crown, eventually realized that neither the Presbyterians nor Congregationalists were suffering the same frequency and intensity of torment. Perhaps fully understanding the political reality of their circumstance they assembled in 1689 in a General Convention and officially adopted [William] Collin's very Westminsterish confession.
>
> **The desire of these tortured brethren to align themselves with the Presbyterians is evident throughout the document.** However, nowhere is it more apparent than in the preamble of the 1677 first edition, which reads in part, "...our hearty agreement with them (Presbyterians and Congregationalists) in the wholesome protestant doctrine, which with so clear evidence of Scriptures they have asserted." The preamble of the second edition of 1688, as adopted in 1689, is less direct but equally obvious in pointing readers to its similarities with the Presbyterian and Congregationalist creeds. It reads, "...And finding no defect in this regard in that fixed on by the Assembly, and after them by those of the Congregational way, we did readily conclude best to retain the same order in our present Confession." Assembly and Congregational, both capitalized, refer to the Presbyterians and Congregationalists respectively. Further this statement indicates the London Confession was written, as much as possible, with the same topical format as the Westminster Confession.
>
> **We must not think harshly of these tortured brothers' willingness to seize this opportunity to gain official tolerance.** None today have lived under constant threat of imprisonment or worse for practicing their religion. None have seen their pastors drawn upon the rack and quartered. None have gone to their meeting house and found their pastor's head mounted on a pike in the church yard.
>
> Also, it is reasonable to conclude that the 1689 London Confession accurately represents the beliefs of its ratifiers and their congregations. To think otherwise is to accuse the Particular Baptists of surrendering conscience to political opportunity. Such a possibility flies in the face of all they suffered prior to 1689. Liberty of Conscience was, from the beginning, a fundamental tenet of the Particular Baptists. It seems highly unlikely these courageous brethren would have abandon certain elements of their doctrine

simply to gain religious toleration.[14]
(emphasis mine)

Mr. Duncan gives good counsel about avoiding the presumption that we can know the motives of these long-dead men; we are not to judge the motives of those we live and serve and fellowship with, or those brothers who have gone before us. At the same time, we know that no man has pure motives and must admit that *we* would likely have taken some pragmatic steps to lessen the pain of constant harassment and persecution. The world and their culture were also complex 500 years ago; we do not have that market all to ourselves and our 21st century minds. History is not a crystal clear ball into which we can peer without careful discernment.

One of the oldest known confessions from outside the Magisterial Reformation is attributed to Hendrik Terwoort & Jan Pieters, part of a Dutch Baptist group that fled Holland and found apparent safety in England. But, as has been documented in many books, the state church in England also persecuted those who did not agree with and practice her theology. Terwoort and Pieters wrote their simple 3-page confession while in prison in London, in July 1575, shortly before they were executed. They are said to be the first witnesses for liberty of conscience in England, having appealed to Queen Elizabeth, in vain. Some in the Reformed community do not regard Terwoort and Pieters, considering them "Anabaptists" in the most radical sense (see chapter 1). But their confession is biblical and orthodox in its declaration of basic Christian doctrines including believer's baptism and the autonomy (under the Lordship of Christ) of the local church. Unlike the later, more well-known confessions, this early document defines and defends marriage from the Scriptures, something to which in our day we need to pay special attention (see chapter 8). In 1590, an English congregational church fled to Holland and two of her leaders, Henry Barrowe and John Greenwood, published A True Confession in 1596. While the English Congregationalists were paedobaptists, they were also Calvinist. When the English particular Baptists saw the need to declare their beliefs, they used this document as their template for the First London Baptist Confession, first published two years before the so-called divines published the Westminster Confession. Presbyterians have the Westminster Confession; paedobaptist congregationalists have the Savoy; Baptists have two London Baptist Confessions, the 1644/46 First LBC and the 1689 Second LBC. There are others, many of which are slight modifications to the 1689 as Baptists spread into the New World; but there has not been much activity in writing confessions after the 17th century. From a review of church history one sees that confessions are useful and common, at least among certain churches; and central to the identity of some churches. It would appear that there is no need perceived by confessional Christians to continue to write confessions, being content to use those written 500 years ago, as if those documents express an unquestionable level of human understanding of the unfathomable truths of Scripture. The lack of religious persecution has, no doubt, lessened the need for Christians to defend and define themselves in this manner.

While some churches hold to confessions too tightly, there's a ditch on the other side of the road as well, as a good friend of mine likes to put it. Within the evangelical Baptist world, there are many who distain all creeds and confessions, crying. "No creed but Christ!" or "No creed but the Bible!" Since every document written by man has the possibility, if the not dominant presence of error, at first glance it may appear that these "no creed" folks are doing right by sweeping aside all the creeds and confessions and standing only on the work and Word of Christ Jesus. But is that really a good thing and is that, in fact, what they do? When anyone declares something vague, he has in mind something specific that he does not wish to discuss. Talk with any pastor who embraces the creedal statement, "No creed but the Bible" and you will find out he has specific doctrines he holds close and has certain expectations of church members. And members of such churches will discover over time what they are supposed to hold dear and believe. And while these churches refuse to write their confessions or creeds, they have them just as certainly as any person has opinions about anything important to him. It's better to be honest and tell people what the church believes so they can decide whether to join and the pastor can be held to account. I visited a church several years ago that had a page on its web site showing four categories of evangelical doctrines and indicating in each column which stands they agree or disagree with. While some will not be satisfied because this church does not hold to a specified confession, they are very clear and open about what they believe and hold to; and isn't that the main reason confessions exist?

In the next chapter, we will review some of the inconsistencies and errors (as I see them) in the 1689 LBC; yet I do not advocate throwing it out. The Apostle's Creed has some unclear language in it, but I don't think we should throw it out. These documents have value and need to be understood and held in their proper place, subordinate to Scripture. The Apostles' Creed says that Jesus "was crucified, dead, and buried. He descended into Hell. The third day He rose again from the dead." The Bible does not say that Jesus descended into Hell. This is an unfortunate consequence of certain English translations. A common heresy is to declare that Jesus *did* go to Hell, having been abandoned by the Father, was under the domain of Satan; that He died spiritually and was tormented for our sins by Satan, as Kenneth Copeland taught: "He [Jesus] allowed the devil to drag Him into the depths of hell....He allowed Himself to come under Satan's control...every demon in hell came down on Him to annihilate Him....They tortured Him beyond anything anybody had ever conceived. For three days He suffered everything there is to suffer."[15] Such nonsense denies the sufficiency of the cross and it rails against the clear teaching of Scripture. So should we avoid the Apostles' Creed? Probably not. Perhaps, as with historical confessions, ancient creeds need to be studied and explained so that the glorious truths therein can edify the saints and the ambiguous language or errors are properly explained and avoided. Jesus did not descend into hell; He did not pay for any sins there. His salvation work was completed on the cross as He suffered the Father's wrath for our sins. That is the punishment for sin, the wrath of God, not the torment of Satan. Those who are tormented by Satan in hell are merely gaining their reward for their service of their spiritual father while living on the earth. No matter how one interprets 1 Peter 3:18-19 it is clear that where He went after His crucifixion, and when He went, He went *in the spirit*. He died in the flesh, not the spirit. He is alive evermore (Revelation 1:18), He was not abandoned by His Father. Peter said of Jesus, quoting David, "*For you will not abandon my soul to Hades, or let your Holy One see corruption.*" (Acts 2:27). He told the thief "*today you will be with me in Paradise.*" (Luke 23:43) No matter what one thinks "Paradise" is, it is not hell.

If we are serious about being people of the book, we must be careful to keep our traditions and confessions in their rightful place – subordinate to the Word of God, not held up as an interpretative grid for God's Holy Scriptures. We must continue to grow in the grace and knowledge of our Lord (2 Peter 3:18), and the Scriptures are authoritative and sufficient for this.

Recommended reading on this topic:
First London Baptist Confession* (see also Appendix 3)
Second London Baptist Confession*
Westminster Confession of Faith
40 Questions About Christians and Biblical Law – Thomas Schreiner
The Fatal Flaw of the Theology Behind Infant Baptism – Jeffrey D. Johnson
The Works of the English Reformers - William Tyndale and John Frith
Confessions of faith: and other public documents, illustrative of the history of the Baptist Churches of England in the 17th century*
The Pilgrim's Progress* – John Bunyan
The Sabbath Complete – Terrence D. O'Hare

Chapter 6 - Semper Reformanda: The Call to Biblical Renewal.

This brings me to a sticky wicket, so to speak: non-compliance with certain doctrines espoused by the WCF and the 1689 LBC. Confessions are good and useful tools to codify core doctrines around which a local church can grow and have close fellowship. They are subordinate to the Scriptures, not a tool by which to interpret the Scriptures. They are documents written in a particular historical context by men who were limited in their comprehension of Scripture and somewhat blind to their own presuppositions, as are all men. Standing on and under the Word of God, resisting the siren call to rely on the traditions of men (men we love and thank God for), and ever growing in our love and knowledge of God and His Word means we may discover errors in our confessions, wording that is no longer clear, or conclusions that don't appear as evident as they must have to those brothers 500 years ago. Our confessions as well as our personal presuppositions need to be tested in light of Scripture, always reforming for the glory of our God. This is the call to be truly *Semper Reformanda*! Not seeking change for cultural convenience, but in response to the command that we grow as Christians and churches and hold only to that which is good, Truth as God has revealed.

How does a Reformed church or Christian keep from allowing the confession to dictate beliefs on secondary issues as if it were the ruling document? This is evident in many Reformed churches, where people defend their confession first, or only; having forgotten which document is their foundation. Brothers, this should not be so! To cling to one's confession of faith, no matter how sound it may be, as one's first priority is *not* Reformed. Such a priority reflects the carnal priorities of all false religions, and turns a good confession into another golden calf. Bob Gonzalez notes the effect of what he terms *confessionally colored glasses*, and cites as an example the description of the Westminster Confession of faith in Herman Hoeksema's systematic theology, *Reformed Dogmatics*, found inside the dust jacket of that book:

> **Here is a thoroughly Scriptural and Reformed exposition of the faith once delivered to the saints**.... In the view of the author, there are three factors essential to a sound dogmatics. The first is that dogmatics must be faithful to the Scriptures, and therefore thoroughly exegetical. The second is that fundamentally all of dogmatics must be theologically construed, and must therefore be theocentric. **The third is that sound dogmatics must be faithful to the Reformed creeds and to the dogma of the church.**[1] (emphasis added)

When the documents of man are held as an authority in the same as Scripture, they will overshadow Scripture. Guy Prentiss Waters makes it clear the perspective from which he views Scripture, which will delight his fellow paedobaptists but ought to give Baptists a bit of caution. "This commentary is Reformed in its orientation. **It proceeds from the conviction that the Westminster Standards**

are the best summary of the Bible's teaching in the church's possession. It believes that Reformed theology and sound exegesis are not mutually exclusive alternatives, but the very best of friends."[2] (emphasis added)

These are very clear and honest declarations that some people do hold their documents and traditions up as a filter through which to determine what its official teaching will be. With changes to a couple of words, Hoeksema's third point would well have come from Rome: "Sound dogmatics must be faithful to the Magisterium and to the dogma of the Church." The concepts are the same, the extra-biblical documents and ecclesiological history are different only in the context of who is speaking. This is how *any* Christian or church can get stuck in the mud of an inner-look rather than pressing forward to willingly be more and more conformed to Christ, what might be called *Semper Torpor* (always lethargic) instead of *Semper Reformanda*. This is *not* to say that historical orthodoxy is unimportant; it is a vital guardrail that helps keep us from drifting.

Gonzalez examines another sample of this way of thinking and notes that "there seems to be an underlying assumption that the only right way to interpret and apply the Bible is through the medium of Reformed creeds. The unfortunate result is that one can begin interpreting the Bible in light of John Calvin instead of interpreting Calvin in light of the Bible."[1] This observation is particularly wry in my opinion, as John Calvin has been widely seen as viewing the Scriptures in light of Augustine. Gonzalez wisely urges his readers to respect, not revere, the confessions written by those who have preceded us in this spiritual battle to which all saints are called. He quotes James Williamson: **"Documents gain an unsightly prestige over time when they are foundational documents for a given body of believers. They are invested with a sense of authority and regarded as virtually untouchable by succeeding generations.** We have seen this happen with the King James Version of the Bible."[1] (emphasis mine) One last quote from brother Bob, an elder who respects the 1689 LBC but does not revere it:

> Instead of "confessionalism," we need to promote and cultivate "something close to biblicism." Instead of expending the bulk of our energies exegeting the Confession and the writings of Luther, Calvin, and the Puritans, we need to go back farther in history and find the answers and solutions to modern questions and problems as they're provided in the writings of Moses, the Prophets, and the Apostles.[1]

This was the counsel of Spurgeon, as he wrote in his introduction to the 1689 LBC used in the Metropolitan Tabernacle, quoted earlier. This was also the counsel of our Lord as He explained the meaning of the Scriptures to the two disciples He met on the Road to Emmaus (Luke 24); the Scriptures, God's special revelation, are all about Him. The only good a book can do is to point back to the Scriptures, which focus on the Lamb of God who was slain to reconcile sinners to Holy God. To the degree books help us better comprehend God's Truth, praise

God – let us read! To the degree books distract us or, worse, lead us astray from God's Truth – let us repent! Confessions or books, the same rules apply; undergirded by the reality that all works of man are influenced to some degree by the sin that has infected and affected every person in every generation of the human race.

As Baptists learn more about the covenants of Scripture (explored in more detail in Part 3: A Baptist View of Covenant Theology), apart from the Presbyterian hermeneutic so prevalent in Reformed publications, will we be willing to examine what our confessions say about the secondary doctrines that flow out from one's view of the covenants? We will if we are to be true to our calls of *Sola Scriptura* and *Semper Reformanda*. And we will also not be willing to defend our confession by mere argument, but with a clear conscience led by the teaching from the Word of God.

This does not mean that aggressive "inquiries" that appear to be meant only for tearing down confessional doctrines should be entertained. It does mean that honest inquiries from saints who want to sincerely understand how a given doctrine is defended from Scripture should be welcomed. A clear indication of trouble is when secondary documents are not allowed to be questioned, this is a sign of cultish behavior. From a description of the dispute in 1524 between Ulrich Zwingle and Martin Luther over the nature of Christ's presence in the Lord's Supper, D'Aubigne provides this snippet as a response to Luther's dogged declaration that Jesus was physically present and his reliance on un-named "doctors" of the early church:

> "If this be the case," said Oecolampadius, "we had better leave off the discussion. But I will first declare, that, if we quote the Fathers, it is only to free our doctrine from the reproach of novelty, and not to support our cause by their authority." No better definition can be given of the legitimate use of the doctors of the Church.[3]

Once again, insight from the history of God's people to show us the right use of human authority, be it from second century doctors or seventeenth century confessions.

To have a clear and proper perspective on any confession we must bear in mind that it is not inspired, not inerrant, and not infallible. Therefore, it must be tested, as with all things of man. We must reject any errors and cling only to that which is good (1 Thessalonians 5:21), that which is true to the Word of God, following the examples of the Bereans who were willing to test what the apostles were teaching.

It is clear from the historical notes surrounding the publication of the Second London Baptist Confession, including the authors' introduction, that the English Baptists had grown tired of being harassed and persecuted by the English government. Having suffered far more than the Presbyterian and congregational paedobaptists, the Baptists looked to those groups to see how to take advantage of their standing with the government and present the particular Baptists as no greater threat to society than these others, putting more distance between themselves and the "radicals" which people tended to align with the non-conforming Baptists.

The introduction to the 1689 LBC in the Spurgeon version tells us "It was based upon, and drew its inspiration from the Confession drawn up by the Westminster Assembly of Divines a generation earlier, and indeed differs only from it in its teaching upon those matters, such as baptism, the Lord's Supper, and church government, upon which among the Reformed churches the Baptists differ from the Presbyterians."[4] While some within the 1689 camp insist on putting the Savoy between the Westminster Confession of Faith and the 1689 LBC, this is an argument without substance; as the Savoy was a clone of the Westminster, differing only on church government. The 1689 LBC *is* largely a clone of the Westminster.

The matter of church government noted above must include the difference in how each group saw its relationship with the civil governments. These issues (baptism, ecclesiology, church/civil relationships) are those which are easy to detect, *above the water line* one might say. What our Baptist forefathers did was to knock these matters out of the way and replace them with Baptist alternatives. What the early Baptists apparently did not do is carefully examine the foundation that was *below the water line*.

If one studies the theology and related history of the Westminster Confession, it is clear that their theological framework was established to provide the foundation for the doctrines they had developed and devoted themselves to. These *above the water line* matters did not grow out of their theological framework; these key distinctives formed the "foundational" basis of the Presbyterians' theology which was codified in the Westminster Confession of Faith.

One, perhaps *the* major area in which it appears the Baptists erred in cloning the Westminster regards the treatment of the Decalogue. As this piece of the Mosaic Law does not directly relate to baptism, ecclesiology, or church/civil relationships there apparently was no perceived need to examine how it was treated in the Westminster and carried over in the 1689 LBC. Yet, as presuppositions are more powerful than abstract arguments, the importance of rightly understanding the rationale for how the Decalogue is treated in the Westminster cannot be overstated. Presbyterians need the covenant with Israel to be directly applicable to the New Testament church because they see the church and Israel as the same thing under the same covenant; we Baptists do not. God had a remnant of saints within national Israel, but they were not "the church". The conclusion of Hebrews 11 makes this clear: *And all these, though commended through their faith, did not receive what was promised, since God had provided something better for us, that apart from us they should not be made perfect* (complete) (Hebrews 11:39-40). The church, as the New Covenant community, was not fully formed until late in the life of the last Apostle, as the teachings entrusted to those men were the last foundation stones to be laid (Ephesians 2:20). Those saints in the Old Covenant were not complete until the fulfillment of time, they looked forward to Christ's day and rejoiced (John 8:56). *For he was looking forward to the city that has foundations, whose designer and builder is God* (Hebrews 11:10).

We rightly teach people to take the biblical and historical context into consideration when interpreting Scripture, using Jeremiah 29:11 as a primary text for teaching on this. Christians are not Israel, we have not been exiled to Babylon, we have not been promised restitution in 70 years. And that is the context for the famous promise found in verse 11, preceded by 10 other verses which culminate with *For thus says the LORD: When seventy years are completed for Babylon, I will visit you, and I will fulfill to you my promise and bring you back to this place* (Jeremiah 29:10). Yes, there are spiritual applications of this passage that should bring great comfort to Christians: God is faithful to His promises to His chosen people! But the explicit promise of temporal wealth and restitution He promised national Israel is not applicable to us. Many Reformers make this very argument, and rightly so. This makes it all the more mysterious when they do not see the context of the Decalogue and the importance it has on one's proper interpretation and application of that text. The Decalogue is presented as the primary witness, or testimony to the Sinai Covenant being given by God to Israel; not as an eternal moral law of God for all people. The Decalogue does not exist anywhere else in Scripture (although some claim otherwise. See the article, An Ethical Manifesto" by Richard Barcellos, in Appendix 4), only in the context of God's covenant with the nation-state of Israel.

It does make perfect sense for the Presbyterians to appropriate the covenants given specifically to the nation of Israel, because they see equivalence between the church and ancient Israel, both members of the same Mosaic covenant with wheat and chaff therein. It does not make sense for Baptist to embrace their view; ancient Israel was temporal, the church is spiritual. Baptist ought to see the nation of Israel mainly as a type, fulfilled in Christ in the New Covenant in His blood, wherein only the redeemed enjoy the far greater benefits of that covenant. The Decalogue partially reflects God's "moral law" given to Adam after the fall as it was deployed within the Sinai Covenant with terms that were types and shadows of Who was to come, marking His temporal people as distinctly His, as His Spirit marks His eternal people as distinctly His.

This paedobaptist influence is found predominately in chapter 19 of the 1689 LBC, but also in one paragraph of chapter 22, addressing the "Christian Sabbath". Chapter 19 (footnotes as they appear in Sam Waldron's *Modern Exposition of the Second London Baptist Confession*) addresses the volatile concept and use of "the law." One thing that makes this concept volatile is the plain fact that it has various meanings, not always referring to the Decalogue. Context helps the careful reader determine what is meant when he reads about "the law." Here then, is a short review of what I see as paedobaptist ideas carried over from the Westminster Confession into the 1689 LBC.

1689 LBC – Chapter 19.

Paragraph 1. "God gave to Adam a law of universal obedience written in his heart." The references for this statement are Genesis 1:27; Ecclesiastes 7:29; Romans 2:12a, 14-15. The first two passages talk about man being made in God's image and upright; Romans 2 reveals the law given to all men who were not given the Mosaic Covenant. This law given to Adam must be the "moral law" of God; that which operates on the conscience of all whom the Holy Spirit has not given over to their sinful desires. It is not specified as the Decalogue or the Mosaic Covenant.

Paragraph 2. "The same law that was first written in the heart of man continued to be a perfect rule of righteousness after the fall." We see this at work beginning in Genesis 3 as Adam gained knowledge of good and evil, continuing throughout biblical and world history. This law must be the that same law referred to above, in Romans 2, because the confession says, "the same law". Yet the Scriptures referenced in footnote 1 point to various places where the Mosaic Law is written in Scripture, not the law given to Adam. Herein is a conflict within the confession. The balance of this paragraph declares that the Ten Words given on Sinai are the same law as written on Adam's heart, citing (footnote 2) the same passage from Romans which reveals the law at work in Gentiles who do not have the law of Moses.

How can the law given to Adam be the law of the Gentiles, who are without the law of Moses, then be described as the Ten Words which were given to Moses as law that the Jews had possession of? And how does using Romans 2:12a & 14-15 as the proof text prove that? Other versions of the 1689 LBC refer to Deuteronomy 10, which describes the tablets but that passage does not indicate that they are the same law as given to Adam. This is conjecture, not exegesis. And it conflicts with itself regardless of which footnotes are used in a given version of the confession.

Further, how could Adam know the Decalogue or *any* version of the "moral law" prior to having knowledge of good and evil? Only *after* he and Eve ate the forbidden fruit did Adam know he was naked (Genesis 3:11). Only then God said *the man* **has become** *like one of us in* **knowing good and evil** (Genesis 3:22). It is clear that Adam did not know evil before he sinned, though he clearly knew the goodness of God. Since knowledge of the Law incites sin (Romans 3:20; 5:20; 7:7), one can only conclude that Adam was given the "moral law" conjunction with The Fall; not when he was created nor when he walked in innocence. There is no warrant in Scripture to take the Decalogue as an eternally binding "moral law" for all people: it was given to Moses and the infant nation of Israel (Nehemiah 9:13 & 14) and the tablets sit in an ark that is to be forgotten (Jeremiah 3:15-16).

Paragraph 3. "Besides this law, commonly called moral ..." It appears that the previous reference to the ten words given on Sinai is "this law" being here mentioned. There is no proof text for this assertion, that the ten words are the moral law. What is the biblical defense for the Decalogue being called *the* moral law? John Reisinger has observed that when theologians have no biblical support for a doctrine, they defend it as "commonly called", etc. He further observes "A moral act is the opposite of an immoral act. A moral person is the opposite of an immoral person. However, the people who employ this term theological forms do not use the word 'moral' as the opposite of 'immoral.' They make the opposite of 'moral' to be 'ceremonial' and 'civil.' This has created a new and unique use of the work 'moral' that is used to justify a preconceived theological position."[5] "A Jew living under the Old Covenant could not make the same distinctions that we can make today. A Jew obeyed "the law of God" in its entirety. He did not make sure to keep certain laws because they were on the moral list, while not worrying too much about observance of other laws because they were on the 'ceremonial' list. "God said" was the Israelite's sole authority for all his behavior, whether it concerned loving his neighbor or mixing different kinds of seeds in his garden (Leviticus 19:18, 19)."[6]

Since the Hebrews under the Mosaic covenant rightly saw all the commands of YHWH as moral (why else would picking up sticks on the Sabbath be a capital offense? – Numbers 15:32-36), it dawned on me that the right nomenclature would be *universal law* (do not murder, marriage, etc.) and *covenantal law* (do not eat pork, stay in your home on the Sabbath, etc.). Many people refer to a "natural law" that applies to all people, but since such a law is instituted and communicated by Creator God, it's a supernatural law which applies universally. Hence my preference for that label. The covenant one is in determines which laws apply, apart from the universal laws which apply to all men. If one uses the tri-part distinction embraced by reformed folks, one must recognize "ceremonial" and/or "civil" law within the Decalogue, varying to some small degree between the two records of it. If the record in Exodus 20:1-17 is all and only God's "moral" law, then Moses was a false prophet for changing some of that "moral" law with he recounted them in Deuteronomy 5. These labels are misleading more than helpful.

Where in Scripture is the Decalogue declared to be the law written in the heart of man? If all men have the Decalogue written on their hearts, what is the new law that will be written on the hearts of the redeemed (Jeremiah 31:33)? If Christians get the Decalogue written on their hearts, it's not a new law; it's the same old law. Again, this fits well within the paedobaptist view of one covenant of grace under two administrations. Just a bit of cleanup and the old covenant will look brand new! We will see this is *not* how God describes these two covenants.

There is no argument that the Decalogue contains universal law, but it contains more; specific instructions and commands that are part of the Mosaic covenant with national Israel and no other nation or people. Rather than *being* the universal law of God, it would seem that the Decalogue is a particular *application* of law given in the Mosaic Covenant to the Jews.

In a critique of New Covenant Theology, Richard Barcellos quotes John Owen from his *Works*, 22:215. Owen follows the common Presbyterian construct in referring to ancient Israel as the church. While discussing the functions of the Decalogue and arguing for the morality and immutability of the essence of the fourth commandment, Owen makes this statement concerning the nature and function of the Decalogue under the Old Covenant:

> The nature of the decalogue, and the distinction of its precepts from all commands, ceremonial or political, comes now under consideration. The whole decalogue, I acknowledge, as given on mount Sinai to the Israelites, **had a political use**, as being made **the principal instrument or rule of the polity and government of their nation**, as peculiarly under the rule of God. It had a place also in that economy or dispensation of the covenant which that church was then brought under; wherein, by God's dealing with them and instructing of them, they were taught to look out after a further and greater good in the promise than they were yet come to the enjoyment of. Hence the Decalogue itself, in that dispensation of it, was a schoolmaster unto Christ.
>
> But in itself, and materially considered, it was wholly, and **in all the preceptive parts of it, absolutely moral.** Some, indeed, of the precepts of it, as **the first, fourth, and fifth, have either prefaces, enlargements, or additions, which belonged peculiarly to the then present and future state of that church in the land of Canaan**; but these especial applications of it unto them change not the nature of its commands or precepts, which are all moral, and, as far as they are esteemed to belong to the Decalogue, are unquestionably acknowledged so to be.[7] (emphasis mine)

In this quote, both Owen invalidates the common assertion that what we see in Exodus 20 is nothing but the "moral" law, although he did specify the "prescriptive parts" as "absolutely moral;" which is the universal law shining through the tablets. Walter Chantry asserts, "the Ten Commandments *per se* are free of all ceremonial and judicial peculiarities of the Mosaic covenant."[8] Chantry does not tell us what he considers "the Ten Commandments *per se*" to be, but we know the Decalogue communicates "that law commonly called moral" in the context of the covenant God made with Israel. A close reading of the text reveals, as Owens said, there are "prefaces, enlargements, or additions, which belonged peculiarly to" Israel in the 2nd through 5th and the 10th words of the tablets; more places within the Decalogue than Owen cited, indicating more words that what were carved on the tablets.

Terrence O'Hare tell us that Thomas Aquinas appears to be the first to develop this line of thought, "asserting that the old law contains moral (emanating from natural law), judicial (laws regarding justice among men), and ceremonial (laws touching on worship, holiness, and sanctification) precepts; and that these three can be distinguished in the Decalogue as well."[9] This appears to be the first teaching of what is now cherished reformed doctrine; that the Law of Moses can be separated into these three categories and dealt with appropriately for New Covenant saints. There should be no denying these three elements are found in the Law of Moses, but, as noted above: one man's ceremonial law is another man's moral law. Accepting such a novel teaching from anyone is treading on thin ice; that the originator was a Roman Catholic makes it all the more important that we examine it closely before declaring it truth that binds everyone.

Paragraph 5. "The moral law does for ever bind all, as well justified persons as others, to the obedience thereof." We cannot understand the meaning of this statement without knowing what was meant by the word, "bind". Which of these definitions (from a modern dictionary, but in alignment with Webster's 1828 dictionary) applies to the law of Moses and the Christian?

> *a* : to make secure by tying
> *b* : to confine, restrain, or restrict as if with bonds
> *c* : to put under an obligation <*binds* himself with an oath>
> *d* : to constrain with legal authority

I do not see the law of Moses performing any of these functions for the Christian, though the last definition certainly applies the *universal* law to all persons not justified in Christ.

The footnotes for this assertion mention a Jew trying to keep the law of Moses (Matthew 19:16-22); the same Romans passage as above, having to do with Gentiles without the Law of Moses; Jews who are condemned by the of Moses (Romans 3:19-20); and Christians who now *serve in the new way of the Spirit and not in the old way of the written code* (Romans 7:6). This passage contrasts the man living under the Law of Moses (*the old way of the written code*) with the man who serves *in the new way of the Spirit* (HCSB). The Apostle had just described how Christians are free from the law by having died to it in the same way we have died to the world (Galatians 6:14). How can the Law of Moses bind the Jewish Christian who is freed from it? How can the Law of Moses bind the Gentile Christian who was never subject to it? Further, Ephesians 2:11-22 provides a glorious look at the unity all saints have in Christ Jesus, Who gained our reconciliation with God and Who *is* our peace; accomplishing this *by* **abolishing the law of commandments expressed in ordinances**, *that he might create in himself one new man in place of the two, so making peace, and might reconcile us both to God in one body through the cross, thereby killing the hostility* (verses 15 & 16). **How are we free** from *the old way of the written code*, have peace in Christ by His *abolishing the law of commandments* that spoke against us **and still be bound by the law** of commandments as this confession states?

Next in the footnotes is a verse attesting to the victory we have in God (Romans 8:3); and Paul's statement that the law is good if used lawfully (1 Timothy 1:8-11). Is "*using the law lawfully*" the same as "binding all people" with it?

If Christians are freed from the condemnation of the law, and live in the new way of the Spirit, then lawful use of the law (and it does appear Paul meant the law of Moses) is to restrain and punish the lawless and disobedient, the ungodly and sinners, and myriad others who engage in gross sin. This does not say the law of Moses is used to bind all people to the obedience thereof; it is to bind those who are not in Christ, rebellious against God. Those are the people this text tells us the law is for, not *the just* who have been justified by faith in Christ (Romans 3:26). (See "An Ethical Manifesto" in Appendix 4 for the opposing view.)

The next citation has Paul summing up the second table of the law of Moses as doing no wrong to a neighbor, which is proper love for one another (Romans 13:8-10); then we see the law of Moses held up as the perfect standard of obedience (1 Corinthians 7:19), which is possible only for the Lord Jesus; and then we are referred to two statements in which circumcision (often a summary of the law of Moses) is described as nothing, but faith in Christ as the only thing that matters (Galatians 5:6 & 6:15). Then we have a large section of Ephesians (4:25-6:4) which does not mention the law of Moses but does show the demands of the universal law; and James 2:11-12, which shows us the condemnation of the law of Moses contrasted with *the perfect law, the law of liberty* under which Christian shall be judged. Christians are not bound by the law of Moses, we are informed by it as we are with all of God's Word. We are bound by and judged by the law of liberty, which only comes by being set free from the penalty of sin by being made a new creature in Christ.

This is a sign of trouble in any document, when the Scripture passages used as references do not support the point being made. Thomas Schreiner observed, in reviewing the Apostle James' view on the "Royal Law" found in James 2:1-10: "What is striking, however, is what is absent. James never mentions circumcision, Sabbath, or food laws. The ceremonial dimensions of the law are entirely absent, and this fact is all the more notable when we recall that James was addressed to Jewish Christians (James 1:1)."[10] The Tablets and the sign of the Mosaic Covenant (the Jewish Sabbath) are not mentioned by the Apostle as he describes to Jewish Christians how to fulfill God's law, which must be His "moral law." It appears that "Royal Law" is God's universal law, and it also appears that the Royal Law (which grants liberty) is not equal to the Decalogue (which is the ministry of death – 2 Corinthians 3).

This paragraph in the 1689 LBC ends with, "neither does Christ in the Gospel any way dissolve, but much strengthen this obligation"; meaning the obligation and binding of the Mosaic law is greater for the Christian than for the lost. Matthew 5:17-19 is cited, which refers to the totality of the Old Covenant law which the Jewish leaders were to teach and live; it does not seem to bind Christians to obedience to the law of Moses. Then we are led to Romans 3:31, where man's inability to keep the law of Moses and the prophets is said by Paul to establish the law, to confirm it as God's covenant that must be kept and was kept by Christ alone. The law, in total, stands as vindication of man's inability to justify himself, opposing the Jews (the law of Moses) and the Gentiles (the universal law). The entire argument that the Decalogue equals God's "moral" law and is binding on every man fails to stand up under the illumination of the very Scripture called upon to defend that view.

Consider this view of how the law was used in the Old Covenant and is to be used in the New:

> if we were to grab Paul and sit down with him to have a larger discussion about the law, he would tell us that in the Old Covenant era another proper use of law was to tell believers (the tiny minority in Israel) how to love God (so David says "Oh how I love Your law!"). He would also tell us that in the New Covenant era, the Law of Christ is used both ways: (1) to tell unbelievers that they are under God's wrath: "For the wages of sin is death, but the gift of God is eternal life in Christ Jesus our Lord" (Romans 6:23) and (2) to tell believers how to show their love for God: "This is how we know that we love the children of God: by loving God and carrying out his commands. This is love for God: to obey his commands. And his commands are not burdensome, for everyone born of God overcomes the world. This is the victory that has overcome the world, even our faith" (1 John 5:2-4).[11]

Not a list of things to do and not do; a reminder of Who we belong to and Who enables us to love as we were loved.

1689 LBC – Chapter 22: On the "Christian Sabbath"

> <u>Paragraph 8.</u> "The sabbath is then kept holy unto the Lord, when men, after a due preparing of their hearts, and ordering their common affairs aforehand, do not only observe a holy rest all day, from their own works, words and thoughts, about their worldly employment and recreations,[30] but are also taken up the whole time in the public and private exercises of his worship, and in the duties of necessity and mercy."[31]
> [30] Isa. 58:13; Neh. 13:15-22
> [31] Matt. 12:1-13

Before we consider the applicability of this command, we will examine it to see if it what is portrayed in the 1689 LBC. There is no question about the Sabbath command to rest, from all "works, words, and thoughts about their worldly employment and recreation." Exodus 34:21 makes this clear: even in plowing time and harvest, Israel was to rest from their work on the seventh day just as YHWH had rested from His work on the seventh day. This is a continuation of what He began teaching them in Exodus 16: God's people are to work (itself a gift from God, mired in a creation cursed by Adam's sin) yet see every good thing as provision from Him. So on the seventh day, work for even the basics of life was prohibited. This seems to be the same message our Lord Jesus taught in His

Sermon on the Mount, in Matthew 6:19-34 as He encourages being heavenly-minded, avoiding covetousness, being solitary in their focus on being obedient to their God. And then He says to not worry, *be not anxious, saying, 'What shall we eat?' or 'What shall we drink?' or 'What shall we wear?' For the Gentiles seek after all these things, and your heavenly Father knows that you need them all. But seek first the kingdom of God and his righteousness, and all these things will be added to you.* If we consider His provision for Israel as they were led out of Egypt, the parallel is amazing. In their exodus from Egypt, YHWH had provided Israel manna and quail to eat (Exodus 16:13 & 14), water from a rock (Exodus 17:1-7), and clothes that did not wear out (Deuteronomy 8:4). God provided for His temporal people the necessary things of life in this temporal age. He continues to provide these things for His spiritual children, just as He will discipline us as He disciplined them. *Thus you are to know in your heart that the LORD your God was disciplining you just as a man disciplines his son* (Deuteronomy 8:5 NASB). All that was done was to teach Israel to trust YHWH, to honor Him, to glorify His name amongst the pagan world. These are the continuing messages from our God, who *causes all things to work together for good to those who love God, to those who are called according to His purpose* (Romans 8:28, NASB). This "good" that God orchestrates is for our spiritual good, which is eternal. He will provide what we need in this life, but He works all things together for our eternal good, adding *all these things* to us in His time. This is the theme of the Sabbath: rest from temporal work, trusting God to provide. This is the spiritual application of the Sabbath: cease from your works of self-righteousness, trusting God to impute His to you and find your rest in Christ. God ceased from creation work when it was finished and He declared it very good. He has ceased from His work of re-creation and He declared *"It is finished!"* (John 19:30); and He bids us find our rest in Him (Matthew 11:28). Jesus is the Sabbath for the Christian, in this age and the one to come.

The 1689 LBC cites a passage from Isaiah (chapter 58 verse 13) wherein Creator God holds up the Sabbath as a touchstone of His relationship with Israel. Is this text rightly applied to the New Covenant church? In this passage, not for the first time, a prophet of God is rebuking His temporal people for failing to keep His covenant made with them. The religious people in Israel had turned their Sabbath into the day before the important things of life, as Amos recorded: *Hear this, you who trample on the needy and bring the poor of the land to an end, saying,* **"When will the new moon be over, that we may sell grain? And the Sabbath, that we may offer wheat for sale**, *that we may make the ephah small and the shekel great and* **deal deceitfully with false balances**, *that we may buy the poor for silver and the needy for a pair of sandals and sell the chaff of the wheat?"* (Amos 8:4-6). This is the same behavior found as the nation returned from exile and Nehemiah rebuked them for polluting the Sabbath by conducting business on that day of rest (Nehemiah 13:15-22).

It is clear that Sabbath breaking by those in the Mosaic Covenant was a serious affront to God. But is Sabbath keeping required of those in the New Covenant as well? Ancient witnesses give their perspective:

Justin Martyr [circa 100-165], in controversy with a Jew, says that ...
Christianity requires not one particular Sabbath, but a perpetual
Sabbath. He assigns as a reason for the selection of the first day for
the purposes of Christian worship, because on that day ... Jesus rose
from the dead and appeared to his assembled disciples, but makes
no mention of the fourth commandment.[12]

Moreover, all those righteous men already mentioned [after
mentioning Adam. Abel, Enoch, Lot, Noah, Melchizedek, and
Abraham], though they kept no Sabbaths, were pleasing to God;
and after them Abraham with all his descendants until Moses. And
you were commanded to keep Sabbaths, that you might retain the
memorial of God. For His word makes this announcement, saying,
"That you may know that I am God who redeemed you."[13]

Barnabas [thought by many to be the companion of Paul the
apostle] ... calls this day the eighth day, in distinction from the
seventh-day sabbath of the Jews, and which he says is the beginning
of another world; and therefore we keep the eighth day, adds he,
joyfully, in which Jesus rose from the dead, and being manifested,
ascended unto heaven.[14]

This concept of the eighth day is something we who claim Christ should study
and seek understanding. "From another angle, redemption is also the beginning.
Hence, the redeemed are free on the eighth day, that is, the first day of the new
week. The new week designates a new period of time, a better epoch, and a new
generation. It is built upon that which preceded but brings us closer to that which
is anticipated; it reaps the blessings earned or bestowed in previous days, and
hopes for fulfillment of greater promises."[15] O'Hare goes on to demonstrate from
Scripture how the number eight portrays hope and promise that comes only in the
promised seed. "Based on the root word for fatness or abundance, the first
mention of eight occurs in Genesis 5, of the number of years that Adam lived
after his son Seth was born, years marked by the prodigious growth of his
family."[16] "Noah in a sense was "translated" to the new world as a family of eight
on the eighth day, signifying again the association of eight with the resurrection
to immortality in a new day."[17] O'Hare bases this observation on the record in
Genesis 7, wherein the animals were led into the ark by YHWH and seven days
later the flood came. On that day, Noah and his family entered the ark, God shut
them in, and the ark foreshadowed the rescue of sinners that the Lord Jesus brings.
The first day of safety in the midst of the world-destroying flood, was the eighth
day after the ark was opened as a refuge. David was the eighth son of Jesse (1
Samuel 17:12-14). "When David's eighth-position antitype arrives (Jesus Christ),
said Isaiah, His kingship and kingdom will be unlike anything that preceded it
(Isaiah 9:6-7)."[18] The eighth day signifies our redemption and the resurrection of
our Savior. The seventh day is the Jewish Sabbath, which was a type of the rest
promised in the Messiah. The eighth day is our rest, begun when we are raised up
by the Spirit of God to new life in Christ and to be consummated when He returns

to take us home. We should agree with these dear brothers and joyfully keep the eighth day by fellowshipping and worshiping our King with others He has called to Himself.

The 1689 LBC uses the 4th word to claim Sabbath-keeping includes worship, citing Matthew 12:1-13. Clearly the worship of God is an essential reason Christians gather on the first day of the week, but neither the passage from Matthew nor any other text in the Bible mandates or describes worship as a component of Sabbath-keeping. The one reference to the Sabbath that some think commands worship must be examined. Does Leviticus 23 convey a Sabbath command for worship, and does that create a "Christian Sabbath" with the same command? Here's the introduction to this chapter in God's Holy Word, which describes the many feasts He gave to Israel: *The LORD spoke to Moses, saying, "Speak to the people of Israel and say to them, These are the appointed feasts of the LORD that you shall proclaim as holy convocations; they are my appointed feasts. "Six days shall work be done, but on the seventh day is a Sabbath of solemn rest, a holy convocation. You shall do no work. It is a Sabbath to the LORD in all your dwelling places* (Leviticus 23:1-3). This passage goes on to describe various feasts as "holy convocations," with repeated reference to and emphasis on faithful obedience to the Sabbath command. And how was the Sabbath command defined? It was a day of *solemn rest, a holy convocation … in all your dwelling places.*

> The Sabbath has the precedence given to it, and it was to be "a holy convocation," observed by families "in their dwellings"; where practicable, by the people repairing to the door of the tabernacle; at later periods, by meeting in the schools of the prophets, and in synagogues.[19]

Neither this text nor any other reveals, much less commands, weekly worship as part of the Sabbath; nor does it bring this mythical command into the New Covenant gathering of called-out ones. The Sabbath given to Israel was a command to rest from their work, typifying the command to cease working to be reconciled to God and find rest in the completed work of the Christ.

Many people argue for the perpetual and universal application of the 4th commandment by pointing out the word, *"Remember"*, in the version from Exodus 20; claiming this shows that the Hebrews knew of this law from ancient times, despite no record of observance by man prior to being taught about the Sabbath in Exodus 16. They *might* have been told to remember what YHWH had taught them in the desert. These Sabbath commands were given to national Israel are not directly applicable to New Covenant Christians, unless one flattens out the distinctives between the old and new covenants and their participants. God's Holy Scriptures (Nehemiah 9:13-14) tell us the Sabbath was given by God to the nation of Israel at Mt. Sinai, not from the garden and not to all people; YHWH revealed His holy Sabbath to the Jews.

> *You came down on Mount Sinai, and spoke to them from heaven. You gave them impartial ordinances, reliable instructions, and good statutes and*

commands. You revealed Your holy Sabbath to them, and gave them commands, statutes, and instruction through Your servant Moses. You provided bread from heaven for their hunger; You brought them water from the rock for their thirst. You told them to go in and possess the land You had sworn to give them. Nehemiah 9:13-15 (HCSB)

This seems to easily a.) exclude the creation ordinance argument, and b.) show to whom the Sabbath was given.

The word, "remember" can also mean to "keep in mind", as when a mother tells her young son to "remember your coat." She is not telling him to keep in his mind a memory of his coat; she is telling him to keep her command in mind and not leave his coat at school. This word does not prove the case of those who hold to alleged long-time practice of keeping the Sabbath. YHWH reminds the Hebrews of His resting on the first 7th day as the reason for this commandment. Creation ends with the 7th day, upon which Creator God rested from His creation work. This served as a model to help the nascent nation keep His commandment in mind. The same commandment in Deuteronomy begins with, "*Observe*", reinforcing the idea that "remember" (in Exodus) means "to keep in mind" and goes on to provide reasons why the Hebrews should keep His Sabbath: remember how the Lord brought them out of Egypt; that their exodus from Egypt, reminding them of God's protection and His promised rest, etc. is the reason they, the people of Israel, are to keep the Sabbath. Again, does not this show us that some of what is recorded in the Decalogue is temporal and "ceremonial" or "civil?" Ezekiel 20:1-8 tells of YHWH reminding Israel how He had provided for them, how they turned aside and His wrath burned towards them. Verses 9-20 tells us His provision for them, with the Sabbath as a sign between God and the Hebrews; marking their exodus from Egypt:

> But **I acted for the sake of my name**, *that it should not be profaned in the sight of the nations among whom they lived, in whose sight I made myself known to them in bringing them out of the land of Egypt. So I led them out of the land of Egypt and brought them into the wilderness. I gave them my statutes and made known to them my rules, by which, if a person does them, he shall live.* **Moreover, I gave them my Sabbaths, as a sign between me and them, that they might know that I am the LORD who sanctifies them.** *But the house of Israel rebelled against me in the wilderness.* **They did not walk in my statutes but rejected my rules, by which, if a person does them, he shall live; and my Sabbaths they greatly profaned.** *"Then I said I would pour out my wrath upon them in the wilderness, to make a full end of them. But* **I acted for the sake of my name**, *that it should not be profaned in the sight of the nations, in whose sight I had brought them out. Moreover, I swore to them in the wilderness that I would not bring them into the land that I had given them, a land flowing with milk and honey, the most glorious of all lands, because* **they rejected my rules and did not walk in my statutes, and profaned my Sabbaths; for their heart went after their idols.**

Nevertheless, my eye spared them, and I did not destroy them or make a full end of them in the wilderness. "And I said to their children in the wilderness, Do not walk in the statutes of your fathers, nor keep their rules, nor defile yourselves with their idols. **I am the LORD your God; walk in my statutes, and be careful to obey my rules, and keep my Sabbaths holy that they may be a sign between me and you, that you may know that I am the LORD your God.**

The Sabbath is a sign of the Mosaic Covenant, a reminder to sinful Israel of their identity as God's marked-out people. Scripture tell us (Exodus 34:27 & 28) that the covenant was made with Israel; *his covenant … that is the ten commandments he wrote on two tablets of stone* (Deuteronomy 4:13). Further, Moses emphasizes (Deuteronomy 5:2 & 3) this covenant was made with national Israel, not the patriarchs; and not, by implication, with Adam. The entire history of the nation of Israel serves as a shadow of the spiritual journey God's redeemed go through to find their rest in Jesus. The Jewish Sabbath is not listed as a sign for the church any more than water baptism is a sign and seal of the New Covenant.

Terrence O'Hare provides a refreshing, Christocentric view of the fourth commandment:

> The Mediator is on the first table (of the Decalogue) because, unlike Moses, Christ truly comes from God and is fully God. Yet Christ, by becoming fully man, joins with man to make him complete. Man cannot become complete simply by keeping the law, but he must experience through faith a life-altering union with Christ. The ceremonial Sabbath is the evangelion within the Ten Commandments that addresses the redemption of man. It is Christ Himself who takes the place of the Sabbath in the Decalogue. The Lord's Day is not a continuum of the Sabbath or its replacement; it is a fresh ordinance for the church of God based upon the completion of redemption that was twice sealed by the Lord, first by His resurrection and second by the descent of the Holy Spirit.[20]

This puts the Decalogue in the absolute best light for new covenant saints to understand it and relate to it, with Christ front and center.

We read in Colossians 2 not to let anyone judge us on questions of *food and drink, or with regard to a festival or a new moon or a Sabbath because these are a shadow of the things to come, but the substance belongs to Christ.* This pattern of days refers to all of the holy days of the Jews, from yearly feasts to the weekly Sabbath, and comes from repeated descriptions of the Mosaic ritual, found in 1 Chronicles 23:30-31; 2 Chronicles 2:4, 8:12-13, 31:3; Nehemiah 10:33; Isaiah 1:13-14; Ezekiel 45:17; and Hosea 2:11. This is another indication that the Mosaic code, of which the Decalogue is part, does not apply to Christian as a law, but as a type or shadow of the Christ to come. Our exodus is not from the nation of Egypt; that country serves as a type for sin and wickedness. The universal law, though it is revealed within the Mosaic code, is eternal and no more uniquely part of that Sinai covenant than the New Covenant is; though the covenant of redemption was progressively revealed over time, even within the era of the Mosaic Covenant.

There is no record in Scripture of any mention or observance of a "Christian Sabbath." History shows a creeping incrementalism towards that idea, being codified by the Roman Catholic Thomas Aquinas, who opined that the Decalogue was God's "moral" law, binding on all people. Early reformers, including John Calvin, did not hold to a Christian Sabbath, although Sunday worship was normal since apostolic times and embraced by these men. The moral aspects of the law were clearly seen, the ceremonial or civil brought into the visible church over time by men who were not satisfied with God's design for the church. The New Testament shows Christians gathering for worship, teaching, fellowship, and much more on the first day of the week ("the day after the Sabbath" in the Greek; does this not make the use of the term "Christian Sabbath" all the more strange?); but there is no record of keeping the Jewish Sabbath on the next day as some claim. This argument is akin to the paedobaptists' argument for infant baptism based on the several "household baptisms" found in Scripture, claiming a practice so common place that nobody mentioned it. The sabbath rest promised in Hebrews 4:8-11 refers to our resting in Christ, ceasing from our works as God ceased from His work of creation on His Sabbath; not keeping a pale imitation of the Jewish Sabbath on the day after the Sabbath. The word for rest in this passage is unique to that verse, it portrays the rest of God that He has provided for His people, the *children of Abraham according to the promise*. This rest is fulfilled when we die the first death and cease from our war with sin (Revelation 14:13).

The prophet Jeremiah tells us the Ark of the Covenant, which contained the tablets of testimony, is to be forgotten: *And I will give you shepherds after my own heart, who will feed you with knowledge and understanding. And when you have multiplied and increased in the land, in those days, declares the LORD, they shall no more say, "The ark of the covenant of the LORD." It shall not come to mind or be remembered or missed; it shall not be made again* (Jeremiah 3:15-16). Does not this align with what Hebrews 8 says about the old and new covenants? Might these testimonies of the Mosaic Covenant be types and shadows that point us to something greater, as so much of what God gave Israel in that covenant is properly recognized as?

There are those who claim that since God wrote the Decalogue on stone tablets with His own finger, the Ten Words are eternal and morally binding. The first set of tablets was destroyed and the second set of tablets (which may or may not have been written on by God, see Exodus 34:27-28) has been lost, intentionally, to antiquity. Why would almighty God allow this if those tablets of stone were His moral law? It does make sense for YHWH to allow this if that ark and its contents represent the old, worn out covenant. We do not have a record in Scripture of exactly what was written on these tablets; we have what Moses told Israel as part of the Sinai Covenant; more words, in two different versions of "the ten commandments." Of note, it appears that no Bible translated the ʿeser dābār as "ten commandments" until the Geneva Bible was published. The Hebrew is "ten words", hence the Latin term Decalogue.

Are the stone tablets sacred? We see in Scripture that temporal objects made of stone are not eternal. Hearts of stone are replaced with hearts of flesh (Ezekiel 36:26); the message of Christ is written (by God) on the hearts of His people, not on tablets of stone (2 Corinthians 3:3); the fine Jewish temple of noble stones would be torn down (never to be useful again) and replaced by a temple of Christ's body (John 2:19-20). The tablets are a ministry of death and condemnation (2 Corinthians 3:7 & 9), contrasted with the ministry of righteousness, life, and freedom (verses 6, & 17). This is the contrast between the Old Covenant and the New Covenant (verses 6 & 14). There is no reason to conflate or confuse these two covenants or their signs; one condemns and one liberates. Christ fulfilled the first to bring about the second (more on this in chapter 9 on the covenants between God and man).

To better understand the scope of this issue, let us review how the biblical description of the weekly Sabbath compares with the confessional view of the "Christian Sabbath" according to the Second London Baptist Confession in chapter 22. Let the reader decide if the Puritans and those confessions had it right or followed traditions of man.

Biblical Sabbath	"Christian Sabbath"
Every 7th day (Ex 16:27-30, Ex 20:8-11, 31:15, 35:2; Lev 23:3; Deut 5:14)	Para 7: Claims One day in Seven (Ex20:8). Changed from the last day of the week to the first day of the week (citing 1 Cor 16:1-2; Acts 20:7); claiming "Christian Sabbath" as the Biblical Sabbath was abolished (no Scripture citation).
Rest from all work (Ex 16:23, 25; 20:8-10; 35:2; Lev 23:3; Num 15:32; Deut 5:12-15; Jer 17:21)	Para 8: Rest from all things (Isaiah 58:13; Neh 13:15-22).
Remain in your dwelling (Ex 16:29; Lev 23:3)	Private and public worship are commanded (para 8; no Scripture citation)
It is a sign to the Israelite (Ex 31:13, 16, 17; Lev 24:8; 2 Chr 2:4; Neh 9:14; Ezek 20:12, 20)	
Death penalty for violating it, even minor activities such as picking up sticks (Ex 31:14-15; Num 15:32-36)	
No fires for cooking, Sabbath day meals were prepared the day before (Ex 35:3)	

Ceremonial bread, made in accordance with a strict formula, was presented (Lev 24:8; 1 Chr 9:32)	
Offerings – consisting of lambs, grain, and drink (Num 28:9, 10)	
Soldiers/priests guard the temple (2 Kings 11:5-12; 2 Chr 23:4-8)	
Gentiles not bound (Deut 5:15; Neh 10:31)	Para 7: Claims "law of nature … by Gods appointment" a "moral, and perpetual commandment, binding all men, in all ages" (no Scripture citation).
Prohibited from business (buying or selling) with Gentiles (Neh 10:31, 13:15-19)	
Gentiles invited to join with God's people and keep the Sabbath (Isaiah 56:1-7)	
Israel to keep the Sabbath (Isaiah 58:13)	
	Duties of necessity and mercy are permitted (para 8; Matt 12:1-13)
No bearing of burdens (Jer 17:21-27)	

Notes:

1. The 1689 LBC cites Exodus 20:8 for setting the Sabbath one day in seven and for binding all men. That verse does not mention the frequency of the Sabbath; verses 10 & 11 both specify the 7th day, that day which ended the week for the Hebrew nation. Every 7th day, not one day in seven; that's the consistent record in Scripture. Neither does that passage mention anyone other than national Israel as the subjects of this covenant and this specific command.

2. The 1689 LBC then claims 1 Corinthians 16:1-2 and Acts 20:7 as a record of God having changed the day of observing the Sabbath. Read the texts: narratives showing the practice of the new church on "the day after the Sabbath." No instruction or record of changing the Sabbath; no record of establishing the "Christian Sabbath" or abolishing the 7th day Sabbath, which continued on during the Lord's time on earth and the apostolic era.

3. Because of the death penalty for minor infractions of the Sabbath command to rest (as shown in Exodus 31 & Numbers 15), it was common in Israel for the people to ask the religious leaders for clarification of what was permissible. This developed into the complex, legalistic list of rules that were infamous in the time of Christ.

4. The "holy convocation" mentioned in Leviticus 23:3 is widely considered to have been a call to prayer, praise, and instruction from the Word of God. But the biblical record (Exodus 12; Leviticus 23; Numbers 28 & 29)

shows a consistent requirement to cease work, with cooking meals being the only exception. There is the occasional mention of humbling one's self, making offerings to God, and the blowing of trumpets. Some of these convocations lasted several days or weeks. There is nothing in Scripture to indicate this was a weekly occurrence of prayer, praise, and preaching; although extra-biblical history does show the post-exile nation adopting the weekly synagogue practice that was well established by the time of Christ.

5. There are many special Sabbaths, such as the Day of Atonement (Leviticus 23:32) and the Sabbath year (Leviticus 25). This comparison is restricted to the weekly Sabbath.

6. Nehemiah 13:20-22 reveals the only passage in Scripture wherein Gentiles are told about the Sabbath, their merchants being warned to leave the Jews alone on the Sabbath so the Jews won't be led astray. Gentiles are not commanded by Nehemiah to keep the Sabbath.

7. There is not one Scripture cited by the 1689 LBC showing the weekly Sabbath being addressed to, defined for, imposed on, or required of anyone other than those under the rule of Moses. Nor is there any biblical record of Christians keeping the Sabbath.

In the mid-17th century, English Baptist John Grantham was defending the doctrine of the credibility of then-modern Bibles as the Word of God. He saw the wisdom of God in allowing the autographs to be lost, as men would revere them as relics and be led astray as in the Roman Catholic Church. With numerous credible copies, he argued, all men would be more peaceable since God had given to all equal access to His word. Does the reverence some men give to the Decalogue approach relic worship? How bad might it be if God had not "lost" the ark and its contents? All things considered, it does not appear that the stone tablets of testimony are sacred to God. We remind ourselves that what He has revealed to us in Scripture is sufficient for life and godliness, so pointing to stone tablets He has withheld from us is not a proper argument for interpreting the written Word He has given us.

The 1689 LBC, in chapter 1 paragraph 1, declares something not found in the Westminster document: "The Holy Scripture is the only sufficient, certain, and infallible rule of all saving knowledge, faith, and obedience." May we rightly see this as a call for us Baptists to be faithful to the doctrine of *Sola Scriptura*, and not be misled by what men have built up as tradition.

In summary, I believe the 1689 LBC suffers from paedobaptist influence in its perception of The Law, resulting in unavoidable conflicts within itself. Baptists ought not to embrace this unless we embrace their view of the covenants as well, for therein lies the basis for the view espoused in chapter 19 and chapter 22.8 of the 1689 LBC. All of this is not to say I think the 1689 LBC has no worth or value. It is a broad scoped examination of basic Christian issues that should cause

Christians to think biblically and dig into the Word. This entire topic would not be worth discussing if these confessions were not held up as authoritative, with the "Christian Sabbath" as the main point of contention. And this should not be, as *One person considers one day to be above another day. Someone else considers every day to be the same. Each one must be fully convinced in his own mind. Whoever observes the day, observes it for the honor of the Lord* (Romans 14:5-6, HCSB). We who are Baptists and reformed and reforming have much in common that is central to the faith; holding to one day above another should not be a point of conflict among us.

I first became aware of these errors and inconsistencies in the 1689 LBC when I was teaching this confession to prospective members of the church I belonged to, and was in the elder training program. When I approached my mentor, one of the elders therein, with these observations, asking him to correct me if I was in error, I was met with an almost cavalier dismissal. Future discussions with the elders of that church about my view of these issues were only focused on them determining that I did not claim to fully subscribe to that confession, which would settle my status with them. There was virtually no interest in *seeing if these things be so*; only an interest in holding to the 1689 LBC. I was reminded of this, as well as conversations with a few others who hold to something written or spoken by man too tightly, when I read the following:

> There is a secret consciousness in error that makes it shrink from examination, even when talking most of free inquiry.[21]

Whether Billy Graham or Benjamin Cox is one's favorite author, the Christian should only bow the knee to the Author of Holy Writ and be willing to discuss anything man has written.

An astute observation from a news story wherein Paul McHugh, a respected psychiatrist at Johns Hopkins, refuted self-identification of sex is most appropriate here: "gird your loins if you would confront this matter. Hell hath no fury like a vested interest masquerading as a moral principle."[22] So it is in discussing the "Christian Sabbath" with those who hold to it.

If I may quote John Calvin with just a slight change, to show how he understood this issue:

> We do not despise the writings of ~~the Fathers~~ *these confessions*, but in making use of them we remember always that 'all things are ours' (1 Cor 3:22); that they ought to serve, not govern us; and that 'we are Christ's,' (1 Cor 3:23). Whom in all things, and without exception, it behoves us to obey.[23]

That is basically what our modern Baptist brother Bob Gonzalez advocates, as noted above. And yet this healthy perspective of how we ought to consider godly men who have preceded us is looked down upon by many who, as Gonzales wrote, see through *confessionally colored glasses*. Brothers, this should not be so!

If being reformed truly includes the concept of ever reforming to Scripture and always seeking to grow in the grace and knowledge of our Lord, then we ought to realize that our brothers from the 17th century no more had it all together than do you and I. Therefore, we should *test everything, hold to that which is good;* and be willing change documents written by other sinful men when we see one or two things more clearly, by God's grace. Change for its own sake is rarely a good thing. But change when we see more clearly from the Word of God is always a good thing. And we must not allow our own wisdom or that of men who went before us to stand in the way. How can we claim to be reformed if our confession is unchangeable, sacred? No man arrives at a full understanding of God's Word while living in this age; how can a confession be considered inviolate? While our confessions are good and useful, they must always submit to the Word of God and we must be willing to entertain honest questions from saints wishing to understand them better or examine them in light of Scripture, with the aim of being more accurate and, therefore, honorable to our God and useful to His children.

Always reforming to the image of Christ by growing in grace and knowledge of our Savior, being transformed more and more by the on-going renewal of our minds in His Scripture, means we cannot afford to stop learning or growing complacent in what we (or our favorite author) "knows." Guarding against the human tendency to build a fence around what he already believes and refusing to grow in grace and knowledge, the reformer Philip Melanchthon said, "The destruction of learning brings with it the ruin of everything that is good: religion, morals, Divine and human things. The better a man is, the greater his ardour in the preservation of learning; for he knows that of all plagues, ignorance if the most pernicious."[24]

And for us as individual Christians to guard against falling prey to our own opinions, it continues to be vital for life and godliness for us to belong to and participate in life in a healthy, local church.

Conclusion.

Apart from these truths, each one based solely on the Word of God, many will be led astray from the narrow path of God's Truth. The reminder that we, as sinful creatures, will never stop learning about the Lord, and ourselves in this age is necessary for our own spiritual health. While some in the history of the church have claimed that perfection is possible, the Apostle Paul; likely one of the most mature Christians we know of; declared, *Not that I have already obtained this or am already perfect, but I press on to make it my own,* **because Christ Jesus has made me his own**. *Brothers, I do not consider that I have made it my own. But one thing I do: forgetting what lies behind and straining forward to what lies ahead, I press on toward the goal for the prize of the upward call of God in Christ Jesus* (Philippians 3:12-14).

In commenting on this need to ever be seeking conformity to Christ, Gary Long observed:

> John Murray, one of one of CT's greatest exegetical paedobaptist theologians, has acknowledged that "theology must always be undergoing reformation, [because] the human understanding is imperfect" and [because] "*covenant theology, notwithstanding the finesse of analysis with which it was worked out and the grandeur of its articulated systematization, needs recasting.*"[25]

(Emphasis in Long's citation)

It's a sad commentary in that neither Westminster nor 1689 LBC advocates see this; the basic reality of the human condition: we cling to what we're comfortable with; the conflict between our imperfect understanding and the higher ways that comprise the mind of God (Isaiah 55:8 & 9).

There is a paragraph from James Pendleton's *Baptist Church Manual* addressing church discipline; his review and analysis of Scripture is well suited to the current topic. Grant me the liberty to change his introductory phrase to fit this topic.

> The doctrine of *always reforming to the Word of God* is taught in such passages as these: "In whom all the building fitly framed together growth unto a holy temple in the Lord: in whom ye also are builded together for a habitation of God through the Spirit." "For the perfecting of the saints, for the work of the ministry, for the edifying of the body of Christ; will we all come in the unity of the faith, and of the knowledge of the Son of God, unto a perfect man, unto the measure of the stature of the fullness of Christ." "Giving all diligence, add to your faith virtue; and to virtue knowledge; and to knowledge temperance; and to temperance patience; and to patience godliness; and to godliness brotherly-kindness; and to brotherly-kindness charity." "Grow in grace, and in the knowledge of our Lord Jesus Christ." Ephes. 2:21, 22; 4:12, 12; 2 Pet. 1:5-7; 3:18.

It is clear from these Scriptures that Christians should ever be in a state of progressive spiritual improvement. We must not be retrograde nor remain stationary, but be constantly advancing in the divine life. The *perfecting of the saints* is an object of vast importance. The perfection referred to has to do not so much with absolute freedom from sin, as some suppose, as with the symmetrical development and maturity of Christian character. The new convert to the faith of the gospel is a "babe," a spiritual infant, that has *need of milk*, and not of *strong meat*. While the Holy Spirit is the teacher of every Christian, so also has our Creator given us the local assembly of believers where we are to grow in grace and knowledge. In addition to those passages cited by Pendleton, we see instructions to Timothy that every Christian ought to heed:

Do your best to present yourself to God as one approved, a worker who has no need to be ashamed, rightly handling the word of truth. So flee youthful passions and pursue righteousness, faith, love, and peace, along with those who call on the Lord from a pure heart. Have nothing to do with foolish, ignorant controversies; you know that they breed quarrels. And the Lord's servant must not be quarrelsome but kind to everyone, able to teach, patiently enduring evil, correcting his opponents with gentleness. God may perhaps grant them repentance leading to a knowledge of the truth, and they may come to their senses and escape from the snare of the devil, after being captured by him to do his will. (2 Timothy 2:15, 22 – 26)

This concept of *always reforming to the Word of God* appears to be rooted in a sermon from Pastor John Robinson in the 1620s. He had been an Anglican minister who renounced his position in that church in 1606, having become convinced the Church of England was insufficiently biblical. In a short article, "The Implications of Semper Reformanda," Andrew Atherstone reports:

> Moving to Leiden in the Netherlands to pastor a separatist congregation he was a vocal advocate of the reformed doctrines expounded by the Synod of Dort. In 1620 over forty members of his congregation joined the puritan pilgrimage to New England on the Mayflower. Before they left Robinson exhorted them to follow Jesus Christ and him only – not to be disciples of Luther, or Calvin, or Pastor Robinson, but disciples of Christ. He urged them to be willing, in Christian humility, to continue learning from Scripture. 'For he was very confident', says the earliest account of that farewell sermon, that 'the Lord had more truth and light yet to break forth out of his holy Word.' [26]

Semper Reformanda is not an invitation to depart from God's Word and use our imagination to come up with some new thing. It is to recognize we each and collectively have the on-going need to be transformed by the renewing of our minds, so that we will be able to discern the will of God (Romans 12:2). We find the will of God in the Word of God. From the near-ancient Roman Catholic mystics to the new-age apostasy of those called "Emergent" – if man is not content with God's revelation in Scripture, he will display an ever increasing tendency toward self-idolatry and rebellion against God.

The process of growth in a Christian (progressive sanctification) is an area we are commanded to actively engage in (see Colossians 1:9-12). Yet it is not something we can do apart from being found in Christ as a new creature, indwelt by the Holy Spirit, *for it is God who works in you, both to will and to work for his good pleasure* (Philippians 2:13) and apart from Christ Jesus we can do nothing (John 15:5). The Christian life is full of tension: we love our God because He first loved us (1 John 4:19), we seek to honor Him with our lives (Romans 12:1). Yet sin plagues us (Hebrews 12:1), our fleshly desires (Galatians 5:17) never give up (Romans 7:23), and the enemy of our souls (1 Peter 5:8) is always eager and active to drag us astray and bring dishonor to the Lamb. We must be watchful (Ezekiel 3:17), on guard (1 Peter 5:8), and *stand fast in the faith, quit you like men, be strong* (1 Corinthians 16:13 KJV); knowing He is our refuge and strength and ever present help (Psalms 46:1). Anyone who claims to belong to Christ and has no interest in fighting this good fight should not be encouraged as a brother. The brother who weeps because he struggles with sin and is horrified that he has dishonored the Lamb who bought him ought to be encouraged as a brother. To struggle against sin is our life. To "go with the flow" is the enemy's plan: the path of least resistance makes both men and rivers crooked. Our personal goal of *Semper Reformanda* must be a life-long deliberate focus on finding our strength, sufficiency, and reward in our Savior; He will make our paths straight (Proverbs 3:6). We must follow the Apostle Paul's counsel, following the passage cited earlier from Philippians 2:

> *Brothers, join in imitating me, and keep your eyes on those who walk according to the example you have in us. For many, of whom I have often told you and now tell you even with tears, walk as enemies of the cross of Christ. Their end is destruction, their god is their belly, and they glory in their shame, with minds set on earthly things. But our citizenship is in heaven, and from it we await a Savior, the Lord Jesus Christ, who will transform our lowly body to be like his glorious body, by the power that enables him even to subject all things to himself.* (Philippians 3:17-21)

There is no demilitarized zone in the Christian's life. The contrast between the two kingdoms is explicit. We have instructions and examples from God's Holy Word to guide us. To continue to grow in grace and knowledge of our Lord Jesus, we must be always reforming to the glory of our God. That's *Semper Reformanda!*

Recommended reading on this topic:
Tablets of Stone – John Reisinger
The Danger of Reformed Traditionalism* – Bob Gonzalez
Is the Mosaic law tripartite? * – Mael
Absolute Predestination* - Jerome Zanchius
Baptists - Thorough Reformers* – John Quincy Adams
What is Reformed Christianity* – Tony Warren
The Essential Sabbath – David H. J. Gay
The Sabbath Complete – Terrence D. O'Hare

Conclusion.
Being reformed simple yet complex. It's simple in concept: always be reforming to the Word, conforming to Christ. It's complex in practice because men have developed systems that, while mostly solid, include error that has been adopted as truth. This is the human condition and we must imitate those good Bereans and seek out the Scriptures to see if what man teaches us is so.

Part 3: A Baptist view of Covenant Theology

Introduction

Reformed theology is often referred to as covenant theology, based on the presupposition that God deals with us primarily through covenants. Nobody reading the Bible can deny that there are many covenants revealed to us therein. How many covenants, how do they relate to one another, who are party to any given one? The answers to those questions are what divide us. Determining how the various covenants relate to the covenant of grace (also referred to as the covenant of the promise or the covenant of redemption) helps us rightly determine how they apply to Christians, who are members of the New Covenant. The most common connotation of "covenant theology" is the long-standing and widely held paedobaptist view, documented in the Westminster Confession of Faith and the associated catechisms. The details of how Baptist *ought to* differ from our Presbyterian brothers will be clarified as each covenant is reviewed. Some differences are semantic, some are fundamental.

One's view of the biblical covenants has great influence over myriad doctrines, or reflects underlying presuppositions that are difficult to defend from Scripture. If one holds to the Aquinas notion that the Decalogue is the moral law of God, the Mosaic Covenant becomes something more than the centerpiece of the Old Covenant. This requires artificial distinctives to allow one to set aside much of the Mosaic Covenant as "ceremonial"; something unknown to the Jews and Christians until the 13th century (see chapter 6). Many Baptists, including those who hold to a dispensational perspective, deny the existence of a Covenant of Works, mainly due to their basic rule of interpretation which relies heavily on a literal view of Scripture and the absence of certain terms in the creation account. Others, many holding to New Covenant Theology, dislike the terms Covenant of Works and Covenant of Grace, mainly due to the way they are presented in the Presbyterian system with the latter encompassing both the Old and New Covenants. As we will see, the differences one may have with New Covenant Theology brothers are small and deal in large part with defining our terms. The differences we have with our Presbyterian brothers has to do with the content, participants, fulfillment, and application of these two covenants; their covenantal view apparently being determined by their desire to defend certain doctrines that were developed before they generated their confession and catechisms. There are more than these two covenants mentioned in Scripture and I will focus on those which reveal man's relationship with God, as that is the critical aspect of everyone's life.

One of our old Baptist brothers, C. H. Spurgeon, had this to say about the importance of understanding the covenants of Scripture:

> The doctrine of the covenant lies at the root of all true theology. ...
> I am persuaded that most of the mistakes which men make
> concerning the doctrines of Scripture are based upon fundamental
> errors with regard to the covenants of law and grace. ... The

covenant of works was, "Do this and live, O man!" but the
covenant of grace is, "Do this, O Christ, and thou shalt live, O
man!"[1]

To clarify Spurgeon's quote, the covenant of law or works challenges man (who is
"hard-wired for works righteousness," as Voddie Baucham has often said) to see
that he cannot fulfill the Law's demands. Likewise, when Spurgeon said the
covenant of grace is a command for Christ Jesus to "do this," he must be referring
to the covenant of works as that which Jesus had to fulfill so He would be worthy
to shed His blood to enact the covenant of grace (or fulfill the Covenant of
Promise) by issuing the New Covenant to provide eternal life to God's elect. Being
born under the curse of the Law (Galatians 4:4), Jesus had to keep the entire Law
to earn the right to sacrifice Himself for us to be reconciled to God the Father.
The covenant of works (this covenant must be carefully defined) is revealed by
the light of nature; nature's light teaches self-righteousness (Romans 2:15), leading
to judgment. The Covenant of Promise is revealed by the Spirit of God (1
Corinthians 2:13) Who reveals Christ's righteousness, which leads to eternal life.
John Reisinger put it this way: "The old covenant said, "If you obey, then you will
be blessed" (Ex 19:5,6), but the New Covenant says, "I have obeyed for you,
believe and live" (Heb 10:14-22)."[2] I am inclined to refer to the Eternal Covenant
as that which conveys God's promised redemptive plan and the fulfillment thereof,
rather than the commonly used "Covenant of Grace" as I think it is a better
reflection of what the Bible reveals to us. These concepts will be more fully
developed later as we review the covenants in some detail.

Some claim that the covenants in Scripture are the key to understanding the Word
of God. Others claim having a right view and understanding of Christ Jesus and
His role and work is the key to understanding the Word of God, with the
covenants helping that view. This basic foundation is a major influence on the
difference between a paedobaptist view of Scripture and a proper Baptist view of
Scripture. Here's how one of the most revered paedobaptist brothers of our day
summed it up:

> Reformed theology, as many have said, is covenant theology, for **the
> concept of covenant has shaped the development of
> Reformed thinking.** We should expect as much because of our
> doctrine of sola Scriptura, which says that the Bible is the only
> infallible authority for Christian faith and practice. Therefore, we
> want to structure all theological understanding according to
> Scripture. **This demands covenant theology, since covenant is
> an organizing principle in Scripture.**[3] (emphasis mine)

Mr. Sproul ties "the concept of covenant" to "the development of Reformed
thinking," meaning his paedobaptist view. Nowhere in his article does Sproul
defend from Scripture his statement that "covenant is an organizing principle in
Scripture;" he merely asserts it as if it is clear on its face. If this is true, one ought
to be able to easily show it from the Word of God, rather than merely assert the

point while describing several of the covenants that we agree are found in Scripture.

Read how Baptist John Reisinger addresses this topic:

> **The gospel promise of Christ Himself is the heart of both the Old and New Testament Scriptures.** The Advent and work of Christ is the fulfillment of that gospel promise, and the personal advent of the Holy Spirit on the Day of Pentecost and His subsequent indwelling of every New Covenant believer are the absolute proofs that the Gospel promise has been fulfilled. Understanding **that the gospel of salvation by grace is what is being promised in all of Scripture, and further, that Christ Himself is the "Seed" Who fulfills that gospel promise**, is the only Biblical way to see and consistently maintain the unity of God's purpose in Redemption.[4] (emphasis mine)

There is a huge difference in seeking God's Truth between trying to figure out all the minutia in the arguments about this covenant or that one and seeking to find out how His Word progressively reveals the glorious Christ promised to our failed father so many generations ago. To shallow-thinking men in His day, Christ Jesus declared: *"O foolish ones, and slow of heart to believe all that the prophets have spoken! Was it not necessary that the Christ should suffer these things and enter into his glory?"* **And beginning with Moses and all the Prophets, he interpreted to them in all the Scriptures the things concerning himself** (Luke 24:25-27). The Scripture **does not** say, "And beginning with Moses and all the Prophets, he interpreted to them in all the Scriptures the things **concerning the covenants**." If we look for another message than the one He has given us, we will end up with a wrong image of Him in our theology. This does not mean that covenants are unimportant, as some declare. Covenants do communicate truths from God so we do need to comprehend them; in light of the gospel, not as an end to themselves. This rule will keep the child of God from drifting astray as he might if he allows covenants to be the organizing rule he follows.

There are three categories of covenants in the Bible: those among men, those between man and God, and the one called eternal which is among the trinity. In each of the first two categories there exists typological connections between the temporal subject and the spiritual truth portrayed therein; I will explore these enough to demonstrate this fact. Each covenant has a basic reason for existence and specific requirements for being fulfilled as well as specific stipulations for inclusion and being eligible for the benefits thereof. All of the covenants explored herein also have as their main focus the eternal covenant and its fulfillment as Christ cut the New Covenant to usher in the Kingdom of God to mankind. There is no higher purpose in God's special revelation to us than this.

It is not my intention to present the 17th century Baptist view on the covenants, as if theirs was the ultimate expression of Baptist thought. Pascal Denault's book,

The Distinctiveness of Baptist Covenant Theology, is an excellent review of that position and the folks at http://www.1689federalism.com/ have been doing a very good job explaining some of the historic Baptist distinctives and how they differ from the Westminster Confession of Faith. My intention is to present what I, a particular Baptist, see as the biblical view of the covenants. Conforming to what particular Baptist have historically believed is not my main concern. I desire to conform the Scriptures, not to 16th and 17th century brothers who no more had perfect theology than you or I. We are not to be disciples of mere men (1 Corinthians 3:1-9), but disciples of the Lord Jesus; thankful for those who have been faithful and gone before us but not trapped in their teachings. Hence the title of this part of the book: *A* Baptist View of Covenant Theology; not ***The*** Baptist View of Covenant Theology. There are, today, many variants of how Baptists view the covenants in Scripture; far be it from me to speak on behalf of those with whom I disagree on topics relevant to this (such as reviewed in Part 2: A Baptist View of Reformed Theology). My desire is to be captive to the Word of God; not captive to a 17th century confession nor a system of theology developed by men.

Chapter 7: The Eternal Covenant

This covenant was agreed to by the godhead before time and space were created; revealed to man in time with more and more clarity as redemptive history unfolded. Here is how YHWH told of it:

> ***Behold my servant, whom I uphold,***
> ***my chosen, in whom my soul delights;***
> *I have put my Spirit upon him;*
> ***he will bring forth justice to the nations.***
> ***He will not cry aloud or lift up his voice,***
> *or make it heard in the street;*
> *a bruised reed he will not break,*
> *and a faintly burning wick he will not quench;*
> ***he will faithfully bring forth justice.***
> ***He will not grow faint or be discouraged***
> ***till he has established justice in the earth;***
> *and the coastlands wait for his law.*
> *Thus says God, the LORD,*
> *who created the heavens and stretched them out,*
> *who spread out the earth and what comes from it,*
> *who gives breath to the people on it*
> *and spirit to those who walk in it:*
> ***"I am the LORD; I have called you in righteousness;***
> ***I will take you by the hand and keep you;***
> ***I will give you as a covenant for the people,***
> ***a light for the nations,***
> ***to open the eyes that are blind,***
> ***to bring out the prisoners from the dungeon,***
> ***from the prison those who sit in darkness.***
> (Isaiah 42:1-7)

More than seven hundred years before the birth of Christ, the Holy Trinity spoke through the prophet Isaiah to proclaim, once again, the promise of the seed that would crush the head of the serpent and deliver His people from the enemy, bringing them from all nations under the spiritual lineage of Abraham. While national Israel longed for a king who would fulfill the description given here by "their" prophet, we know this passage speaks of the then-coming Christ. For only He can truly meet the superlative descriptions found throughout the Old Testament wherein national Israel imagined YHWH would provide them the righteous man to be their prophet, judge, and king. All the while they were largely unknowingly working out His plan to display His power to the world and His faithfulness to true Israel as He called wayward sheep from every nation, tribe, and tongue in the fullness of time.

The Spirit spoke through the author of the letter to the Hebrews to insure this covenant was mentioned, almost in passing, as the benediction is pronounced. Notice: it is the eternal covenant by which sinners are redeemed and sanctified:

Now may the God of peace who brought again from the dead our Lord Jesus, the great shepherd of the sheep, **by the blood of the eternal covenant, equip you with everything good that you may do his will,** *working in us that which is pleasing in his sight, through Jesus Christ, to whom be glory forever and ever. Amen.* (Hebrews 13:20 & 21)

Here's how our Baptist forefather, Benjamin Keach, described it, referring to it as the Covenant of Peace:

> This Covenant of Peace was entered into between the Father and the Son before the World began. Hence the Apostle saith, alluding to this Covenant, *God hath saved us, and called us with an holy Calling, not according to our Works, but according to his own purpose and Grace which was given us in Christ Jesus before the World began.* Moreover, Our Lord Jesus saith, that he was set *up from everlasting, from the beginning, or ever the Earth was.* That is ordained, substituted, and anointed to be the great Representative and Covenanting-Head in behalf of all the Elect of GOD.[1]

I would include the Holy Spirit as a participant in this covenant. All of the covenants between God and man are the working out of God's redemptive plan which was established and granted prior to the foundations of creation. This eternal covenant is between the eternal members of the triune God; not that they need a document to bind themselves to one another, but as an expression of the oneness that exists by their very nature!

The existence of this covenant is denied by some who claim covenants are always between a greater and a lesser being. While that structure is the consistent arrangement in ancient near-east culture, we must bear in mind that YHWH often uses anthropomorphic terms to describe Himself to us so we might grasp His meaning. In doing so, He violates the normal terms of language by using "carnal" terms to describe Himself *and calls into existence the things that do not exist.* I think an honest look at Scripture will reveal a covenant between the only beings that existed before time; all equal to one another. The foundation of this perspective is the biblical record that God has always been one God eternally existent as Father, Son, and Holy Spirit. As all three members of the Holy Trinity are involved in the salvation of sinners, so are all three involved in the entire redemptive process. This Eternal Covenant is the recognition of this unity in purpose that preceded the created order and endures for eternity.

We see this unity in many places in Scripture. When God the Father completed His creation work, He rested from that work. He continued to guide redemptive history and the Scriptures, actively involved in shaping history and the lives of men. When the Lord Jesus had finished His work of atonement, He sat down at God's right hand, resting from His work of redemption. He yet works, serving as our high priest and advocate, our protector and shepherd. And so it is with the third person in the holy trinity; the Holy Spirit worked during and after Pentecost to bring about the birth of the church, with many signs and miracles. Though the bulk of these miracles has ceased, the foundation of the church having been completed, the Holy Spirit continues His work of giving us illumination as we read the Scriptures; convicting the world of sin and revealing the righteousness of Jesus. In each of these creation works and in all of the ongoing works, the three persons of the trinity are completely unified. Recall that the world was created by the Father through the Son, and we read that the Spirit hovered over the waters during this event, as if giving birth. The Father chose those to be redeemed, Jesus atoned for them, and the Spirit has sealed them until the Day of Judgment. They each had a time of one-time creation work and in regeneration work, followed by resting from that work, while continuing on, in unity, with other work required for our good and their glory. This is the work of the Trinity, each completely unified with the other two; one God, three persons in covenant with one another for the redemption of sinners to bring glory to their name, all of which is revealed clearly and concisely in Ephesians 1:3-14:

> **Praise the God and Father** of our Lord Jesus Christ, who **has blessed us in Christ** with every spiritual blessing in the heavens. For **He** (God the Father) **chose us in Him** (our Lord Jesus Christ)**, before the foundation of the world**, to be holy and blameless in His sight. In love **He predestined us to be adopted through Jesus Christ for Himself,** according to His favor and will, **to the praise of His glorious grace** that He favored us with in the Beloved. **We have redemption in Him through His blood, the forgiveness of our trespasses, according to the riches of His grace that He lavished on us** with all wisdom and understanding. **He** (the Holy Spirit) **made known to us the mystery of His will, according to His good pleasure** that He (God the Father) planned in Him (our Lord Jesus Christ) for the administration of the days of fulfillment—to bring everything together in the Messiah, both things in heaven and things on earth in Him. **We have also received an inheritance in Him**, predestined according to the purpose of **the One** (the Holy Trinity) **who works out everything in agreement with the decision of His will**, so that we who had already put our hope in the Messiah **might bring praise to His glory.** When you heard the message of truth, the gospel of your salvation, and **when you believed in Him, you were also sealed with the promised Holy Spirit. He is the down payment of our inheritance, for the redemption of the possession, to the praise of His glory.** (HCSB)

The God Who saves is a gloriously complete, competent, omnipotent, eternal, sovereign Lord of all things Who works out everything as He has willed it; to bring sinners into His glorious light and have His name praised in all the earth and heaven for all time and beyond. If you are in Christ, this ought to give you much comfort and confidence in Him. Let no saint seek such in his flesh, *for all flesh is like grass and all its glory like the flower of grass. The grass withers, and the flower falls, but the word of the Lord remains forever* (1 Peter 1:24 & 25). While *the name of the LORD is a strong tower; the righteous man runs into it and is safe* (Proverbs 18:10). Our God saves and He is greatly to be praised!

In His high priestly prayer, the Lord Jesus gives us a look behind the scenes of the Holy Trinity before time and space were created: *Father, I desire those You have given Me to be with Me where I am. Then they will see My glory, which You have given Me* **because You loved Me before the world's foundation** (John 17:24 HCSB). One critical difference between the eternal covenant and every other covenant is the beginning of the covenant. The eternal covenant began before time, established between the only beings that were; the great I AM. Every other covenant was established in time between those so ordained by God; each of which has its roots and deepest meaning in its connection with the Eternal Covenant of Promise.

The tale of the "suffering servant" in Isaiah 53 is another look into this redemptive covenant God entered into, reminding us of many things; the relevant point for this discussion being the unity of the Father and the Son as the prophecy of Jesus' suffering and reward were declared seven hundred years before He came in the fullness of time. God's plans will come to fruition; hear Him!

> **To whom will you liken me and make me equal, and compare me, that we may be alike?** ... *Remember the former things of old; for* **I am God, and there is no other; I am God, and there is none like me, declaring the end from the beginning** *and from ancient times things not yet done, saying,* **'My counsel shall stand, and I will accomplish all my purpose,'** *calling a bird of prey from the east, the man of my counsel from a far country.* **I have spoken, and I will bring it to pass; I have purposed, and I will do it.** (Isaiah 46:5, 9-11)

There is none who is like our God! Unconstrained by time and space, the biblical God set the world in order, having predetermined the means, method, and recipients of His great Eternal Covenant. And by this means alone, sinful man is reconciled to Holy God.

This covenant is first (partially) revealed in Genesis 3:15, when man first rebelled against Creator God and the promise of a seed who would crush the head of the serpent was spoken in the presence of man. Redemption and reconciliation are possible! But pain and suffering follow after man as a consequence of his sin. As redemptive history unfolds, we see what might appear as a chess game of sorts, with the serpent seeking to kill the seed of the woman in hopes of defeating the promised Seed and God revealing He is the omniscient One, making use of the second-born son (Genesis 25:19-23), the Gentile harlot (Hebrews 11:31), and Moabite widow (Ruth 4:13-17) to demonstrate His faithfulness and omniscience. Unlike a chess match, this unfolding history was determined beforehand by One no one can withstand; the outcome is not in question.

We also see more clarity of how this covenant will be fulfilled. Man, trusting his efforts more than the promise of YHWH, tries substituting the son of flesh known as Ishmael to "kick-start" his legacy (Genesis 16). But God said, *"No, but Sarah your wife will bear you a son, and you shall call his name Isaac; and **I will establish My covenant with him for an everlasting covenant for his descendants after him"*** (Genesis 17:19). This everlasting covenant is an eternal one, established and fulfilled by God, reconciling elect sinners with holy God. This is testified to by the apostle in Galatians 4:21-31 as he identifies the covenant represented by Sarah as the covenant with the heavenly Jerusalem, which is liberty (John 8:36); sharply contrasted with earthly Jerusalem, which is slavery, condemnation, and death (2 Corinthians 3:7-9). Note how this eternal aspect of our redemption is stated in 1 Peter:

> *For you know that **you were redeemed** from your empty way of life inherited from the fathers, not with perishable things like silver or gold, but **with the precious blood of Christ**, like that of a lamb without defect or blemish. **He was chosen before the foundation of the world** but was **revealed at the end of the times** for you who through Him are believers in God, who raised Him from the dead and gave Him glory, so that your faith and hope are in God.* (1 Peter 1:18-21)

These passages show us how the Eternal Covenant is foundational to the plan of redemption. If the triune God did not establish the purpose, the means, and the timing of redeeming sinners, we would be without hope because God does not answer to us and is not responsible for our fallen condition.

We must take note of this: not all "everlasting" covenants are eternal; they often last only as long as the lesser participant lives. The Noahic Covenant is a prime example of an everlasting covenant that has an end (Genesis 9:16 & 8:22). The everlasting promise of land for the nation of Israel is another example. We will examine both of these in Chapter 10 as we discuss the Old Covenant and how it relates to other covenants between us and our Creator.

We saw how Hebrews 13:20 & 21 reinforce this idea that the Eternal Covenant is directly related to our redemption and sanctification. The blood of Christ is a sign of the New Covenant, at which we will take a more detailed look below. Albert Barnes explains this connection:

> *Through the blood of the everlasting covenant.* The blood shed to ratify the everlasting covenant that God makes with his people (Hebrews 9:14, Hebrews 9:15-23). This phrase, in the original, is not connected, as it is in our translation, with his being raised from the dead; nor should it be so rendered, for what can be the sense of *"raising Christ from the dead by the blood of the covenant?"* In the Greek it is, *"The God of peace, who brought again from the dead the shepherd of the sheep, great by the blood of the everlasting covenant, our Lord Jesus,"* etc. The meaning is, that he was made or constituted the great Shepherd of

the sheep-the great Lord and Ruler of his people, by that blood. That which makes him so eminently distinguished; that by which he was made superior to all others who ever ruled over the people of God, was the fact that he offered the blood by which the eternal covenant was ratified. It is called everlasting or eternal, because

> (1.) it was formed in the councils of eternity, or has been an eternal plan in the Divine Mind; and

> (2.) because it is to continue for ever. Through such a covenant God can bestow permanent and solid "peace" on his people, for it lays the foundation of the assurance of eternal happiness.[2]

Note how our brother helps us see in this passage that the blood of Christ is tied to the Eternal Covenant. In addition to these two key characteristics that set off this covenant as being *the* Eternal Covenant, we see that the Lord Jesus and those He would save were *chosen before the foundation of the world* (1 Peter 1:20; Ephesians 1:4; Revelation 13:8; 17:8), binding His propitiating death to those He was sent to save. This is confirmed by the apostle: *So don't be ashamed of the testimony about our Lord, or of me His prisoner. Instead, share in suffering for the gospel, relying on the power of God. He has saved us and called us with a holy calling, not according to our works, but* **according to His own purpose and grace, which was given to us in Christ Jesus before time began.** *This has now been* **made evident** *through the appearing of our Savior Christ Jesus, who has abolished death and has brought life and immortality to light through the gospel* (2 Timothy 1:8-10 HCSB). Our redemption was given to us before time began, made evident in time, and is provided by the blood of Christ who was also chosen to die for the church (John 10:14 & 15; Ephesians 5:25) before the foundation of the world. The Eternal Covenant is the Covenant of Promise, they are one in the same, speaking of its nature and its purpose; established before time, worked out in time until the end of time.

We have **peace with God** *through our Lord Jesus Christ* (Romans 5:1). The Bible supports the notion of referring to the Eternal Covenant as the Covenant of Peace, because through it we have peace with God. Chapter 34 of Ezekiel makes this clear, where YHWH describes Himself as the Good Shepherd who searches for and rescues His sheep, bringing peace to them while they dwell among wolves. If you recall the sermon from Thabiti Anyabwile, mentioned in the discussion about elders in chapter 3, this scene will be familiar. The first 10 verses of Ezekiel 34 recount the sorry state of the shepherds of national Israel. Beginning in verse 11, Creator God reveals His faithfulness to His people, spiritual Israel, as He describes how He will gather His sheep, tend to their injuries, judge between sheep and goats, and provide justice for them. And then in verse 25 we see the promise of eschatological fulfillment of the peace promised to national Israel (Leviticus 26:6) coming through the promised seed (Isaiah 11:6-9; 35:9; Hosea 2:18) Who brings eternal peace to the children of promise (Galatians 3:15-29). This Covenant of Peace is described in temporal terms familiar to national Israel but is clearly tied to the peace God's children will enjoy in the age to come, as sin and death are put away and Israel will be the people of God and the sheep of His pasture. This view is validated by Hebrews 8, which states that the Mosaic/Levitical religion served primarily as types which pointed to and were fulfilled in the New Covenant and the eternal tabernacle of God, His people. Here's how our Baptist brother Arthur Pink described it:

> Finally, let it be pointed out that this compact made between the Father and the Son on behalf of the whole election of grace is variously designated. It is called an "everlasting covenant" (Isa. 55:3) to denote the perpetuity of it, and because the blessings in it devised in eternity past will endure forever. It is called a "covenant of peace" (Ezek. 34:2, 5; 37:26) because it secures reconciliation with God, for Adam's transgression produced enmity, but by Christ the enmity has been removed (Eph. 2:16), and therefore is He denominated the "Prince of Peace" (Isa. 9:6). It is called the "covenant of life" (Mal. 2:15), in contrast from the covenant of works which issued in death, and because life is the principal thing pledged in it (Titus 1:2). It is called the "holy covenant" (Luke 1:72), not only because it was made by and between the persons of the Holy Trinity, but also because it secures the holiness of the divine character and provides for the holiness of God's people. It is called a "better covenant" (Heb. 7:22), in contrast from the Sinaitic arrangement, wherein the national prosperity of Israel was left contingent on their own works.[3]

There are some who claim the sovereign creator and judge of all things saves people in response to their actions or decisions. If this were true, man would certainly deserve credit for being wise enough to seek his redemption. And God would be less than sovereign. His Holy Writ tells us that none seek after Him (see the Biblical Gospel in chapter 3), but that before He created all things **He chose to save some, not try to save all**. His faithfulness is what makes His covenant, the eternal covenant, binding on our behalf. The eternal covenant: it truly is good news for those who are loved by YHWH and love in Him in response.

Recommended Reading:
Divine Covenants – A. W. Pink*
The Display of Glorious Grace - Benjamin Keach*

Chapter 8: The Covenant Between Man and Woman.

Of the covenants between men, the one that binds two people, *a man and a woman*, into becoming one flesh, is the one of eternal significance. So many people think of marriage as a contract of convenience that it appears in large part even many Christians have lost sight of the glorious meaning inherent in this institution created by God. But is it a covenant? Where does YHWH describe marriage as a covenant? The prophet Malachi is used by God to rebuke His temporal people, specifically the Jewish priests, calling them to remember their standing before God, reminding them of things they had forgotten. They had turned from YHWH's instruction, caused many to stumble because of their negligence (Malachi 2:8 & 9). And then he says:

> *And this second thing you do. You cover the LORD's altar with tears, with weeping and groaning because he no longer regards the offering or accepts it with favor from your hand. But you say, "Why does he not?" Because* **the LORD was witness between you and the wife of your youth, to whom you have been faithless, though she is your companion and your wife by covenant.** *Did he not make them one, with a portion of the Spirit in their union? And what was the one God seeking? Godly offspring.* **So guard yourselves in your spirit, and let none of you be faithless to the wife of your youth.** *"For the man who does not love his wife but divorces her, says the LORD, the God of Israel, covers his garment with violence, says the LORD of hosts. So guard yourselves in your spirit, and do not be faithless."* (Malachi 2:13-16)

As He reveals elsewhere, it is God Who makes one flesh from two people, creating a spiritual union between a man and a woman. This has implications lost on many people who profess faith in Christ, as they are conformed to the pattern of this world and evolve in their thinking, concluding that Holy God approves of what He calls sin. One thing God cannot do is approve of sin; He hates sin and those who are marked by it (Psalms 5:5 & 6; 11:5; 78:59; Proverbs 11:20; Jeremiah 12:8; and Hosea 9:15). And those who encourage sin will be judged harshly (see below).

The system of this world is at war with the creator of this world. Because they cannot see the One Who created this world they conclude He is imaginary. The Bible says people like this have become futile in their understanding (Romans 1:21 & Ephesians 4:18). Redefining or reducing this covenant to something akin to a grocery bag, to be discarded when used, is a key element of Satan's plan to seek and destroy God's people. When Christians put away their spouses, the name of Christ is profaned in the nation. Many years ago I served as a deacon in a small Baptist church. Several years after a job moved us away, I found out from the wife of a friend who served with me as a fellow deacon that he was seeking to divorce her. I called Mark (as I will call him) to see if he would listen to the Word of God. We talked on the phone for nearly two hours, most of which was Mark complaining about how difficult the marriage had been for him and how nobody, including me, knew the depths of his difficulties. I told him how marriage was a picture of Christ and His church and asked Mark if he had bled for his bride. I told him I didn't need to know the depth of his trouble, but the Lord does and He cares for His own. Mark was selfish and had determined to put his wife away; he had no interest in listening to biblical reason. I contacted the man identified as pastor of the church Mark had joined and offered to drive the four hours to meet with him so we could confront Mark in person. This man who called himself a pastor told me there was no need for me to make the journey as he would simply "pray for God's perfect will to be done." Was there a question in that man's mind whether Mark's course of action was God's will? Is marriage something to be thrown aside when one member therein decides he has had enough? How many of you reading this have a spouse like I do, who put on Christ and loved you in spite of yourself and what you had done, refusing to cooperate with Satan? *That* is biblical marriage!

The creature cannot redefine what God created, though he imagines many a vain thing. The Creator of the world is the Creator of marriage; Scripture gives Moses the reason and composition for this relationship that was announced to the creature before the Fall (Genesis 2:24). Jesus confirmed this as YHWH's plan in Matthew 19, adding, *So they are no longer two but one flesh. What therefore God has joined together, let not man separate.* Notice this: **what God has joined together**, marriage is a covenant that God created that He calls each couple into when He joins them together. This is made clear even when man doesn't consider a relationship marriage, as Paul teaches that that *he who is joined to a prostitute becomes one body with her. For, as it is written, "The two will become one flesh"* (1Corinthians 6:16).

This teaches us two things regarding the July 2015 U.S. Supreme Court ruling. Firstly, when two or three men get a marriage license, they are not married. The creator of marriage defined it as between *a* man and *a* woman. Man is by nature a liar and when the man known as Obama celebrated this ruling with a perverse delight and when the judicial oligarchy declared marriage to be a right for anyone and all combinations of people, they are all defying God and heaping up judgment on themselves. Those who claim Christ yet join with the reprobates celebrating this abominable ruling are revealing themselves as enemies of Christ, not brothers and sisters of His redeemed people.

Marriage is the only place given where sex can be enjoyed, as a gift from God: *Marriage is honourable in all, and the bed undefiled: but whoremongers and adulterers God will judge* (Hebrews 13:4, KJV). YHWH declares He will judge adulterers and sexually immoral (the phrase used in other translation where the KJV has *whoremongers*). Man is a fool in thinking he can contrive myriad relationships that will be fun (for a season), for he soon thinks something is not right for he tries to get society to approve of his sin (Proverbs 16:5; Romans 1:18, 32; 1 Peter 4:1-5). Judgment for violating the marriage covenant called for death in the Old Covenant (Genesis 38:24; Leviticus 20:10-16) and calls for excommunicating a church member (1 Corinthians 5:1, 9-11). Paul teaches us *"The body is not meant for sexual immorality, but for the Lord, and the Lord for the body."* (1 Corinthians 6:13) and tells Christians to *"Put to death therefore what is earthly in you: sexual immorality, impurity, passion, evil desire, and covetousness, which is idolatry. On account of these the wrath of God is coming*" (Galatians 5:19-21). He also tells us that it is God's will that Christians *abstain from sexual immorality* (1 Thessalonians 4:3).

The second aspect of marriage that makes it unacceptable for man to redefine is that YHWH uses it as a metaphor to describe the relationship between the church and Jesus (Ephesians 5:31 & 32). This is why the attempted deconstruction of marriage by our political leaders is so seriously evil. Judgment is coming for those who celebrate such wickedness, see Revelation 2:14, 20; 14:8; 19:1 & 2. Read those passages and see how those evil persons will end. Creator God is a jealous God and He will not allow the guilty to go free.

God has given us marriage as the only release for our sexual desires: *But because of the temptation to sexual immorality, each man should have his own wife and each woman her own husband* (1 Corinthians 7:2). There is no provision for a man to have a man or woman to have a woman; those desires are sinful and God will not honor them. And man, as much as he tries to cover it up and talk louder about how sin is not sin, will not escape God's judgment.

In Ephesians 5:25-32, the Apostle Paul compared marriage to Christ's relationship to His bride, the church. Jesus cleanses His bride by washing her with His Word. He nourishes it and cherishes it, working to present her to the Father without stain or blemish. He gave Himself for the church, this referring to His work on the cross. The fullest description of marriage is beyond the Apostle's command of language, reinforcing the notion that it is more about Jesus than a simple voluntary relationship between two humans. Even redeemed people are unable to comprehend any aspect of God (His love, holiness, wisdom, wrath, etc.) in its fullest. We are finite beings; He is infinite. Marriage is primarily a picture of the work of redemption and sanctification the Lord provides for the people purchased by His blood. This ought to impress upon the Christian a higher, Christo-centric view of marriage and of all biblical covenants tied to God's redemptive plan.

Marriage is a holy, God-given covenant that binds a man and woman, making them one; just as in Christ Jesus there is no male or female, no Jew or Greek, no bond or free. Christ has broken down the wall of hostility and made the two (Jew and Gentile) one man (Ephesians 2:13-16). Let us who name Christ hold fast to His word on this topic and tremble when people mock Him and the covenant He created between man and wife and never give into the prince of the air to redefine marriage or reduce it. Either compromise gives our flesh room to blossom and profanes the name of the Savior. It should not be so with us!

Recommended Reading:

Talks on Getting Married – Thomas Treadwell Eaton*
Sex, Romance, and the Glory of God – C.J. Mahaney
Anchor Man – Steve Farrar
The Faithful Parent – Martha Peace & Stuart W. Scott
The Duty of Parents – J.C. Ryle

Chapter 9: The Covenants Between God and Man.

A Baptist View of the Covenants

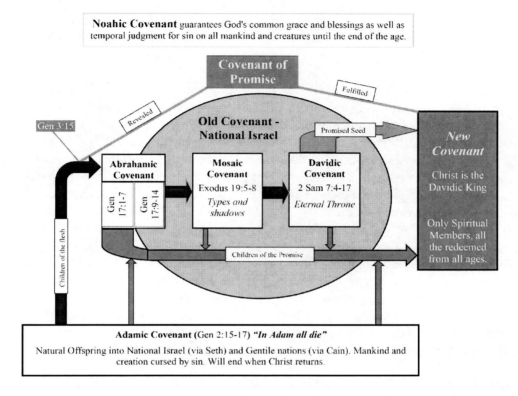

The diagram above is my attempt to show the relationship between the various covenants between God and man discussed below. The covenants with Adam and Noah were with mankind and all the created order. Adam fell and we all are dead in him, our federal head. So too all of creation was cursed because of Adam's sin (Genesis 3:17 & 18).

From the dust of men YHWH called out a people for Himself to be custodians of His Word, to shine forth His glories in the wicked world, and to preserve the promised seed as it was carried through the generations from Adam to Christ Jesus. The Old Covenant represents God's relationship to national Israel, and includes the three major covenants contained therein, although the Abrahamic Covenant is only partially in this arena. This began to close with the Davidic Covenant, coming to a final close when the son of David who was his Lord fulfilled all the requirements of Moses and the prophets and cut the New Covenant (Galatians 3:24). The Old Covenant was worn out and ended.

Some may protest that Jews were not in the Adamic Covenant; they were in the Mosaic Covenant. But if not all men are in Adam's Covenant, then all men could not die in Adam. And since all men die in Adam, we must see those that God formed into the Hebrew nation were born dead in Adam. The covenant of circumcision and the Mosaic covenant applied to them as God's temporal people, but in Adam they all died. Some of them were redeemed by faith in the promised Christ and were brought out of the Adamic covenant into the covenant of redemption, to be sealed in Christ in the fullness of time. While they lived in the flesh, they were in the Mosaic Covenant as God's temporal people. So all national Israel was at all times members of two covenants - one identifying their spiritual condition (in Adam or in Christ), the other identifying them as God's temporal people (under Moses).

The Adamic Covenant runs parallel to the Old Covenant, but does not expire until the end of the age. All people in history are ruled by this covenant, with God's universal law at work in the nations; the works of which are written on the hearts of these people (Romans 2:12-16). Those who are in the First Adam remain in this covenant unless, in time, God redeems them. From God's covenant with Abraham come children of the flesh (being held captive by the Law of Moses – Galatians 4:21-25) and children of promise (being set free by faith in the promised seed – Galatians 3:29 & 4:26-31). This ever-increasing family gathers members from all races, creeds, and covenants. Sons of Adam who are redeemed have Abraham as their spiritual father (Galatians 3:29) with Jesus as *the* promised son of David (Acts 2:22-39), being born under the law and its curse (Galatians 3:10-14), and giving Himself as a ransom to buy the elect (John 6:37-40). His work of redemption fulfilled the demands of the Old Covenant and all the types that pointed to His coming. This work made the Old Covenant obsolete and introduced the New Covenant which displays the glories of Christ in the lives of the redeemed (Hebrews 8).

The covenant with Noah is outside the redemptive chain, as it is an unconditional promise of God to provide for man and beast *seedtime and harvest, cold and heat, summer and winter, day and night* until the end of the age. It is included to remind us of God's kind provision even to those whose best life is now. It mitigates the wrath of God for those in Adam while this age winds down. With Noah as our federal head, we have so-called common grace from our Creator, both man and creation. The curse of Adam remains throughout this age, conquered but not eliminated, as we wait for the age to come; so the blessings through Noah remain throughout this age, to be made all the more glorious in the age to come.

The Covenant of Promise was revealed to man as God cursed the serpent, recorded in Genesis 3:15 and fulfilled in the New Covenant, being revealed with increasing clarity as redemptive history unfolded. The eternal covenant called out in Hebrews 13 was a supralapsarian[1] agreement within the holy trinity. It was revealed progressively until it was fulfilled by Christ and the issuing of the New Covenant. What the eternal covenant does is provide redemption for sinners (Ephesians 1 and others). 2 Timothy 1 shows us that our redemption was effected before the foundation of the world. I consider this covenant to be the guardian for the elect through redemptive history, until the New Covenant was issued, as was the Old Covenant for national Israel. Hebrews tells us the Old Testament saints waited until Christ came to get their full reward, while saved looking forward to the promised seed, *"they did not receive that which was promised, since God had provided something better for us, so that they would not be made perfect without us."*

Of the covenants between God and man, there is a lack of consensus amongst reformed folk as to how many covenants there are or by what names they ought to be called. But most would agree that there are two main covenants that encompass all else; but even the names of these two vary depending on your view of the Covenant of Grace. Baptists and Presbyterians see a Covenant of Grace throughout the redemptive history in Scripture, but in fundamentally different ways. Both see a Covenant of Works given to Adam, but we differ in what is meant by it and where it ends.

The Adamic Covenant – *In Adam all die*

Unlike all who followed him, Adam was able not to sin; he had the ability to meet the demands of his covenant. If the reader disagrees in calling Adam's relationship with God a covenant, preferring to call it a promise, that is fine with me. I submit that a promise from God *is* a covenant, for when YHWH promises something He is bound to His Word to bring it to pass. We will see this explicitly stated in the apostle's commentary on the covenant with Abraham. The Adamic covenant was made between God and Adam, unstained with sin, whence Adam would maintain life based on obedience to God (Genesis 1:28-30; 2:15). I agree with Augustine who understood Ecclesiasticus 14:17 to be referring to the Adamic Covenant. There is nothing in the Scripture to support the notion widely held by some in the paedobaptist world of Covenant Theology that Adam had a "time of probation" that hypothetically held out access to the Tree of Life. This notion implies a "plan B" in God's mind, which Scripture flat-out proscribes (Acts 2:23 for example) yet open theology embraces. Our God is in His heavens and does what He pleases. When he fell, Adam was kept from this tree; that is all that Scripture reveals. Many consider the Tree of Life to be the sign of this covenant (Genesis 2:9), reminding Adam of the promise of life if he obeyed God, reinforced by the role played by the Tree of Life in the age to come (Revelation 2:7; 22:1 & 2). I see this as a remarkable connection by our God between Adam and Jesus, that the Tree of Life in the garden *was* a sign of His covenant with Adam: the first Adam failed to keep his covenant and was forbidden from partaking from the Tree of Life, with his descendants building earthly Jerusalem. The Last Adam fulfilled all that was required by the covenants with Abraham, Moses, and David and He provides the Tree of Life to all who inhabit and make up New Jerusalem.

I believe this covenant is fundamental to a biblical understanding of covenants and is misunderstood by many folks, most of whom fail to account for the ever increasing number of Gentiles who are under its bondage. One of the strongest arguments for mankind's standing in this covenant is found in Romans 5: *Therefore, just as* **sin came into the world through one man**, *and death through sin, and so* **death spread to all men** *because all sinned … Yet death reigned from Adam to Moses … many died through one man's trespass … the judgment following one trespass brought condemnation …***because of one man's trespass, death reigned through that** *one man ... one trespass led to condemnation for all men ... **by the one man's disobedience the many were made sinners...*** (Romans 5:12-19). The Apostle summed this up for the fine folks in Corinth: ***For as by a man came death ... in Adam all die*** ... (1 Corinthians 15:21-22). The governance given Adam by God was simple, the consequences for his disobedience were astounding. Our identity with Adam is that he died, spiritually at first, physically later. When we are born physically we are spiritually dead, in need of a savior, and in the grip of death. Unless one is born again in Christ, he is still in Adam; Adam's covenant did not end when he sinned, the punishment phase began. The consequences of disobedience cannot continue if the covenant is not in force.

There are some evangelicals who deny the concept of covenant theology, properly objecting the paedobaptist system, arguing that there is no mention of a covenant with Adam. With regards to this, we must consider what all of Scripture does say and what it means. We see the construct of a covenant with Adam in Genesis 2:15-17, even if the text does not reveal a full blown covenant nor contain the word covenant. *The LORD God took the man and put him in the garden of Eden to work it and keep it. And the LORD **God commanded the man**, saying, "You may surely eat of every tree of the garden, but of the tree of the knowledge of good and evil you shall not eat, **for in the day that you eat of it you shall surely die.**"* (Genesis 2:15-17)

The command of the superior with penalties for non-compliance of the inferior are classic covenant elements in the ancient near-east culture of Moses. "Do this and live, do that and die." So it was spoken to Adam in the garden and to the Hebrew nation; both covenants required "work" to fulfill the obligations therein. The covenants under the realm of the Old Covenant added legal burdens and revealed more about the One Who would fulfill them all. More than once, covenants between God and man are promised years before they are fully documented or completed; we see this clearly with the Covenant of Redemption, established before time, promise made in Genesis 3:15, but not fully revealed or fulfilled for generations thereafter. When Adam sinned, not only was mankind sentenced to death, creation was cursed (Genesis 3:17-19). George Whitefield declared that every time a dog barks at man, every time a bear growls at man, it's as if they are saying, "You have sinned against God, and we take up our Master's quarrel."[2]

In discussing the question of a covenant with Adam, Peter Gentry and Stephen Wellum offer this evidence from Scripture about the covenant with Noah and how it reveals the covenant with Adam:

> Therefore the construction *hēqîm běrît* in Genesis 6 and 9 indicates that God is not initiating a covenant with Noah but rather is upholding for Noah and his descendants a commitment initiated previously. This language clearly indicates a covenant established earlier between God and creation or God and humans at creation. When God says that he is confirming or upholding his covenant with Noah, he is saying that his commitment to his creation, the

care of the creator to preserve, provide for, and rule over all that he has made, including the blessings and ordinances that he initiated through and with Adam and Eve and their family, are now to be with Noah and his descendants.[3]

This helps us understand why we can confidently believe God had a covenant with Adam and His covenant with Noah is tightly linked to it. We will see more of this when we review the covenant with Noah, the second Adam.

To determine if this covenant can rightly be called a covenant of works, we need some historical context. The concept known today as the Covenant of Works began to be developed in the late 16th century, preceded in theological discussions by the expression *foedus naturae*. This is a covenant of nature, most likely referring to God's covenant made with Adam in the Garden, as God instructed Adam to mind the garden. This is more completely described in Pascal Denault's *The Distinctiveness of Baptist Covenant Theology*. Advocates of this construct have acknowledged that this phrase is not found in Scripture and we must be careful not to follow those who allow their view of covenants to determine their interpretation of Scripture. Since only a few of Adam's descendants found themselves in national Israel, regarding the Adamic Covenant as THE covenant of works simply won't stand up to scrutiny. To national Israel were given several covenants of work under the umbrella of the Old Covenant that were all swept away when Christ Jesus fulfilled their demands. Yet Adam was commanded by God to "do this and live" (*You may surely eat of every tree in the garden*, Genesis 2:16) and "do that and die" (*but of the tree of the knowledge of good and evil you shall not eat, for in the day that you eat of it you shall surely die*. Genesis 2:17). Though very narrow in scope, this relationship required obedience by Adam for him to remain in fellowship with Creator God. And by his disobedience, death came to every man (Romans 5:12-19; 1 Corinthians 15:21 & 22), Jew and Gentile without distinction.

Much of the support for the Baptist view of this early covenant is found in the parallels between Adam and Christ, as aptly demonstrated by A.W. Pink:

1. Adam, the one with whom the covenant was made, entered this world in a manner that none other ever did. Without being begotten by a human father; so with [the incarnate] Christ [by the virgin birth].
2. None but Adam of the human family entered this world with a pure constitution and holy nature; so was it with Christ.
3. His [Adam's] wife was taken out of him, so that he could say, "*This is now bone of my bones, and flesh of my flesh*" (Gen. 2:23); of Christ's bride it is declared, "*We are members of His body, of His flesh, and of His bones*" (Eph. 5:30).
4. Adam voluntarily took his place alongside of his fallen wife. He was not deceived (I Tim. 2:14), but had such a love for Eve that he could not see her perish alone; just so Christ voluntarily took on Himself the sins of His people (cf. Eph. 5:25).

5. In consequence of this, Adam fell beneath the curse of God; in like manner Christ bore the curse of God (cf. Gal. 3:13).

6. The father of the human family was their federal [covenant] head; so is Christ, the "*last Adam*," the federal [covenant] head of His people.

7. What Adam did is imputed to the account of all those whom he represented; the same is true of Christ. "*For as by one man's disobedience many were made sinners, so by the obedience of one shall many be made righteous*" (Rom. 5:19).[4]

(Words within [square brackets] were added for clarification.)

There are several parallels between Adam and Christ that are not found in any other man that stands as an Adam. As the first, Adam is unique and all men are in him when conceived in the womb. The other men who stand as Adam represent certain aspects of man and his relationship with God.

Each man who stood as "Adam" was in covenant with God, including Jesus as the last Adam (this is discussed in some detail, below). As noted above, in Romans 5:12-14 Adam is identified in Scripture as a type of Christ. This is one the clearest examples of how the imperfect is used to point to the perfect; a device we see throughout Scripture if we are using the right lens through which to view Scripture.

John Owen, a paedobaptist who shared much in common theologically with Baptists, agreed with Pink on this point in his commentary on Hebrews 8:6 (emphasis mine):

> There was an original covenant made with Adam, and ***all mankind in him***. The rule of obedience and reward that was between God and him, was not expressly called a covenant, but it contained the express nature of a covenant. For it was the agreement of God and man concerning obedience and disobedience, rewards and punishments. Where there is a law concerning these things, and an agreement upon it, by all parties concerned, there is a formal covenant. Wherefore it may be considered two ways.
>
> 1st. As it was a law only; so it proceeded from, and was a consequent of, the nature of God and man, with their mutual relation unto one another. God being considered as the Creator, Governor, and Benefactor of man: and man as an intellectual creature, capable of moral obedience; this law was necessary, and is eternally indispensable.
>
> 2dly. As it was a covenant; and this depended on the will and pleasure of God. I will not dispute whether God might have given a law unto men, that should have had nothing in it of a covenant

properly so called as is the law of creation unto all other creatures, which hath no rewards nor punishments annexed unto it. Yet this God calls a covenant also, inasmuch as it is an effect of his purpose, his unalterable will and pleasure, Jer. 33:20, 21.[5]

Benjamin Keach addressed the question of whether Adam was party to a covenant with God:

> Proposition: That the Breach betwixt God and Man, was occasioned by the violation of the First Covenant which God entered into with Adam, as the Common or Public Head and Representative of all Mankind; which Covenant was a Covenant of Works; I say, God gave a Law, or entered into a Covenant of Works with the First Adam and his Seed, and in that Covenant he gave himself to be our God, even upon the strict and severe condition of perfect Obedience, personally to be performed by Man himself, with that Divine Threatening of Death and Wrath if he broke the Covenant, In the Day thou eats thereof thou shalt surely die. Yet some may doubt (as one observes) whether this was a Covenant of Works, because here is only a threatening of Death upon his Disobedience to this one positive Law.[6]

In the style of 17th century apologetics (often called diatribes), Keach stated the propositions and provided the answers. This is his answer to the above proposition:

> Man in his First Creation was under a Natural Obligation to universal compliance to the Will of God, and such was the Rectitude of his Nature, it imports an exact Conformity to the Divine Will, there being an inscription of the Divine Law upon Adam's heart, which partly still remains, or is written in the hearts of the very Gentiles (though much blur'd) which is that light which is in all, or that which we call The light of Nature.[7]

The covenant made with Adam was a covenant of works which did not comprehend sin and the need for redemption; it was a nascent form of the covenant of works, giving way to more full expressions with Abraham, Moses, and David. We know Adam was in a covenant with God, because the Lord's Word so declares: *But like Adam they transgressed the covenant; there they dealt faithlessly with me* (Hosea 6:7). While the Hebrew word for Adam is sometimes interpreted "man," meaning the human race, such an understanding does make sense in this context. The human race did not transgress a covenant; Adam did. The prophet is recounting how Israel and Judah rebelled against YHWH and broke the covenant (the Mosaic Covenant) God made with them just like Adam broke the covenant God made with him. Jeremiah 33:19-22 and Isaiah 24:5 & 6 confirm that the Judge of all flesh considered His relationship with the first Adam to be a covenant relationship. "The covenant" mentioned by these three prophets is a covenant of works given to Adam before the Fall and continuing until the end of the age ("everlasting" as Isaiah put it) and being renewed in subsequent covenants given to national Israel as reminders of God's wrath for sin and His standard that no sinner be admitted into His presence. As Adam fell, his covenant became the first revelation of the binding yoke of perfection in word, thought, and deed which no mortal man can bear. With differing promises, signs, and fulfillments the Abrahamic, Mosaic, and Davidic covenants demanded the same level of perfect obedience. We will also see that the Abrahamic Covenant had unconditional promises, making it unique in this line of redemptive covenants between Creator and creature.

We must take note of something unique about the Adamic Covenant. It is a stand-alone covenant in one very important aspect. While this covenant could not deliver eternal life, neither does it exclusively lead to the Abrahamic covenant. Once Able was murdered, Adam was left with two lines: Cain and Seth, representing the people of the world and the people of God, respectively. Some of Adam's offspring became Hebrews, through Noah, Shem, and Abram; coming under the Old Covenant. From others of Adam's children came the world of Gentiles, among them are some of the elect, including Melchizedek, about whom we learned a bit in chapter 2 and who prefigured the Lord Jesus as did no one else. Some of Adam's progeny constitute the mass of humanity that is bound for the wide gate that leads to the broad road that ends in destruction; apart from the Covenant of Works and condemned by the works of the law written on their hearts (Romans 2:12-16). Here is its unique characteristic: men are trapped in it and will be until the Lord returns to judge the nations. Only those called by God into His rest will be counted as children of Abraham according to the promise. This covenant, disputed by many, is the one most relevant to the vast majority of people, holding them captive and unable to deliver them to eternal life just as those fleshly children of Abraham who are rolled up in the Old Covenant.

Many theologians refer to the Lord Jesus as the "second Adam," as both of them stood as federal heads for mankind in different times. However, Scripture does not refer to Jesus as the "second Adam;" it calls Him the "last Adam" – *Thus it is written, "The first man Adam became a living being"; **the last Adam** became a life-giving spirit* (1 Corinthians 15:45). What is the significance of this? If we bear in mind the meta-story of God's Word and look for the progressive unfolding of redemptive history in the Scriptures, we will see various men who stand in as types pointing to the promised Christ. This is merely one way YHWH helps us see Him more clearly, with Adam as the first one. With Scripture calling Jesus the last Adam, who, if anyone, does Scripture reveal as an "Adam;" one who stands as the federal head for all mankind or all the elect? I will show from God's Word that we have Adam, Noah, Abraham, Isaac, Jacob (together as Israel), Moses, and David; then Christ. Others are types of Christ (Joseph, Daniel, et.al) but not all are "Adam."

Noah as Adam
From the loins of Adam many sons were born, but not until Noah do we find the culmination of all that had gone before and one man standing as God's

representative for all creation, as the world would be consumed by a great flood and only those humans and animals that God led into the ark Noah built would be saved; God's remnant for a new beginning (Genesis 6:5-7:24). As the flood waters abated, YHWH gives Noah the same creation mandate (*be fruitful and multiply on the earth*, Genesis 8:17) He had given Adam (*Be fruitful and multiply and fill the earth and subdue it*, Genesis 1:28). Adam's mandate to *subdue* the earth was given to Noah in a slightly different way: *The fear of you and the dread of you shall be upon every beast of the earth and upon every bird of the heavens, upon everything that creeps on the ground and all the fish of the sea. Into your hand they are delivered* (Genesis 9:2 & 3). As the chosen head of the new earth Noah stood as did his father, Adam, as the first man in a new world. And, as with Adam, it went downhill almost immediately (Genesis 9:20-28); both of these Adams showing us mortals cannot stand (Psalm 76:7, Revelation 6:12-17).

Noah's family grew and *spread abroad on the earth after the flood* (Genesis 10:32); and *the whole earth had one language and the same words.* Noah's grandchildren and their kids built the Tower of Babel in the city built by Nimrod (Genesis 10:8-10), wanting to make a name for themselves (Genesis 11:4). Our God is a jealous God and will not share His glory with another (Isaiah 42:8 & 48:11), so He destroyed the earth again, but in a different fashion than before. The people with a common language and culture were *dispersed from there over the face of all the earth* and YHWH confused their language (Genesis 11:9).

Abraham as Adam
There were nine generations between Adam and Noah; ten generations stood between Noah and the next Adam – Abram. Out of this sea of humanity, the world lost in re-learning how to communicate and rediscover their place, one genealogy is highlighted and traced down to a solitary man God would call to stand as the father of many nations; and the father of all the redeemed. The first Adam had two sons, representing two categories of people; this Adam had two sons, representing those same two categories, with more clarity as to the extent of alienation from God Ishmael represents and the extent of peace with God Isaac represents. As the destruction of the world preceding Abram's fall was not absolute, his federal headship is not absolute. As a temporal father of nations (Genesis 17:1 & 2), Abraham (as he was later named) is claimed by Jews and Muslims; pointing to Isaac and Ishmael, respectively. He does not stand as the father of all nations in the flesh. YHWH claims Abraham as the father of promise (Romans 4:9-12; Galatians 3:29) for Jew, Muslim, Gentile; *all* who are called to be reconciled to Him through faith in Christ Jesus (Romans 10:12-15). As the chosen head of a new kingdom, Abraham stood, as did his father Noah, as the first man in this new world. And, as with Noah, this mortal was unable to stand; and though he served YHWH faithfully, death claimed him (Genesis 25:7 & 8). As Adam was created from the dust of the earth, so Abram was called by God from the dust of post-flood humanity. One man, chosen by God to serve as the federal head of the human race. And to dust he returned.

Before we take a brief look at Isaac and Jacob as Adams, let us see from Scripture how tightly these two men are tied to Abraham; the three of them known as the Patriarchs of the Jewish and Christian faiths. Note how Peter ties them all together in his sermon to Jews; and ties them to Christ. *Men of Israel, why are you amazed at this? Or why do you stare at us, as though we had made him walk by our own power or godliness?* **The God of Abraham, Isaac, and Jacob, the God of our fathers, has glorified His Servant Jesus.** Acts 3:12 & 13 (HSCB) This identification is also found in Exodus 3:6 & 15; 4:5; Deuteronomy 9:27; 2 Kings 13:23; Matthew 22:32; and others. The Hebrews saw these patriarchs (and the 12 sons of Jacob) as the foundation of their faith; not ours. But even their Scriptures tell them the truth about Jesus as do the New Testament. The Word of God (Isaiah 28:16; Ephesians 2:20; 1 Peter 2:6) tells us the God-man Jesus is the chief cornerstone of the foundation of true faith in YHWH for people of all nations, tribes, and tongues!

A quick survey of the key promises to each of these three patriarchs will show why they are tied together with more than a human bloodline. While only of one of them was named Israel, they are each and all together the foundation stones of that nation, which had Moses as its prophet.

Promises Made

Abraham	Isaac	Jacob
Nations would be blessed – Gen 12:1-3	Nations would be blessed – Gen 26:3-5	Nations would be blessed – Gen 28:14
Father of many nations – Gen 17:1-7		
Descendants would be as the stars in the sky – Gen 15:5	Descendants would be as the stars in the sky – Gen 26:3-5	Descendants would be as the dust of the earth – Gen 28:14
The promise was to his seed – Gen 12:7; Gal 3:16	Isaac's seed would be blessed – Gen 26:24	Jacob's seed would be blessed – Gen 28:14

Although there are some differences, and a critical promise is made to Abraham that is not given to Isaac or Jacob, we do see commonality in the essentials among these three patriarchs of the Jewish and Christian faiths. Each of them were heirs to the same promise (Hebrews 11:9), each of them knew what God had promised was better than the picture of the promise seen in Canaan (vs 16). Their descendants were numerous, as promised (vs 12) as YHWH counted the *heirs according to promise* (Galatians 3:29). Fulfillment is found in Christ, not in the flesh. Through each of them the promised seed would pass. As with each of the fathers of Israel, when we look at Israel as a people, we see them as another Adam, as the chart below reveals.

Comparing Adam and Israel

ADAM	ISRAEL
Formed by God from the dust of the earth. (Gen 2:7; 1 Cor 15:47)	Formed by God from the dust of the people of the world. (Gen 11:10 – 11:3; Deut 7:7)
Was brought to life by the word and breath of God. (Gen 1:26 & 27; 2:7)	Was brought into being by the word of God. (Gen 12:2 & 3; 15:1; Ex 3)
Had close fellowship with God. (Gen 2:15ff; 3:8a)	Had close fellowship with God. (Gen 15; Ex 15; 2 Kings 23:1 – 27)
Was given a covenant within which to live and prosper. (Gen 2:16 & 17; Hosea 6:7)	Was given a covenant within which to live and prosper. (Gen 17:14; Ex 19:3 – 6; 24:3 – 8; Neh 9 & 10)
Broke the covenant and received the penalty of death, which was carried out in due time. (Gen 3:6 & 7; 22 – 24; 5:5)	Broke the covenant and received the penalty of death, which was carried out in the fullness of time. (Deut 31:16 – 18; Judges 2:11 – 15; Jer 11:10 – 13; 1 Kings 11:9 – 11; Ezek 44:1 – 7; Hosea 6:7)
Was cast out of the garden, cursed to walk and work in the world which was wrecked by The Fall. (Gen 3:23 & 24; 3:17 – 19)	Was divorced by God, left desolate, cursed to walk and work in darkness until the light of Christ. (Jer 3:6 – 10; Matt 15:12 – 14; 23:37 & 38; 2 Cor 3:12 – 17; Gal 4:4)
As a type of Christ, Adam points us to the antitype, Christ Jesus, in whom there is life for Adam's children who are secure in the Last Adam. (1 Cor 15:45)	As an echo of Adam, Israel points us to the antitype, Christ Jesus, in whom there is life for Abraham's children of promise. (Gal 4:21 – 31)

There is support for Israel serving as a type of Christ as well, as the last line in the chart points out. YHWH calls Israel His first-born son (Exodus 4:22) and He refers to Jesus as His first-born son (Colossian 1:15). In the most direct fashion, Jesus and His spiritual people are called *the Israel of God* (Galatians 6:16), showing the deepest meaning God had in mind when calling together the nation of Israel. Just as its religious rituals were types and shadows of the heavenly realities (Hebrews 8:4 & 5), Israel as a nation stood as a type or shadow of the heavenly reality of the eternal people of God. Rather than a tall man of the world as her king (1 Samuel 8), the Israel of God has God Himself as her king, redeemer, judge, advocate, defender, and shepherd. In Jesus, all the promises of God find their yes and amen (2 Corinthians 1:20), which means that every judge, prophet, priest, and king that national Israel had are fulfilled perfectly by Christ Jesus. National Israel and her leaders were all disobedient to various degrees; just as every person or practice that serves as a type is. The antitype, the reality to which all the less-than perfect types pointed to, is perfect. And when the antitype comes, the types pass away, unneeded. We can easily agree that Jesus is perfect, but do we see His bride, the church, that way? Not in this age, while we are still plagued by sin and temptation and while tares grow up alongside the wheat. But He is sanctifying us and has cleansed us from our sin so that at the wedding feast we will be in white robes, clothed in His righteousness. Perfect as He is and always has been.

With the redeemed being true Israel, national Israel serves primarily as a picture of the spiritual people of God. Serving as such and protecting the chain of humanity leading to the promised seed were the crucial reasons for national Israel to exist. This concept of representation, revealed in Romans 5, is where something or someone historical (as opposed to a mere concept or mythical person or thing) depicting, imperfectly, the spiritual reality that is the meta-story of Scripture. As YHWH called His people out of Egypt to occupy the Promised Land (Deuteronomy 26:1-10) and find rest in a land that was prepared for them, so He called His Son out of Egypt (Matthew 2:13-15) to be the Promised Land for His people (Hebrews 4:1-11), providing spiritual rest (Matthew 11:28-30).

Another way in which we can see YHWH's use of types which point us to Christ is how the people of God are described by God in Scripture. Part of the promises made to the patriarchs is almighty God's promise to protect and defend His people and take retribution out on those who attack them. This becomes all the more sweet to those of us who have been adopted into His family and are called His temple and His body. Let us see how this protection of God is portrayed for Israel – the Israel of God.

Abram. Genesis 12:2 & 3: *I will make of you a great nation, and I will bless you and make your name great, so that you will be a blessing. I will bless those who bless you, and him who dishonors you I will curse, and in you all the families of the earth shall be blessed.*

Jacob. Genesis 27:29: *Let peoples serve you, and nations bow down to you. Be lord over your brothers, and may your mother's sons bow down to you. Cursed be everyone who curses you, and blessed be everyone who blesses you!*

Israel. Numbers 24:8 & 9: *God brings him out of Egypt and is for him like the horns of the wild ox; he shall eat up the nations, his adversaries, and shall break their bones in pieces and pierce them through with his arrows. He crouched, he lay down like a lion and like a lioness; who will rouse him up? Blessed are those who bless you, and cursed are those who curse you.*

True Israel. 1 Corinthians 3:16-17: *Do you not know that you are God's temple and that God's Spirit dwells in you? If anyone destroys God's temple, God will destroy him. For God's temple is holy, and you are that temple.*

The patriarchs are the foundation of physical Israel. Jesus and His prophets and apostles are the foundation of true Israel with Him and His people being the temple thereof. As with the shadows and types of the heavenly things given us in the Levitical religion (Hebrews 8), so physical Israel serves as a shadow and type of the heavenly reality of God's people. As noted previously, when the fullness of the antitype is here, the types and shadows pass away (Hebrews 8:13). In Christ, there is no Jew or Greek, slave or free, male or female; all people are one in Christ (Galatians 3:28). This is the fullness of true Israel.

After the patriarchs of the faith, we come to Moses. Four hundred years after Jacob found rest in Egypt (Genesis 47), God raised up Moses to lead His people out of Egypt, providing a temporal picture of the spiritual rest to which Christ calls us (Hebrews 3 & 4). Moses also stands in two-fold role, as an Adam and as a type of Christ.

Moses as Adam

God created Adam from the dust of the earth; He called Moses from the dust of Midian (Exodus 3:1-6), much as Abram had been called. YHWH tells Moses to go back to Egypt, to *"Say this to the people of Israel, 'The LORD, the God of your fathers, the God of Abraham, the God of Isaac, and the God of Jacob, has sent me to you.'"* (Exodus 3:15) At this early phase in the Hebrew nation, their identity is already set as being those people identified with the God who claims Abraham, Isaac, and Jacob; their fathers in the flesh. Over the next 8 chapters of Genesis, Moses' role as the federal head of national Israel is solidified, as he confronts the most powerful man on the planet. Unlike Adam's experience with the serpent, Moses relied upon God and struggled to obey Him, and was used to bring his people out of slavery (chapter 14); an inverse reflection of Adam who led *his* people *into* slavery when he sinned. There was a time when Moses used a serpent to save his people (Numbers 21:8); reflecting Adam (Genesis 3:1) and prefiguring Christ (John 3:14).

Yet Moses, like Adam, was felled by sin. It was a simple thing: speak to the rock and trust YHWH to bring water from it (Numbers 20:8). The man Moses, so much like Adam and so much like you and me; could not quite discipline himself to do what God had told him. He was angry with the people God entrusted to him and to express that anger, he struck the rock twice with his staff (20:9-11). And the One who called him to this position told him he would not fulfill his role; he would not accompany his people into the Promised Land (20:12) for giving this vent to his anger and, in doing so, disobeying YHWH. There are some who think Creator God was too harsh on Adam, and all of us, because of his eating fruit from the forbidden tree. They likely think God was too harsh on Moses in telling him he would die and not enter the Promised Land for hitting a rock. But we creatures tend to look at sin too lightly, failing to rightly comprehend how hateful it is to holy God. The Bible is replete with people being punished harshly for "light sins" (Leviticus 10:1 & 2; 2 Samuel 6:6 & 7 for example). YHWH uses the promise of rest in Canaan and shows how a "light sin" keeps the priest and prophet of Israel from entering that rest. By striking the rock, Moses did not treat God as holy in the midst of the people of Israel. For that, he would not enter that rest (Deuteronomy 32:48-52). There is another rest spoken of elsewhere, the antitype of the rest found in Canaan. And we have faith that Moses has entered *that* rest.

This common man served not only an Adam and as the federal head of national Israel; Moses also served as a type of Christ. During the time in which Moses was born, the King of Egypt had ordered all the Jewish boys to be killed at birth (Exodus 1:15 & 16). This he did because he feared the growth and influence of the Hebrew people (verses 8-10). But the midwives refused to obey, provoking Pharaoh (verses 18 & 19) to order all the male Hebrew babies be thrown into the Nile River and drowned (verse 22). Note: God protected and rewarded the midwives for their stand against evil (verses 17, 20, & 21). When Moses was born, his mother put him into a basket, floated into the river (Exodus 2:1-3). YHWH's providential care provided Pharaoh's daughter who took him to raise as her own son (verses 5-10).

Moses was sent into the inner Egyptian court to save him from the King of Egypt. He was tried, persecuted by his own people (Exodus 2:11-14), and called personally by God to rescue the Jews from Egypt. Out of Egypt he led the people, towards the Promised Land where they would have rest.

During the time in which Jesus was born, the King of Israel had ordered all the Jewish boys in and around Bethlehem, 2 years and younger, to be killed (Matthew 2:16). This because he feared the Hebrew people and was troubled at the news of a king (verses 1-4). But the magi refused to obey King Herod, not telling him where to find the promised child. And YHWH spoke to Joseph through an angel, telling him to flee to Egypt to avoid Herod's wrath (verses 13 & 14).

Jesus was sent into Egypt to save him from rulers of Israel. He came out of Egypt, to be tried and persecuted by His own people (John 19:12-16), having been sent by the Father to rescue His people from their sins. Out of Egypt He came, to lead God's chosen people into eternal rest.

Hebrews 3:1-6 records Moses as having been appointed by God to be over His household (national Israel), calling him a faithful servant as a testimony of what was to be spoken of later (Jesus). This same passage calls Jesus the apostle and high priest of our confession of faith and faithful to the One who appointed Him. And while Moses was a faithful servant, Jesus is spoken of here as being faithful over God's house as a son. And while Moses built a tabernacle for God to meet with His people, Jesus is building the spiritual house where God will dwell with His people; both made to YHWH's specifications.

Moses served as an Adam, representing man and failing to do so perfectly. Moses also served as a type of Christ, giving us an imperfect picture of the One Who was promised to Eve and Abraham.

David as Adam

The last mortal man that I believe stands as an Adam is King David. As with earlier Adams, David was called by God out of the dust of Israel, both the country and the people, to serve as the federal head of national Israel (1 Samuel 16:1-13; 2 Samuel 7). When the giant taunted Israel (1 Samuel 17:1-11), David ran to the challenge, relying on God for his success (17:36 & 37). Adam stood and watched his wife get deceived by the serpent; he took and ate from the forbidden tree with her (Genesis 3:6 & 7). Yet as Eve fell prey to the lust of her eyes and her husband followed suit (Genesis 3:6), failing to protect her, so it was with David. It was in the spring of the year, when kings went out to battle, David stayed home, allowed boredom and lust to take hold of his mind. He failed to discipline himself, to guard against weakness. And while looking around (the eye never tires of seeing - Ecclesiastes 1:8), David saw that Bathsheba looked good (2 Samuel 11:1-4), just as the fruit did in the garden so many years earlier. So while David had victory by his faith in God, he also had failure by his inability to stay focused on God. And so the greatest king in Israel's history was slain by sin. In Adam all die.

With each of these men who stood as an Adam, there was a covenant issued by God that defined their role as such. All but the covenant with Noah demanded perfect obedience and several were part and parcel of the Old Covenant, requiring perfect compliance with the terms of the covenant in order to merit the favor of God. As David stood as the penultimate Adam, his covenant is perhaps studied more than the ones preceding it, with widely variant perspectives. We will discover more about this when we review that covenant.

Jesus – the last Adam

In the fullness of time, the last Adam arose as God Himself, in the form of a man, to fulfill the demands of the Old Covenant and earn the right to issue the New Covenant, bringing the promise revealed in the garden after the Fall to completion. The New Covenant is, in essence, ancient, being conceived before time and revealed beginning with the first Adam. Yet it is most certainly the last covenant, as there will be no need for the guardianship covenants provide once He returns to make all things new and dwell among His people. Again we will turn to a long-dead Baptist brother who has made an important, relevant point (as most do, Bunyan refers to the Adamic Covenant as "the Covenant of Works"):

> Again; if at any time you do find in Scripture that the
> Covenant of Works is spoken of as the first covenant that

was manifested, and so before the ~~second~~ *last* covenant, yet you must understand that it was so only as to manifestation–that is, it was first given to man, yet not made before that which was made with Christ; and indeed it was requisite that it should be given or made known first, that thereby there might be a way made for the ~~second~~ *last*, by its discovering of sin, and the sad state that man was in after the Fall by reason of that. And again, that the other might be made the more welcome to the sons of men. Yet the ~~second~~ *last* Adam was before the first, and also the ~~second~~ *last* covenant before the first. This is a riddle].

And in this did Christ in time most gloriously answer Adam, who was the figure of Christ, as well as of other things. Romans 5. For, Was the first covenant made with the first Adam? so was the ~~second~~ *last* covenant made with the ~~second~~ *last*; for these are and were the two great public persons, or representators of the whole world, as to the first and ~~second~~ *last* covenants; and therefore you find God speaking on this wise in Scripture concerning the new covenant–"My covenant shall stand fast with HIM." "My mercy will I keep for HIM for evermore," saith God: "My covenant shall stand fast with HIM" (Psa 89:28,34,35); this HIM is Christ, if you compare this with Luke 1:32, "My covenant will I not break"–namely, that which was made with HIM–"nor alter the thing that is gone out of My mouth. Once I have sworn by My holiness that I will not lie unto David," [David here is to be understood Christ.] to whom this was spoken figuratively in the Person of Christ; for that was God's usual way to speak of the glorious things of the Gospel in the time of the Law, as I said before.[8] (changes made to the second covenant and second Adam by this author)

By His life of perfect obedience to all that was given to Moses and the prophets, by fulfilling the demands of the Adamic, Abrahamic, Mosaic, and Davidic covenants Jesus earned the right to offer Himself as the Lamb of God, without spot or blemish, so He could redeem those His Father chose. This is the glory of our Savior: He surrendered His rights to become a man, to redeem Himself from the law by being found innocent, to gain victory over death as one having no sin, and to ransom sinners for the glory of the Father Who would bestow upon the Son more glory than He had before His humiliation. YHWH cares about His glory more than we can truly understand. This characteristic of God is often overlooked by His people, leading us to have too low a view of YHWH and too high a view of man. God's desire for His creation to glorify Him is as high a calling as the love He has set upon His elect. The former makes the latter possible.

The biblical God is a jealous God (Exodus 20:5) and will not sit by and allow agents of Satan to destroy His people. And since Jesus is the last Adam, we should gain great comfort from seeing how our Savior and Lord identifies with those in need, providing what we need most. We see in this next covenant the kindness of YHWH to provide temporal goodness to all mankind and even the animals of the earth; a type of the Covenant of Redemption by which sinners are reconciled to Holy God without accepting sin. Seeing Adam rightly, as the Word portrays Him, should encourage us to have less confidence in ourselves and all confidence in the last Adam.

The Noahic Covenant – *A new beginning*.

This covenant was between God and Noah, who stood as a federal head of all men and all the creatures of the earth. It is a covenant between Creator God and His creation. This covenant was the promise by God to never destroy the earth again by flood and provide food and seasons for all the beasts of the earth until the end of the age (Genesis 8:20-22; 9:8-17). The sign of the covenant is the rainbow (Genesis 9:13). As we learned in our review of the Adamic Covenant, this covenant is most likely a confirmation by God of that covenant with this man who is the second Adam. These two men are tightly connected as being God's chosen representatives of the entire human race; it makes sense that this covenant confirms the Adamic, and brings new temporal blessings and consequences for all men until Christ returns.

> *Then Noah built an altar to the LORD and took some of every clean animal and some of every clean bird and offered burnt offerings on the altar. And when the LORD smelled the pleasing aroma, the LORD said in his heart, "I will never again curse the ground because of man, for the intention of man's heart is evil from his youth.* **Neither will I ever again strike down every living creature as I have done. While the earth remains, seedtime and harvest, cold and heat, summer and winter, day and night, shall not cease."** *… Then God said to Noah and to his sons with him,* **"Behold, I establish my covenant with you and your offspring after you, and with every living creature that is with you, the birds, the livestock, and every beast of the earth with you, as many as came out of the ark; it is for every beast of the earth. I establish my covenant with you, that never again shall all flesh be cut off by the waters of the flood, and never again shall there be a flood to destroy the earth."** *And God said, "This is the sign of the covenant that I make between me and you and every living creature that is with you, for all future generations: I have set my bow in the cloud, and it shall be a sign of the covenant between me and the earth.* **When I bring clouds over the earth and the bow is seen in the clouds, I will remember my covenant that is between me and you and every living creature of all flesh.** *And the waters shall never again become a flood to destroy all flesh. When the bow is in the clouds, I will see it and remember the everlasting covenant between God and*

every living creature of all flesh that is on the earth." God said to Noah, **"This is the sign of the covenant that I have established between me and all flesh that is on the earth."** (Genesis 8:20-22 & 9:8-17)

Since my wife and I moved to south-east Oklahoma from Houston, Texas, having real seasons (rather than summer with a dash of cool weather) has reminded me of the personal providential aspect of YHWH's covenant with Noah and all of us. *While the earth remains, seedtime and harvest, cold and heat, summer and winter, day and night, shall not cease.* That's a personal, gracious, kind God; even for those who hate Him (as we all did until He rescued us). Do not lose sight of this promise: the Creator of all things (Colossians 1:15 & 16) Who holds all things together (Colossians 1:17) declares that until Christ returns (as long as the earth remains, 2 Peter 3:8-13) *seedtime and harvest, cold and heat, summer and winter, day and night* will be sustained by the will of almighty, sovereign YHWH! That is unearned kindness from One Who owes nothing to anyone.

Adam's two sons served as types for humanity; so did the three sons of Noah. From Ham's children came Nimrod and Babel, Canaan and Assyria: the people of the world who war against the people of God. Japheth fathered Elishah, Tarshish, and Magog: people who grew rich and fat. Shem was the representative of God's chosen people and the promised seed, giving rise to Abram nine generations later. The safety of the ark was not for the sake of all the people Noah fathered; which, considering only he and his sons (and their wives) survived the great flood, means everyone. It was for the sake of the promised seed that these eight were saved and Shem's line was produced. Everyone else after Noah is the beneficiary of almighty God's kindness and providential care; because God is faithful and will keep His Word. This covenant provides the only goodness many folks will ever see, with Ham and Japheth as representatives of those who will not find peace with God. In this age, He graciously provides seed time and harvest, so they might have life, even if only for a season. For those who are in Christ, Shem points us to the promise of God that brings eternal life to those who are called. These two groups of people are a constant presence in this age. While Adam's Covenant brought death to all men, Noah's Covenant provides a respite until that great Day of Judgment, when Christ shall come to judge the nations and all men must give an account to their Creator.

The Abrahamic Covenant – *Two Peoples, Four Seeds.*

Since the Abrahamic Covenant is a major point of departure between Baptist and Paedobaptist views on the covenants, we must examine it closely to see what the intended meaning is; not what our favorite theological system teaches. Without an accurate view of the Abrahamic Covenant it is impossible to understand the relationship between the various covenants of the Bible and who are the mediators and members therein; which we need to understand if, as Spurgeon said, we are to rightly comprehend the Scriptures.

The promise given to Abram sprang forth from the Eternal Covenant, as do all of God's redemptive actions. Contrary to what many theologians claim, the Author of our salvation did not put together His rescue plan in reaction to what Adam did in the garden. The promise was conceived before time by the Holy Trinity, revealed to man in the garden, confirmed in Abram, secured in national Israel, and fulfilled in Christ Jesus and His body, the church.

We cannot comprehend what the Old Testament tells us about the covenant with Abraham without properly understanding how the Author interpreted those passages for us in the New Testament. Since much of the New Testament is commentary or interpretation on the Jewish Scriptures, we cannot ignore what God has spoken through His Spirit to shed light on that which was hidden in types and shadows. So we turn to the chief Pharisee of his time to see the true meaning given in the Abrahamic Covenant.

In his letter to the Galatian church, the apostle Paul was shining the light of God's grace into the then-growing darkness of legalism which was based on the dominant Jewish perspective of their Scriptures, a perspective he was very familiar with. In the first two chapters, Paul accuses his audience of leaving the truth; defends his apostleship and gospel as that of Christ rather than mere man; and begins explaining the dangers of creeping legalism. In chapter 3, he turns to Abraham, the father of the Jews, as an example of being reconciled to YHWH by faith rather than works as required by the Law of Moses. He tells them Jesus was cursed for our disobedience *so that in Christ Jesus the blessing of Abraham might come to the Gentiles*. Now to his inspired interpretation of God's covenant with Abraham:

> *To give a human example, brothers: even with a man-made covenant, no one annuls it or adds to it once it has been ratified.* **Now the promises were made to Abraham and to his offspring.** *It does not say, "And to offsprings," referring to many, but* **referring to one, "And to your offspring," who is Christ.** *This is what I mean: the law, which came 430 years afterward, does not* **annul a covenant previously ratified by God**, *so as to make the promise void. For if the inheritance comes by the law, it no longer comes by promise; but* **God gave it to Abraham by a promise.** (Galatians 3:15-18)

The *promises* made to Abraham were communicated to him by *a promise*. In several places, God promised several things to Abraham and his offspring. The apostle is precise in correcting the Jewish perspective wherein they supposed all national Israel was being spoken of as that offspring. Paul has even confused some modern commentators here, but clearly he means that what was promised to Abraham's offspring was not to national Israel and its countless members; it was promised to one offspring, the promised seed that national Israel had been formed to protect as it was delivered through 43 generations (Matthew 1:17). Here is how one commentary explains it:

promises—plural, because the same promise was often repeated (Gen 12:3, 7; Gen 15:5, 18; Gen 17:7; Gen 22:18), and because it involved many things; earthly blessings to the literal children of Abraham in Canaan, and spiritual and heavenly blessings to his spiritual children; but both promised to Christ, "the Seed" and representative Head of the literal and spiritual Israel alike.[9]

There were four specific places wherein the promises to Abraham are made and they explain how the body of Christ, His redeemed, are included in the person of Christ, to whom the promises are extended and guaranteed by the covenant ratified by God. We will turn to a well-known reformer to explain why the Law was added, because some even in our day don't understand this. A Baptist brother dear to my soul considers the Law as necessary for leverage to exert on church members to get them to Sunday services. Is this why the Law was given, 430 years after the promise? That is the question. Here's Martin Luther's answer:

> Why was the Law added to the promise? Not to serve as a medium by which the promise might be obtained. The Law was added for these reasons: That there might be in the world a special people, rigidly controlled by the Law, a people out of which Christ should be born in due time; and that men burdened by many laws might sigh and long for Him, their Redeemer, the seed of Abraham. Even the ceremonies prescribed by the Law foreshadowed Christ. Therefore the Law was never meant to cancel the promise of God. **The Law was meant to confirm the promise until the time should come when God would open His testament in the Gospel of Jesus Christ.**[10] (emphasis mine)

One reason for the Law, meant here as the Mosaic Covenant, was to form up a special people, national Israel, to guard the promised seed until the fullness of time. Another reason is found in Galatians 3:19: the Law of Moses *was added because of transgressions, until the offspring should come to whom the promise had been made.* The phrase, *because of transgressions,* only makes sense when viewed as meaning *for the sake of transgressions,* to better shine the light of Truth on the sin that would consume this infant nation. The Law of Moses was given to provide guardrails for life to national Israel, that they might not pollute themselves with the world, and to weigh them down with their own sin so they might see their need of the promised seed; the One Who would keep the Law and ascend to God. This law was given to the Jews, not to the world. It was intended, as Luther wrote, to confirm the promise by reminding national Israel of their need of atonement and to keep them as a people until the promised was fulfilled in Jesus.

This brings the apostle to a key point which is another common opportunity for misunderstanding. Peter wrote about the difficulty in rightly comprehending some of the things Paul had written (2 Peter 3:16), so this should not surprise us. One caution we must exercise is to carefully examine context to determine what is meant when we see the word "law" in Scripture. It can mean the law Gentiles are to themselves, it can mean the first five books of the Bible, it can mean the Mosaic Covenant, and it can mean the Decalogue. Read Romans 1:12ff to see several of these meanings being referred to with no clear indication as to which law he means. Here in Galatians, however, it is clear that Paul is talking to those who want to earn righteousness by works of the Mosaic Law; he tells them the purpose of that law has been fulfilled.

> **But now that faith has come, we are no longer under a guardian**, *for in Christ Jesus you are all sons of God, through faith. For as many of you as were baptized into Christ have put on Christ. There is neither Jew nor Greek, there is neither slave nor free, there is no male and female, for you are all one in Christ Jesus. And* **if you are Christ's, then you are Abraham's offspring**, **heirs according to promise.** (Galatians 3:25-29)

The Mosaic Law was a guardian to national Israel, designed to keep that nation until the fulfillment came. This code was never meant to provide salvation to the Jews, it was meant to keep the Jews so that from them salvation would come to the world. When Jesus came, in the fullness of time, the Law no longer served this purpose. We will see more about this in the review of the Mosaic Covenant.

Verse 29 makes it very clear that when Paul interpreted "offspring" as singular, meaning Christ (Galatians 3:16), he also had in mind all those who would be redeemed, *being one in Christ, heirs according to promise, and Abraham's offspring* (verse 29). In Jesus the line of David comes to an end without end. He, Jesus, ever lives and reigns as the antitype king to David's type. We who are *heirs according to promise* are such because the faithful witness satisfied the Father's wrath on our behalf.

What the Law could not do and was never intended to do, the promised seed, the offspring of Abraham brought to completion. Christ Jesus, born under the curse of the Law, was obedient to every perfect, unbending expression of God's holiness expressed therein so He could bring many sons to glory. Jesus is the *promise* by which God would fulfill the *promises* made to Abraham. The covenant with Abraham is foundational to the Christian faith. It was the cornerstone of the Old Covenant giving the promise of the One Who would prove Himself to be the cornerstone of the New Covenant.

As noted above, there are four passages that reveal God's covenant with Abraham. I've extracted from those passages the essence of the promise/covenant in each so we can see what I think is an interesting pattern.

> **The Promise.** ... *I will make of you a great nation, and I will bless you and make your name great ... in you all the families of the earth shall be blessed.* (Genesis 12:1-3)

> **The Covenant: Heirs & Land.** ... *"This man shall not be your heir; your very own son shall be your heir." And he brought him outside and said,*

"Look toward heaven, and number the stars, if you are able to number them." Then he said to him, "So shall your offspring be." And he believed the LORD, and he counted it to him as righteousness. ... "Know for certain that your offspring will be sojourners in a land that is not theirs and will be servants there, and they will be afflicted for four hundred years. But I will bring judgment on the nation that they serve, and afterward they shall come out with great possessions. ... On that day the LORD made a covenant with Abram, saying, "To your offspring I give this land ..." (Genesis 15:1-21)

The Covenant: The Sign of Circumcision. ... *"Behold, my covenant is with you, and you shall be the father of a multitude of nations. ... I will establish my covenant between me and you and your offspring after you throughout their generations for an everlasting covenant, to be God to you and to your offspring after you. ... As for you, you shall keep my covenant, you and your offspring after you throughout their generations. This is my covenant, which you shall keep, between me and you and your offspring after you: Every male among you shall be circumcised. You shall be circumcised in the flesh of your foreskins, and it shall be a sign of the covenant between me and you. ...* (Genesis 17:1-13)

The Promise Restated. ... *I will surely bless you, and I will surely multiply your offspring as the stars of heaven and as the sand that is on the seashore. And your offspring shall possess the gate of his enemies, and in your offspring shall all the nations of the earth be blessed...* (Genesis 22:15-19)

Before the covenant with its clear and conditional promise of natural heirs and possessions was given, God gave Abram an unconditional promise that only makes sense in the eschatological view, as only in the fullness of time would all nations be spiritually blessed in Abraham, as people from all nations, tongues, and tribes are called to new life in Christ Jesus. *After* the covenant with its clear and conditional promise of natural heirs and possessions was given, God confirmed the true scope and intent of what the shadows and types of the natural promises were meant to portray as He reconfirmed the unconditional promise that shows Jesus as victorious over His enemies and effective in redeeming His elect.

In these four passages we find two peoples, children of Abraham according to the flesh (Ishmael's people and national Israel) and children of Abraham according to the promise (spiritual Israel, the redeemed saints). This is clearly spelled out by the same apostle used to bring the Galatian epistle to us, a man highly educated and trained in Jewish religion who was called into the glorious light that only a new life in Christ can bring. Paul is conflicted by the realization that many of his *kinsmen of the flesh* will perish, though they were entrusted by God with *the adoption, the glory, the covenants, the giving of the law, the worship, and the promises. To them belong the patriarchs, and* **from their race, according to the flesh, is the Christ**, *who is God over all, blessed forever. Amen* (Romans 9:4-5). When we read that *salvation is from the Jews* (John 4:22), this is the meaning: Jesus came from national Israel, *according to the flesh*. The apostle then tells the saints in Rome of what he told those in Galatia: *But it is not* *as though the word of God has failed. For **not all who are descended from Israel belong to Israel**, and not all are children of Abraham because they are his offspring, but "Through Isaac shall your offspring be named." This means that it **is not the children of the flesh who are the children of God, but the children of the promise are counted as offspring*** (Romans 9:6-8, see also Romans 2:28 & 29). This is the true meaning of YHW's covenant with Abraham.

This covenant was between God and Abraham, with duality in fulfillment: one physical, the other spiritual (Gen 12:2-8; 15:13-16; 17:1-27), with two categories of seed within each. The physical had physical circumcision as its sign (Gen 17:10-14); the spiritual sign of this covenant is being found in Christ (Gal 3:27-29). Abraham gave rise to many nations on the earth, as promised by God. All of those descendants are a child of the flesh or as a child according to the promise. He is claimed as father by Jews, Muslims, and Christians – though Christians are of a different seed than the others (Romans 4:9-12). The paedobaptist covenant system is unable to see this complexity because it would expose the error in their "covenant children" doctrine, which requires all within the covenant be of one nature.

This dual nature of the Abrahamic Covenant has been written about by many. In various ways, writers make the same point:

> the Abrahamic Covenant was first fulfilled physically in the Old Covenant and in the nation of Israel and then fulfilled spiritually in the New Covenant and the church.[11]

Lehrer describes types and shadows by saying that spiritual truths were portrayed in Old Covenant times by pictures. The New Covenant temple comprised of the spiritual stones (God's redeemed) was portrayed by the tabernacle; the efficacious atonement of Christ was pictured by the endless and intricate liturgy of animal sacrifices and sinful priests. As has been mentioned before, when the antitype has come, the type ceases. The spiritual fulfillment is the true fulfillment of this covenant; the temporal fulfillment cannot ever deliver the promise.

> *For when God made a promise to Abraham, since he had no one greater by whom to swear, he swore by himself, saying, "Surely I will bless you and multiply you." And thus Abraham, having patiently waited, obtained the promise. For people swear by something greater than themselves, and in all their disputes an oath is final for confirmation. So when God desired to show more convincingly to the heirs of the promise the unchangeable character of his purpose, he guaranteed it with an oath, so that by two unchangeable things, in which it is impossible for God to lie, we who have fled for refuge might have strong encouragement to hold fast to the hope set before us.* (Hebrews 6:13-18)

There is nothing greater, nothing more binding, nothing as eternal as an oath from God. He Who created all things, Who sustains all things, Who will judge the quick and the dead needs nothing more than His will to insure what He has promised. In His kindness to Abraham and us (verse 17), God guaranteed His promise with an oath, reminding us *it is impossible for God to lie*. There can be nothing more sure than this! And thus God condescended, again, so that we would *have strong encouragement to hold fast to the hope set before us*. Herein is our God glorified: that His children exhibit trust in Him in the midst of the wicked culture we find ourselves. God's redemptive plan would be accomplished without His promise to Abraham or His oath to guarantee it. These are for our benefit and His glory. That is, in a nutshell, why all good things are given to us.

But the covenant with Abraham is more complex yet, as the following description taken from Jeffrey D. Johnson's excellent book, *The Fatal Flaw of the Theology Behind Infant Baptism* reveals for us:

The Abrahamic Covenant included at least four major promises:
> A seed
> A land of rest
> That Abraham would be the father of many nations
> And, ultimately, that Abraham's children would be the "People of God"

The key to understanding these promises is distinguishing their two-pronged fulfillment; that is the dual nature to the Abrahamic Covenant. By studying the Old and New Testaments, we learn there is a physical and spiritual fulfillment to each of these promises.

Included in the physical fulfillment were:
1. A natural seed (Genesis 17:7 & 10). This includes both a.) all Jews and Arabs, and b.) national Israel.
2. Types and shadows pointing to the arch-type, Jesus
3. Bilateral
4. A condition which man must meet.

Included in the spiritual fulfillment were:
1. A spiritual seed (Galatians 3:16 & 29). This is a.) uniquely Christ Jesus, and b.) all who have been purchased by His blood.
2. Spiritual realities – people reconciled to God by the blood of Jesus, Who is the antitype
3. Unilateral
4. An unconditional guarantee from God[12]

Whether one calls Genesis 12 a promise or a covenant, there is no possible means to conflate the membership, benefits, or mediator with the covenant in chapter 17. The Lord provides this exposition through Paul's pen:

> *Tell me, you who desire to be under the law, do you not listen to the law? For it is written that Abraham had two sons, one by a slave woman and one by a free woman. But the son of the slave was born according to the flesh, while the*

son of the free woman was born through promise. **Now this may be interpreted allegorically: these women are two covenants. One is from Mount Sinai, bearing children for slavery; she is Hagar. Now Hagar is Mount Sinai in Arabia; she corresponds to the present Jerusalem, for she is in slavery with her children. But the Jerusalem above is free, and she is our mother.** *For it is written, "Rejoice, O barren one who does not bear; break forth and cry aloud, you who are not in labor! For the children of the desolate one will be more than those of the one who has a husband."* **Now you, brothers, like Isaac, are children of promise.** *But just as at that time* **he who was born according to the flesh** *persecuted* **him who was born according to the Spirit**, *so also it is now. But what does the Scripture say? "Cast out the slave woman and her son, for the son of the slave woman shall not inherit with the son of the free woman."* **So, brothers, we are not children of the slave but of the free woman.** (Galatians 4:21-31)

The Abrahamic covenant: dual in nature, one of works, one of grace; one of earthly shadows, one of heavenly realities. Two peoples; children according to the flesh, marked by circumcision of the flesh and those according to the promise, marked by the circumcision not made by human hands – the unconditional promise of God to His elect.

> Although they recognized that the posterity of Abraham was both physical and spiritual at the same time, the paedobaptists refused to see two posterities, because, according to them, Abraham had only one posterity made up of the mixed people of the Covenant of Grace. … The paedobaptists refused to separate the dualities of the Abrahamic Covenant in order to preserve their model of the Covenant of Grace which integrated these dualities. … The Baptists saw two posterities in Abraham, two inheritances and consequently two covenants.[13]

There are those who claim the Abrahamic Covenant is of grace – and they are right. Others claim the Abrahamic Covenant is of works – and they are right! How can both of these claims be right? Scripture has the answer, of course; if one cares to study it humbly, rather than cling to beloved traditions. Paul shows us that the Abrahamic Covenant is of grace as we read in Galatians 3:17 & 18 and in Romans 4:13-25. In both passages the Apostle is used of God to contrast the Law given to Moses with the promise of redemption given to Abraham. Nothing which comes after a promise made by God can annul God's promise; He cannot lie and does not change. The promise God gave Abraham was under, was part of, the Covenant of Redemption; pointing to the promised Savior. This is made clear by what preceded verse Galatians 3:17, when Paul stated that the promise was made to one seed, not many; and that one seed is Christ. This promise is extended to all the elect in Romans 4:16 & 23-25. Man can do no work to be made right with

God. We are brought into His family by grace alone through faith alone in Christ alone.

Yet the Scripture also shows that the Abrahamic Covenant is of works. In John 8:33, Jews claim Abraham as their father, and Jesus confirms this in verse 37; while in verse 39 denying it, going on to say that their father is the devil. How can these things be? This is but one passage shedding light on the true nature of the Abrahamic Covenant: it is either two covenants, made with two people-groups – one temporal and one spiritual; or it is one covenant, as John Bunyan said, like a coin, with two sides – a dual covenant with terms for the same two people-groups. It cannot be a simple covenant with one people-group, for some of Abraham's offspring are spiritual children of Satan and some are spiritual offspring of God. And there are no children of Satan in the New Covenant.

This passage brings us the benefit of demonstrating the use of allegorical interpretation of Scripture as well as making the dual nature of His covenant with Abraham explicit. If one holds the promise of Genesis 12 and 22 separate from the covenant of Genesis 15 and 17, this passage in Galatians shows us that the promise of God given to Abraham is a covenant. Those who trust in their lineage and their feeble attempts to keep the Law and the Prophets are in bondage, even though, as did the Jews in John 8, they claim to be free. Paul explained what freedom truly is when he described it as being associated with heavenly Jerusalem, children of the free woman (Galatians 4:21-31), about which Reisinger observes:

> It is important to note that Paul does not demonstrate and prove the doctrine of election by comparing a "covenant child" (seed of Abraham) and a "non-covenant" child (Gentile), but he compares two "covenant" children.[14]

The slave woman and her children will be cast out and will not inherit the kingdom of God. True freedom only comes from being liberated from sin by the work of the Holy Spirit, being made citizens of New Jerusalem. We who have been born of the Holy Spirit are not children of the slave woman, we are not bound by her covenant, made on Mount Sinai. We are children of the promise, freed from the bondage of sin and made free in Christ, being bought and brought into the New Covenant of His blood. The Abrahamic Covenant was made with two different people-groups, with different promises. Understanding the dual nature of the Abrahamic Covenant is crucial to rightly comprehending the Baptist view of covenant theology.

We now come to the second aspect of this covenant that is often overlooked. Within these two groups of people are *four* seeds. These were alluded to in the discussion of the duality of this covenant. Here is how John Reisinger describes them:

> 1. Abraham has a NATURAL seed. This seed includes all of his physical progeny or every person who was in any way physically

descended from Abraham. The natural seed includes Ishmael, as well as Isaac; Esau, as well as Jacob; the Arabs, as well as the Jews; and Judas, as well as Paul. In this sense, Gentile believers can never be Abraham's seed. Some of the same promises were given to both Ishmael and Isaac because they were both Abraham's natural seed. The same is true of Jacob and Esau.

2. Abraham has a SPECIAL NATURAL seed. All of the natural children of Jacob, Abraham's grandson, became the "Nation of Israel." This nation was a "special" or "chosen" nation before God. Most of the people in that nation perished because of unbelief, but they were still a special natural seed of Abraham with special and unique promises from God which no other nation, before or since, ever had. However, despite their special national status before God as a physical nation, they were still only the fleshly natural seed of Abraham. An unregenerate Israelite had no more claim or right to spiritual blessing than did Ishmael or Esau. This must be constantly remembered.

3. Abraham has a spiritual seed. Every true believer in every age since the time of Abraham is Abraham's spiritual seed. This seed is the true "election of grace." In this sense, Gentile believers are part of Abraham's seed and Jewish unbelievers are not. It is this seed alone, through Christ, that inherits the true "promises made to Abraham and his seed."

4. Abraham has one unique seed who is Christ the Messiah. This Seed is the One who is the most important of all of Abraham's seeds. As mentioned earlier, any spiritual blessing that any of the other three seeds ever enjoyed, or ever will enjoy, is only because of their union with the true Seed, Christ, to "Whom the promises were made."[15]

I differ with Reisinger a bit with his definition of the 2nd seed and the 3rd seed. What he calls the special natural seed is a sub-set of the natural seed. National Israel, typified by Jacob, came out of Abraham according to the flesh; the only thing that made them special was God's calling them out of the world to be His temporal people for a time. Additionally, Jesus is counted in Scripture as having descended from Abraham according to the flesh, so He must be listed in the second category. If He was not a natural seed of Abraham (humanly speaking), He would not have been born under the law, cursed on our account. And we would be without hope. Regarding the third category, Abraham's spiritual seed includes the redeemed beginning with the first believers, not those since his time. From Adam to the end of the age, all the redeemed are Abraham's children according to the promise, his spiritual seed. Even considering these shortcomings, Reisinger's identification of these four seeds aligns with Scripture and give us a more accurate view of this two-sided covenant (one side, the promise fulfilled in Christ Jesus;

the other side, the unique theocratic nation of Israel) than a superficial read of the initial account in Genesis will provide. Although some details are different, the essential description of this covenant provided by Reisinger and Johnson are in strong harmony.

This *four seed* view of the Abrahamic Covenant shows us more of the depth of meaning in Scripture. God's Word will always take us deeper if we prayerfully seek the redemptive meaning, of how by the predetermined will of the Holy Trinity, sinful men are reconciled to God in Christ Jesus. National Israel had many benefits and responsibilities, but this did not bring them peace with God as nation. Some within national Israel and every tribe of people were chosen by God to become His true people, children of Abraham according to the promise. These are reconciled to God by the special seed of Abraham. Noticeably absent from Abraham's covenant are the non-elect Gentiles; they have no place with Abraham nor with God; Adam is their federal head.

There are those who think the fulfillment of Abraham's covenant is with a renewed national Israel, with a resurrected David as its king (this problem shows up in our discussion of the David Covenant, as well). Abraham did not have this in mind and though he had far less of God's Scripture, he was given faith in the promised seed and was counted as righteous by God. His view of the promise was far more glorious than what is imagined in the novel system known as dispensationalism.

> *By faith Abraham obeyed when he was called to go out to a place that he was to receive as an inheritance. And he went out, not knowing where he was going. By faith he went to live in the land of promise, as in a foreign land,* **living in tents with Isaac and Jacob, heirs with him of the same promise. For he was looking forward to the city that has foundations, whose designer and builder is God.** *By faith Sarah herself received power to conceive, even when she was past the age, since she considered him faithful who had promised. Therefore* **from one man, and him as good as dead, were born descendants as many as the stars of heaven and as many as the innumerable grains of sand by the seashore.** *These all died in faith, not having received the things promised, but having seen them and greeted them from afar, and having acknowledged that they were strangers and exiles on the earth.* **For people who speak thus make it clear that they are seeking a homeland.** *If they had been thinking of that land from which they had gone out, they would have had opportunity to return. But as it is,* **they desire a better country, that is, a heavenly one.** *Therefore God is not ashamed to be called their God, for he has prepared for them a city.* (Hebrews 11:8-16)

For Baptists who belong to the Darby school of thought, the main thought to bear in mind is that the eternally significant aspect of Abraham's status as the father of many nations is his being the father of all who are saved through the seed that was promised him. Ishmael and his nations have no more or less significance in the next age than does the Jewish nation that are children of Abraham according to the flesh. All the promises of God find their yes in Christ Jesus, fulfilling spiritually for eternity what Darby imagined were only physical and only for a time. In Christ there are no ethnic or social distinctives. Reisinger puts it well:

> God does not have two peoples, two programs, two eternal purposes, two gospels, and He most certainly does not have two separate brides for His Son (Eph. 2:11-22).[16]

And as for the question of why this entire covenant was issued and its proper meaning:

> **This is the heart of the issue. God did not cast off a physical nation and then replace it with a physical church. He fulfilled the true promise to Abram by creating a spiritual regenerate nation, the Body of Christ.**[17] (emphasis mine)

As we saw in our study of Adam, Abraham died without anything more than the promise of God. He was buried in the only part of the Promised Land he had come to possess, a field he had purchased wherein to bury his wife (Genesis 23:10-20; 25:7-10). And yet, we know by the Word of God that Abraham looked forward to what was, in truth promised to him: ***For he was looking forward to the city that has foundations, whose designer and builder is God.*** God's covenant with Abraham – two sets of terms with two sets of people represented by four seeds. All of which points us to or brings us into union with the promised seed, Christ Jesus.

The Mosaic Covenant – *Israel's Guardian.*

The Mosaic Covenant was between God and the Israelites (see Exodus chapters 20 through 30), with the Decalogue as the summary thereof (Deuteronomy 4:13). It applied to Gentiles only as they voluntarily joined with Israel (Exodus 12:43-49; Numbers 9:14). National Israel was told they would be a *kingdom of priests and a holy nation* **IF** they kept this covenant (Exodus 19:5 & 6). The sign of the covenant was explicitly stated as being the weekly Sabbath (Exodus 31:12 & 13; Ezekiel 20:10-12). Since Jesus fulfilled this covenant (Matthew 5:17-20; Galatians 4:4) and He is true Israel (2 Corinthians 1:20; Galatians 6:16), all the redeemed constitute the *kingdom of priests and a holy nation* (Galatians 3:8 & 9; 27-29) that national Israel portrayed in types and shadows. This relationship gives a clear picture of the meaning of this covenant, not an end unto itself but a type of the Eternal Covenant.

Unlike the Abrahamic covenant, the Mosaic had no dual nature: it was strictly a covenant based upon works, as clearly spelled out in Exodus 19:5-8: *Now therefore,* ***if you will indeed obey my voice and keep my covenant,*** *you shall be my treasured* *possession among all peoples, for all the earth is mine; and you shall be to me a kingdom of priests and a holy nation. These are the words that you shall speak to the people of Israel." So Moses came and called the elders of the people and set before them all these words that the LORD had commanded him.* **All the people answered together and said, "All that the LORD has spoken we will do."** *And Moses reported the words of the people to the LORD.*

Acknowledging the close connection between the Abrahamic and Mosaic Covenants, many will bring up the promise in Genesis 17:7 wherein YHWH declares He will be the God of national Israel. Does this not prove the unconditional foundation of the Mosaic Covenant? Easily we say, no! Yes, this is an unconditional promise from God within the covenant of circumcision, but that is only part of the story. In the first place, God is the God of all people; in the same way that Christ Jesus is the Lord of all even if most do not recognize Him as such. And, as noted in the discussion of Abraham's covenant, national Israel was a special seed, yet not in the same sense as Abraham's spiritual seed. And this brings us to the second point: for national Israel to be God's people, they had to keep the covenant; all of it, without one failure. Recall the exchange in Exodus 19: Moses set before the people of Israel **all** the words YHWH has spoken. **All the people answered together and said, "All that the LORD has spoken we will do."** They all properly recognized that this covenant God was gracious in giving to them required perfect obedience. And like so many in our day who take Deuteronomy 6:5 as a command one must do to be a Christian, those early Hebrews and most all who followed them, were deceived into thinking they could earn – and, indeed, had earned – God's favor. By the time the Messiah came, they by and large thought they were keeping up rather nicely. Works righteousness will do this to one and all, so we must be on guard to always see superlative commands as reminders that we are sinful and unprofitable servants; that Christ alone was able and was successful in keeping the law completely and He alone earned the favor of God the Father.

This tight connection between Abraham's and Moses' covenants, along with David's, is evidence that they have something fundamental in common. As was pointed out in the introduction to this chapter, these three covenants comprise the Old Covenant, with the recognition that the promise to Abram in Genesis 12 stands outside of that circle.

In order to fulfill its mission as national Israel's guardian, the Mosaic Covenant contained 1.) an outward and visible seed, 2.) various types and shadows, and 3.) inclusion based on works. Gentiles who came to live with the Jews could be circumcised and brought into this covenant. It promised blessings and curses based on the record of obedience of the Jews; it was not established with the physical seed of Abraham to make them righteous, but to show them their sins and point them to the promised Christ. No salvation was forthcoming for members of this covenant without perfection.

Firstly, the outward, visible seed consisted of Abraham's children according to the flesh who took circumcision as the sign and were marked by YHWH's law as given through Moses. Circumcision was first given to Abraham (Genesis 17:9-11) and became an early sign of the covenant with Moses (Exodus 4:24-26; Leviticus 12:3) that was quickly neglected. We see that the generation that left Egypt was circumcised, but none of those born in the wilderness were (Joshua 5:1-7). Not until the younger Hebrew males were circumcised were they allowed to pursue entry into Canaan (Joshua 5:8 & 9). To be uncircumcised was to be considered an enemy of God and a disgrace to Him (Genesis 34:14; Judges 14:3; 15:18; 1 Samuel 17:25 & 26). By Jesus' time, circumcision was seen as the symbol of the Mosaic Covenant (John 7:22 & 23), a burdensome yoke (Acts 15:5-11) that was of no benefit (Galatians 5:1-6). Yet all the while, the members of national Israel trended towards pride and presumption in their standing as God's people. Jesus instructed his disciples telling them not to be like the Pharisees, who were well known for performing pious acts for public view (Matthew 6:1-6; 23:1-8; Luke 16:14-16). These outward acts, including circumcision, were what defined the Jews as a people.

Secondly, all the details of the religion given them by God were various types and shadows of the heavenly realities that comprise YHWH's plans for redeeming sinners. Properly understood, types in Scripture shed light on the redemptive message that is central to rightly comprehending God's Word. O'Hare gives us an example: "Jonah did not just happen to be engulfed by a great fish and later ejected as a random biological event, but this occurred as *designed* by the Lord to shadow forth the death, burial, and resurrection of our Lord. Likewise, the seventh day rest was not a random terminus of creation but a purposed end point to shadow forth the inevitable results of God's work in redemption. ... [A] type occurs by God's design – it is not that a situation arises in history and God uses it an analogy at a later period to express some truth or object lesson."[18] We see this emphasis clearly in Hebrews, with one example beginning in chapter 6 as the promise to Abraham is recounted and Jesus is described as the sacrifice that has gone beyond the curtain into the inner sanctuary (verses 13-20). Chapter seven demonstrates the superiority of Jesus to the Levitical priesthood, being *the guarantee of a better covenant*; having made a one-time sacrifice for sin. If these two links between the temporal and spiritual were too subtle, the Author instructs us as to the main point this part of the epistle (8:1 & 2). In describing the endless rituals and repeated sacrifices made by the Levitical priests, He comments plainly: ***These serve as a copy and shadow of the heavenly things***, *as Moses was warned when he was about to complete the tabernacle. For that was shown to you on the mountain* (verse 5).

One of the types that became clear to me as such only recently is found in the short record in 2 Kings 4, wherein we read of a famine in the land of Israel and starving men came to Elisha for food. Let us look at verses 42-44:

> *A man from Baal-shalishah came to the man of God with his sack full of 20 loaves of barley bread from the first bread of the harvest. Elisha said, "**Give it to the people to eat.**" But Elisha's attendant asked, "**What? Am I***

to set 20 loaves before 100 men? " *"Give it to the people to eat,"* Elisha said, *"for this is what the LORD says: 'They will eat, and they will have some left over.' "* **So he gave it to them, and as the LORD had promised, they ate and had some left over.** (HCSB)

I wonder how the Jews being fed by Jesus (Matt 14 & 15; John 6) were connecting what they were experiencing with what they had heard about this old prophet. In the gospels we have the command to feed the crowd with what appears to be far too little food. Then we have a complaint from the servants that it is not enough, followed by having left-overs. We see Jesus teaching in John 6 that these feedings and the manna in the wilderness were types of the true spiritual food that He is for His sheep. He rebuked those who were following because their bellies were full (John 6:26; see also Philippians 3:18 & 19), admonishing them to work for eternal food (verse 27). That work, He told them, was to believe in Him (verse 29). God provides, directly or through natural means that are multiplied supernaturally, to show His faithfulness and sufficiency. Types in the Bible are always real world objects or practices that have their main purpose as pointing to the antitype, which is the fulfillment of what was spoken of in the shadows. Since all the promises of God find their yes and amen in Christ Jesus, it is appropriate that we look for legitimates types that point to Him, for in Christ alone does anything or anyone find fulfillment and rest.

Thirdly, inclusion by works was noted above as regards outsiders. For Jews, inclusion was contingent upon the same work; males being circumcised and certain laws being kept (Exodus 12:44 & 44; Leviticus 12:3). As we noted in chapter 6 in the discussion of the Decalogue and the 1689 LBC, the weekly Sabbath was the sign of this covenant and was developed over generations to include not only the commands given national Israel by God, but also hundreds of rabbinical commands intended to help the Jews keep their Sabbath, so important was this to that nation (Jeremiah 17:21-27). Inclusion in the Jewish community meant exclusion from pagan nations (Exodus 23:27-33); this was to keep the nation in tact so the promised seed would be protected and to keep the Jews from being polluted by the false gods of the world. This prefigures one of the signs of what James called pure and undefiled religion within the New Covenant: *to keep oneself unstained by the world* (James 1:27). Many of the laws were specific for the worship system and agricultural life of ancient Israel (Exodus 12:14-20, Leviticus 1:10-13, 11:1-23, 15:19-20, 19:19, 19:27-28, 27:30-32, Deuteronomy 25:5-6). These regulations and more comprised a burden too heavy for mortal man to bear; pointing us to the One God-man who would bear them and the reconciliation He provides to those who believe.

The covenant made with national Israel on Mount Sinai was built upon the Abrahamic covenant of circumcision found in Genesis 17, promising land to the natural offspring of Abraham, contingent on the people keeping God's commands. The biblical record is clear: Israel failed, repeatedly, to keep this covenant. No man is justified by the Law of Moses. Is this covenant then futile? If the demands of this covenant are such that no man can keep them and, therefore, no man able to earn the promised reward; what was the purpose of this covenant? One reason was to instruct us by providing a negative example (see 1 Corinthians 10:6-11). We cannot deny that the Mosaic Covenant is the major focus of the Jewish nation; but Galatians 4 and 2 Corinthians 3 show it cannot bring liberty to slaves of sin. Paul asks and answers this same question, in Galatians 3:19, as we have seen earlier in our preview of the covenants between God and man. As with the religion given to national Israel, the promise of land within the Mosaic Covenant serves mainly as a type pointing to the promise of eternal rest found in the offspring to whom the promise was made. Paul went on to say, (3:21-22) *Is the law then contrary to the promises of God? Certainly not! For if a law had been given that could give life, then righteousness would indeed be by the law. But the Scripture imprisoned everything under sin, so that the promise by faith in Jesus Christ might be given to those who believe.* This shows the main reason the law, in this context meaning the Mosaic Covenant, was given: to put the chains of sin on man so the freedom that comes with faith in Christ, the law-keeper, would be all the more evident.

The following discussion of the purpose or goal of the Mosaic Covenant is based on Pascal Denault's *The Distinctiveness of Baptist Covenant Theology*, pages 130ff.

The purpose of the Mosaic Covenant is three-fold: a.) to preserve the messianic lineage which culminated in Christ; b.) to point typologically to Christ; and c.) to imprison everything under sin in order that no hope for the promised inheritance would be found in anything or anyone other than in Christ Jesus. We will look into each of these purposes to validate this assertion.

a. The first purpose of the Mosaic Covenant was to preserve the messianic lineage which culminated in Christ. We find the lineage of Jesus as a focal point of proving His identity in the first chapter of Matthew's gospel account and in the third chapter of Luke's. Matthew finishes his record of the Lord's human lineage by summing up the entire Jewish line: *So all the generations from Abraham to David were fourteen generations, and from David to the deportation to Babylon fourteen generations, and from the deportation to Babylon to the Christ fourteen generations* (Matthew 1:17).

In Romans 9:4-5, the Word of God tells us the Israelites were given many blessings (including the law and the covenants) and the Patriarchs from whom, according to the flesh, came Christ. Denault summed it up well: "The point of the genealogical succession of Abraham was not to establish a perpetual principle in order to include the natural posterity of all the members of a covenant, but only to lead to his ultimate posterity who was, according to this interpretation his only posterity."[19] Romans 9:5 indeed, mentions only Christ as the descendant of the Patriarchs, though there were many children of Abraham according to the flesh. Paul, a Jew of significant import, recognized that all these other children of Abraham were not the reason of keeping the tables of nations. Since Christ came, in the fullness of time, as THE seed of Abraham, the covenant and laws that kept Israel were no longer needed. This is why Hebrews 8, in describing the superiority of the New Covenant, tells us the Old Covenant, which had the Mosaic Covenant as its main feature, is obsolete, ready to vanish. Romans 9:4 reminds us the Jewish people were given the oracles of God, in which the gospel was revealed, in types and shadows.

b. The second purpose of the Mosaic Covenant was to point typologically to Christ. Few Christians would deny that the Jews were blessed by God as a function of being in a covenant relationship with Him. Under the Abrahamic and Mosaic Covenants, the Jews were delivered from Egypt, led to Canaan, given the design and materials for the tabernacle, led by prophets, priests, and kings. In describing several aspects of the Mosaic Covenant (priests, sacrifices, tabernacle), Scripture reveals the higher purpose they served: *a copy and shadow of the heavenly things* (Hebrews 8:5). And in the next two verses, God's Word contrasts the more excellent ministry of Christ with the Old Covenant, which is described as having faults, as the law can never take away sins; the practice thereof can only cover them for a season. The Old Covenant pointed to Christ, in Whom all the promises of God are yes and amen. This is far more excellent than mere temporal blessings.

c. The third purpose of the Mosaic Covenant was to imprison the Hebrew people under sin in order that no hope for the promised inheritance would be found in anything or anyone other than in Christ Jesus. Since man is inherently prideful and prone to self-worship, there is a universal need for the human race to be brought face-to-face with our nature. We are, by nature, children of wrath (Ephesians 2:3), spiritual offspring of Satan (John 8:44), enemies of God (Romans 5:10), dead in sins and trespasses (Ephesians 2:1), following the prince of this present age (Ephesians 2:2). We need to be broken of our sin, and the Law given to Moses as part of that covenant reveals God's uncompromising holiness. Who can stand? This purpose was already shown from Galatians 3 (above) and is also revealed clearly in 2 Corinthians 3:6-9, where the Old Covenant is described. The Decalogue, called the tablets of testimony of the Mosaic Covenant (Exodus 31:18, 32:15, 34:27-29), is called in this passage, *the letter that kills, the ministry of death, carved in letters on stone … the ministry of condemnation.* Death came to creation by sin; the wages of sin is death. Those who are left alone by God, those who remain dead in their sins, are condemned (John 3:18, Romans 5:16 & 18). This is the work of the Mosaic Covenant: to imprison everything under sin and condemn all who do not belong to the sheepfold of Christ Jesus (Romans 8:1). This shows that the Mosaic Covenant has the same foundation as the Adamic Covenant; they both bring death; they both reveal, in part, the holiness of God.

Many paedobaptists protest that the Mosaic Covenant is part of the over-arching Covenant of Grace. This line of reasoning is necessary to sustain their view of "covenant children" and the equivalence of national Israel with the church. As we saw in the covenant with Noah, YHWH was gracious in giving mankind the Noahic Covenant so that even the most reprobate sinner can trust the created order for seed time and harvest. In a similar way, God was gracious with national Israel in giving them the Mosaic Covenant. Both of these covenants provide unregenerate men various benefits; neither secures eternal peace with God. There is no saving grace given to members of these covenants, only to those chosen to be members of the New Covenant.

From Jeremiah 11:1-17 we see how this covenant was broken and how national Israel would come to its end as the guardian of the promised seed and how its people would be told their covenant was to be ended. The entire passage is relevant, but I have extracted the essence in order to be somewhat brief.

> *The word that came to Jeremiah from the LORD: ... Cursed be the man who does not hear the words of this covenant that I commanded your fathers when I brought them out of the land of Egypt,... do all that I command you. So shall you be my people, ... Hear the words of this covenant and do them. For I solemnly warned your fathers when I brought them up out of the land of Egypt, warning them persistently, even to this day, saying, Obey my voice. Yet they did not obey or incline their ear, but everyone walked in the stubbornness of his evil heart. Therefore I brought upon them all the words of this covenant, which I commanded them to do, but they did not." ... They have gone after other gods to serve them. The house of Israel and the house of Judah have broken my covenant that I made with their fathers. Therefore, thus says the LORD, Behold, I am bringing disaster upon them that they cannot escape. Though they cry to me, I will not listen to them. ... The LORD once called you 'a green olive tree, beautiful with good fruit.' But with the roar of a great tempest he will set fire to it, and its branches will be consumed. The LORD of hosts, who planted you, has decreed disaster against you, because of the evil that the house of Israel and the house of Judah have done, provoking me to anger by making offerings to Baal."*

Nehemiah chapters 9 & 10 records the various ways national Israel failed to keep the covenant, some 70 years after Jeremiah's prophesied exile began. Though the city and the temple would be rebuilt, national Israel never regained its temporal glory, and it was on life support until Messiah came.

But is not the Mosaic Covenant described as everlasting? In many places, various practices required in that covenant are spoken of as "eternal" or "everlasting" (Exodus 12:13, 17; 13:10; 28:29, 43; 30:21; 31:16 & 17; and many more), but the covenant itself is not so described. The Hebrew word that comes across as eternal, everlasting, or permanent in our English Bibles is *olam* (Strong's 5769) and does not mean "continually in force throughout infinite time, no matter what happens to the world." It can mean lasting a long time, continual, during a lifetime, or forever. A common use of this word refers to events or conditions that were in the past, further strengthening the view that *olam*, like law, must be examined carefully in its context to see what it means, rather than doggedly assigning one definition to all uses without regard to how context and the balance of Scripture shed light.

Why did I label this covenant as Israel's guardian? In the various ways described above, it kept national Israel for the purposes God had laid out for her. The former Pharisee described it thusly: *Now before faith came, we were held captive under the law, imprisoned until the coming faith would be revealed. So then, the law was our guardian until Christ came, in order that we might be justified by faith* (Galatians 3:23-24). The law, meaning (again) by the context in Galatians, the Mosaic Covenant. This was national Israel's multi-faceted guardian until Christ came. That was the main purpose this covenant was given, for as it is written, salvation comes from the Jews! This short passage also means, and this will be explored more in the discussion of the Old Covenant, that the Mosaic Covenant no longer functions.

As we saw in our study of Adam, Moses died without entering into the Promised Land of Canaan (Deuteronomy 32:48-52); he saw it from afar without possessing it, as did Abraham before him. *By faith Moses, when he was grown up, refused to be called the son of Pharaoh's daughter, choosing rather to be mistreated with the people of God than to enjoy the fleeting pleasures of sin.* **He considered the reproach of Christ greater wealth than the treasures of Egypt, for he was looking to the reward.** *By faith he left Egypt, not being afraid of the anger of the king, for* **he endured as seeing him who is invisible** (Hebrews 11:24-27). By this testimony, we have every good reason and hope that Moses, though he was the mediator of this covenant, was welcomed into his rest by our Savior.

The Davidic Covenant – *The Promise Renewed.*

The David Covenant is first revealed in 2 Samuel 7 as Nathan communicates God's plan for establishing David's throne and kingdom forever. It is very similar to the Abrahamic Covenant in that it is dual-natured, comprised of a conditional promise (made to Solomon and all the natural offspring of David) and an unconditional promise (made to David on account of the surety of Jesus Christ). The difference between the Abrahamic and Davidic Covenants is that Christ is the substitute for all of Abraham's spiritual seed, earning us the right to enjoy the promises made to Abraham; while in the Davidic Covenant, Christ reigns as high priest and rules alone as the King of kings, seated on the throne of David. The Covenant of Abraham secures our position in the kingdom of God. The Covenant of David secures Jesus' position as King of kings and Lord of lords, as a reward for having perfectly kept the law of Moses and the prophets.

Some 400 hundred years after David died, when Israel's status as a nation was a mere shadow of what it was, the Lord God brought word a second time to the prophet Jeremiah while he was in prison. Of this word, recorded in Jeremiah 33, John Gill said, "This chapter is a continuation of prophecies of spiritual blessings on the church of Christ in Gospel times, of which the return of the Jews from captivity, and the benefits following on that, were types."[20] YHWH had told the prophet that He would bring prosperity and healing to the land, restore fortunes of Israel and Judah, and more. These were, as Gill pointed out, types of the spiritual blessings we receive in the New Covenant by being united by faith to

Christ. We find this worked out in the second half of the chapter, which begins with this promise from God:

> *"Behold, the days are coming, declares the LORD, when I will fulfill the promise I made to the house of Israel and the house of Judah. In those days and at that time I will cause a righteous Branch to spring up for David, and he shall execute justice and righteousness in the land. In those days Judah will be saved, and Jerusalem will dwell securely. And this is the name by which it will be called: 'The LORD is our righteousness.' "For thus says the LORD: David shall never lack a man to sit on the throne of the house of Israel, and the Levitical priests shall never lack a man in my presence to offer burnt offerings, to burn grain offerings, and to make sacrifices forever."* (Jeremiah 33:14-18)

The promise was made long before: God would bless the nations through Abraham, Isaac, and Jacob; He says now through the prophet that *a righteous Branch of David* will be raised up in due time, in the fullness of time. David was a king of Israel who exercised some of the privileges of a priest (1 Samuel 21:1-6; Luke 6:4); this Son of David was a divine prophet, priest, and king, the final fulfillment of the hope that king David represented for national Israel. This Branch will rule with justice and righteousness, without the stain of sin that mortal men always bring to even the highest calling. Here, Judah represents true Israel, the elect of God; all of whom will be saved. Jerusalem here is the heavenly city that Abraham looked for (Hebrews 11:8-10) and is not to be confused with earthly Jerusalem, which never provided the security one finds only in Christ Jesus (Galatians 4:25 & 26; Proverbs 18:10). This city is called *YHWH is our righteousness*, something earthly Jerusalem desired but could not possess. The Levite priests have given way to the body of Christ, as everyone therein is a priest with access to the holiest of holies (1 Peter 2:9 & 10) in the holy kingdom of God (Revelation 1:6; 5:10; 20:6). Lehrer provides this insight: "This promise of a "Branch" and his connection to David is very similar to Isaiah 4:2; 6:13; 9:7; 11:1, which are fulfilled in Matthew 2:23. It is clearly a messianic promise in which, according to the language of the text, the Messiah will be doing what is just and right in the land of Palestine."[21] The shadows and types give way to the antitype.

A young brother proving himself to be a diligent workman, accurately handling the Word of Truth gives this account of how it is Christ Jesus rather than Solomon who fulfills the promise made to David:

> 1 Chronicles 28:5-7 demonstrates that the promises of the Davidic Covenant find a near fulfillment in David's son, Solomon. In fulfillment of the son of God promise, the Lord declares of Solomon, "...*for I have chosen him to be my son, and I will be his father*" Jesus Christ is both Solomon's antitype and the ultimate fulfillment of the Davidic 'son' promise (cf. Mark 1:1; Matt. 1:1; Luke 1:30-33) Since the Davidic monarch is typologically analogous to God Himself (as God's son), the Davidic throne must also be

typologically analogous to God's throne. Thus, when Jesus Christ ascended to the right hand of His Father, He did so in fulfillment of the Davidic Covenant. Thus, Christ's enthronement at God's right hand in heaven over the entire cosmos constitutes the ultimate fulfillment of the Davidic Covenant. The Lord Jesus Christ is the One that has ultimately replaced and fulfilled Israel. As He is the True Seed of Abraham and David's Greater Son, Christ fulfills all God's promises, including those given to Israel (2 Cor. 1:20). Not only does He recapitulate Israel's history in His own sinless humanity but He also perfectly succeeds where all God's previous mediators, including Israel, miserably failed.[22]

The deepest, most truthful and God-honoring view of Scripture is that which sees the obedient, faithful servant and Lamb of God as the fulfillment of all things. Christ Jesus said this was the main point of Scripture (Luke 24:25-27) and the "least apostle" said that in Him *all things hold together*, that Jesus is *preeminent* (Colossians 1:17 & 18) and that in Christ *are hidden all the treasures of wisdom and knowledge* (Colossians 2:3). He is the beginning and the end of all things – there is no meaning in any of creation apart from the person and the work of the Son of Man. Without life in Christ, all is vanity (Ecclesiastes 12:8)!

Revelation 3:7 tells us in another fashion how Jesus is the fulfillment of the Davidic Covenant: *"And to the angel of the church in Philadelphia write: The words of the holy one, the true one, who has the key of David, who opens and no one will shut, who shuts and no one opens.* Surely no one thinks the aged apostle is describing anyone other than Jesus in these letters as the Person in authority. It is the Lord Jesus Himself that holds the key of David. No matter how you view The Apocalypse of John, Jesus holding the key of David at this early stage precludes any mortal from standing in as Christ's vice regent during any earthly millennium. As the spiritual fulfillment of Abraham's covenant was the key to truly understanding it, so with David's covenant; for *children of Abraham according to the promise* would have no standing if the One making that promise had failed to keep all the law and the prophets and fulfill this covenant.

In his preaching revealed in Acts 2:22-36 it is clear that Peter was convinced that David understood exactly what was being promised to him in 2 Samuel 7. Peter showed that David understood both when and how the covenant promise to *"raise up his offspring"* and *"establish his kingdom"* would be fulfilled. This very clear "time" reference (when David's days are fulfilled and he is buried with his fathers) is often overlooked by those discussing the establishment of David's throne.

Let us compare David's prophetic words and Peter's interpretation to see if these things be so. Careful observation will show a direct correlation between David's words and Peter's interpretation of them.

2 Samuel 7:12 – the prophecy	Acts 2:29-31 – the fulfillment
When your days are fulfilled and *you lie down* with your fathers,	*Brothers, I can confidently speak to you about the patriarch* **David: He is both dead and buried,** *and his tomb is with us to this day.*
I will raise up your offspring after you, who shall come from your body,	*Since he was a prophet, he knew that God had sworn an oath to him to* **seat one of his descendants on his throne.**
and *I will establish his kingdom.*	*Seeing this in advance, he spoke concerning* **the resurrection of the Messiah**: *He was not left in Hades, and His flesh did not experience decay.*

1. Peter identifies the Messiah as David's offspring. Unless we discount the inspiration of Peter's sermon there is no question as to the subject of the prophecy. Christ is the "seed" that was resurrected to sit in fulfillment of the covenant promise to David. This fulfillment took place when the Christ was raised from the dead; it is not still waiting.

2. The prophecy was more than a promise of the bodily resurrection of Christ. "Peter clearly connected the resurrection and ascension of Christ with the establishment of the kingdom promised to David." Raising up offspring and establishing his kingdom (2 Samuel 7) are equivalent to seating his descendant on the throne of David (Acts 2). "The Holy Spirit specifically tells us that when David spoke of "the raising up of Christ (resurrection) to sit on his (David's) throne" that David was expressly speaking of the resurrection and ascension of Christ that had just taken place (verses 30,31). Peter's words can only mean that David's greater Son was to begin sitting on the promised throne at the time of Christ's resurrection and ascension."

3. The prophecy sets its fulfillment in time when David's days are done and he is asleep with his fathers. While David awaits the second resurrection is when the Messiah will assume His rightful position on David's throne. Peter does not let us forget that Christ has risen and taken His place while David is dead and lies buried in his tomb even to the day when he was preaching. The fulfillment is completely aligned with the prophecy: the Lord assumed the throne when He ascended, while David was still asleep. (See 1 Chronicles 17:11-15 and Acts 13:35 & 36 for the same time reference.)

It makes no sense to say that Jesus is now seated at God's right hand but will sit on a lesser throne as the King of a new temporal nation of Jews. "The gift of the Holy Spirit on the Day of Pentecost is the evidence of Christ's ascension to David's throne as promised in II Sam 7. Pentecost is also a visible expression or exercise of Christ's earned Lordship or present Kingship (cf. Joel 2:28,29). The gift of the Holy Spirit was the direct and earned response to the victorious work of the enthroned King, and it was also the full proof that the Father was perfectly satisfied with that work."[23]

In Acts 4:23-28, the Holy Spirit puts Psalm 2 in the mouth of David and applies it to the death of Christ. Jesus is his anointed one, Herod and Pilate are kings of the earth and rulers, and Gentiles are the nations that rage. Psalm 2 was a coronation declaration; not only did the nations rage against God's anointed, YHWH defeats them and sets His Son on His holy hill, in victory over death which He suffered at the hands of sinful men and God's predetermined plan.

In his second letter to Timothy, Paul is encouraging him and all the saints to stand fast in the strength of YHWH, keeping the heavenly kingdom as first priority. He calls us to *remember Jesus Christ, risen from the dead, the offspring of David* (2 Timothy 2:8). Jesus Christ is THE offspring of David, the ONE who will bring true liberty to the slaves, shackled by chains of sin that no mortal can break.

With these points in mind, and the further testimony of Scripture found in Luke 1, why would anyone think that David would re-take his throne and rule alongside Messiah in any phase of this age or the next? When Mary was told Who she would bring forth as a son, God's messenger told her, *behold, you will conceive in your womb and bear a son, and you shall call his name Jesus. He will be great and will be called the Son of the Most High. And* **the Lord God will give to him the throne of his father David**, *and he will reign over the house of Jacob forever, and of his kingdom there will be no end* (Luke 1:31-33). There is no temporal fulfillment of the promise to David that can be supported from Scripture without ignoring or re-writing passages reviewed herein. The spiritual fulfillment *is* the main thing of the Davidic Covenant.

The dispensational view of this covenant is summed up by one of their foremost modern theologians:

> The Davidic covenant is most important as assuring the millennial kingdom in which Christ will reign on earth. Resurrected David will reign under Christ as a prince over the house of Israel . . . The Davidic covenant is NOT fulfilled by Christ reigning on His throne in heaven . . . It is rather an earthly kingdom and an earthly throne (Mt 25:31). The Davidic covenant is, accordingly, the KEY to God's prophetic program YET TO BE FULFILLED.[24]

Matthew 25:31ff describe the great and terrible day of judgment, not a mythical beginning of a mixed race of glorified and fleshly people in an earthly kingdom that will perish when the end of the age comes.[25]

As with each of the covenants between God and man that are revealed in God's Word, the Davidic Covenant has the promised Messiah and His redemptive work as the main focus. The promise to David renewed the promise made to Abraham so long before, with a fresh and much clearer depiction of the Redeemer given to us. No mortal man can claim the promise that Christ has fulfilled; no mortal man would have hope if the Lord Jesus had not fulfilled all of the Law and the prophets, including this covenant.

Old Covenant – *The Heavy Yoke.*

In Acts chapter 15 we have the familiar scene in which Paul and Barnabas went to Jerusalem to tell of the great work YHWH had been up to in bringing Gentiles into His kingdom (verses 1-4). Not all welcomed the news with rejoicing, as *some believers who belonged to the party of the Pharisees rose up and said,* **"It is necessary to circumcise them and to order them to keep the law of Moses"** (verse 5). These Jews saw the continuity between Abraham's covenant of works and the Mosaic Covenant. We saw above how they assumed the Davidic Covenant would be fulfilled in the flesh, bringing all three of these covenants together, serving a common three-fold purpose: to crush human pride, to provide hope in God's promise, and to deliver the seed so Abraham's children according to the flesh would be reconciled to God. Peter replies to these of the Pharisee party, telling them God makes no distinction between Jew and Gentile and that they *are* **putting God to the test by placing a yoke on the neck of the disciples that neither our fathers nor we have been able to bear** (verses 9 & 10). Reinforcing what we saw of the Davidic Covenant while tying it to the Old Covenant and the Redeemer, James assigned prophecy from Amos and Jeremiah to Jesus: the spread of the gospel to bring Gentiles into God's kingdom was the fulfillment of God's promise to rebuild David's tent (verses 13-18). The Old Covenant, comprised of these three covenants, is as essential and important to God's Covenant of Redemption as the New Covenant is. Nothing done by the Creator is meant to be wasted.

The Scriptures (Jeremiah 31:31-32 and Hebrews 8:8-13) specifically call the covenant between God and national Israel, given from Mount Sinai, the Old Covenant, having Moses as its mediator. As the Covenant of Redemption was progressively revealed, accumulating saints from all ages before it was formally concluded in Christ's sacrifice, so with the Old Covenant as it pulled along into its umbrella the Abrahamic Covenant of Circumcision, the Mosaic Covenant, and the Davidic Covenant. We see this, in part, in John 7:22-23 and Galatians 5:3 as well as Acts 7, Acts 15:5 and 10:11. And we see also that the Covenant of Redemption was working in the same ages as the Old Covenant, saving God's people through faith in the promised Messiah long before He condescended to put on human flesh and dwell among us (see Hebrews 9:15).

In many ways, the Mosaic Covenant is seen as equivalent with the Old Covenant, because the content of the Mosaic Covenant is more broadly and deeply revealed than are the other covenants within the Old. The missions of the Mosaic and Old Covenants have much in common and since national Israel is the lesser participant in both, we would expect terms to be common. Hence when we see Scripture describing one, it usually applies to the other. Such is the case with Deuteronomy 31:26: *Take this Book of the Law and put it by the side of the ark of the covenant of the LORD your God, that it may be there for a witness against you.* The Book of the Law, which in this case refers to the first five books of the Bible, serves as a witness against national Israel. It is placed alongside the ark of the covenant to reinforce the idea that it is part and parcel of the covenant given to national Israel, which is in itself a witness against them. Jesus taught this as He defended His position as God to the Jews, saying, *Do not think that I will accuse you to the Father.* **There is one who accuses you: Moses**, *on whom you have set your hope.* For **if you believed Moses, you would believe me; for he wrote of me.** *But if you do not believe his writings, how will you believe my words?* (John 5:45-47). This lines up with myriad other passages wherein we are taught that all of Scripture has the person and work of the Lord Jesus as its proper focus. Those who think they can merit God's favor are accused by Moses, the lawgiver! He knew this was not the way to peace with God, He was taught by God that lesson and stands ready to warn all who want to follow that path, which leads only to eternal death.

As for those who claim the Mosaic Covenant still stands, as if it is not part of the Old Covenant, let us consider the biblical record. The Jew is no more in the Mosaic Covenant than the Christian is in the Adamic Covenant. The Jew pretending to practice the Mosaic religion is more like the Christian honoring his flesh, which has died and no longer has dominion over him. But even this comparison fails at some point, because many people are still dead in Adam but nobody is still within the Mosaic Covenant.

> The Mosaic Covenant with all of its individual commandments, its Levitical priesthood, sacrifices, and tabernacle, things upon which it was mutually dependent, were all faulty by design (8:5; 10:1). God enacted the old covenant, and all that was inherently linked to it, with a built-in obsolescence. It was never meant to be permanent. It was a temporal, intermediate covenant, always designed to anticipate, to foreshadow, and to typify the good things to come in Jesus Christ (9:11; 10:1).[26]

Much of the epistle to the Hebrews is focused on convincing all who would cling to the Law of Moses that such a path leads to eternal death. The rest prefigured by Canaan is found only in Christ Jesus, Who makes a New Covenant (promised ages ago), and in so doing, makes the Old Covenant obsolete; it was vanishing away during the immediate time after the Lord's assentation to His rightful place on David's throne. When the temple veil was torn from top to the bottom, when the pagans destroyed the temple and took away their altar, when their house was left to them desolate (just as Jesus had declared – see Luke 13:35), national Israel was no more. The antitype had come; the type must decrease and give way just as did John the Baptist.

Among covenant evangelicals, some, mostly paedobaptists, draw a hard and fast distinction between the Old Covenant and the Covenant of Works; claiming the Old and New Covenants are both part of the Covenant of Grace; the Covenant of Works ending with The Fall. This leads to, *or is designed to allow*, unregenerate folk such as small children being included in the New Covenant. This fits with their view of the church being the same as Old Covenant community of Israel, which had elect and non-elect within.

Here is the paedobaptist view, as stated by 17th century Baptist Nehemiah Coxe:

> That the Infant seed of Believers, during their Infancy, have all of them a certain and definite Interest in the Covenant of grace by virtue of which they are completely justified before God from the Guilt of original Sin, both *Originans* [that sin committed by Adam], and *Originatum* [that indwelling sin in all of us]; and yet when they come to Years of Discretion may, (yea must) by their actual chosing with, or refuting the Terms of the Covenant, either obtain the Continuation and Confirmation of the Convenant-Interest, or be utterly and finally cut off from it, and so perish eternally in their Ignorance of God and Rebellion against him.[27] (my comments in brackets)

The paedobaptist view, even though many deny it, is that you may be born into the New Covenant but must keep yourself in it. Charles Hodge, a paedobaptist, said, "*If the Church is one under both dispensations; if infants were members of the Church under the theocracy, then they are members of the Church now, unless the contrary can be proved*"[28] (*italics* mine). Note the requirement that membership is presumed but can be overthrown, and note the assumed equivalence between the church and theocratic Israel, rather than seeing Israel as a temporal shadow of the church eternal. It appears the Presbyterian view of covenant theology is arrived at by first establishing the doctrine of infant baptism and working backward to make everything fit under that basic presupposition. This is not good biblical interpretation.

Because they see the church being equal to theocratic Israel, paedobaptists claim the Abrahamic and Mosaic covenants as part of the Covenant of Grace, pointing out that God was gracious to the Hebrews in giving them this covenant. *All* covenants between God and man, including those which require perfect obedience, are acts of kindness and goodwill – but this kindness of God in these covenants does not mean they are in the New Covenant. That covenant was ratified by the blood of Christ, not the blood of goats and rams. We see at the Jerusalem council, the apostles drew a hard line between being reconciled to God through faith in Christ by saving grace and being bound by "*circumcision and the law of Moses*." They also tied the Genesis 17 Abrahamic covenant to the Mosaic Covenant, both of which required perfect work which only Christ can do. These covenants are meant to point us to Him, not reconcile us to Him. *For **not all** who are descended from Israel* (through circumcision) *belong to Israel* (through faith in Christ). This shows the dual nature of the Abrahamic covenant.

Support for the paedobaptist view is found in passages such as Leviticus 26:12, where we read: *And I will walk among you and will be your God, and you shall be my people.* To see the problem with this view, one must first acknowledge how gracious God is whenever He condescends to provide anything to anyone. This does not mean He is the saving God of all the people He shows any temporal kindness to; He is faithful to the Covenant given to Noah, which is for the ongoing benefit of all of creation. He *is* the God of all people; He is the Creator of all things and peoples and He is God of all. The second thing one must do is examine the context and application of this verse. The paragraph containing verse 12 begins with verse 3, which opens, *"If you walk in my statutes and observe my commandments and do them,"* demonstrating the conditional aspect of this covenant, contrary to the claim it is part of the unconditional Covenant of Redemption.

Again, we turn to Benjamin Keach:

> Though evident it is that God afterwards more clearly and formally repeated this Law of Works to the People of Israel, it being written into Two Tables of Stone, though not given in that Ministration of it for Life, as before it was to Adam; yet as so given, it is by St. Paul frequently called the Old Covenant, and the Covenant of Works, which required perfect Obedience of all that were under it, to their Justification at God's Bar, and so made Sin appear exceeding sinful, and tended to aggravate Man's Guilt and Misery upon his Conscience, though the Design of God hereby was to discover unto Man how unable he was in his Fallen State to fulfill the Righteousness of God, that so that Law, together with the Types and Sacrifices, might be a Schoolmaster to lead us to Christ.[29]

Under the Old Covenant, Israel's obedience procured God's temporal favor: produce, favor with other nations, power, and God's protection. Under the Old Covenant, as one born under the law, Jesus' obedience procured spiritual and eternal favor: redemption, sanctification, righteousness, and Christ's intercession for the New Jerusalem, sealing the New Covenant under which sinners are declared righteous (Romans 5:18-20, 8:3-4, Galatians 3:13, 4:4-5). The Old Covenant, in each of its administrations, demands much, but provides no hope of reconciliation with God. The New Covenant, made possible by Jesus having submitted to the Father's will in all things, points to Jesus' record of meeting all the demands of the Old Covenant, credits the accounts of the saints, providing the sure hope of eternal life, having reconciled each child of God to the Father. "The Law given to Moses was a grace to lead to the grace accomplished by Jesus Christ."[30] In this matter, Martin Luther was right: we serve Christ Jesus, not Moses. The covenants are different, the mediators are different, the purposes and subjects are different; as different as the type is from the antitype, as the shadow is from the reality.

In describing the differences between the Old and New Covenants, Hebrews 8 tells us the New Covenant will be different from the Old, it will be written on the hearts of God's people rather than on stone tablets given to them. Unlike in the Old Covenant where Israel was promised to be God's people *if* they kept all His commandments, people of the New Covenant are *unconditionally* God's people because the faithful One would perfectly keep the Old Covenant on our behalf. Note how the Lord describes the new covenant (Jeremiah 31:31-33, and quoted in Hebrews 8): "*Behold, the days are coming, declares the LORD, when* **I will make a new covenant** *with the house of Israel and the house of Judah,* **not like the covenant that I made with their fathers on the day when I took them by the hand to bring them out of the land of Egypt**, *my covenant that they broke, though I was their husband, declares the LORD. For this is the covenant that I will make with the house of Israel after those days, declares the LORD:* **I will put my law within them, and I will write it on their hearts. And I will be their God, and they shall be my people.**"

Contrast this with the announcement of the old covenant (Exodus 19:3-6): *while Moses went up to God. The LORD called to him out of the mountain, saying, "Thus you shall say to the house of Jacob, and tell the people of Israel: You yourselves have seen what I did to the Egyptians, and how I bore you on eagles' wings and brought you to myself.* **Now therefore, if you will indeed obey my voice and keep my covenant, you shall be my treasured possession among all peoples**, *for all the earth is mine; and you shall be to me a kingdom of priests and a holy nation. These are the words that you shall speak to the people of Israel."*

Both declare the absolute sovereignty of God, Who is the God of all people, but one has an unconditional promise regarding man's relationship to God and the other a conditional promise. God was gracious in giving the Mosaic Covenant to Israel, but a conditional covenant which must be kept to obtain the blessing is of works, not grace. And here's the comment in Hebrews 8 verse 13, after the citation of Jeremiah 31: *In speaking of a new covenant, he makes the first one obsolete. And what is becoming obsolete and growing old is ready to vanish away.* The Mosaic Covenant is a follow-on to the covenant Abraham entered into in Genesis 17; which is only one side of the covenant issued to Abraham, with Genesis 12 & 15 being the other side of that coin. We must comprehend the historical, redemptive, and textual context of each covenant in order to understand how it applies to people in our day.

As Terrence O'Hare observed, "Paul made clear, the old covenant is practically unintelligible without the new perspective of the new covenant (2 Cor 3:12 – 18); that is, it only makes sense as it is interpreted through the ministration of the Holy Spirit who testifies of Christ."[31] The Old Covenant is indeed far too heavy a burden for carnal man to understand and mortal man to bear. In describing how much more excellent the Lord Jesus is compared to Moses, YHWH tells us, *For on the one hand, a former commandment is set aside because of its weakness and uselessness (for the law made nothing perfect); but on the other hand, a better hope is introduced, through which we draw near to God* (Hebrews 7:18-19). The *former commandment*, the Old Covenant typified by the Mosaic Covenant, is set aside because it was unable to reconcile sinners to God; it was weak and useless in that regard. That covenant is the law, which can make nothing perfect. But God has provided a *better hope* through which we are reconciled, drawn near to Him. On this hand, the work and blood of Christ have opened the way to the New Covenant.

The New Covenant – *Promise Fulfilled.*

Just as the epistle to the Hebrews contrasted Moses and Jesus, do did John in his gospel. *For the law was given through Moses; grace and truth came through Jesus Christ* (John 1:17). John sums up his introduction to the fourth gospel with this contrast between law and grace, between old and new. John further describes this Word of grace and truth as *the only God, who is at the Father's side* whom He (God the Father) has made known. Christ revealed in human form is the mystery of the old unveiled in the new. More certain than the creation, based on the character and promises of God, this New Covenant would be fulfilled and many sons brought to glory under the banner of Christ, the heir of David's throne and all things.

> *Thus says the LORD: If I have not established my covenant with day and night and the fixed order of heaven and earth, then I will reject the offspring of Jacob and David my servant and will not choose one of his offspring to rule over the offspring of Abraham, Isaac, and Jacob. For I will restore their fortunes and will have mercy on them."* (Jeremiah 33:25-26)

And from the earliest days of being known as Baptists, our forefathers have protested the conflated view of covenants espoused by our Presbyterian brothers, described earlier.

> In rejecting the paedobaptist model of the Covenant of Grace, the Baptists did not want to do as the Socinians, who had rejected the Covenant of Grace itself and reformed theology as a whole. They (the Baptists) wanted to distance themselves from the latter and identify with reformed orthodoxy. The Baptists maintained unity with the Presbyterians by affirming the unity of the Covenant of Grace. Baptist theology subscribed fully to the notion of there being only one Covenant of Grace in the Bible, which brings together all who are saved as one people.[32]

The 1689 LBC confirms Denault's perspective of the 17th century Baptists; see chapter 7, para 2 & 3 and chap 11, para 6 of that confession. Baptists believed and taught the singularity regarding people being reconciled to God, whether they lived in the Old or New Testament times. John Spilsbery (the spelling is uncertain, some documents spell it Spilsbury), author of the oldest known treatise on Baptist theology, stressed this unity: "The Church of God under the Old Testament, and that now under the new, for nature are one, in reference to the Elect of God, called to the faith, and by the Spirit of God united to Christ, as the branches to their vine."[33] Calling Old Testament saints "the church" is useful to the Presbyterians in their effort to eliminate the distinctions between the Old and New Covenants. Spilsbery would have made the Baptist position more clear by using the phrase "the redeemed people of God" in referring to Old Testament saints. The church, as defined in the New Testament, did not exist as such during the time of Abraham and David; but we count these two and countless others from those ancient times among the redeemed people of God, united to Christ by the work of the Holy Spirit in each life.

In describing the New Covenant, divine and human authors often use contrasts to communicate the idea. As with describing the holiness of Christ Jesus against the dark blackness of sin, Thomas Patient holds up the New Covenant as His finished work, in contrast to the failed efforts of sinful man.

> Now I come in the next place to prove that the Covenant of Circumcision is no Covenant of Eternal Life, but a typical covenant, yea a Covenant of Works. It is also called by the Lord, a Covenant in the flesh, Gen. 17:13. Therefore, to be sure, it is no Covenant of Eternal Life.[34]

The Old Covenant could never provide eternal life to sinners, only the New Covenant can fulfill this need. Early Baptists accepted the notion of a single Covenant of Grace in both testaments, but they refused the idea of two administrations. The Presbyterian view has Moses administering the Covenant of Grace under the Mosaic Covenant and Christ administering the Covenant of Grace under the New Covenant. These Baptists saw the Covenant of Grace being progressively revealed after its announcement in Genesis 3:15, until the full revelation and conclusion in the New Covenant. This growing revelation of the saving covenant parallels that of the covenant of death, announced in the garden before the Fall. While all men after Adam were born into the covenant of death, the redeemed people of God were rescued and born alive into the Covenant of Redemption, still affected by the curse but no longer enslaved to it. Hence the description of Christians as aliens and sojourners in this present age, having our citizenship in heaven.[35]

Baptists believed the New Covenant was the accomplishment of the promise given in Genesis 3:15; they considered the New Covenant alone was the Covenant of Grace. Spilsbery declared that as late as Abraham, the Covenant of Grace was not yet a formal covenant, but a promise. Indeed, though the New Covenant was intimated as early as the 7th day, it did not assume its status as a formal covenant until Christ came, having met the demands of the Law and the Prophets, being punished on our account, glorified by the Father by being raised from the dead, and issuing the New Covenant by His shed blood. Nehemiah Coxe put it this way: "[...] in the wise counsel of God Things were so ordered that the full revelation of the Covenant of Grace, the actual accomplishment of its great promises, and its being filled up with ordinances proper to it, should succeed the covenant made with Israel after the flesh."[36]

The New Covenant binds Christ and His church together, providing redemption and eternal salvation for sinners. The covenant sign is circumcision not made with human hands followed by water baptism (Colossians 2:11-12). The Lord's Supper is another sign within this covenant, reminding us of its Author and His return (1 Corinthians 11:25). Both of these, discussed in some detail in Part 1, primarily serve to remind us of our Lord's sacrifice on our behalf. One dear brother in our century helps us see this:

> Baptism serves as an outward sign of the inward grace of regeneration and union with Christ. It is less than meaningless if there is no inward grace to reflect. Jesus said, "This cup is the new covenant in my blood" (Luke 22:20). What Jesus is saying is that this cup of wine represents the new covenant he is going to ratify by shedding his blood. This cup becomes the sign of that covenant. Every time we take communion we should rejoice that we are heirs of the new and better covenant that was ratified by his blood.[37]

In Hebrews 7-9 the covenant of redemption is featured, contrasted with the covenant of works, especially in chapter 9: *Now even the first covenant had regulations for worship and an earthly place of holiness.* What follows is a description of the tabernacle of the Hebrew religion, featuring lampstands, a table and bread, the Most Holy Place with the ark of the Mosaic covenant containing the tablets of testimony, the golden vial of manna, and Aaron's staff. Levitical priests ever making sacrifices that would cover sin for a time but never able to take away sin. All of these forms of worship are summed up in verse 9 as symbolic for that age and *"imposed until the time of reformation"* (verse 10). Those who hope for a re-institution of those types and symbols dishonor the sacrifice of the Lord Jesus, which satisfied God the Father and finished the redemptive work announced in Genesis 3:15, bringing that reformation.

> *But when Christ appeared as a high priest of the good things that have come,* then **through the greater and more perfect tent (not made with hands, that is, not of this creation** [speaking here of His body of flesh]*) **he entered once for all into the holy places, not by means of the blood of goats and calves but by means of his own blood, thus securing an eternal redemption.** Therefore **he is the mediator of a new covenant**, so that those who are called may receive the promised eternal inheritance, since a death has occurred that redeems them from the transgressions committed under the first covenant.* (Hebrews 9:11-12 & 15)

The differences between the Mosaic covenant and the Covenant of Redemption are further clarified by YHWH:

> *Thus **it was necessary for the copies of the heavenly things to be purified with these rites,** but the heavenly things themselves with better sacrifices than these. For **Christ has entered, not into holy places made with hands, which are copies of the true things, but into heaven itself, now to appear in the presence of God on our behalf.** Nor was it to offer himself repeatedly, as **the high priest enters the holy places every year with blood not his own,** for*

*then he would have had to suffer repeatedly since the foundation of the world. But as it is, **he has appeared once for all at the end of the ages to put away sin by the sacrifice of himself.** And just as it is appointed for man to die once, and after that comes judgment, **so Christ, having been offered once to bear the sins of many, will appear a second time, not to deal with sin but to save those who are eagerly waiting for him.*** (Hebrews 9:23-28)

These two distinct covenants could not have the same substance, which is the claim of the paedobaptists. The Old Covenant (the second part of the Abrahamic covenant, the Mosaic covenant, and the Davidic covenant) required perfect obedience for the people to be considered the "people of God" and receive temporal blessings. These were all and each a covenant of works. The saving grace of God in Christ Jesus was revealed as these covenants were deployed with the Hebrew nation, bringing the elect of God in that nation into relationship with the Father while they walked among the dead men as dual citizens in both covenants. Their temporal lives were bound to the covenant of works, their spiritual lives to the promised Messiah. The non-elect Hebrews had only the eternal death promised by the covenant of works to all who failed to keep that covenant perfectly.

The Old Covenant conferred earthly blessings and long life in the land; the New Covenant confers heavenly blessings and eternal life. Jeff Johnson presents three points describing deficiencies in the Old Covenant: a.) it was not spiritual, b.) it was not eternal, and c.) it had no power to fulfill the promise made to Abraham. He then presents the purposes of the Old Covenant, also known as the Mosaic Covenant and as Mt. Sinai: a.) it manifests guilt, b.) it pointed to Christ, c.) it preserved the nation of Israel, d.) it established the need for bookkeeping the genealogical trace of the Seed, and e.) it established the means of salvation, pointing to the Promised Seed who would be faithful to all of the law and the prophets. The law, which is an over-arching term for what God gave Moses on Mt. Sinai, convicts you and me of guilt and points us to Christ; the law is not the gospel but it works with the gospel. Lastly, he describes four key differences between the Old and New covenants. These differences are a.) participants, b.) substances, c.) durations, and d.) efficacies. Johnson tells us "the law written on stone can never change the heart of stone."[38]

Romans 8:1-3 instructs us, *There is therefore now no condemnation for those who are in Christ Jesus.* **For the law of the Spirit of life has set you free in Christ Jesus from the law of sin and death.** *For God has done what the law, weakened by the flesh, could not do. By sending his own Son in the likeness of sinful flesh and for sin, he condemned sin in the flesh.* What is this *"law of sin and death"*? Paul further tells us in 2 Corinthians 3:3 & 5-11: *And you show that* **you are a letter from Christ** *delivered by us,* **written not with ink but with the Spirit of the living God, not on tablets of stone but on tablets of human hearts.** *Not that we are sufficient in ourselves to claim anything as coming from us, but our sufficiency is from God,* who has made us sufficient to be ministers of a **new covenant, not of the letter but of the Spirit.** For **the letter kills, but** *the Spirit gives life. Now if **the ministry of death, carved in letters on stone,** came with such glory that the Israelites could not gaze at Moses' face because of its glory, which was being **brought to an end**, will not the ministry of the Spirit have even more glory? For **if there was glory in the ministry of condemnation, the ministry of righteousness must far exceed it in glory.** Indeed, in this case, what once had glory has come to have no glory at all, because of the glory that surpasses it. **For if what was being brought to an end came with glory, much more will what is permanent have glory.*** The Old Covenant is *the law of sin and death* mentioned in Romans 8, signified by the tablets of stone which sit in the ark of that Covenant, lost in time according to God's will (Jeremiah 3:15 & 16). It has been ended, rolled up as a worn out garment (Hebrews 8:13).

There can be no greater contrast than what our Creator has provided through His apostle to the Gentiles. Consistently, the Old Covenant is described as stone, slavery, death, condemnation, and being worn out; for it, in all of its individual covenants, requires perfect obedience that no mortal man can deliver and yields salvation to no man. This covenant is contrasted with the New Covenant, described as flesh, liberty, life, righteousness, and eternal; delivered to the saints of God by the perfect life and sacrificial death of Jesus, yielding His righteousness to all the chosen men. The Old Covenant is described as *the law of sin and death*, contrasted with the New Covenant which is described as the *law of the Spirit of life*.

The glory of the New Covenant is so wondrous, Benjamin Keach seems to have been beside himself in trying to describe it.

> It is a Full Covenant; because in it there is the Mediators Fulness Communicated to all such that are united to him as the effects thereof, 'tis not a Creature-Fullness that is in Christ; no, but the Fullness of God: For it pleased the Father that in him all Fulness should dwell; - in him dwelleth the Fulness of the God-head Bodily: The Fulness of the God-head dwells as truly in the Son, as in the Father; and of his Fulness do all Believers partake, Of his Fulness all we receive, and Grace for Grace.

> 1. Therefore in this Covenant, we do not only receive Light, but the Fulness of Light.
> 2. Not only Life, but the Fulness of Life, because Christ is our Life whom we receive in this Covenant.
> 3. Not only Strength, but the Fulness of Strength; The Lord is the Strength of my heart, and my Portion forever.
> 4. Not only Pardon of Sin, but Fulness of Pardon; or, the Fullest pardon, complete Pardon.
> 5. Not only Righteousness, but the Fulness of Righteousness; perfect and complete Righteousness, and you are complete in him
> 6. Not only Peace, but the Fulness of Peace; Peace that passes all understanding.

7. Not only Beauty, but the Fulness of Beauty; for it was perfect, thro' my Comliness which I put upon thee saith the Lord God.
8. Not only Knowledge, but the Fulness of Knowledge; And ye also are Full of all goodness, filled with all knowledge, etc. The parts may be weak, yet where Christ dwells or hath taken possession of the heart, there the Soul hath a Fulness of Spiritual knowledge: Our Vessels may be full though' but small.
9. Not only Joy, but the Fulness of Joy."[39]

This covenant has only one category of people: the redeemed of Christ who have the fullness of Him in Him. There can be no greater hope, no greater joy, no greater peace, no greater salvation than what Christ Jesus provides for the elect in the New Covenant. We are complete in Christ, fulfilled in Him (Colossians 2:10). We have no other argument, we need no other plea, it is enough that Jesus died, and that he died for me and for thee! Let the saints praise His name!

As the Scriptures continually describe these covenants in contrasting the two, as has the Baptist view of the covenants embraced the biblical truth that the New Covenant is *new*. (See Appendix 6 for a comprehensive comparison between the Old and New Covenants.) The paedobaptist view that the New Covenant is the same as the Old, just with a new administer cannot be reconciled to what Scripture says about either. Swiss reformer Francis Turretin, a paedobaptist, said: "It is called "new" not as to the substance of the covenant (which is the same in both) but: (1) as to the circumstances and mode [...] (2) as to the excellence and glory of this dispensation [...] (3) as to perpetual duration."[40] In tackling what Jeremiah wrote about the New Covenant (chapter 31), Turretin claimed, "Although the Sinaitic and the legal covenant are opposed in Jer. 31 to the New Covenant, it is not necessary that this opposition should be as to essence, but it can be as to accidents or diversity of economy."[41 & 42]

We see the Lord of the covenants tell us, through Jeremiah's quill, that the New Covenant *is not* like the old. The Old Covenant was summed up on stone tablets and kept in the Ark of the Covenant as a reminder of all that God has communicated to the Jews through Moses; the New Covenant is written on the soul of each member, each will know the Lord, having been regenerated and indwelt by God's Spirit. The Old Covenant was broken by the ongoing disobedience of Israel; the New Covenant cannot be broken because God the Son mediates it (Hebrews 9:15) and keeps us (John 10:27-30). The sins of Israel were brought up to them time and time again, with petitions from many prophets for them to repent; yet they did not because they could not; and God divorced her (Jeremiah 3:8). The sins of New Jerusalem, the redeemed saints within the New Covenant, are forgiven in Christ and God promises to remember them no more (Isaiah 43:25; Jeremiah 31:34; Hebrews 8:12)! Contrary to popular conventional wisdom, God does not forget our sins. He chose to not remember them. To forget something is symptomatic of flawed recall, something one cannot rightly attribute to God. The proper view of this is to take it as written, in the context of seeing God for Who He is: perfect and without flaws; able to not remember something. You and I can try to forget something, but such memories often return to our minds. God is not like this. When He chooses to *not remember* something, He does not allow that thing to come to His mind. He is perfect.

Some people, including Baptists (recall Spurgeon's unclear statement in the introduction to this topic), make the error of claiming that the New Covenant was conditional for its mediator, that Jesus' redemptive work was His part of the Covenant of Redemption. Scripture tells us Christ fulfilled the *Old* Covenant and earned the right to issue the *New* Covenant. He came to fulfill the Law and the Prophets (Matthew 5:17); this phrase is commonly used "shorthand" to refer to what we call the Old Testament. Although the Old Testament is not equal to the Old Covenant, the Old Testament does give us the complete description of the Old Covenant and we need the New Testament to comprehend the full meaning of that covenant and that which was partially revealed in the Old Testament: God's gracious Covenant of Redemption; the New Covenant cut by the blood of Christ Jesus. If this is not our over-arching focus as we read and study the Bible, we are vulnerable to being led astray into *controversies, genealogies, dissensions, and quarrels about the law, for they are unprofitable and worthless* (Titus 3:9).

With the New Covenant comes the fulfillment of the types. These have been mentioned in several places, but the main emphasis on earth with the advent of the New Covenant is the fulfillment of Israel as a type of the spiritual people of God. The universal body of Christ which is composed of both Jews and Gentiles is the true Israel of God (Romans 2:28-29; 9:6; Galatians 6:16; 1 Peter 1:1; 2:9-10). James, writing to Christians, calls them *the twelve tribes which are scattered abroad* (James. 1:1). Paul taught that all who believe in Christ are the true sons of Abraham (Romans 4:11-17; Galatians 3:7); that the middle wall of partition has been removed by Christ; and that the believing Jews and Gentiles are one body (Ephesians 2:14ff.). The universal church (all the called-out ones) of Christ is one spiritual building (Ephesians 2:20-22), one bride (Ephesians 5:22 & 32; Revelation 21:9ff.), and the New Jerusalem (Galatians 4:26; Hebrews 12:22; Revelation 3:12; 21:1 & 2; 21:9-11).

Thomas Schreiner provides more clarity on this aspect of Israel being fulfilled in the body of Christ (commonly called, the church):

> The temple in Jerusalem points to Jesus as the true temple (John 2:19-22). The manna the Lord provided for Israel in the wilderness is fulfilled in Jesus, who is the true bread who has come from heaven and given his flesh for the life of the world (John 6:25-59). Jesus also fulfills the Feast of Tabernacles (*m. Sukkah* 4:9-10; 5:2-4). The water-pouring rite is fulfilled in Jesus, for one's thirst is satisfied only in him (John 7:37-38). So too, the lighting ritual that was practiced at the feast finds its fulfillment in Jesus as well, for he is "the light

of the world" (John 8:12), which is verified by his ability to grant sight to the blind (John 9).

In the Old Testament Yahweh is the shepherd of his people and promises to shepherd them in the future (Ps 23:1; Ezek 34:11-16, 23-24), but this promise is realized in the ministry of Jesus as the Good Shepherd who gives his life for the sake of of his sheep (John 10:11-18). In the Old Testament the vineyard of the Lord is Israel (Isa 5:1-7), but Israel failed to produce good fruit; Jesus is the true Vine, the true Israel who always does what pleases the Lord (John 8:29; 15:1). The Lord liberated Israel from bondage at the Exodus, and Israel celebrated the Lord's deliverance at Passover, but Jesus is the true Passover Lamb (John 18:28; 39;19:14).[43]

[T]he Mosaic covenant and law had a typological and salvation-historical function. The tabernacle points to the true tabernacle in heaven, where God dwells (cf. 8:1-6; 9:1-10). The Old Testament sacrifices and regulations anticipate the sacrifice of Christ and the era that has dawned in the new covenant (9:11-14, 23-28; 10:1-10). Old Testament sacrifices also point to the need to share with other and to praise God (13:15-16). The promises of land and rest in the Old Testament forecast the heavenly city and the Sabbath rest prepared for the people of God in the age to come (3:7-14; 11:9-10, 13-16; 12:22; 13:14).[44]

And Vern Poythress helps us see how even this is merely a part of the glorious fulfillment that Christ Jesus brought with His perfect life and death.

Israel was not only a nation of priests, but God's "firstborn son" (Exod. 4:22; cf. Deut. 8:5). Israel failed, however, to live in obedience to God. She was corrupted by injustice (Isa. 1:21). Her very failure testified to the need for a final, obedient son who would come from the line of David and would establish justice (Isa. 11:1-5; 9:6-7). In Isaiah God promises to raise up his servant, whom he names "Israel" (Isa. 49:3), but who will also "bring Jacob back to him" (Isa. 49:5). Injustice and impurity are cleansed (Isa. 4:4) by the servant's death as a sacrificial lamb (Isa. 53). Isaiah is speaking, of course, about the work of Jesus Christ. Christ is the final, definitive seed of Abraham (Gal. 3:16). And when Christ comes, Matthew notes that his life is patterned after the life of Israel the son (Matt. 1:15). Or rather, he notes that the Old Testament history of Israel was patterned after the true and final Son.

The church in turn is patterned after the fullness of Christ (Eph. 4:7-16). The experience of Christians is thus in a multifaceted way analogous to that of Israel (1 Cor 10:1-13; Heb 12:14-29; Gal. 4:21-31). We are the firstfruits of a new humanity in a new heavens and new earth (James 1:18; Rev. 14:4; 21:1). Christopher J. H. Wright sums up these matters by saying that Israel as a people is related "paradigmatically" to fallen mankind, "eschatologically" to the whole of redeemed humanity, and "typologically" to the church. He could have added to these observations the fact that Israel is a type pointing to Christ first of all, and only through Christ to the church and to the new humanity. These rich connections indicate the multidimensional significance of the Old Testament for us.[45]

The veil that covers the eyes of unregenerate typifies the temple veil that kept the world out of the Holy place where God met with His priests. The rending of the temple veil by God symbolizes the lifting of the veil on those who have died to self and been resurrected to new life in Christ; no longer separated from Holy God, no longer part of the world.

Historically, early Baptists faced opposition from the politically powerful state churches (see chapters 1 & 6). "It would be difficult to exaggerate the size of the challenge that the Baptists were up against: contesting the majority understanding of the Covenant of Grace by insisting on the discontinuity between the biblical covenants, while disassociating themselves from the Socinians, the Anabaptists and the Arminians. Disassociation from them was made even more difficult by the fact the Anabaptists and Socinians also rejected child baptism and only baptized believers. **It is, therefore, not surprising that the Baptists were called Anabaptists and that they were marginalized, persecuted and that very few of the paedobaptists gave honest consideration to any of their arguments**"[46] (emphasis mine). I observe a similar tension and general environment of condescension within reformed Baptist circles, as we who do not accept the 1689 LBC view of law and the Mosaic Covenant (chapters 6 & 7 herein) are accused of antinomianism and simple mindedness. Check out videos on the Internet of Sam Waldron and Richard Barcellos discussing Tom Wells' New Covenant views to see this in action. It is difficult to dissociate ourselves from antinomians when so few have bothered to defend the Law of Christ (see Charles Leiter's excellent work, *The Law of Christ*, to help understand this topic); all the more so with the Encyclopedia Britannica defining antinomianism as the "doctrine according to which Christians are freed by grace from the necessity of obeying the Mosaic Law."[47] The commonly held definition within the Christian community is "a pejorative term for the teaching that Christians are under no obligation to obey the laws of ethics or morality."[48] NCT is not antinomian, we simply recognize the law that guarded Israel is not the law by which the Holy Spirit leads those who are in the New Covenant. The Spirit of God empowers us to want to obey His commands; the Law of Christ, His royal law, is fulfilled when we love one another rightly (Galatians 6:1-2 & James 2:8-9); and this law of liberty, which is perfect, is a hearer and doer of the Word (James 1:22-25). NCT is not lawless – it embraces and lives the Greatest commandment and the second one.

The newness of the New Covenant cannot be overstated, as there are so many Christians who think it is not really new. But God is unchanging and He gave some Old Testament saints illumination on this topic:

> The New Covenant of Jeremiah 31 was seen as a covenant superseding the Mosaic covenant. The Hebrew Bible sees these two covenants as being in contrast (this New covenant related to the "Old" Covenant of Sinai), and one major difference is that ONLY the Newer Covenant is "olam". The Mosaic covenant is never called an "olam berith" in the Hebrew Bible (unlike other covenants).

> Ezekiel and second Isaiah look forward to an everlasting covenant between God and the nation (Ezek 16:60; Isa 55:3; 61:8) which they describe elsewhere as a covenant in which God's Spirit will indwell the people (Ezek 36:27–28; Isa 59:21). Malachi's "messenger of the covenant" is cast as a priestly figure (Mal 3:1; cf. 2:1–9). Ezekiel 37 again speaks of the great blessings to be enjoyed by the people of God, including cleansing, walking in God's statutes, recognition as God's people, and he says of this era of blessings: "I will make a covenant of peace with them; it shall be an everlasting covenant with them" (v 26). Other important foreshadowings of the new covenant are found in Isa. 54:10; 55:3; 59:21; 61:8; Hos. 2:18–23; Mal. 3:1–4. Jeremiah's words imply the receiving of a new heart by the people, as is expressly promised in the parallel prophecy of Ezek. 11: 19 and 36:26.[49]

The following comparison, presented by Reisinger, shows in two short passages the similarities and the differences between the Old and New Covenants. The Old is conditional and is a type foretelling the New, which is unconditional (as far as mankind's participation in each).

Exodus 19:5-6	1 Peter 2:9
Now therefore, **if you will indeed obey** my voice and **keep my covenant, you shall be**	But you **are** [because Christ kept the covenant for us]
(1) **my treasured possession** among all peoples, for all the earth is mine; and you shall be to me	(1) **a chosen race**, ... a people for his own possession
(2) a **kingdom of priests,** and a	(2) a **royal [kingly] priesthood,**
(3) **holy nation.**	(3) a **holy nation**

"Both the beginning and the ending of Israel's special national standing and privileges are connected with their keeping or breaking the Ten Commandments."[51] As was discussed in Part 2 and in the Mosaic Covenant, the Decalogue existed as the testimony of that Covenant, which was the centerpiece of the Old Covenant.

The centerpiece of the New Covenant is the person and finished work of Christ Jesus. *And the Holy Spirit also bears witness to us; for after saying, "This is the covenant that I will make with them after those days, declares the Lord: I will put my laws on their hearts, and write them on their minds," then he adds, "I will remember their sins and their lawless deeds no more."* (Hebrews 10:15-17) YHWH says He will remember our sins and lawless deeds no more because His Son has suffered on our account, paying our debt in full (Hebrews 9:15 & 16).

As Reisinger put it, the Old Covenant said, ""Do not come near or even touch this mountain or you die," but the New Covenant says, "Come and welcome, the door is wide open.""[52] He cites a passage describing each covenant to demonstrate this.

> To those in the Old Covenant, God spoke: *The LORD spoke to Moses after the death of the two sons of Aaron, when they drew near before the LORD and died, and the LORD said to Moses, "Tell Aaron your brother not to come at any time into the Holy Place inside the veil, before the mercy seat that is on the ark, so that he may not die. For I will appear in the cloud over the mercy seat.* (Leviticus 16:1-2)

> To those in the New Covenant, God spoke: *Therefore, brothers, since we have confidence to enter the holy places by the blood of Jesus, by the new and living way that he opened for us through the curtain, that is, through his flesh, and since we have a great priest over the house of God, let us draw near with a true heart in full assurance of faith, with our hearts sprinkled clean from an evil conscience and our bodies washed with pure water.* (Hebrews 10:19-22)

The nature of the New Covenant reflects the promise made to Abraham: in it are and will be people from every nation. In Christ there is no Jew or Gentile, male or female, slave or free; these ethical and temporal distinctives have no more role in determining one's status in the New Covenant than does the blood or the will of the flesh or the will of man (John 1:13).

The chart below[52], taken from John G. Reisinger's *Abraham's Four Seeds*, shows the biblical relationship of type (national Israel) and antitype (the body of Christ). This builds on the chart which showed how Abraham, Isaac, and Jacob were each given the same basic promise, identifying them as national Israel and as an Adam. In concert with what Hebrews 8 teaches us, national Israel also served, as did Moses, as a type of the Christ. As with all types, once the antitype arrives, the type has no further purpose. Note the conditional promise given to national Israel

(Exodus 19:5 & 6) based on man's performance and the inheritance granted those in the New Covenant due to the God-man's performance. As the man in national Israel was temporal, so was the kingdom promised; while the God-man and His kingdom, true Israel, in the New Covenant are spiritual. Reisinger has a more detailed explanation of this chart in his book, which is well worth reading.

Point of Comparison	The Nation of Israel	The Body of Christ
Promise to Abraham	Same promise given to the nation of Israel	Fulfilled in the Church
"I will make of thee a Great Nation (Gen. 12:3)	"If ye will obey…and keep my covenant, then ye shall be a peculiar treasure unto me…a kingdom of priests, and an holy nation… (Ex. 19:5-6).	"Ye also, as lively stones, are built up a spiritual house, an holy priesthood…Ye are a chosen generation, a royal (kingly) priesthood, an holy nation, a peculiar people… (1 Peter 2:5, 9).
Both chosen "nations"	Isaiah 51:4	1 Peter 2:9
Kind of nation	Physical	Spiritual
Basis of citizenship	Natural birth	Spiritual birth
Spiritual state of citizens	Saved and lost – Romans 9:6	Saved only – Hebrews 8:10, 11
Proof of citizenship	Circumcision of the flesh by human hands	Circumcision of the heart by the Holy Spirit
Both are the "seed of Abraham" by birth	Born "after the flesh" – "natural" seed only	Born "after the Spirit" – "spirtual" seed
Relationship to God	Loved, chosen, redeemed, adopted, as a physical nation among nations	Loved, chosen, redeemed, and adopted as a spiritual family
Both "redeemed"	Physically – from Egypt	Spiritually – from sin
Both "called by God"	Out of Egypt	Out of the world
Covenant foundation of nationhood	Decalogue – "Do" and lived, disobey and die	Blood of Christ; "Finished" – believe
Condition of blessing	Works – obedience	Grace – faith
Government or rule	Whole Mosaic economy	Whole Law of Christ
Goal – become the true "holy nation" of God (Exodus 19:4, 5)	Never realized – the "if" never fulfilled	Realized by every citizen in the nation – "ye are"
Time frame of nation's existence	Began – Exodus 24:8 Ended – Matt. 27:51	Began – Pentecost (1 Cor. 12:12, 13) Never end – Eph. 2:21-23
Conclusion	All finished – Heb. 8	All new – Hebrews 9 and 10

The New Covenant is new; it's not the Old Covenant with its promised curses for disobedience. The New Covenant shines with the glory of the finished work of Christ; it does not promise the future work of the Messiah yet to come. The New Covenant brings the fullness of Christ to every child of God; with the suretyship of our Lord as the guarantee that He will not forsake us. The New Covenant is where new creatures in Christ have been brought into fellowship with the Father. Without the New Covenant, we would still be under the Law of Moses or under the condemnation of Adam, waiting and waiting. But praise God for His faithfulness! Christ has come and fulfilled ALL that the Law and the prophets demanded. And by His blood He has cut the New Covenant, bringing all the lost sheep into the fold of God.

> *I am the good shepherd. I know my own and my own know me, just as the Father knows me and I know the Father; and I lay down my life for the sheep. And I have other sheep that are not of this fold. I must bring them also, and they will listen to my voice. So* **there will be one flock, one shepherd.** *For this reason the Father loves me, because I lay down my life that I may take it up again. No one takes it from me, but I lay it down of my own accord. I have authority to lay it down, and I have authority to take it up again. This charge I have received from my Father.* (John 10:14-18)

The New Covenant provides God Himself as our shepherd, caring for us, tending to us, keeping us unto that great Day of Judgment where He will serve as our advocate. The New Covenant gives us the fullness of Christ Jesus! We can trust Him in this, for He is faithful to Himself. We trust our souls to the only wise God, who is truly God and truly sovereign over time and space.

> **It is he who made the earth by his power, who established the world by his wisdom, and by his understanding stretched out the heavens.** *When he utters his voice, there is a tumult of waters in the heavens, and he makes the mist rise from the ends of the earth. He makes lightning for the rain, and he brings forth the wind from his storehouses. Every man is stupid and without knowledge;* **every goldsmith is put to shame by his idols, for his images are false, and there is no breath in them.** *They are worthless, a work of delusion; at the time of their punishment they shall perish.* **Not like these is he who is the portion of Jacob, for he is the one who formed all things, and Israel is the tribe of his inheritance; the LORD of hosts is his name.** (Jeremiah 10:12-16)

If you be in Christ, He is sufficient and all glorious! Behold your God:

> **And he who was seated on the throne said, "Behold, I am making all things new." Also he said, "Write this down, for these words are trustworthy and true." And he said to me, "It is done! I am the Alpha and the Omega, the beginning and the end.** (Revelation 21:5-6a)

Recommended reading on this topic:
*The Everlasting Covenant** – Benjamin Keach
*The Display of Glorious Grace** – Benjamin Keach
*Divine Covenants** - A. W. Pink
The blood of the covenant – Charles H. Spurgeon
New Covenant Theology - Steve Lehrer
Abraham's Four Seeds – John Reisinger
Tablets of Stone & The History of Redemption – John Reisinger
The Fatal Flaw of the Theology Behind Infant Baptism - Jeffrey Johnson

*The Doctrine of Law and Grace Unfolded** – John Bunyan
The Distinctiveness of Baptist Covenant Theology – Pascal Denault
*The works of William Bridge, Vol 3**
*A Friendly Examination of the Pacifick Paper** - Isaac Chauncy
The Shadow of Christ in the Law of Moses - Vern S. Poythress

Conclusion.

The covenants of Scripture are essential to our proper understanding of the over-arching story of the Bible, God's redemptive plan being revealed in time through types and shadows that gave increasing clarity of the Promised Seed Who would take away sins. Properly seeking Christ in all of the Bible is the goal. Comprehending the covenants therein are a help. May God keep us from getting these two reversed.

.

Part 4: How it works together in a local church

Introduction.

As Paul often spent most of a letter explaining theology before he turned to the practice associated with it (Romans), so we now come to the application in this work. With the theology of Baptists in hand, as reviewed in parts 1 through 3, we now turn to the practice: how are these Baptist distinctives deployed properly in the local church? We will examine four areas, using the epistle to the Colossians as our context, to explain how the Bible applies the theological topics to a.) The structure of the local church, b.) Membership within the local church, c.) Worship within the local church, and d.) Evangelism by the local church. These are complimentary to what are known as the 4 marks of a biblical church: i) Biblical ordinances, ii) Biblical offices, iii) Biblical gospel, and iv) Biblical church discipline. My decades of experience reveal that many Baptist churches give little thought to these issues and some give priority to traditions of man rather than biblical principles. My prayer is for those who read this book to be provoked to think and live biblically without allowing man's traditions to rule in their personal and church lives. This is how we should live, even though we will disagree here and there about the proper interpretation or application of Scripture.

Chapter 10. Structure: The Form of the local church.

He is the image of the invisible God, the firstborn of all creation. For by him all things were created, in heaven and on earth, visible and invisible, whether thrones or dominions or rulers or authorities—all things were created through him and for him. And he is before all things, and in him all things hold together. And he is the head of the body, the church. He is the beginning, the firstborn from the dead, that in everything he might be preeminent. For in him all the fullness of God was pleased to dwell, and through him to reconcile to himself all things, whether on earth or in heaven, making peace by the blood of his cross (Colossians 1:15-20).

We cannot comprehend the structure of the church if we know not its Head. Since Christ is Lord of all things, creator of all things, God in the flesh Who gave Himself to His body, the church; how can we not seek to honor Him by how we order the local church?

In chapter 3 – The Nature of the Local Church, the nature and function of the offices were described, as well as the qualifications of those who serve in them. What, if any, structure for the local church is given to us? How are the men who answer the call to these roles supposed to work together in the local church? Practice varies, by style, culture, and size of fellowship; but the Scriptures reveal only one structure: two or more men serving as elders responsible for the spiritual health of the flock YHWH has gathered together with deacons being primarily responsible for temporal matters therein. There is no indication that size, location, or physical structure of a building are the least bit important. As we will see, all instructions are given to insure the spiritual growth of the saints while keeping body and soul together. No church can fulfill its mission of being salt and light in this wicked age unless it is spiritually healthy and physically active.

The average size of the local church in the United States continues to be around 75 members.[1] There are many small churches that have only one elder and no deacons. I have seen how this can run a man ragged and have also seen how pride keeps the "pastor" from having others serve in one of these capacities. While there may be times in the life of a church when deacons are not there, all members should be on the watch for men that YHWH is calling and equipping for service as deacons or elders, recognizing them as such when they have demonstrated the character, skills, and willingness for such service. Even in a small church, having only one elder can lead to a kind of "cult of personality" as a solitary man is seen as the public face and voice of that church. One man alone, coping with a job, his family, and the ministry is vulnerable to being drawn aside by pragmatism in what may start as an innocent desire to do all things well and unto the Lord but which soon go astray. I have seen a man present others' sermons as his own, with no indication he had done so, proving himself not to be able to show himself a workman unashamed (2 Timothy 2:5). If the saints YHWH has gathered and gifted in the local church (1 Corinthians 12:4-11) are encouraged to serve the body, those serving as elders and deacons will have a much lighter load and the local church will marvel to see the Lord working in their midst!

Having two or more men who preach and teach provides several benefits, in addition to aligning with the examples and teachings from Scripture (Acts 11:27-

30; 14:21-23; 20:7; Titus 1:5; James 5:14; et. al.). Two or more men can sharpen one another and hold each other accountable, while the church sees the true Shepherd more clearly when they see Him work through more than one man. The church will see strengths and weaknesses in each man and those men will have the opportunity to be examples of how to serve in unity without letting egos derail the ministry. As they seek to identify others and train them for this service, more men will have opportunity to serve the saints in myriad ways. This is part of life in the body of Christ that is vital and often undervalued.

Some large churches have numerous elders, often with an unbiblical distinction between paid staff "professional" elders and "lay elders" who are not paid. Even with this arrangement, there are Baptist churches with a senior elder/pastor supported by "lesser men" who shepherd some members but do not preach, following the Presbyterian model. Churches built around a person are likely to grow larger and larger without serious regard to equipping and sending men to plant new churches, due to the often unspoken acknowledgment that pastor-man is too important; nobody can be without him. So it is more and more common to see multiple services and/or locations, either option creating different congregations, different churches with a shared eldership. This is not a Baptist practice! When Second Baptist in Houston first stretched beyond its large campus on the west side of town, they beamed Ed Young to their several remote locations for the sermon. The implicit message is the pastor is the message. This same message is implicit in the operation of multiple services, where the same man preaches to two or more groups. Not only do both of these practices emphasize the "senior pastor" to an unhealthy degree, they produce separate congregations under one leader. Neither practice is recommended to us in Scripture and neither one should be embraced by people who fear God.

Whether there is a solitary elder or too many to number, there is a sober warning that elders are to shepherd the flock of God that is among them, being examples to them (1 Peter 5:1-3). Recall from chapter 3 the discussion of what it means to be an "under shepherd" of God's people. Being mindful of to Whom we answer should keep the child of God who serves as an elder from taking those responsibilities too lightly or himself too seriously. As the mission of the local church is summed as equipping the saints for ministry, that the body of Christ would be strong and not tossed about by human cunning and the deceitful schemes of the devil (Ephesians 4:11-14), all men serving as elders should be looking for God to raise up others to work alongside them rather than protecting their turf as if they are a separate class, which reflects the false dichotomy of the clergy/laymen view of the church that the Bible knows nothing about.

I recommend Sam Waldron's contribution on this topic in *Who Runs the Church? (4 Views on Church Government)*, as he provides a good historical, theological, and biblical defense of the plurality of elders and what their duties are with the local church. He reviews six passages of Scripture to provide a biblical analysis of role of the elder, concluding that Scripture makes no distinction between teaching and ruling elders (as many claim for 1 Timothy 5:17). Rather the distinction is between "elders who rule well and those who labor in the Word and doctrine. ... The contrast is not between no teaching and teaching. It is between some teaching and a greater degree of teaching."[2] As discussed in the Deacon section of chapter 3, our human frailties are somewhat kept in check if caring for the sheep is systematic, relational, and comprehensive.

Men working closely together for the good of God's people must be humble men so egos and fleshly conceits do not inhibit the proper function of these watchmen. This is taught in Scripture, as the apostle gives instruction to Timothy:

> *Show yourself in all respects to be a model of good works, and in your teaching show integrity, dignity, and sound speech that cannot be condemned, so that an opponent may be put to shame, having nothing evil to say about us. Bondservants are to be submissive to their own masters in everything; they are to be well-pleasing, not argumentative, not pilfering, but showing all good faith, so that in everything they may adorn the doctrine of God our Savior.* (Titus 2:7-10)

This short passage gives us an excellent overview of the role elders play. Be an example to the flock (1 Peter 5:3) and to those outside (1 Timothy 3:7); this so that YHWH's name is not profaned (Romans 2:17-24; 1 Timothy 6:1). Good works are to adorn the life of the elder, and these will be mostly caring for the sheep of God He has gathered there (Acts 20:28). Teaching and preaching is a hallmark of those called as elders (1 Timothy 3:2; 4:6-16; 2 Timothy 4:2; Titus 1:9). These men will be submissive to Christ and His Word (1 Corinthians 1:18; 2:10; 2 Timothy 2:8); and they will be hospitable & honest (2 Timothy 2:24 & 25; 1 Peter 4:9-11 & 5:2; 1 John 3:16 & 17) all for the glory of our God and Savior and the good of His people.

It is almost comical, yet unspeakably sad that so many elders call themselves "pastor" and take no thought as to what the Bible means by this word. As reviewed in chapter 3, the word pastor communicates the act of care for the spiritual condition of the flock God has gathered before you. This is not a title to communicate one's standing as a Christian or leader in the church. In practical ways, pastoring shows up when elders visit their people in their homes, getting to know them, encouraging them and counseling them as to how to live godly lives, train up their children, and evangelize their neighbors. How can a pastor care for his sheep if he does not know how they live nor what they think and do when away from the Sunday gathering? Once more, recall the sermon about the role of elders in the local church from Thabiti Anyabwile in chapter 3. YHWH takes this role very seriously; we who serve have no license to reduce this role to a title.

This fondness of titles shows up as we see elders called "Reverend," which puts a more spiritual weight on them. There are men with earned or honorary doctorate degrees and like to be called "Doctor," which confers more authority as a learned man. No matter the title, the impact is consistently contrary to the teaching of Scripture that elders are no different from those they serve, save for the role they have been called to and responsibility they have to God for that service. Far too many "pastors" see themselves as *the* teacher/preacher with members sitting and learning, whereas Scripture does show that God Himself has gifted each member of the local church with the expectation that each will serve as gifted (1 Corinthians 12). Titles tend to lend credence to this structure, though the Word of God does not.

Whether visiting members or preaching and teaching, such service is not the job only for the elders. Each member of the local church is to be equipped for ministry and the simple act of visiting one another, sharing a meal, praying, being a part of each other's struggles and joys and for teaching and rebuking one another (2 Timothy 3:16). Such active ministry will do as much to mature the Christian as nearly anything else. In most of the churches I have been a part of this ministry was either minimized or ignored, mainly because people have been conditioned that such service is the domain of the clergy and the local church is little more than a social club. This attitude towards church elders reflects an unbiblical view of the church, harkening back to the Old Covenant and its need of priests. Christ is our high priest, we have no need of any mortal to stand in our stead, no matter how many titles, degrees, or honors other men may bestow upon him.

Because we are prone to forget what we have been taught (2 Peter 1:12) and we tend to wrap ourselves up in our own traditions (Galatians 1:14), each local church would be well served to have a concise statement of faith that effectively communicates what is taught and held as essential for faith and unity within that fellowship. Such documents must not seek to impose rules not found in Scripture, such as the "Christian Sabbath" rules found in the 1689 London Baptist Confession, reviewed in chapter 6. Without a clear, biblical statement of faith (and the Baptist Faith and Message does not work; it is so broad and shallow that everyone from Rick Warren to Al Mohler can claim agreement), new members will find out what the "hot button" items are by bumping into them. Depending on the issue and the church, these experiential discoveries of church doctrine might be pleasant or more akin to walking through an unmarked mine field. It is far more honest and open (as we should be with one another) for the local church to have a statement that declares what they see as essential for unity within that fellowship. Not only will this let guests decide if they want to belong, it will provide an opportunity for the members to see the diversity of beliefs they hold and make decisions as to which are foundational. This will strengthen the fellowship as people learn from one another in humility as we see how limited our understanding is and how awesome our God is.

Not directly related to the structure of the local church, but important within the teaching ministry therein, the question of discipleship must be addressed. A key component in most churches is Sunday School, supplemented by Vacation Bible School in the summer. As with most programs supported in the church today, there is no biblical instructions or examples of these specific activities. When England was caught up in the early days of the Industrial Revolution, scores of children were pressed into the world of manufacturing; working six days a week and causing trouble on the seventh. Historically, education was the purview of parents and poor working people simply were unable to do much in the way of teaching the 3 Rs. Sunday School was introduced in England in the 1780s as a Christian outreach to these poor children; providing a well-rounded education with the Bible as the main text book. This practice spread to the United States and as towns grew, community schools were opened to educate children during the week. Sunday School was slowly relegated to religious education with the community handling the academics.[3]

Vacation Bible School has a similar history, beginning in New York in the early 20th century as Christians sought ways to provide a religious education to children. With lost people being unregenerate, they had little interest in what the church could offer, so "safe" venues were used and sensational themes were developed. Homer Grice, a Baptist elder of the 1920s, developed and "promoted a plan that gave children a daily program to minister to physical, mental, moral, and spiritual needs. He incorporated a patriotic regimen with the still-familiar opening exercises of pledges to the United States flag, the Christian flag, and the Bible. Grice wrote the pledge to the Bible for use in Vacation Bible School."[4]

Both of these programs started off as a means to reach lost and wayward children. Both of them relied on extra-biblical methods to attract and keep the attention of children who knew not the Lord. Both of them brought age-segregation into the church. All three of these things were learned from the world. Many churches have become so concerned with maintaining these programs that they have forgotten what evangelism and discipleship are. Children who were given a marginally Christian education in one or both of these programs grew into parents who desired the same for their children. And so the dramatic, sensational, and often unbiblical messages proliferate and fool people into thinking we are doing good for the children.

The Word of God (Colossians 3:21; Deuteronomy 6:4-7 & 10; 11:19) shows us that parents have the main responsibility of training children in the Word and ways of God, that the Word is to be taught. YHWH has also told us, rather than grouping people by age, younger people are to be taught by older people within the local church (Titus 2:1-6) just as they are at home as their parents fulfill their God-given roles. The education programs of the local church, from small children up to "young adults" must be Word and Lord focused and avoid falling into the trap of what Charles Finney called "new methods." If we trust in the Spirit of God to bring people into the kingdom of lights, we will be faithful to use His methods, the proclamation of His gospel, to do our part. It is too easy to get fooled into thinking the sensational children's programs are doing good because small children and teenagers can easily be influenced to change without being changed by God. We cannot trust in our "new methods" or traditions unless they are clearly taught in Scripture; in which they will not be new.

The goal of raising children is to produce responsible adults. It would do children and adults much good to focus on this and incorporate children around 12 years and older into the normal activities with adults. In this environment they will see how Christian adults behave and learn; we who are such should be sober minded and provide good examples!

Considering Who the local church represents, it is incumbent on every member of every church to be diligent and engaged to contribute to the building of the saints, bringing them to maturity so they won't be tossed about by deceiving spirits and misguided men. No solitary pastor can do this by himself for he stands in need of the same common means of grace God gave the church as those he is supposed to shepherd. And the saints will see God more clearly when they see Him working in two or men laboring in the Word and doctrine and the care for His sheep.

Recommended Reading:
*Ecclesiology** - Edwin Charles Dargan
A Portrait of Paul – Rob Ventura and Jeremey Walker
The Church: Why Bother? – Jeffrey D. Johnson
Building Blocks of the Church – Anton Bosch
The Pastor: Does He Exist? – David H. J. Gay
The Deliberate Church – 9 Marks
*The Glory of a True Church** - Benjamin Keach
*The Church of Jesus Christ as Seen in Biblical Types and Metaphors** - Benjamin Keach
*The Church** - J.C. Philpot
Biblical Eldership - Alexander Strauch
Shepherding a Child's Heart – Tedd Tripp
The Faithful Parent: A Biblical Guide to Raising a Family - Martha Peace and Stuart W. Scott
What Is the Mission of the Church?: Making Sense of Social Justice, Shalom, and the Great Commission – Kevin DeYoung & Greg Gilbert

Chapter 11. Membership: The Body of Christ.

Put on then, as God's chosen ones, holy and beloved, compassionate hearts, kindness, humility, meekness, and patience, bearing with one another and, if one has a complaint against another, forgiving each other; as the Lord has forgiven you, so you also must forgive. And above all these put on love, which binds everything together in perfect harmony. And let the peace of Christ rule in your hearts, to which indeed you were called in one body. And be thankful. Let the word of Christ dwell in you richly, teaching and admonishing one another in all wisdom, singing psalms and hymns and spiritual songs, with thankfulness in your hearts to God (Colossians 3:12-16).

The relationships implied in what Paul wrote about in this passage cannot exist apart from people indwelt by the Holy Spirit loving one another and spending time in all circumstances with each other.

Membership was discussed in Chapter 3, as a fact and its significance. Here we will see the application of these principles. While the physical make-up of each local church will reflect the people who belong thereto, no church ought to make a point of being identified by any social demographic, such as skin color or sub-culture status. A country church in the United States might be completely populated by folks who make their living as or who simply identify as "cowboys," yet it is an insult to Christ Jesus for such a fellowship to call itself a "Cowboy Church." By His blood Jesus bought the saints and calls them His body (Ephesians 5:30) and His temple (1 Corinthians 6:19), wherein there is no Jew or Gentile, free or slave, male or female (Galatians 3:28). Our identity is Christ; why then would anyone think it proper to modify that identify or that of a local church, by name or practice, such as a "Cowboy Church" or a "Black Church" or a "White Church?" If language divides, that is more rational as we are to communicate well with those within and outside our local body. But we must be careful to not allow our culture to conform our local churches to its image just as we must be careful not to allow the world to conform us individually to it. The body of Christ is composed as it pleased Him to do so (Romans 12:3-8; 1 Corinthians 12:14 & 25), we have no cause for thinking we can shape it according to our fleshly desires. We are, as individuals and as local expressions of His body, to glorify His name and not make a name for ourselves.

How are new members brought into the local body of Christ? It is common among Baptist churches for new members to be accepted into membership by "transfer of letter."[1] This process takes the member out of the membership process, with the accepting church taking the word of the previous church that the candidate is a "good Christian." There are at least two problems with this process, apart from the lack of biblical warrant for it. In our day of hyper litigation even among the body of Christ, how likely is it the referring church would issue anything but a good reference? Secondly, it reduces church membership to an impersonal transaction. As we will see below, on church discipline, the Bible records a vital and personal relationship amongst the members of each local church. If membership is reduced to a third party perfunctory reference, it will be much more difficult to teach the people how precious the fellowship our Lord intends for us to have. New members ought to be brought in after expressing a desire join and a simple conversation with the elders to see if they know the gospel and have a credible witness as a redeemed child of God.

Jeff Johnson helps us understand the importance of belonging to a local church, observing that "Although all Christians have an individual and personal relationship with Christ, they are also all called by God to live out their Christianity within the community of God's people. The same Spirit that unites believers to Christ has also united believers to each other."[2] He then provides a concise list reminding us of our Lord's revelation on this topic:

> Those who have a heart for God and His people need no other reason to meet together. But with today's reservations, here are a few additional reasons why being formally dedicated to a local church is a biblical necessity:
>
> 1. Christ instituted the church for the saints; to shun it, therefore, is to view oneself wiser than God (Matt 16:18)
>
> 2. There are Biblical commands which cannot be obeyed outside the membership of a local church:
> > A. One could not obey ruling elders (Heb 13:17; I Tim 5:17)
> > B. One could not properly partake in the Lord's Supper
> > C. One could not come together with other Christians for corporate worship (Col 3:16).
>
> 3. Christians are mutually interdependent (1 Cor 12; Eph 4:16)
>
> 4. The church is a means of sanctification (Eph 4:11-13); therefore, to neglect the church is to neglect the care of one's soul
>
> 5. There are promised blessings for those who assemble together (Matt 18:19-20)
>
> 6. Scripture commands us not to forsake the local assembly (Heb 10:25)
>
> 7. The local church brings God glory (Eph 3:21)[3]

Terrence O'Hare explores the historical context of church membership as the religious war of Europe continued to unfold. As in the first century, when the new-born Christian community was persecuted by Jewish and Roman leaders, so in the time of the Reformation, Christians who did not submit to the state church (mainly the Roman Catholic Church) were fiercely persecuted and many were killed. This situation continues unabated in many countries around the world, where official religions refuse to tolerate and accept those who worship the one true God. This condition, being hated by the world, has made being known and identified as a Christian something of a risky proposition for much of the world's population. But public identification as a Christian, where a child of God aligns himself with a local church, has lost much of its meaning in places where doing so carries little or no risk. The result is that many churches have reduced membership to something less than what is required by most local fitness clubs, being composed by trite rituals with little or no spiritual significance. Historically, there have been two memberships with overlapping requirements and evidence of new birth, as O'Hare sums it up: "we distinguish between 1) the minimum requirements to belong to Christ's universal church – faith alone, in particular soteriological doctrines (Rom 10:10), 2) formal minimum requirements that identify membership in Christ's church – baptism and communion (Acts 2:41 – 42), and 3) the evidential minimum requirements of a plausible faith – an appetite for God's word, acceptance of sound doctrine, a desire to fellowship, a hatred of sin, and love for the saints and the lost (John 8:31 – 32; 1 John 4:1- 6 ; Jas 2:17 – 18)."[4]

We must not allow ourselves into being deceived, thinking we love the body of Christ if we do not care to be around those who locally comprise that body. Some saints stay home and watch a preacher on TV or the Internet but care nothing to worship, pray, fellowship, rejoice, or grieve with brothers and sisters. Christians far away that we empathize with cannot take the place of those we know well enough to admit our differences so we can live out the walk of humility our Lord calls us to. While are citizenship is in heaven, we are commanded to be reconciled to one another in the love of Christ Jesus as His body; by this the world will know we are His (John 13:35)!

Many churches have membership covenants that are intended to teach and remind the saints why they belong to one another in the local church. Such documents must not seek to impose rules not found in Scripture, such as the standard Baptist membership covenant from the 19th century which requires that members "abstain from the sale and use of intoxicating drinks as a beverage."[5] The Bible forbids getting drunk and warns about "strong wine" but does not prohibit the sale or use of alcohol for any but a few, such as Nazarites (Numbers 6:1-7). At the end of the time of his vow, the Nazarite was permitted to drink wine (Numbers 6:13-20). A covenant that saints can embrace as the pure milk of God's Word will help unify them as a local expression of Christ's body. Some form of membership covenant can be most useful if it does not impose extra-biblical constraints on people. Since most American Christians have a very low view of church membership, having a good membership covenant can help them grow in understanding how important this fellowship is.

The Bible is clear: if we love God we will love our brothers and sisters who have been bought by the blood of Christ. And with every aspect of our Christian life, we must be on guard lest we drift away (Hebrews 2:1). O'Hare gives us a good summary of how easy it is for elders to drift off the narrow path: "We have church leaders who are intolerant of any deviation in secondary issues and others that promote a "casual, come-as-you-are attitude (quoted from Ken Sande's "Taking Church Membership Seriously")." Underlying this phenomenon is a pastorate that underestimates the power of the Holy Spirit to lead and guide the saints into truth through Christ-like leadership and the power of their own example."[6] How many Christians have been led astray by a fog in the pulpit on this topic, thinking so little of belonging to one another that they accept a few minutes of polite conversation on Sundays as the fellowship Christ purchased?

Membership in a local church is not a matter of casual convenience nor for the purpose of making one's life easier or having their best life now. Belonging to other Christians is the way He has given us to function as His body in this age; it is the way we can make John 15:35 come alive in our generation. We cannot count on God to honor what He has not given us with regards to His body and how we function together. Obedience to His Word is key to for successful church membership. And fellowship with one another brings opportunity for conflict, as our flesh is always on the prowl to offend and take offense. Hence the need for biblical church discipline.

As often as people and churches get the gospel wrong, likely more Christians are unaware that the Bible has much to say about discipline. The section on church membership in chapter 3 touched on discipline as a way of demonstrating that membership in a local church is a biblical construct. In this section, we will closely examine the texts and how they have been historically applied by those calling themselves *Baptist*.

For most of us, the concept of discipline is likely to be unpleasant, based on the notion that discipline, by its nature, involves punishment for wrong doing. While it is true that correction is one aspect of discipline, athletes, military folk, and many others will recognize the other side of the coin: discipline also covers the positive side of instruction and training. Many Christian authors have summed these two concepts of discipline up in the terms formative and corrective. The first, reflecting discipleship, training, equipping; the second being in response to wrong doing, to correct thinking, behavior.

It is important for us to realize that behavior modification is not the primary aim of Christian life; soul transformation is. This makes it critical that, in the family and in the local church, formative discipline is where we should focus. We are to be making disciples, of our children and of the people of the world, teaching them all that the Lord has said, praying that He would have mercy on them and give them a new heart of flesh. We disciple in the hopes of salvation, we disciple Christians with an eye towards maturity in Christ, so that we will not be tossed about by false teaching (Ephesians 4:11-14). All the while we do this we must acknowledge that we are planting and watering, but God alone grants the increase. We cannot effect soul transformation; God alone saves and He alone satisfies spiritual thirst. And He has condescended to entrust us with His Word, promising to attend its proper teaching to bring about that which we so desire, transforming spiritually dead sinners into new creatures in Christ that thirst for His righteousness. Discipleship, formative discipline, takes place on both sides of this transformation. This is perhaps made most clear in the Great Commission: make disciples, baptize them, teach them. And we want behavior to match the testimony, so the name of Christ is not maligned.

Read how formative discipline is described in a 19th century Baptist church manual:

> The doctrine of formative discipline is taught in such passages as these: "In whom all the building fitly framed together growth unto a holy temple in the Lord: in whom ye also are builded together for a habitation of God through the Spirit." "For the perfecting of the saints, for the work of the ministry, for the edifying of the body of Christ; will we all come in the unity of the faith, and of the knowledge of the Son of God, unto a perfect man, unto the measure of the stature of the fullness of Christ." "Giving all diligence, add to your faith virtue; and to virtue knowledge; and to knowledge temperance; and to temperance patience; and to patience godliness; and to godliness brotherly-kindness; and to brotherly-kindness charity." "Grow in grace, and in the knowledge of our Lord Jesus Christ." Ephes. 2:21, 22; 4:12, 12; 2 Pet. 1:5-7; 3:18
>
> The new convert to the faith of the gospel is a "babe," a spiritual infant, that has "need of milk," and not of "strong meat." Formative church discipline contemplates the vigorous growth of the "babe in Christ" till it is developed into "a perfect man." Bringing the baptized disciples into local church organizations has this purpose in view. They are to be taught "to observe all things whatsoever Christ has commanded." By such observance alone can a church edify itself in love, building up its members on their most holy faith. By such observance is promoted the symmetry of Christian character, and in it are included all the activities of the Christian life.
>
> Formative discipline, in its sanctifying influences, ought to reach every church member. The old, with their gray hairs, should exhibit its beneficial power in the ripeness of the fruits of the Spirit. The middle-aged, in the perfection of physical strength, should also show that it makes them "strong in the Lord and in the power of his might." And the young, in the morning of life, should yield to its plastic touches, that they may become useful laborers in the vineyard of the Lord. All have been redeemed with the precious blood of Christ, and "should live, not to themselves, but to him who died and rose again."[7]

Pendleton went to classify offenses into two categories: personal and general. Some classify offenses into private and public, which designate between the types: certain offenses are against individuals, in private and are no direct, immediate concern of the public. This is based on what we are taught in Matthew 18:15: *If your brother sins against you, go and tell him his fault, between you and him alone. If he listens to you, you have gained your brother.* At this point, the offense is of no direct concern of anyone other than the two involved, the sin and its resolution are private, though the sin committed may indeed end up affecting many other people – at this point, we cannot know. A public offense is contrasted with the private one by being committed in public, where mere observers can be affected. Such offenses may be of a nature as to be contrary to common morality, such as public drunkenness. Pendleton, for reasons he declines to tell us, prefers personal instead of private and general instead of public. Of private offenses, he says,

> Any offence committed by one brother against another, which, if acknowledged and forgiven by the parties, would leave the fellowship of the church undisturbed, is personal. Such an offence, whether committed in private or public, has to do with the two brethren, and not with the church. It can not be brought before the church legitimately till the directions of Christ, in Matt. xviii. 15, 16, are complied with. The offended brother, presuming to bring his grievance before the church, in disregard of these directions, would subject himself to church censure; and the church by considering the grievance would violate the law of her Head. The more this law is studied the more will its wisdom be seen; and the less surprise will be felt at the unhappy consequences resulting from its neglect.[8]

The goal of confronting a brother or sister over a personal offense is not to get vengeance nor to humiliate; it is to pursue reconciliation: *If he listens to you, you have gained your brother.* This is a call for humility, on the part of the offender and the offended, for it is all too easy for our sense of personal pride to rear its ugly head and insist on our way; that which makes us feel vindicated. And lest we think the offended one must initiate reconciliation (as we see in Matthew 18:15), we see instructions (even though in a Jewish synagogue setting) that either party involved is to initiate reconciliation: *So if you are offering your gift at the altar and there remember that your brother has something against you, leave your gift there before the altar and go. First be reconciled to your brother, and then come and offer your gift. Come to terms quickly with your accuser* (Matthew 5:23-25a). This shows us that the one who has caused offense, given his brother something against him, is to seek reconciliation before performing acts of worship. The offender is often blinded by pride and unable to see, unwilling to admit his sin. The offended is often blinded by pride, unwilling to admit he has been wounded and seek reconciliation; each "knowing" the other person should seek reconciliation. We are all blinded by our own pride and need the work of God's Spirit within us to be humble enough to see the truth; we are broken people who need His grace to love one another rightly. This is the bottom line purpose of biblical discipline.

Personal offenses that are not resolved between the two (in accordance with Matthew 18:15) are addressed in the same passage, showing us that the Lord knows us, our weaknesses and sin; and He makes provision for how we are to live with one another. *But if he does not listen, take one or two others along with you, that every charge may be established by the evidence of two or three witnesses* (Matthew 18:16). This hearkens back to the Law given Moses: *A single witness shall not suffice against a person for any crime or for any wrong in connection with any offense that he has committed. Only on the evidence of two witnesses or of three witnesses shall a charge be established* (Deuteronomy 19:15). This is a safeguard established by our Creator and Judge, to protect His people from vindictive men and willful judges. Within the local church we should not expect our brothers and sisters in Christ to have such attitudes, but we know that within us, that is in our flesh, there is nothing good and there are times we act out in the flesh rather than in submission to the Holy Spirit. Hence the safeguard; no charge may be brought before the church on the evidence of a single witness. An unrepentant sinner may deny the charge, he may have a "reasonable" excuse for it. Two or three witnesses are more difficult to mislead than one and less likely for a rogue judge to ignore or manipulate.

The next step in Matthew 18 is: *If he refuses to listen to them, tell it to the church. And if he refuses to listen even to the church, let him be to you as a Gentile and a tax collector.* Pendleton is firm on a point here: "The church, till this point is reached, has nothing to do with the matter. The discipline, strictly speaking, has not been church discipline but the discipline of brethren in their individual character."[9] No charges should be heard by the church unless the preceding steps have been followed. This is another safeguard from the Shepherd of our souls. No rush to judgment upon a mere allegation. Credible evidence, weighed by two or three witnesses, are needed before a brother or sister can be brought up on charges to the church. Once it is taken to the church, the charge must be heard and a decision must be made. If the "defendant" and the two or three witnesses can agree on the facts and the church accepts either the confession and repentance of the one or the recantation by the two or three, the matter ends and all is forgiven. If, however, the one charged refuses to hear the evidence brought by the witnesses, refuses to submit to the church, is contrary to good order and truthful fellowship; then he is the expelled from membership, excluded from fellowship, and treated as the least desirable person. In another passage on church discipline, Paul wrote that we are *not even to eat with such a one* (1 Corinthians 5:11). Don't even eat with this person then purge him. Recall the reaction from the Jews when Jesus ate with tax collectors: *And Levi made him a great feast in his house, and there was a large company of tax collectors and others reclining at table with them. And the Pharisees and their scribes grumbled at his disciples, saying, "Why do you eat and drink with tax collectors and sinners?"* (Luke 5:29-30) Tax collectors were as low and beyond civil discourse as were Samaritans. As the Samaritan woman (John 4) was surprised that Jesus, a Jew, would accept water from her, so the Pharisees and their scribes were dismayed that a Jew would eat with tax collectors and sinners! This was not how Jews were supposed to act! So when Jesus tells us to treat an unrepentant sinner like a tax collector, Paul reminds us that one thing this means is we don't even share a meal with them. This prohibition certainly forbids the fellowship and brotherly love that meals historically brought to participants; it also forbids the sharing of the Lord's Supper with those who are expulsed. Paul went on to say, *Purge the evil person from among you* (1 Corinthians 5:13), this being a citation from many instances in Deuteronomy chapters 13-24, where sinners are punished by expulsion and, often death. Those who refuse to listen to the church are to be dismissed from membership and our only interaction with them should be to treat them as "Gentiles" – those who are separated from God and need the gospel. All our personal friendships and family members are temporal and nothing more if they know not the Lord Jesus. What could be more important than putting the gospel in front of one who professed Christ but has denied the faith by clinging to his pride? This is the goal of all church discipline, both personal and general, private or public: reconciliation and restoration. These steps in discipline are means of grace our Lord has given us to bring about these good ends.

In a short booklet widely published in the 19th century, Eleazer Savage summed up 5 categories of offenses with biblical methods for handling each:

> 1. Minor; the smaller offences; such as should be borne. The distinctive feature of this class is, they are infirmities, natural or acquired. The rule: *We, then, that are strong, ought to bear the infirmities of the weak, and not to please ourselves.*

> 2. Private, or such as cannot be proved. The distinctive feature of this class, is, a lack of evidence. The rule: *Go and tell him his fault between thee and him alone*; or, *Debate thy cause with thy neighbor himself, and discover not a secret to another.*

> 3. Personal, as when one brother injures another in his person, reputation, or property, and there is proof of the fact. The distinctive feature of this class, is, personal injury and proof of it. The rule: *If thy brother shall trespass against thee, go and tell him his fault between thee and him alone; if he shall bear thee thou hast gained thy brother. But if he will not hear thee, then take with thee one or two more, that in the mouth of two or three witnesses, every word may be established. And if he shall neglect to hear them, tell it unto the church; but if he neglect to hear the church, let him be unto thee as an heathen man and a publican.*

> 4. Public, or such as equally injure all the members of the church, and for which all require an equal satisfaction. The distinctive feature of this class, is, equal injury of all, and equal satisfaction to all, the members. The general rule: *Them that sin rebuke before all, that others also may fear.*

> 5. Insufferable. The distinctive feature of this class is, such enormity of offence as requires prompt exclusion for the honor of the cause. The rule, *Put away from among yourselves that wicked person.*

Now this classification of offences, with the distinctive feature of each class; and the rule of treatment in each case, should be as familiar to every church member, as the multiplication table is, to every active arithmetician. To be able to class ever-occurring offences; and to select the rule of treatment, is a great and noble attainment. A good disciplinarian is a good physician. He can heal the difficulty. And why may not all become such?

Discipline is far less difficult of understanding, than we, at first, might suppose. The Saviour's provision for the correction of offences, has a most instructive simplicity. He knew that *offences must needs come*; and offences, too, of various type; and that they must be corrected. And yet, all that he himself has said, and all that his inspired servants have said, is embraced in a few, brief, simple sentences. The direction has meaning enough, for the tallest intellect; and plainness sufficient, for the weakest understanding. The essence of all divine principles and rules of discipline, is this. Now, your brother has done wrong. You must not suffer the sin to pass uncorrected. It would injure your brother, and hurt the cause. You must pity him and go and see him, and show him his fault. And if you do not succeed in helping him to see, and realize, and retrace his wrongs; then you must get one or two to go with you to see him; and to use their influence with him; and if still unsuccessful, you must bring his case to the Church. And if all your kindness and care and effort to save him prove unavailing; then you must, still kindly, but solemnly, and formally, and promptly, exclude him from the Church.

This, we repeat, is the essence of all divine principles and rules of Discipline. How plain! How easy of understanding! Why, then, are individuals and Churches so often whelmed in deepest difficulty, in correcting the wrongs of an offender? We answer; plainly, because simple, as are the principles of discipline; easy, as is the classification of offences; and plain, as are the methods of treatment, few have so accurate knowledge of these things, as to know what to do, in any given case. We fully believe that, in nine cases out of ten, for the want of such knowledge, the injured brother or Church has settled upon some improper course of procedure. And *Behold, how great matter a little fire kindleth!* Zion's sorest troubles have arisen, from the wrong treatment of offences, rather than from the offences themselves, simply considered. Let, then, all thoroughly acquaint themselves with this subject. Let each kind of offence be learned and remembered, in its distinctive feature, and rule of treatment. And we add, with emphasis, let it be done at the right time, when no case is on hand to bias the judgment, if possible. Discipline is generally studied, when we want the knowledge of it, rather than when we may want it.[10]

Why does there seem to be such a wide-spread ignorance of the need, the provision, and the means of discipleship the proper discipline brings? I dare say much of the reason is we do not like discipline and we avoid that which we dislike. But proper personal and general discipline are part of God's grace in chastising

His children. Have we forgotten that those who are not chastised are not true children of God?

> Hebrews 12:3-11 *Consider him who endured from sinners such hostility against himself, so that you may not grow weary or fainthearted. In your struggle against sin you have not yet resisted to the point of shedding your blood.* **And have you forgotten the exhortation that addresses you as sons? "My son, do not regard lightly the discipline of the Lord, nor be weary when reproved by him. For the Lord disciplines the one he loves, and chastises every son whom he receives."** *It is for discipline that you have to endure.* **God is treating you as sons. For what son is there whom his father does not discipline? If you are left without discipline, in which all have participated, then you are illegitimate children and not sons.** *Besides this, we have had earthly fathers who disciplined us and we respected them. Shall we not much more be subject to the Father of spirits and live? For they disciplined us for a short time as it seemed best to them, but* **he disciplines us for our good, that we may share his holiness.** *For the moment all discipline seems painful rather than pleasant, but later it yields the peaceful fruit of righteousness to those who have been trained by it.*

17th century Baptist preacher Benjamin Keach summed up church discipline very well. The over-arching purpose for Christian discipline, he said, is "to *sympathize* with the *afflicted*, *succor* the *tempted*, and *relieving* the *poor* and *distressed*; *rejoicing* with them that *rejoice*, and *mourning* with them that *mourn*."[11]

Church discipline – it's one of the marks of a biblical church; and it cannot be experienced apart from the unity of believers in the local church.

Recommended Reading:
The Church and the Surprising Offense of God's Love: Reintroducing the Doctrines of Church Membership and Discipline – Jonathan Leeman
The Church: Why Bother? – Jeffrey D. Johnson
*Manual of Church Discipline** - Eleazer Savage
*Corrective Church Discipline** - Patrick H. Mell
The Pastor: Does He Exist? – David H.J. Gay
*Baptist Church Manual** - James Madison Pendleton
The Priesthood of All Believers: Slogan or Substance? – David H.J. Gay

Chapter 12. Worship: When We Gather.

If then you have been raised with Christ, seek the things that are above, where Christ is, seated at the right hand of God. Set your minds on things that are above, not on things that are on earth. For you have died, and your life is hidden with Christ in God (Colossians 3:1-3).

When we walk as children of God, individually or together, our focus is on Him Who died to bring us into His kingdom. When we gather to worship Him, if He is not our focus, our worship is false. How, then, should we worship Him?

The main reason the church gathers is to worship our Creator and Savior and Lord. The way we worship Him is in praise, prayer, reading, preaching, giving, and ordinances. These are the things we see practiced in the church as recorded in Scripture. We see several of these things (preaching, praying, taking the Lord's Supper) displayed early in the life of the church (Acts 2:42) and others (giving and reading Scripture) developed later (2 Corinthians 9:12; 1 Timothy 4:13). Worship is also summed up by Paul in Colossians 3:16: *Let the word of Christ dwell in you richly, teaching and admonishing one another in all wisdom, singing psalms and hymns and spiritual songs, with thankfulness in your hearts to God.* The proper preaching of the Word, teaching and correcting each other in His wisdom, praising Christ in song; all done with a thankful heart that owes all to God. That is biblical worship.

As mentioned in Chapter 4 on Sola Scriptura, there is more than one view of how Christian worship should be governed. In addition to the affective principle previously discussed, historically many people held to the normative principle, which claims all things are permitted unless forbidden in Scripture, while others held to the regulative principle. The regulative principle asks such question as "Is our worship God-centered?" "Are our song lyrics faithfully teaching the truths of Scripture?" "Does our worship focus on God and not ourselves?" "Is every element contained in our worship service grounded in God's Word?" "Does it seek to glorify God?" This is a far more biblically solid way to approach the question of how to worship and does not need to be reduced to a list of rules to be followed. The regulative principle seeks to govern the content of worship by Scripture, not the circumstances. This means the building is not important, our prayer, praise, reading, preaching, giving, and ordinances are! Since the people Christ Jesus has redeemed are His temple, using biblical means to build up the saints is the way we honor our God and make the biggest impact in this present age. Let us take a quick look at how these six things mentioned can be done so as to impact the life of the local church and glorify our God.

Here is a short piece from Jeff Johnson that helps us see the importance of Scripture to our corporate worship:

> According to Scripture, the church is to worship in Spirit and in truth (John 4:24). No doubt, worship needs to be objectively based in the truth and subjectively felt and expressed within the heart. Even so, the church is called to fix its worship not upon the

subjective feelings and various "spiritual experiences," but upon the objectivity of the fixed Word of God.

A. Worship must be regulated by the Word because the Spirit convicts, comforts, empowers and sanctifies the saints by the Word. That is, the Spirit works in and by the Word and the subjective feelings must flow from the objective truth of God's Word. The Word is the sword of the Spirit that cuts to the heart. That is to say, the Spirit has chosen to use the Scriptures (which He has inspired) to inflame faith, love and devotion to God.

B. Worship must be regulated by the Word because the church does not have the authority or the ability to impart the Holy Spirit (John 3:8). Therefore, the church must focus upon what it has been given the responsibility to do—preach and teach the truth.

C. Worship must be regulated by the Word because it is the Word that the Spirit has given us to test and examine various spiritual and subjective experiences (1 John 4:1).

For these reasons, worship must be Word-centered.[1]

Sadly, this is often not the case. In many Baptist churches veterans, firemen, et al. are celebrated on Memorial Day and Veterans Day, honoring those who served the public in myriad ways. In one church we belonged to for one very long year, American flags covered the entire interior of the room in which the worship services were held during the week of July 4th. Political flags advertise allegiance to an earthly realm and can do nothing but distract and detract from the worship of God. Why do so many saints embrace the display of political flags alongside the so-called Christian flag? This practice got its start in 1897, as a compliment to the then-common use of the American flag within local churches. There is a pledge of allegiance and a code for the Christian flag. The only thing that can be said in favor of its use is that it portrays the cross. The Bible tells us to preach Christ crucified (1 Corinthians 1:18-24), acknowledging the shame of the cross He bore on our account (Hebrews 12:2). Yet we must bear in mind that we owe no allegiance to any flag, only to our King. And any graphic image we hold up before us can lead us astray as our minds fill in meaning that the image cannot communicate. During the Dark Ages, the Roman Catholic Church discovered the power of images: having vague meaning with various interpretations lent credence to their doctrine that meaning (for images or Scripture) can only be as Rome teaches it. Other things, such as announcements, birthday celebrations, etc., are not worshipful of God, not found in Scripture; they celebrate and honor the creature rather than the Creator.

This leads me to another means of using art in worship that most reformed Christians embrace: architecture. What comprises the basis for the architectural style of a church building? We have no Scripture that directly sheds light on this question, so we must rely on principles that Scripture may provide and history. The types and shadows revealed in the Mosaic Covenant clearly define what structure they were to build for worship, but there appears to be no biblical principles guiding us under the New Covenant in the type of building to use as we gather to worship the Lord.

Holding to the regulative principle, reformers rightly abhor the use of art as elements of worship unless prescribed in Scripture, as with music. We find no such commands for other forms of art to be used in worship. The question for consideration: why are we content to use architecture as an element in our worship? How is the cruciform, described below, not considered art? Church buildings have been described as reaching up to God, by use of high arches and bell towers and steeples, laid out in the form of a cross; clearly an element of worship. Clearly art.

How did the cruciform, the cross-shaped floorplan, come into use?

> As the Western Roman Empire crumbled in the fifth century, illiteracy became the norm. The church was desperate to teach matters of doctrine and faith to a people who had neither access to Scriptures nor an ability to read them. The architectural layout of the worship edifice served as a tool. The church was built in the shape of a cross to teach that the foundation of the church was the cross of Christ. The church faced east because of an understanding that Christ would return to earth from the east (Matt 24:27).
>
> At the head of the edifice were three windows to represent the Trinity as the head of the church. The center of the church (the dome) was elevated to signify that the heart of the cross was closest to heaven and the heart of God.[2]

It is clear from the description above that the church mentioned is the Roman Catholic Church. She did her best to keep her subjects illiterate and ignorant of the Bible. Simple graphics are less specific than the written word, leaving the people more susceptible to being deceived by an unbiblical false gospel. This is implicit in all use of religious art, including architecture.

> Early in the fourth century Constantine the Great became Emperor, and in the course of his reign (from A.D. 312 to 337) he recognised Christianity, and made it the religion of the State. It then, of course, became requisite to provide places of public worship. Probably the Christians would have been, in many cases, reluctant to make use of heathen temples, and few temples, if any, were adapted to the assembling of a large congregation. But the large halls of the baths and the basilicas were free from associations of an objectionable character, and well fitted for large assemblages of worshippers. The basilica, at least in Italy, was followed, to the

exclusion of all others, when new buildings were erected for the purpose of Christian worship; and during the fourth century, and several succeeding ones, the churches of the West were all of the basilica type.[3]

The basilica was a key product of the Ancient Roman and Greek pagan religious cultures, with notable examples in the early 4th century being the Thermae of Diocletian and the Basilica of Constantine. The inexpensive, low-tech construction and wide spread availability of existing buildings built as basilicas made for a natural fit for the newly legal Christian church. "Essentially, the basilica consisted of a rectangular hall separated into three aisles by two rows of columns. The central part, or nave, was carried up above the roofs of the side aisles in order that celestory windows above the side aisle roofs might flood it with light. At the end of the nave was a large aspe, replacing the pagan Roman bema."[4] "In these Roman basilicas we find almost all the essential distinguishing marks of the Christian church building as a type – the nave and side aisles, the aspe and transept, the celestory lighting, the glorified altar, the separated choir."[5]

The Roman Catholic Church, being THE recognized church, built upon this basic form, adding grandiose decorations and architectural details over time; and in the 4th century, developed the cruciform plan that spread to churches all over Europe. With Rome's ecclesiastical model, their churches and associated buildings became town centers, the focus of most all activity in any given town; the better to control their subjects. Based on the basilica, "this type of church was the form and type that has continued in Eastern Christendom to the present day, and has undergone surprisingly little variation."[6]

When the Magisterial Reformers took over church buildings from the cult of Rome, modifications of architectural details (location of altar, pulpit, use of bell tower) were made; and the protestants adopted the *form* of a church building that has its roots in pagan Rome and the Roman Catholic Church because it was less expensive than building new, and – perhaps – because some still held some traditions learned from Rome.

While certain elements of these "traditional" church buildings may be properly used in a church building, it is unclear how we can be enthusiastic about spending money and constructing a church building that echoes its historical roots in the city on seven hills and has no warrant in Scripture.

Considering the history of the architecture normally associated with church buildings, should the form developed by the Roman Catholic Church as an essential part of her ecclesiology and theology be considered good, something to be pursued, as an element of corporate worship? As in other aspects of our Christian lives, we must be willing to sacrifice the idols of our beloved traditions and presuppositions if they do not align with Scripture. We should *not* build doctrine and theology to support them if they are not clearly taught in the Word of God. At the 2016 Together for the Gospel conference in Louisville, KY, Phillip

Jensen (an Anglican from New Zealand) told Mark Dever (a Baptist), that the Baptist talk about the "sanctuary" rubbed him wrong. His sanctuary, Jensen said, was in heaven with Christ! The building was merely a rain shelter. This is the right perspective, avoiding sacred spaces and buildings and rooms and avoiding talking about them as though they are sacred.

In one church we belonged to, the "senior pastor" hired a local man who was a Muslim to paint a logo on the building. He said he had invited the man to our service to worship God with us. Contrary to what some famous Baptists have said, Muslims do not worship the same God that Christians worship.[7] As such, the only reason a Muslim should enter a place of Christian worship is to be confronted with the gospel of Jesus Christ; not as a fellow worshipper of God.

Worship must be God-focused and word-based; not sensual. Old Covenant worship was based on rituals and locations that God had ordained for that people and time, described as temporal types of eternal things (Hebrews 8:1-6). Pagan religions use art, rituals, and sacred locations in their worship. One thing the Lord was teaching with His encounter with the Samaritan woman at the well (John 4) was that sacred places have no place in the true worship of God as revealed in the New Covenant. Far too many Baptists call the church building "God's house," as if it were a modern day temple in the Mosaic Covenant, as if the people were not clearly described as God's temple (Ephesians 2:21 & 22; 1 Peter 2:4 & 5; Revelation 21:1-3) as reviewed in chapter 4. And there are many Baptist churches wherein the space behind the pulpit is a sacred spot only the pastor can stand. This reveals a priestly view of the building and the elder that one cannot find supported in the biblical revelation of the New Covenant church.

All of these practices, and more, reveal a distorted view of the kingdom we serve and in which have our being. It is a spiritual kingdom and all children of God must consistently examine what we believe and practice to see if aligns with holy writ. The wisdom of the age and religion of our youth call to us sweetly but are not the foundation of Truth.

Now we turn our attention to the six activities of worship commended to us by God's Holy Scriptures.

a.) Praise: we lift our voices. Not every song about Jesus is fit or meant to be sung in corporate worship, and some should not be sung at all. The lyrics of every song communicate a message; the theology of hymns and spiritual songs that we sing together ought to be mainly focused on what God in Christ has done to redeem us and glorify His name. Songs that talk about what we have done or will do for Him tend to honor us, draw our attention off our Savior, and should be avoided. We are inclined by nature to think more highly of ourselves than we ought and songs that reinforce that perspective are generally not healthy. Songs that present any member of the Trinity in a common, familiar way, as if He were a gentle old uncle who always buys us gifts do not glorify Him. While we have intimate relationships with each person in the Trinity, He is God – Creator,

Sustainer, Redeemer, Judge, and King over all things and we are the sheep of His pasture. Let us not bring Him down to our level, but recognize what He has done to bring us up to His!

There are far too many Scriptures that tell us to praise God for what He has done, will do, for who He is than can be listed here. One example should convince all that the focus of our praise is to be our God. In Exodus 15 Moses sings a song testifying of the victory YHWH had just given them over Pharaoh's army. Such a great overthrow of the world's greatest military and this entire song has not one phrase about those who were delivered; all is about boasting in our great and mighty God Who won the victory! *The LORD is my strength and my song, and he has become my salvation; this is my God, and I will praise him, my father's God, and I will exalt him. ... Your right hand, O LORD, glorious in power, your right hand, O LORD, shatters the enemy. ... "Who is like you, O LORD, among the gods? Who is like you, majestic in holiness, awesome in glorious deeds, doing wonders? You stretched out your right hand; the earth swallowed them.* All this and more, God's people praising Him for that temporal victory, which would soon fade from their memories. How much worthy is God of our praise for giving us the eternal spiritual victory that we have in Christ Jesus! How much more important is it that we remind one another of His victory over sin and death as we gather together in song! Let us banish songs that focus on the benefits we have gained or will gain because of our standing in Christ. Let us boast in Him and His strength and power and might for His glorious victory over hell and death and sin!

Carefully consider the songs you love; do they praise the finished work of Jesus? Carefully consider the songs used in your worship service; do they relate to the topic of the sermon? If our worship services are not properly planned so the praise and Scripture reading and preaching are all in one accord, the people gathered together can easily get a mixed message that confuses them rather than one that works together to edify them. Our God commands us to worship Him with our minds as well as with our strength. He has given us a mind that can comprehend His truths and He has instructed us to do all things for the glory of His name. Let us be deliberate in choosing the songs we sing as His gathered people.

b.) Prayer: we lift our hearts. In Paul's letter to the Colossians he tells them how he has been praying for them, giving us insight as to what God-honoring prayer looks like. His constant prayer for them was that they would be filled with the knowledge of God's will in all spiritual wisdom and understanding so they their lives would honor YHWH, being fully pleasing to Him and bearing spiritual fruit through good works, patience, and joy. Always giving thanks to God for making us heirs with Christ, having been delivered by Him from death and darkness and transferred into the kingdom of His beloved Son Who has redeemed us from the endless death we were due because of our sin (Colossians 1:9-14). Prayer should mainly be about praise to God and spiritual needs as highlighted above. Fleshly needs are not unimportant but they are secondary as they relate to this age while spiritual needs relate to eternity (Luke 12:29).

In the decades I have been in Baptist churches, the overwhelming number of requests and prayers have been for temporal aches and pains rather than spiritual ones. I recall a friend who asked the Sunday school class to pray for his brother, who had kidney cancer. After a couple of weeks of people praying for his cancer to be healed, my friend cried for these brothers and sisters to pray for his brother's salvation; he was not sure his brother was saved and knew that was far more important than his physical health. This is the right concern, for our time in these fleshly tabernacles is short and we know not our days. Eternity is hard to comprehend because of our nature as time-based creatures. But God has put eternity in our hearts and we must not be satisfied with seeking contentment and comfort in this age while we neglect the age to come.

The main point of prayer is for us to be drawn closer to God. Our purpose is not to inform Him of anything. Whether we are crying out for broken marriages to be healed or confessing our own sin, He knows of these and we are not adding information to His knowledge (Matthew 6:8 & 32). As we recognize His sovereignty and faithfulness, we will be humbled and want to seek refuge in Christ all the more. This He uses to conform us to His Son, which is the purpose He has for each Christian (Romans 8:29; 1 Corinthian 48 & 49).

We ought to be diligent to pray for one another (James 5:16), brothers and sisters being persecuted throughout the world (Hebrews 13:3), and our government officials (1 Timothy 2:1 & 2). We are to ask our elders to pray for us (James 5:14), we are to pray for ourselves (James 5:13), and we are to pray for and with one another (James 5:16). How often have we been in churches where there seems to be no knowledge of those on the prayer list and people simply ask God, Who knows all those who are hurting, to care for those people on the list? We don't truly love these people enough to know their names or spiritual needs. How many prayer lists contain the names of people remotely related to someone, unknown to anyone? Such maudlin sentiments feel good to the carnal heart but cannot satisfy the Christian's desire to draw nigh unto God on behalf of the spiritual warfare raging throughout this age.

Another important aspect of prayer is thanksgiving to God for His provision. *For everything created by God is good, and nothing is to be rejected if it is received with thanksgiving, for it is made holy by the word of God and prayer.* Prayer is serious work for the saints, given to us by our God (1 Timothy 4:4-5). It is common in today's Christian walk to "bless the food" in our prayers. I do not find this taught in the Bible. We do, however, see the Lord Jesus giving thanks for the cup and the bread during the Last Supper (Luke 22:14-19). Being thankful reflects a humble soul who knows his food is a gift, a provision, from Creator God. Recall the Noahic Covenant, wherein YHWH promised to provide the natural means of food generation so saints and sinners would be able to sustain life and prosper to a degree until He returns. He gives us our daily bread, we are to thank Him. By asking Him to bless our food, so we would be strengthened, etc. is closer to superstition than biblical Christianity. Thanking our God for His care for us, providing food and shelter and brothers and sisters in Christ, is far more likely to draw us closer to Him than asking Him to bless our food to the nourishment of our bodies. The object of prayers for blessing is our bodies; the object of biblical prayers is Christ! Even when we are asking God for healing, salvation, reconciliation, etc. our prayers are to be made with thanksgiving, knowing that we are secure in Christ and He will provide what we need even when we don't know what that might be (Philippians 4:6 & 7).

Let us be deliberate in seeking to pray biblically for the people He has told us to pray for and things He has told to pray for. As with our faith, the object of our prayer is important; and the Lord Jesus must be the object of both.

c.) Reading Scripture: We Honor His Word. As pointed out in *The Deliberate Church*, reading Scripture as part of our worship is a God thing, even when there is no explanation or exegesis. Making time to do this declares the value we place on God's Word, showing its authority over us as well as its foundation under us. As men stand and preach, God's people need to know His Word has rule over the preacher rather than his own agenda. Reading the Word and preaching the Word demonstrate this. "Scripture is powerful – even when the person reading it doesn't try to explain it (Jer. 23:29; 2 Tim. 3:16; Heb. 4:12)!"[8] Preaching must be Christocentric and true to the meaning of the text. If you have a deliberate plan for reading from Scripture, you will be amazed at how often it reinforces the sermon (if the sermon is a proper exegesis of His Word).

Dan Phillips provides excellent instruction on how important this is and how it should be approached. Here are his six pointers for doing well in this service.[9]

> **1. Always practice reading the passage aloud.** This may be the most important single pointer. What works inside your head may not get out your mouth, intact. So give it a go, at least once.
>
> **2. Make sure you understand the passage.** That's why, given the option, I always do my own reading. Ostensibly I've studied it, pored over it, marinated my soul in it. I should be ready to read the passage with thought and meaning and proper emphasis. Of course, it isn't a necessity that the preacher also be the reader. But the reader of the passage should first have been a student of the passage.
>
> **3. Don't rush it.** It is an important part of the service. God is speaking to His people. It's not a box to check on the way to the Real Deal. This is the Word of God.
>
> **4. Read it with life.** The last thing a Bible reading should feel like is lifeless and bloodless and monotonous. "Cry aloud; do not hold back; lift up your voice like a trumpet" (Isaiah 58:1) would be good counsel to the man who reads stirring, passionate passages in

assembly. No need for histrionics; but no excuse for soporifics. These are the words of God! Our readings should never sound like Ben Stein ("Beulah? Beulah?").

5. Know how to pronounce difficult words or names. There are plenty of dictionaries. Or, you can ask an authority. Zurishaddai, Kiriath-jearim, or Magor-missabib are just as much part of the inspired text as grace, forgiveness, or love. If they're in the portion you're to read, that's your ministry today. Say them with equal clarity.

6. Read the psalm titles. If your assignment is to read Psalm 32 or 51 or 90, read the title. I was cheered to hear the great Bruce Waltke say (far better) what I've also said for years: the titles and ascriptions (and notations) are as much a part of the text as the rest, and there is no historical reason for rejecting them. They're part of the text we have as the word of God. In Hebrew, the title often is verse one. Skipping the title isn't reading the psalm. Don't leave off part of the Word.

Scripture is the Word of God, it is profitable for life and godliness. When we neglect the reading of God's Word we are passing judgment on ourselves, declaring we treasure worldly things (in the moment) more than the solid gold of Scripture. We ought to be reading it at home and we ought to be reading it in church, with care and thoughtfulness, for our good and the equipping of the saints.

d.) Preaching: We Embrace His Word. Paul's letter to the Colossians also provides rich insight as to how preaching ought to be done and how it is possible. Paul was made a minister of the Gospel by God; given a mission to make the Word of God fully known, making clear what was a mystery wrapped in types and shadows for generations. He was to make known among the people of the world how great and glorious the riches of God in Christ are for those being saved. To this end, Christ is preached and people are warned and taught with all wisdom so God's people will become mature in Christ. To this end, he toils and struggles with all the energy God is working within him (Colossians 1:25-29). Preaching is a glorious task appointed by God make Christ and the Word of God fully known to all the world. It requires work on our part and trust in Him to make it profitable to His saints.

Many consider preaching to be the most important part of a worship. Some consider it unimportant. Since we see preaching as a regular part of New Testament worship (Acts 5:42; 10:42; 1 Corinthians 1:17; 1 Timothy 5:17; 2 Timothy 4:1-4), we know it is of some importance. How we preach, therefore, is important, even if we do not conclude it is most important. Fundamentally, one cannot preach Scripture if he does not comprehend Scripture; one cannot comprehend Scripture rightly if he is not a spiritual being (1 Corinthians 2:14). We know there are many points of view of how we interpret the Word; how does one determine which one is the best? As discussed in Part 3, we need a proper understanding of the covenants found in the Bible in order to properly determine how certain passages and principle apply to the various people we may be preaching to: lost folks or the saints. Each group needs the gospel; the first for salvation, the second for encouragement and reminders of what God in Christ has done for us. No matter what your sermon is about, if it does not present the gospel, you are missing *the* point of Scripture.

There are at least three ways to interpret Scripture, only one of which is correct. Exegesis is reading the Word to see what the Author's intended meaning and application are. Eisegesis is when one goes to the Word to see if your idea can be justified and determining meaning and application by assigning your view to the passage. Narcegesis is reading yourself into Scripture, as if you were Israel, David, et al. and assigning promises or doctrines to yourself that have principles for us, but were only given directly to them.

Properly exegeting the text is essential to equipping the saints; other methods of preaching may satisfy fleshly desires but the hard work of digging truth out and applying it to your life and the lives of the sheep gathered with you is what God calls us to do. One does not need a seminary education to preach well, but he does need to study hermeneutics and preaching skills. David Murray has offered up two short lists that will help anyone who desires to preach well get started. One must select a passage from which to preach rather than deciding what to preach and then find a passage or two that can be used to support his topic. Here is brother Murray's first list:

> **Preacher's Checklist: Selecting a Text**
> 1. Does the text start at the beginning of a thought/passage/paragraph? (By far the most common problem is starting and finishing in the wrong places; breaking into a thought or else finishing before the thought does.)
> 2. Does it finish at the end of a thought/passage/paragraph?
> 3. Is it too long/too short?
> 4. Does it contain one important point?
> 5. Does it contain too many important points?
> 6. Is it the best text for teaching this subject?
> 7. Is it suitable for the congregation, the occasion, the time of year?
> 8. Does it contribute to a balanced preaching diet? [9]

Murray does not make the case for systematic exegetical preaching (the deliberate plan to preach, over time, the whole counsel of God's Word to His people), but he does make the case for paying close attention to the text and how we approach it. If we are to be faithful to the calling as preachers and teachers, Murray's counsel will serve us well. Further, a systematic approach to cover each genre of the Bible in both testaments is what we must do for to do otherwise leaves too much to the wisdom of man and his traditions. God's sheep need sheep food; His elders are to be apt to teach His Word. If we are faithful to be in the Scriptures and seeking to present the story of Christ as redeemer from narrative, poetry, wisdom literature, the prophets, apocalyptic, and epistles, we need to train ourselves to stay in the Word and cover each genre in all of the canon. If we do not, we cannot stand with our brother Paul who said, *I testify to you this day that I am innocent of the blood of all, for I did not shrink from declaring to you the whole counsel of God.* (Acts 20:26-27)

Secondly, our brother Murray provides:

Preacher's Checklist: Exegeting the Text
1. Have I explained the historical background and canonical context?
2. Have I taken account of the genre of the passage?
3. Have I explained who wrote the text, when, why, and to whom?
4. Have I distinguished between what is central and what is peripheral?
5. Have I shown the connections between the text and the previous verses?
6. Have I explained every significant word in the text? (the most common area of failure)
7. Have I incorporated relevant Scripture cross-references?
8. Have I connected the passage with systematic theology, biblical theology, and Christology?
9. Have I checked my exegesis with reliable commentators?
10. Where is the Gospel in this text?[10]

Each of these ten points reveal the depth and breadth of study required to properly stand before God's people and preach His Word to them. No casual reading can pierce our dull minds with the historical and biblical context of any passage; what the main point is; how it connects to other relevant passages; does it properly lead people to the Lord; is something new that nobody has ever presented. There is one sure thing: if you or I are the first one to "discover" a given meaning in Scripture, we can be sure we are wrong! The essential things have been made clear by God to His people from the beginning, giving more light as redemptive history unfolded and more of His special revelation was added to the canon of Scripture. Novelty is loved by the flesh (Ecclesiastes 1:8) but is not found in God's Word. Let this serve as another reminder of the goodness of God in showing us there is more than one man serving as elder in the local church during the apostolic era. No man is strong in every area and two or three elders can sharpen one another in ways not possible with just one standing before the flock of our God.

One point not on Murray's lists that must be in a sermon is the application; how does the text and message preached apply to those listening? A message without an application does not give the hearers a personal identification with the sermon. This last point in the message is the preemptive strike against a "so what?" response. If we are to walk as children of the light, the sermon should help us do that. And that is the role of the application.

"Throughout the history of the church the greatest preachers have been those who have recognized that they have no authority in themselves and have seen their task as being to explain the words of Scripture and apply them clearly to the lives of their hearers. Their preaching has drawn its power not from the proclamation of their own Christian experiences or the experiences of others, nor from their own opinions, creative ideas, or rhetorical skills, but from God's powerful words."[11] The skill of communication is not being put down, it's being put in its rightful place. Only the Word of God pressed by the Spirit of God can change people, this is the authority that comes from the One who had the authority to lay down His life and take it back up again.

Spurgeon told a story of an elderly Scottish preacher who was attending the first service of a young preacher. When the young man had finished, he sought out the older gentleman to ask him what he thought of the sermon. The old man looked the young man in the eye and said, "Not much." "What was the problem with the message?" the young man asked. "There was no Jesus in your message, young man!" "But sir," he replied, "there was no mention of Jesus of the text!" The elder preacher leaned in close and told him, "Son, there's a saying that in England all roads lead to London. Not all of them go straight there, but they all lead there. Every sermon must lead your people to the cross. It may not be a direct route as in the gospel accounts, but even if you have to take them over the hedges and through the swamps, you must take your people to Christ!" (That is my paraphrase of Spurgeon's tale; the essence is the same, his eloquence exceeds mine.)

The point is one that Murray makes: all our preaching must lead people to see their need of Christ, either for salvation or for encouragement to grow not weary in well doing. God forbid we should preach anything that does not include the cross of our Lord Jesus!

e.) Giving: We Love in Deed. Giving to the church may be one of the most contentious topics in the realm of religion. Those who have a form of religion but not the power of God are suspicious that preachers are money-hungry (and, sadly, some are). The early church had a love for Christ and His body that was not inhibited by our natural self-interest (2 Corinthians 8:1-5). If we love God, we will want to give to brothers and sisters in need and not have our own comfort as our first love.

The Bible teaches us the dangers of quick riches (1 Timothy 6:9) because the love of money amounts to idolatry (1 Timothy 6:10). But wealth itself is not sinful and Scripture has instructions on how we are to handle it (1 Timothy 6:17 & 18). Work is honorable and God's people are, if able, to work for their bread and share with brothers and sisters in need and not bring shame on the church or the name of our Savior (Ephesians 4:28; 1 Thessalonians 4:11 & 12). This was practiced by the early church (Acts 4:32-37; 1 Corinthians 16:1 & 2; 2 Corinthians 8 & 9), and in all the record of the early church sharing its wealth with those in need we find no record of one of the modern church's favorite means of encouraging giving, the tithe.

All the talk about tithing in the New Testament falls into one of two categories: activity within the Jewish community (Matthew 23:23; Luke 11:42; 18:11-12) or Abram giving tithes to Melchizedek (Hebrews 7:1-10). Abram's tithe was a one-time offering of war spoils, demonstrating the superiority of Melchizedek. There is nothing to indicate this was part of a weekly tithe. Additionally, Abram gave the other 90% of his spoils back to the king of Sodom so YHWH's enemies could not take credit for Abram's wealth (Genesis 14, see verses 21-24 in particular). Those who teach tithing in the New Covenant do not, to my knowledge, instruct their people to give 10% of their earnings to God and return the balance to those paid it to them. This example fails to support tithing in the New Covenant.

Since Christians are not in the Mosaic Covenant (see part 3 on the covenants), we know that requirements of that covenant do not apply directly to us, but may have a spiritual meaning for us. In these gospel accounts that mention tithing, we see prideful Jewish men who are manipulating the law to their own benefit or boasting of their giving. It is not difficult to see the New Covenant principles that we are to appropriate: our money is a gift from God, just as everything we have is (1 Corinthians 4:7), and we are not to be selfish or prideful in how we handle it. Our wealth is not to become our identity nor our goal, because our flesh will work against us to make it into an idol. And those who trust in uncertain riches will be disappointed (Luke 12:13-21; James 5:1-3). Also, recall from chapter 11 in the discussion of church discipline, the lesson from the Jewish synagogue about giving: in Matthew 5:23 & 24 Jesus portrays giving gifts to God as worship, worship that should not take place when two brothers have something against one another. This highlights the unity in faith and love for one another as essentials in worship.

Since giving to God and His people is an act of worship, as we see it as part of the weekly gathering of saints in the early church (1 Corinthians 16:1 & 2), we must not take lightly the gifts He has given in order that we can share with others. Giving weekly is not a requirement; it is convenient for some. It is not the act of dropping our money in the offering plate that constitutes worship, it is our motive for doing so; although I would caution that our attitude while putting our offering in the basket or plate is important. If our offerings to God through our local church is seen as merely another bill, we need to honestly examine ourselves to see if we are in the faith (2 Corinthians 13:5) more than we need to be giving money. If our heart's desire is not to do good to the brotherhood, then our giving is in vain. We see this in our Lord's Sermon on the Mount, as He describes characteristics of Godly people:

> Beware of practicing your righteousness before other people in order to be seen by them, for then you will have no reward from your Father who is in heaven. "Thus, when you give to the needy, sound no trumpet before you, as the hypocrites do in the synagogues and in the streets, that they may be praised by others. Truly,

I say to you, they have received their reward. But when you give to the needy, do not let your left hand know what your right hand is doing, so that your giving may be in secret. And your Father who sees in secret will reward you. (Matthew 6:1-4)

As with other acts of worship, giving as worship cannot be performed by those who are not clothed in the righteousness of Christ (Proverbs 21:27) and the money earned by sin should not be offered to God (Deuteronomy 23:18). In the passage above we see that the praise of men is the only reward hypocrites have for their giving; it is not accepted by God as are the gifts from the saints on behalf of the saints (Philippians 4:14-18). In one church we were members of for a while, a regular practice was to have little children parade to the front during worship service to toss money (given to them by adults in the congregation as they marched up front) into an offering plate as music is played. As they march out to children's church, people clap. What are these children being taught? It appeared to me that these children played the part of the hypocrites in the passage cited above, with the adults playing the part of the "others" who praised the hypocrites. If we want to teach our unregenerate children the things of God from the Word of God (and we should, praying for YHWH to save them as we teach them), we must be careful to teach them rightly. In this case, to give in such a way as to not bring attention on themselves, for the good of God's people.

It is God that gives us the ability to earn a living; He is the One who gives us all good things (recall the Noahic Covenant). Spending the money He has given us ought to be done soberly, realizing from Whom and to Whom all things come and will return (Colossians 1:16). Let us not take lightly the opportunity to do good to the household of faith (Galatians 6:6-10). For with such sacrifices, by His people, God is pleased.

f.) Ordinances: We Portray the Gospel in Actions. In chapter 2 we reviewed the ordinances given by God to His church: baptism of believers and the Lord's Supper. Herein is a simple reminder that these are God's ordinances, not ours. As with other aspects of worship, we are to follow His instructions rather than our traditions or imaginations. These are "common means of grace" intended to draw us closer to Him as we recall His mercies on us as portrayed in these visible forms echoing His sacrifice and our sacred honor in being called into new life as His people.

We should not impose restrictions nor grant liberties as to who participates or what is performed in each ordinance beyond what is clearly taught in Scripture. Young people who want to be baptized should be closely interviewed by their parents (if they are Christians) and elders to see if there is evidence of new life in Christ. It is very easy for a young child to mimic others and learn the language; it is deceptive for a church to baptize false converts. The author was familiar with church life as a young boy and baptized at eight years of age. But, in the providence of God, I was not saved at the time; there were no signs of new life, no interest in the people or Word of God. I was accepted into membership by several churches before I was redeemed at 38 years of age, demonstrating the ease with which lost people are accepted as members if the local church fails to carefully examine those who desire membership. There is fruit in the life of the redeemed that will testify to the church that he is one of them. Christ did not shed His blood and suffer the wrath of God for people outside His flock. We should not treat goats as sheep; but only offer the means of grace given the church to those who show a credible evidence of having been raised up from spiritual death.

Similarly with the Lord's Supper, since the instructions in Scripture are clear about confessing to one another before taking this ordinance (1 Corinthians 11:27-32) we must be aligned with our Lord in how and to whom we offer it. From the passage Paul wrote it seems clear the context is the local church, not individuals. Within the local church, who should be invited to take this ordinance? While some Baptist churches insist one be baptized and a member of the local church wherein the supper is offered in order to partake, others accept all baptized believers who are members in good standing with any like-minded church. Still other Baptists accept anyone who is willing to accept God as their judge, after giving the warning from Scripture. It seems to me that the restrictions of the first two types go beyond Scripture, though not without reasonable support based on what some would term "good and necessary inference."

For far too many Christians, we "do church" the way we learned from others without regard to seeking to know what the Word of God may say about these matters. Whether one is a Roman Catholic or a Baptist, the danger of traditions of men claiming control over what our worship practice (liturgy — all churches have liturgy) is ever present.

> Church belief — what we call Church tradition — tends to deteriorate in the course of time. It never abides fixed. Tradition is so variable that we cannot depend upon it. There is modification and subtraction. We find this in Jewish history: "making the word of God of none effect through your tradition" (Mark 7:13). Bishop Gore wrote some years ago concerning the Jewish Church, and the Medieval Church, that they had "merged Scripture in a miscellaneous mass of authorities." We must not do this, but keep it separate and supreme.[12]

How we practice the ordinances our Lord has given us should be just as sober minded as our giving, acknowledging our frailty and tendency to do what pleases us rather than worship God with our minds and humbly seek to comprehend how He wants us to worship in these actions required by the ordinances. Before the Lord's Supper is taken, people in the church are to be reminded of the sacrifice of Christ for sin, encouraged to examine themselves to see if they be in Christ. Little children should not be permitted by their parents to partake of the Lord's Supper if they are not able to follow the Lord's instructions that He gave the apostle. By telling small children to let the cup and bread pass them by, parents are given a wonderful opportunity to explain this ordinance and the gospel it portrays. This is the best use of this time given to us when our children are young and curious and without guile. God forbid we should take this ordinance casually, without recognition of the glorious atonement it represents, costing the life of God's Son.

Conclusion.

The Bible reveals the six main activities we reviewed as comprising the worship of God by the early disciples. One thing missing from these elements is *koinonia*, or close fellowship. Fellowship, while a consistent element of the apostolic church, was part of their sharing life together rather than part of their corporate worship. True biblical fellowship is largely missing or misrepresented in church life today. In some local churches the "meet and greet" during worship is considered fellowship while in others time around the coffee pot during Sunday School suffices. But the type of closeness portrayed in Scripture and captured in the Greek word, *koinonia* is more glorious, rewarding, and demanding than the brief, casual interaction found in most gatherings. We get glimpses of this close interpersonal contact believers had with one another in numerous passages, some of which were referenced in the section on church discipline and membership (chapter 11). Hebrews 10:19-25 shows us how the early Christians had a common faith that held them together, had a common expression or confession of that faith, and knew they had to be in each other's lives so they could stir one another to good works and encourage one another, often sharing meals. One will find similar functions of life together in 1 Corinthians 12 and Romans 14. And in the epistle to the church at Philippi (Philippians 2:1-8), we see that Christians are not to be selfish but walk in humility, counting others better than self, and looking to the interests of others; having seen these qualities lived out in the life and death of our Savior. See also 1 Peter 3:8, 4:9, and 5:5 for instruction and encouragement on this topic.

Unless we are willing to submit ourselves to one another in Christ, getting to really know each other to share in the pain and joy, to be used of God to comfort (2 Corinthians 1:3-7), encourage (1 Thessalonians 5:11), instruct (Colossians 3:16), correct (Proverbs 27:6) one another we cannot lay claim to loving one another as our Lord has commanded and equipped us to do. Biblical fellowship within the local church cannot be contained within a couple of hours on Sunday; it can only be experienced by those who are willing to set aside their personal priorities and seek out brothers and sisters with whom they can truly share life. In this our Lord would be truly pleased. Biblical fellowship is not part of our corporate worship, but it is a hallmark of the life of a worshipper.

Recommended Reading:
Why Johnny Can't Preach – T. David Gordon
Why Johnny Can't Sing Hymns – T. David Gordon
*Studies in Strong Doctrine** - Davis W. Huckabee

*Studies On Church Truth** - Davis W. Huckabee
*Why We Do Not Use The Invitation System** – William R. Downing
Dangers of the Invitation System – Jim Ehrhard
Christ-Centered Worship – Brian Chappell
Christ-Centered Preaching – Brian Chappell

Chapter 13. Evangelism: When We Scatter.

Continue steadfastly in prayer, being watchful in it with thanksgiving. At the same time, pray also for us, that God may open to us a door for the word, to declare the mystery of Christ, on account of which I am in prison— that I may make it clear, which is how I ought to speak. Walk in wisdom toward outsiders, making the best use of the time. Let your speech always be gracious, seasoned with salt, so that you may know how you ought to answer each person (Colossians 4:2-6).

With Paul's persistent desire to take the gospel to all the world, he asked a gathered group of God's people to pray for him to have the way opened up to keep on proclaiming the gospel. He told them and us to be wise in how we engage lost people, always speaking truth with grace to each person (see also Ephesians 6:19 & 20). We are ambassadors of His gospel; we should seek to honor Him as we scatter to take His message to our area and the world.

One of the major purposes we are left on this planet after being raised from spiritual death is to take the gospel to every nation, tongue, and tribe; being evangelists and ambassadors of reconciliation. We need to clarify what evangelism is and will begin by identifying a couple of popular practices that are *not* biblical evangelism. First is the idea that inviting lost people to church is evangelism. This reflects the false notion that evangelism is for the "professionals" and it also lets those who are ashamed of or disinterested in Christ Jesus off the hook of being familiar with His message. 1 Corinthians 14:23-25 shows that unbelievers are welcome but not the focus or even normal attendees in the regular worship of the local church. Ephesians 4 teaches that the local church is to be equipped so the sheep will not be tossed about by the wiles of men. Contrary to the idea of inviting lost people to church, YHWH tells us, *So Jesus also suffered outside the gate in order to sanctify the people through his own blood. Therefore let us go to him outside the camp and bear the reproach he endured* (Hebrews 13:12-13). By this, God means we are to *go therefore and make disciples of all nations* (Matthew 28:19); making disciples of those that have answered the call. Evangelism is our outward work; discipleship is our inward work. No church is healthy unless she is active and obedient in both endeavors.

Secondly, many church leaders put emphasis on the personal testimony of those witnessing, rather than making sure they can communicate the gospel. Some even acknowledge that the reason for doing so is because no one can argue with your personal testimony, as it is subjective, whereas the gospel is objective and demands a response. They might argue about the content and the demand of the gospel, but not about what God did for you. This is post-modern thinking and goes directly against the biblical instruction we have as ambassadors of our Lord and Savior (2 Corinthians 5:16-21). While one's personal testimony may reflect the gospel, it is not the gospel.

The essential element in all evangelism is proclaiming the biblical gospel (this was covered in some detail in Chapter 3). By doing so, we take the pressure of our performance and insure we don't contribute to false converts, and we also get confidence in the Word and Spirit of God as we see them do the work that only they can do. Being familiar with the Scriptures will embolden us as we see YHWH has gone before us preparing the soil for the seeds we sow, insuring a good return for His kingdom; see Mark 4:1-9 and:

> *For as the rain and the snow come down from heaven*
> *and do not return there but water the earth,*
> *making it bring forth and sprout,*
> *giving seed to the sower and bread to the eater,*
> *so shall* **my word be that goes out from my mouth;**
> **it shall not return to me empty,**
> **but it shall accomplish that which I purpose,**
> **and shall succeed in the thing for which I sent it.**
> (Isaiah 55:10 & 11)

It is His Word, sent out as He intended, that will not return void, not the 3 minute summary of our personal testimony or a twisted version that He has not commissioned.

As we go about faithfully proclaiming our Lord's message, we would do well to bear in mind that there are two calls involved in evangelism: we give a general call to every creature (Mark 16:15) and God gives an effective call to His elect (John 6:44). Our call is universal, general, and outward, as we do not know who He has chosen to save. His call is specific, effectual, and internal, as He alone knows those chosen before time to be His adopted children (Ephesians 1:3-10) and He will give ears to hear to His elect. We see this graphically portrayed in Scripture in several places, including the scene wherein Paul and Barnabas had been preaching in Pisidia and gained the attention of many people.

> **The next Sabbath almost the whole city gathered to hear the word of the Lord.** *But when the Jews saw the crowds, they were filled with jealousy and began to contradict what was spoken by Paul, reviling him. And Paul and Barnabas spoke out boldly, saying, "It was necessary that the word of God be spoken first to you. Since you thrust it aside and judge yourselves unworthy of eternal life, behold, we are turning to the Gentiles. For so the Lord has commanded us, saying,*
>
> *"'I have made you a light for the Gentiles,*
> *that you may bring salvation to the ends of the earth.'"*
>
> *And* **when the Gentiles heard this, they began rejoicing and glorifying the word of the Lord, and as many as were appointed to eternal life believed.** *And the word of the Lord was spreading throughout the whole region.* **But the Jews incited the devout women of high standing and the leading men of the city, stirred up persecution against Paul and Barnabas, and drove them out of their district.** *But they shook off the dust from their feet*

against them and went to Iconium. And the disciples were filled with joy and with the Holy Spirit. (Acts 13:44-52)

The message preached is found in verses 16-41. Gentiles and Jews heard the same general call, bringing them the good news that what God had promised to the Fathers He had fulfilled by raising Jesus from the dead. The seed fell on some rocky and thorny soil, but it fell on some good soil that had been prepared in advance by the good husbandman (John 15:1). As we see in the well-known road to Emmaus scene, it is YHWH Who keeps people from seeing or understanding until the right time (Luke 24:15 & 16; 30 & 31).

Jesus gave this general call in Matthew 11:28 and John 7:37, as people without respect to their persons were called to come to Him and find rest, to come to Him and satisfy their thirst. This is also the context of Peter's sermon recorded in Acts 2, as men from myriad countries and religious beliefs (verses 9-11) were called to repent and be baptized (as a sign of their belief). The problem with this call is the same problem the Jews had with their Law: neither one can save or enable the hearer to be saved. People can claim to obey the law (Luke 18:18-23) and they can ignore or refute the words of men (Luke 14:15-24).

The general and effectual calls are likewise revealed to us explicitly in Acts 16, wherein we see Paul, Timothy, and Silas making a journey which finds them in Philippi where they stayed for a while. *And on the Sabbath day we went outside the gate to the riverside, where we supposed there was a place of prayer, and* **we sat down and spoke to the women who had come together. One who heard us** *was a woman named Lydia, from the city of Thyatira, a seller of purple goods, who was a worshiper of God.* **The Lord opened her heart to pay attention to what was said by Paul.** *And after she was baptized, and her household as well, she urged us, saying, "If you have judged me to be faithful to the Lord, come to my house and stay." And she prevailed upon us* (verses 13 - 15). A good number of women who were somewhat aware of God had gathered at the river and all had heard Paul's gospel message as the *general call* went out without restriction. At least this one had her heart opened by YHWH so that she heard the *effectual call* and was obedient to follow in believer's baptism.

There are some who think the Law ought to be a part of the gospel, as people need to be convicted of their sin before they can see the need of grace. The law provokes us and reveals sin in us, but cannot grant eternal life. John Bunyan is thought to have written this little poem (which appears to be based on one by John Berridge), showing us with memorable lines the difference between the Law and the Gospel:

> Run, John, Run! The Law commands;
> But gives me neither feet nor hands.
> Far grander news the gospel brings;
> It bids me fly and GIVES ME WINGS!

Our Savior has said something similar, in Paul's Roman epistle: *For God has done what the law, weakened by the flesh, could not do. By sending his own Son in the likeness of sinful flesh and for sin, he condemned sin in the flesh, in order that the righteous requirement of the law might be fulfilled in us, who walk not according to the flesh but according to the Spirit* (Romans 8:3 & 4).

The gospel is the good news of what Jesus has done to save sinners. Our focus must be on that message, not 4 spiritual laws or any other nifty scheme man may have invented to make witnessing easy. We are not called to a life of ease; we are called to obedience. We are ambassadors of His message of reconciliation, not a one-off message of our own making. While the Law may rightly be used to show a self-righteous religious man his sin; it is not part of the gospel that every spiritually dead person must hear. Seeing the holiness of God in Christ, even in part, will do more to crush self-righteousness (as in the opening scene in Isaiah 6) than all the heavy yoke of the Law can bring to bear for the one who is being called to new life by the Spirit of the living God.

Much of the activity in a local church under the flag of evangelism takes place in what are called revivals. This is a logical progression under the previously mentioned idea that evangelism is bringing lost people to church. It appears that there is a belief that a specially called meeting with an out-of-town preacher will create an environment for sinners to be saved. I cannot commend revival meetings because I do not find them revealed or recommended in Scripture; I do not find them practiced by the early church; they presume man can schedule the work of the Holy Spirit; they rely on someone other than the shepherd of the local flock to feed them; and they influence many to chase numbers rather than spiritual growth. A century ago, a brother sounded a warning to the church regarding this practice:

> The modern "revival," the work of the "revivalist" who comes under the title of an evangelist, but works as a religious promoter in the organized church, is unexpected in Scripture, except as the word "revival" is used to denote a forward movement in the spiritual life of the church, without including the idea of attempting to regain some spiritual position once held, but now lost. The use of the word usually means, however, a getting up after having fallen down, or a waking after sleeping, or a coming to strength after a period of weakness; while, on the other hand, the Scripture pre-supposes a continual erect, wakeful and aggressive position for service on the part of every Christian (Eph. vi. 10-17). **Thus, it may be seen, a "revival" is abnormal rather than normal. It may have a function when needed, but in no way should become a habit, much less a sanctioned method of work.** Having regained vitality, believers are not warranted in habitually returning to an anaemic state. ... **The fact that a "revival" is planned for is a confession on the part of a church of a condition which would render the normal movements of the**

Spirit in salvation impossible. The call for the evangelist, under those conditions, also reveals the fact that the expectation of the church, to a great extent, is toward the man that is invited, rather than toward the Holy Spirit and His appointed ministry through the church itself.[1] (emphasis mine)

Evangelism, like all kingdom work, must be in accordance with the instructions and principles clearly given to us by our God. As discussed in chapters 4 and 5, regarding the nature and use of Scripture, when we use what man has developed to further kingdom work rather than what God has given us, we are revealing a greater trust in man than we have in our Creator. And this should never be the case for people of the Book! God is a jealous God and He will not give His glory to another. There is safety in our standing on and under the Word of God; it is His authority and revelation to us. History aligns with Scripture in bearing this out, as the following short extract from an early debate between the reformers and Rome reveals.

Charles Eck had been sent by Rome to Germany to refute what Luther, Melanchthon and others had written in the Augsburg Confession; a document intended to declare essential doctrines and not to be the handmaid or rival to the Word of God. The Duke of Bavaria was the judge. After listening to the reaction to the confession, he asked Rome's defenders, "can you refute by sound reasons the Confession made by the elector and his allies?" – "With the writings of the apostles and prophets – no!" replied Eck; "but with those of the Fathers and of the councils – yes!"[2] As was pointed out in chapter 5 regarding the use of confessions, this peek into history reveals the absurdity of using man's documents to defend Christian disputes. If we cannot, by sound reason, defend our beliefs and practices by the writings of the apostles and prophets, we have no business expounding them as Christian doctrine or practice.

When man claims to accomplish by the flesh what only God can do, we steal glory from God and He will not allow that to continue. It is His work to raise sinners to life, as He breathed life into Adam, as He gave life to 4-days dead Lazarus by calling him forth. Let us abandon the false hope that we can defer to pastor-man or that we can cause God to respond to our schedule and schemes. It is His kingdom, His Word, His temple; He is building the New Jerusalem with spiritual stones that He gathers from every nation, tribe, and tongue. We can work with Him or against Him. 'Tis a far better thing for professing Christians to work with God than in opposition to Him. May it be so with us, as we herald His glorious name throughout the world.

Recommended Reading:

True Evangelism* - Lewis Sperry Chafer
The Art of Manfishing* - Thomas Boston
Reformed Approach to Evangelism* - Kim Riddlebarger
The Altar Call* - Fred G. Zaspel
The Gospel Worthy of All Acceptation, Or, the Duty of Sinners to Believe in Jesus Christ* - Andrew Fuller
The Plain Man's Pathway to Heaven* - Arthur Dent
Evangelism and the Sovereignty of God – J.I. Packer
The Soul Winner – Charles Haddon Spurgeon
What Is the Mission of the Church?: Making Sense of Social Justice, Shalom, and the Great Commission – Kevin DeYoung & Greg Gilbert

Conclusion.

Being Baptist is not important for the sake of that name; it is important for the sake of His name. The doctrines we hold to must be His doctrines and not the outworking of our traditions. While we will have traditions, let us not drift into holding those as sacred but cling only to the clear teachings of Scripture. We need to recognize that our theology will influence how we live; we must work to keep our theology Christ-focused.

As we examine ourselves and our churches, let us submit to the Word of God and one another in the love of Christ, for His glory alone. As we do so we will discover there are two spheres in which the local church works. Here is how one brother summed it up:

> There are two movements in the Church: one is effected inwardly, and its object is its preservation; the other is effected outwardly, and its object aimed at is its propagation. There is thus a doctrinal Church and a missionary Church. These two movements ought never to be separated, and whenever they are disunited, it is because of the spirit of man, and not the Spirit of God prevails.[3]

Many people try to make church overly simple and claim it is only about evangelism or only about discipleship. This argument has no more merit than that over the nature of Christ: is He a man or is He God? He is both! And His body, the church universal and each local church is to be focused on making disciples and sowing the seeds so the harvest will be full. It is not our job nor is it within our capability to save anyone, nor can we truly disciple anyone that YHWH has not saved. We must be diligent in our work inside and without our church, trusting God to grant the increase; knowing He will be faithful to gather all His elect, having condescended to allow us to participate in His plan of redemption.

One cannot be a casual Christian, for the world will never stop trying to conform us to its image. We must continually strive to honor the Lord Who bought us and mortify the sinful desires of our flesh. A wise man once observed, "The path of least resistance makes both men and rivers crooked." The Lord of Heaven will make our paths straight.
Seek Him while He may be found and grow not weary in well doing, for in due time you will reap if you faint not.

May all who claim the name of Christ be understanding the times in which live and constantly on guard, to be not captive to man's traditions, confessions, or systems. Let us search out the truths in Scripture and be only *Captive to the Word of God.*

Appendix 1: Guidance for Deacon Ministry

This is a document intended to inform the members of a local church how the deacons and elders would work together to provide temporal and spiritual guidance and support to the flock gathered there and to make clear to the members their responsibilities to their families and fellow sheep.

Public Guidance for Managing Benevolence Funds

The elders entrust to the deacons management of the church's benevolence funds, according to the following guidance and the approved church budget. The goal in providing benevolence includes meeting the current need of and equipping the recipient for the future provision of the family through work. The benevolence ministry structure is designed to systematically teach Godly stewardship, careful management of money and adequate provision for the family.

Any two deacons can approve the expenditure of up to $250, no more than monthly; additional expenditures by any other combination of two deacons are permitted. Four deacons are required to approve expenditures greater than $250. All expenditures are to comply with the church's budget.

The deacons will provide to the elders a monthly report on families in need and year-to-date expenditures.

The church's benevolence funds will be used only for church members. (Galatians 6:10 & James 2:15 – 17)

The deacons will prioritize orphans and widows who are not assisted by their own families. (James 1:27 & 1 Timothy 5:9 – 16)

The church's benevolence funds will not be used to pay off mortgages on homes, loans on businesses, or to pay off debts of families who have worked their way into bankruptcy or foreclosure. (1 Timothy 5:8)

The following criteria are among those that will be used by the deacons to identify those in need and their specific needs:
* Do you have any savings that can be used?
* Present the family budget to your deacon for review or work with him to develop one.
* What is the plan to generate additional cash flow into the household?
* Have you asked your family for assistance?

Assistance for needs caused by calamities & emergencies, such as accidents, storms, flood and fire may be provided for without regard to the needs-based criteria described elsewhere in this document, at the discretion of the deacons.

Family resources (including savings, retirement, and home equity) should be applied first before church funds made available for recurring needs. For recurring requests, sons older than 14 would be required to seek work to help support the family. (1 Timothy 5:8)

Any family receiving regular monthly support will receive 2 to 4 visits from deacons and at least one visit from an elder in a given month, in order to maintain careful spiritual and financial accountability.

For the purpose of this ministry, family consists of the children, parents, grandparents and siblings within each generation (1 Timothy 5:4) and "recurring" means 3 or more requests for assistance within any 12 month period. Only adult family members have obligations to support their family.

Any exceptions to the above guidance must be approved the elders of the church. (1 Tim 5:17 & 1 Peter 5:1 & 2)

Appendix 2: A Comparison Between Arminianism and Calvinism

THE "FIVE POINTS" OF ARMINIANISM	THE "FIVE POINTS" OF CALVINISM
Free Will or Human Ability Although human nature was seriously affected by the fall, man has not been left in a state of total spiritual helplessness. God graciously enables every sinner to repent and believe, but He does not interfere with man's freedom. Each sinner possesses a free will, and his eternal destiny depends on how he uses it. Man's freedom consists of his ability to choose good over evil in spiritual matters; his will is not enslaved to his sinful nature. The sinner has the power to either cooperate with God's Spirit and be regenerated or resist God's grace and perish. The lost sinner needs the Spirit's assistance, but he does not have to be regenerated by the Spirit before he can believe, for faith is man's act and precedes the new birth. Faith is the sinner's gift to God; it is man's contribution to salvation.	**Total Inability or Total Depravity** Because of the fall, man is unable of himself to savingly believe the gospel. The sinner is dead, blind, and deaf to the things of God; his heart is deceitful and desperately corrupt. His will is not free, it is in bondage to his evil nature, therefore, he will not — indeed he cannot — choose good over evil in the spiritual realm. Consequently, it takes much more than the Spirit's assistance to bring a sinner to Christ — it takes regeneration by which the Spirit makes the sinner alive and gives him a new nature. Faith is not something man contributes to salvation but is itself a part of God's gift of salvation— it is God's gift to the sinner, not the sinner's gift to God.
Conditional Election God's choice of certain individuals unto salvation before the foundation of the world was based upon His foreseeing that they would respond to His call. He selected only those whom He knew would of themselves freely believe the gospel. Election therefore was determined by or conditioned upon what man would do. The faith which God foresaw and upon which He based His choice was not	**Unconditional Election** God's choice of certain individuals unto salvation before fore the foundation of the world rested solely in His own sovereign will. His choice of particular sinners was not based on any foreseen response or obedience on their part, such as faith, repentance, etc. On the contrary, God gives faith and repentance to each individual whom He selected. These acts are the result, not the cause God's choice. Election

given to the sinner by God (it was not created by the regenerating power of the Holy Spirit) but resulted solely from man's will. It was left entirely up to man as to who would believe and therefore as to who would be elected unto salvation. God chose those whom He knew would, of their own free will, choose Christ. Thus the sinner's choice of Christ, not God's choice of the sinner, is the ultimate cause of salvation.

therefore was not determined by or conditioned upon any virtuous quality or act foreseen in man. Those whom God sovereignly elected He brings through the power of the Spirit to a willing acceptance of Christ. Thus God's choice of the sinner, not the sinner's choice of Christ, is the ultimate cause of salvation.

Universal Redemption or General Atonement

Christ's redeeming work made it possible for everyone to be saved but did not actually secure the salvation of anyone. Although Christ died for all men and for every man, only those who believe on Him are saved. His death enabled God to pardon sinners on the condition that they believe, but it did not actually put away anyone's sins. Christ's redemption becomes effective only if man chooses to accept it.

Particular Redemption or Limited Atonement

Christ's redeeming work was intended to save the elect only and actually secured salvation for them. His death was a substitutionary endurance of the penalty of sin in the place of certain specified sinners. In addition to putting away the sins of His people, Christ's redemption secured everything necessary for their salvation, including faith which unites them to Him. The gift of faith is infallibly applied by the Spirit to all for whom Christ died, therefore guaranteeing their salvation

The Holy Spirit Can Be Effectually Resisted

The Spirit calls inwardly all those who are called outwardly by the gospel invitation; He does all that He can to bring every sinner to salvation. But inasmuch as man is free, he can successfully resist the Spirit's call. The Spirit cannot regenerate the sinner until he believes; faith (which is man's contribution) precedes and makes possible the new birth. Thus, man's free will limits the Spirit in the

The Efficacious Call of the Spirit or Irresistible Grace

In addition to the outward general call to salvation which is made to everyone who hears the gospel, the Holy Spirit extends to the elect a special inward call that inevitably brings them to salvation. The eternal call (which is made to all without distinction) can be, and often is, rejected; whereas the internal call (which is made only to the elect) cannot be rejected; it always results in conversion. By mean, of this application of Christ's saving work. The Holy Spirit can only draw to Christ those who allow Him to have His way with them. Until the sinner responds, the Spirit cannot give life. God's grace, therefore, is not invincible; it can be, and often is, resisted and thwarted by man.

special call the Spirit irresistibly draws sinners to Christ. He is not limited in His work of applying salvation by man's will, nor is He dependent upon man's cooperation for success. The Spirit graciously causes the elect sinner to cooperate, to believe, to repent, to come freely and willingly to Christ. God', grace. therefore, is invincible; it never fails to result in the salvation of those to whom it is extended.

Falling From Grace
Those who believe and are truly saved can lose their salvation by failing to keep up their faith. etc. All Arminian, have not been agreed on this point; some have held that believers are eternally secure in Christ — that once a sinner is regenerated. he can never be lost.

Perseverance of the Saints
All who are chosen by God, redeemed by Christ, and given faith by the Spirit are eternally saved. They are kept in faith by the power of Almighty God and thus persevere to the end.

According to Arminianism: Salvation is accomplished through the combined efforts of *God* (who takes the initiative) and *man*(who must respond)—man's response being the determining factor. God has provided salvation for everyone, but His provision becomes effective only for those who, of their own free will, "choose" to cooperate with Him and accept His offer of grace. At the crucial point, man's will plays a decisive role; thus man, not God, determines who will be the recipients of the gift of salvation.

According to Calvinism: Salvation is accomplished by the almighty power of the Triune God. The Father chose a people, the Son died for them, the Holy Spirit makes Christ's death effective by bringing the elect to faith and repentance, thereby causing them to willingly obey the gospel. The entire process (election, redemption, regeneration) is the work of God and is by grace alone. Thus *God,* not man, determines who will be the recipients of the gift of salvation.

REJECTED by the Synod of Dort. This was the system of thought contained in the "Remonstrance" (though the "five points" were not originally arranged in this order). It was submitted by the Arminians to the Church of Holland in 1610 for adoption but was rejected by the Synod of Dort in 1619 on the ground that it was unscriptural.	**REAFFIRMED** by the Synod of Dort. This system of theology was reaffirmed by the Synod of Dort in 1619 as the doctrine of salvation contained in the Holy Scriptures. The system was at that time formulated into "five points" (in answer to the five points submitted by the Arminians) and has ever since been known as "the five points of Calvinism."

Appendix 3: The Forgotten Confession

The First London Baptist Confession of Faith, 1646

The first edition was published in 1644. This second edition "corrected and enlarged" was originally published in 1646.

A confession of faith of seven congregations or churches of Christ in London, which are commonly, but unjustly called Anabaptists; published for the vindication of the truth and information of the ignorant; likewise for the taking off those aspersions which are frequently, both in pulpit and print, unjustly cast upon them. Printed at London, Anno 1646.

I. The Lord our God is but one God, whose subsistence is in Himself; whose essence cannot be comprehended by any but himself, who only hath immortality, dwelling in the light, which no man can approach unto; who is in Himself most holy, every way infinite, in greatness, wisdom, power, love, merciful and gracious, long-suffering, and abundant in goodness and truth; who giveth being, moving, and preservation to all creatures.
1 Cor. 8:6, Isa. 44:6, 46:9, Exod. 3:14, 1 Tim 6:16, Isa. 43:15; Ps. 147:5, Deut. 32:3; Job 36:5; Jer. 10:12, Exod. 34:6,7, Acts 17:28; Rom. 11:36.

II. In this divine and infinite Being there is the Father, the Word, and the Holy Spirit; each having the whole divine Essence, yet the Essence undivided; all infinite without any beginning, therefore but one God; who is not to be divided in nature, and being, but distinguished by several peculiar relative properties.
1 Cor. 1:3; John 1:1, 15:26, Exod. 3:14; 1 Cor. 8:6

III. God had decreed in Himself, before the world was, concerning all things, whether necessary, accidental or voluntary, with all the circumstances of them, to work, dispose, and bring about all things according to the counsel of His own will, to His glory: (Yet without being the [chargeable] author of sin, or having fellowship with any therein) in which appears His wisdom in disposing all things, unchangeableness, power, and faithfulness in accomplishing His decree: And God hath before the foundation of the world, foreordained some men to eternal life, through Jesus Christ, to the praise and glory of His grace; [having foreordained and] leaving the rest in their sin to their just condemnation, to the praise of His justice.
Isa. 46:10; Eph. 1:11, Rom. 11:33, Ps. 115:3; 135:6, 33:15; 1 Sam. 10:9, 26, Prov. 21:6; Exod. 21:13; Prov. 16:33, Ps. 144, Isa. 45:7, Jer. 14:22, Matt. 6:28, 30; Col. 1:16, 17; Num. 23:19, 20; Rom. 3:4; Jer. 10:10; Eph. 1:4,5; Jude 4, 6; Prov. 16:4.

IV. In the beginning God made all things very good; created man after His own image, filled with all meet perfection of nature, and free from all sin; but long he abode not in this honor; Satan using the subtlety of the serpent to seduce first Eve, then by her seducing Adam; who without any compulsion, in eating the

forbidden fruit, transgressed the command of God, and fell, whereby death came upon all his posterity; who now are conceived in sin, and by nature the children of wrath, the servants of sin, the subject of death, and other miseries in this world, and for ever, unless the Lord Jesus Christ set them free.
Gen. 1:1, Col. 1:16, Isa. 45:12, 1 Cor. 15:45, 46; Eccles. 7:29; Gen. 3:1,4,5; 2 Cor. 11:3, 1 Tim. 2:14; Gal. 3:22; Rom. 5:12, 18, 19, 6:22; Eph. 2:3.

V. God in His infinite power and wisdom, doth dispose all things to the end for which they were created; that neither good nor evil befalls any by chance, or without His providence; and that whatsoever befalls the elect, is by His appointment, for His glory, and their good.
Job 38:11; Isa. 46:10,11, Eccles. 3:14, Mark 10:29,30; Exod. 21:13; Prov. 16:33, Rom. 8:28.

VI. All the elect being loved of God with an everlasting love, are redeemed, quickened, and saved, not by themselves, nor their own works, lest any man should boast, but, only and wholly by God, of His own free grace and mercy, through Jesus Christ, who is made unto us by God, wisdom, righteousness, sanctification, and redemption, and all in all, that he that rejoiceth, might rejoice in the Lord.
Jer. 31:2; Eph. 1:3, 7, 2:8,9; 1 Thess. 5:9, Acts 13:48; 2 Cor. 5:21; Jer. 9:23,24; 1 Cor. 1:30,31; Jer. 23:6.

VII. And this is life eternal, that we might know Him the only true God, and Jesus Christ whom He hath sent. And on the contrary, the Lord will render vengeance, in flaming fire, to them that know not God, and obey not the gospel of Jesus Christ.
John 17:3; Heb. 5:9, 2 Thess. 1:8; John 6:36.

VIII. The rule of this knowledge, faith, and obedience, concerning the worship of God, in which is contained the whole duty of man, is (not men's laws, or unwritten traditions, but) only the word of God contained [viz., written] in the holy Scriptures; in which is plainly recorded whatsoever is needful for us to know, believe, and practice; which are the only rule of holiness and obedience for all saints, at all times, in all places to be observed.
Col. 2:23; Matt 15:6,9; John 5:39, 2 Tim. 3:15,16,17; Isa. 8:20; Gal. 1:8,9; Acts 3:22,23.

IX. The Lord Jesus Christ, of whom Moses and the Prophets wrote, the Apostles preached, He is the Son of God, the brightness of His glory, etc. by whom He made the world; who upholdeth and governeth all things that He hath made; who also when the fulness of time was come, was made of a woman, of the tribe of Judah, of the seed of Abraham and David; to wit, of the virgin Mary, the Holy Spirit coming down upon her, the power of the most High overshadowing her; and He was also tempted as we are, yet without sin.
Gen. 3:15, 22:18, 49:10; Dan. 7:13, 9:24, etc.; Prov. 8:23; John 1:1,2,3; Heb. 1:8; Gal. 4:4; Heb. 7:14; Rev. 5:5; Gen. 49:9,10, Rom. 1:3, 9:10; Matt. 1:16; Luke 3:23,26; Heb. 2:16; Isa. 53:3,4,5; Heb. 4:15.

X. Jesus Christ is made the mediator of the new and everlasting covenant of grace between God and man, ever to be perfectly and fully the prophet, priest, and king of the Church of God for evermore.
1 Tim. 2:5; Heb. 9:15; John 14:6; Isa. 9:6.7.

XI. Unto this office He was appointed by God from everlasting; and in respect of his manhood, from the womb called, separated, and anointed most fully and abundantly with all gifts necessary, God having without measure poured out His Spirit upon Him.
Prov. 8:23; Isa. 42:6, 49:15; 11:2,3,4,5, 61:1,2; Luke 4:17, 22; John 1:14, 26, 3:34.

XII. Concerning His mediatorship, the Scripture holds forth Christ's call to His office; for none takes this honor upon Him, but He that is called of God as was Aaron, it being an action of God, whereby a special promise being made, He ordains His Son to this office; which promise is, that Christ should be made a sacrifice for sin; that He should see His seed, and prolong His days, and the pleasure of the Lord shall prosper in His hand; all of meer free and absolute grace towards God's elect, and without any condition foreseen in them to procure it.
Heb. 5:4,5,6, Isa. 53:10,11; John 3:16; Rom. 8:32.

XIII. This office to be mediator, that is, to be prophet, priest, and king of the Church of God, is so proper to Christ, that neither in whole, or any part thereof, it cannot be transferred from Him to any other.
1 Tim. 2:5; Heb. 7:24; Dan. 7:14; Acts 4:12; Luke 1:33; John 14:6.

XIV. This office to which Christ is called, is threefold; a prophet, priest, and king: This number and order of offices is necessary, for in respect of our ignorance, we stand in need of His prophetical office; in respect of our great alienation from God, we need His priestly office to reconcile us; and in respect of our averseness and utter inability to return to God, we need His kingly office, to convince, subdue, draw, uphold and preserve us to His heavenly kingdom.
Deut. 18:15; Acts 3:22,23; Heb. 3:!, 4:14,15; Ps. 2:6; 2 Cor. 5:20; Acts 26:18; Col. 1:21; John 16:8, Ps. 110:3; Song of Sol. 1:3; John 6:44; Phil. 4:13; 2 Tim. 4:18.

XV. Concerning the prophecy of Christ, it is that whereby He hath revealed the will of God, whatsoever is needful for His servants to know and obey; and therefore He is called not only a prophet and doctor, and the apostle of our profession, and the angel of the covenant, but also the very wisdom of God, in whom are hid all the treasures of wisdom and knowledge, who for ever continueth revealing the same truth of the gospel to His people.
John 1:18; 12:49,50; 17:8; Deut. 18:15; Matt. 23:10; Heb. 3:1; Mal. 3:1; 1 Cor. 1:24; Col. 2:3.

XVI. That He might be a prophet every way complete, it was necessary He should be God, and also that He should be man; For unless He had been God, He could

never have perfectly understood the will of God; and unless He had been man, He could not suitably have unfolded it in His own person to men.
John 1:18; Acts 3:22; Deut. 18:15; Heb. 1:1.

Note: That Jesus Christ is God is wonderfully and clearly expressed in the Scriptures. He is called the mighty God, Isa. 9:6. That Word was God, John 1:1. Christ, who is God over all, Rom 9:5. God manifested in the flesh, 1 Tim. 3:16. The same is very God, 1 John 5:20. He is the first, Rev. 1:8. He gives being to all things, and without Him was nothing made, John 1:2. He forgiveth sins, Matt. 9:6. He is before Abraham, John 8:58. He was and is, and ever will be the same, Heb. 13:8. He is always with His to the end of the world, Matt. 28:20. Which could not be said of Jesus Christ, if He were not God. And to the Sone He saith, Thy throne, O God, is forever and ever, Heb. 1:8, John 1:18.

Also, Christ is not only perfectly God, but perfect man, made of a woman, Gal. 4:4. Made of the seed of David, Rom 1:3. Coming out of the loins of David, Acts 2:30. Of Jesse and Judah, Acts 13:23. In that the children were partakers of flesh and blood He Himself likewise took part with them, Heb. 2:14. He took not on Him the nature of angels, but the seed of Abraham, verse 16. So that we are bone of His bone, and flesh of His flesh, Eph. 5:30. So that He that sanctifieth, and they that are sanctified are all of one, Heb.2:11. See Acts 3:22, Deut. 18:15; Heb. 1:1.

XVII. Concerning His priesthood, Christ having sanctified Himself, hath appeared once to put away sin by that one offering of Himself a sacrifice for sin, by which He hath fully finished and suffered all things God required for the salvation of His elect, and removed all rites and shadows, etc. and is now entered within the vail into the holy of holies, which is the presence of God. Also, He makes His people a spiritual house, an holy priesthood, to offer up spiritual sacrifice acceptable to God through Him. Neither doth the Father accept, nor Christ offer to the Father, any other worship or worshippers.
John 17:19; Heb. 5:7,8,9,10,12; Rom. 5:19, Eph. 5:2; Col. 1:20; Eph. 2:14, etc.; Rom. 8:34; Heb. 9:24; 8:1; 1 Pet. 2:5; John 4:23,24.

XVIII. This priesthood was not legal or temporary, but according to the order of Melchisedec, and is stable and perfect, not for a time, but forever, which is suitable to Jesus Christ, as to Him that ever liveth. Christ was the priest, sacrifice, and altar: He was a priest according to both natures; He was a sacrifice according to His human nature; whence in Scripture it is attributed to His body, to His blood: Yet the effectualness of this sacrifice did depend upon His divine nature; therefore it is called the blood of God. He was the altar according to His divine nature, it belonging to the altar to sanctify that which is offered upon it, and so it ought to be of greater dignity than the sacrifice itself.
Heb. 7:16, etc.; Heb. 5:6, 10:10; 1 Pet. 1:18,19; Col. 1:20, 22; Heb. 9:13; Acts 20:28; Heb. 9:14, 13:10,12,15; Matt. 23:17; John 17:19.

XIX. Concerning His kingly office, Christ being risen from the dead, and ascended into heaven, and having all power in heaven and earth, He doth spiritually govern His church, and doth exercise His power over all, angels and men, good and bad, to the preservation and salvation of the elect, and to the overruling and destruction of His enemies. By this kingly power He applieth the benefits, virtue, and fruits of His prophecy and priesthood to His elect, subduing their sins, preserving and strengthening them in all their conflicts against Satan, the world, and the flesh, keeping their hearts in faith and filial fear by His Spirit: By this His mighty power He ruleth the vessels of wrath, using, limiting and restraining them, as it seems good to His infinite wisdom.
1 Cor. 15:4; 1 Pet. 3:21,22; Matt. 28:18,19; Luke 24:51; Acts 1:1, 5:30,31; John 19:36; Rom. 14:9; John 5:26,27; Rom. 5:6,7,8; 14:17; Gal. 5:22,23; Mark 1:27; Heb. 1:14; John 16:15; Job 2:8; Rom. 1:21, [9:17-18]; Eph. 4:17,18; 2 Pet. 2.

XX. This His kingly power shall be more fully manifested when He shall come in glory to reign among His saints, when He shall put down all rule and authority under His feet, that the glory of the Father may be perfectly manifested in His Son, and the glory of the Father and the Son in all His members.
1 Cor. 15:24,28; Heb. 9:28; 2 Thess. 1:9,10; 1 Thess. 4:15,16,17; John 17:21, 26.

XXI. Jesus Christ by His death did purchase salvation for the elect that God gave unto Him: These only have interest in Him, and fellowship with Him, for whom He makes intercession to His Father in their behalf, and to them alone doth God by His Spirit apply this redemption; as also the free gift of eternal life is given to them, and none else.
Eph. 1:14; Heb. 5:9; Matt. 1:21; John 17:6; Heb. 7:25; 1 Cor. 2:12; Rom. 8:29,30; 1 John 5:12; John 15:35, 3:16.

XXII. Faith is the gift of God, wrought in the hearts of the elect by the Spirit of God; by which faith they come to know and believe the truth of the Scriptures, and the excellency of them above all other writings, and all things in the world, as they hold forth the glory of God in His attributes, the execellency of Christ in His nature and offices, and of the power and fulness of the Spirit in its [His] workings and operations; and so are enabled to cast their souls upon His truth thus believed.
Eph. 2:8; John 6:29, 4:10; Phil. 1:29; Gal. 5:22; John 17:17; Heb. 4:11,12; John 6:63.

XXIII. All those that have this precious faith wrought in them by the Spirit, can never finally nor totally fall away; seeing the gifts of God are without repentance; so that He still begets and nourisheth in them faith, repentance, love, joy, hope, and all the graces of the Spirit unto immortality; and though many storms and floods arise, and beat against them, yet they shall never be able to take them off that foundation and rock, which by faith they are fastened upon; not withstanding, through unbelief, and the temptations of Satan, the sensible sight of this light and love, be clouded and overwhelmed for a time; yet God is still the same, and they shall be sure to be kept by the power of God unto salvation, where they shall enjoy their purchased possession, they being engraven upon the palms of His hands, and their names having been written in the book of life from all eternity.

Matt. 7:24,25; John 13:10, 10:28,29; 1 Pet. 1:4,5,6; Isa. 49:13,14,15,16.

XXIV. Faith is ordinarily begotten by the preaching of the gospel, or word of Christ, without respect to any power or agency in the creature; but it being wholly passive, and dead in trespasses and sins, doth believe and is converted by no less power than that which raised Christ from the dead.
Rom. 10:17; 1 Cor. 1:28; Rom. 9:16; Ezek. 16:16; Rom. 3:12, 1:16; Eph. 1:19, Col. 2:12.

XXV. The preaching of the gospel to the conversion of sinners, is absolutely free; no way requiring as absolutely necessary, any qualifications, preparations, or terrors of the law, or preceding ministry of the law, but only and alone the naked soul, a sinner and ungodly, to receive Christ crucified, dead and buried, and risen again; who is made a prince and a Savior for such sinners as through the gospel shall be brought to believe on Him.
John 3:14,15, 1:12; Isa. 55:1; John 7:37; 1 Tim. 1:15; Rom. 4:5, 5:8; Acts 5:30,31, 2:36, 1 Cor. 1:22,24.

XXVI. The same power that converts to faith in Christ, carrieth on the soul through all duties, temptations, conflicts, sufferings; and whatsoever a believer is, he is by grace, and is carried on in all obedience and temptations by the same.
1 Pet. 1:5, 2 Cor. 12:9, 1 Cor. 15:10; Phil. 2:12, 13; John 15:5; Gal. 2:19,20.

XXVII. All believers are by Christ united to God; by which union, God is one with them, and they are one with Him; and that all believers are the sons of God, and joint heirs with Christ, to whom belong all the promises of this life, and that which is to come.
1 Thess. 1:1; John 17:21, 20:17; Heb. 2:11, 1 John 4:16; Gal. 2:19,20.

XXVIII. Those that have union with Christ, are justified from all their sins by the blood of Christ, which justification is a gracious and full acquittance of a guilty sinner from all sin, by God, through the satisfaction that Christ hath made by His death for all their sins, and this applied (in manifestation of it) through faith.
1 John 1:7; Heb. 10:14, 9:26; 2 Cor. 5:19; Rom. 3:23; Acts 13:38,39; Rom. 5:1, 3:25,30.

XXIX. All believers are a holy and sanctified people, and that sanctification is a spiritual grace of the new covenant, and an effect of the love of God manifested in the soul, whereby the believer presseth after a heavenly and evangelical obedience to all the commands, which Christ as head and king in His new covenant hath prescribed to them.
1 Cor. 12; 1 Pet. 2:9; Eph. 1:4; 1 John 4:16; Matt. 28:20.

XXX. All believers through the knowledge of that justification of life given by the Father and brought forth by the blood of Christ have as their great privilege of that new covenant, peace with God, reconciliation, whereby they that were afar off are made nigh by that blood, and have peace passing all understanding; yea, joy in God through our Lord Jesus Christ, by whom we have received atonement. 2 Cor. 5:19; Rom. 5:9,10; Isa. 54:10; Eph. 2:13,14, 4:7; Rom. 5:10,11.

XXXI. All believers in the time of this life, are in a continual warfare and combat against sin, self, the world, and the devil; and are liable to all manner of afflictions, tribulations and persecutions, being predestined and appointed thereunto, and whatsoever the saints possess or enjoy of God spiritually, is by faith; and outward and temporal things are lawfully enjoyed by a civil right by them who have no faith. Rom. 7:23,24; Eph. 6:10,11, etc.; Heb. 2:9,10, 2 Tim. 3:12; Rom. 8:29; 1 Thess. 3:3; Gal. 2:19,20; 2 Cor. 5:7; Deut. 2:5.

XXXII. The only strength by which the saints are enabled to encounter with all oppositions and trials, is only by Jesus Christ, who is the captain of their salvation, being made perfect through sufferings; who hath engaged His faithfulness and strength to assist them in all their afflictions, and to uphold them in all their temptations, and to preserve them by His power to His everlasting kingdom. John 16:33, 15:5; Phil. 4:11, Heb. 2:9,10; 2 Tim. 4:18.

XXXIII. Jesus Christ hath here on earth a [manifestation of His] spiritual kingdom, which is His Church, whom He hath purchased and redeemed to Himself as a peculiar inheritance; which Church is a company of visible saints, called and separated from the world by the word and Spirit of God, to the visible profession of faith of the gospel, being baptized into that faith, and joined to the Lord, and each other, by mutual agreement in the practical enjoyment of the ordinances commanded by Christ their head and king. Matt. 11:11; 2 Thess. 1:1; 1 Cor. 1:2; Eph. 1:1; Rom. 1:7; Acts 19:8,9, 26:18; 2 Cor. 6:17; Rev. 18:4; Acts 2:37, 10:37; Rom. 10:10; Matt. 18:19,20; Acts 2:42, 9:26; 1 Pet. 2:5.

XXXIV. To this Church He hath made His promises, and giveth the signs of His covenant, presence, acceptation, love, blessing and protection. Here are the fountains and springs of His heavenly graces flowing forth to refresh and strengthen them. Matt. 28:18, etc.; 1 Cor. 11:24, 3:21; 2 Cor. 6:18; Rom. 9:4,5; Ps. 133:3; Rom. 3:7,10; Ezek. 47:2.

XXXV. And all His servants of all estates (are to acknowledge Him to be their prophet, priest and king;) and called thither to be enrolled among His household servants, to present their bodies and souls, and to bring their gifts God hath given them, to be under His heavenly conduct and government, to lead their lives in this walled sheepfold, and watered garden, to have communion here with His saints, that they may be assured that they are made meet to be partakers of their inheritance in the kingdom of God; and to supply each others wants, inward and outward; (and although each person hath a propriety in his own estate, yet they are to supply each others wants, according as their necessities shall require, that the name of Jesus Christ may not be blasphemed through the necessity of any in

the Church) and also being come, they are here by Himself to be bestowed in their several order, due place, peculiar use, being fitly compact and knit together according to the effectual working of every part, to the edifying of itself in love.
Acts. 2:41,47; Isa. 4:3, 1 Cor. 12:6,7, etc.; Ezek. 20:37,40; Song of Sol. 4:12; Eph. 2:19; Rom. 12:4,5,6; Col. 1:12, 2:5,6,19; Acts 20:32, 5:4, 2:44,45, 4:34,35; Luke 14:26; 1 Tim. 6:1; Eph. 4:16.

XXXVI. Being thus joined, every [local] church hath power given them from Christ, for their wellbeing, to choose among themselves meet persons for elders and deacons, being qualified according to the word, as those which Christ hath appointed in His testament, for the feeding, governing, serving, and building up of His Church; and that none have any power to impose on them either these or any other.
Acts 1:23,26, 6:3, 15:22,25; Rom. 12:7,8; 1 Tim. 3:2,6,7; 1 Cor. 12:8,28; Heb. 13:7,17; 1 Pet. 5:1,2,3,4:15.

XXXVII. That the ministers lawfully called, as aforesaid, ought to continue in their calling and place according to God's ordinance, and carefully to feed the flock of God committed to them, not for filthy lucre, bat of a ready mind.
Heb. 5:4; John 10:3,4; Acts 20:28,29; Rom. 12:7,8; Heb. 13:7,17; 1 Pet. 5:1,2,3.

XXXVIII. The ministers of Christ ought to have whatsoever they shall need, supplied freely by the church, that according to Christ's ordinance they that preach the Gospel should live of the gospel by the law of Christ.
1 Cor. 9:7,14; Gal. 6:8; Phil. 4:15,16; 2 Cor. 10:4; 1 Tim. 1:2; Ps. 110:3.

XXXIX. Baptism is an ordinance of the New Testament, given by Christ, to be dispensed upon persons professing faith, or that are made disciples; who upon profession of faith, ought to be baptized, and after to partake of the Lord's Supper.
Matt. 28:18,19; John 4:1; Mark 16:15,16; Acts 2:37,38, 8:36,37, etc.

XL. That the way and manner of dispensing this ordinance, is dipping or plunging the body under water; it being a sign, must answer the things signified, which is, that interest the saints have in the death, burial, and resurrection of Christ: And that as certainly as the body is buried under water, and risen again, so certainly shall the bodies of the saints be raised by the power of Christ, in the day of the resurrection, to reign with Christ.
Matt. 3:16; Mark 15:9 reads (into Jordan) in Greek; John 3:23, Acts 8:38; Rev. 1:5, 7:14; Heb. 10:22; Rom. 6:3,4,5,6; 1 Cor. 15:28,29. The word baptizo signifies to dip or plunge (yet so as convenient garments be both upon the administrator and subject with all modesty).

XLI. The person designed by Christ to dispense baptism, the Scripture holds forth to be a disciple; it being no where tied to a particular church officer, or person extraordinarily sent the commission enjoining the administration, being given to them as considered disciples, being men able to preach the gospel.

Isa. 8:16; Eph. 2:7; Matt 28:19; John 4:2; Acts 20:7, 11:10; 1 Cor. 11:2, 10:16,17; Rom. 16:2; Matt. 18:17.

XLII. Christ hath likewise given power to His Church to receive in, and cast out, any member that deserves it; and this power is given to every congregation, and not to one particular person, either member or officer, but in relation to the whole body, in reference to their faith and fellowship.
Rom. 15:2; Matt. 18:17; 1 Cor. 5:4,11,14, 12:6, 2:3; 2 Cor. 2:6,7.

XLIII. And every particular member of each church, how excellent, great, or learned soever, is subject to this censure and judgment; and that the church ought not without great care and tenderness, and due advice, but by the rule of faith, to proceed against her members.
Matt. 18:16, 17:18; Acts 11:2,3; 1 Tim. 5:19, etc.; Col. 4:17; Acts 15:1,2,3.

XLIV. Christ for the keeping of this church in holy and orderly communion, placeth some special men over the church; who by their office, are to govern, oversee, visit, watch; so likewise for the better keeping thereof, in all places by the members, He hath given authority, and laid duty upon all to watch over one another.
Acts 20:27,28; Heb. 13:17,24; Matt. 24:45; 1 Thess. 5:2, 14; Jude 3,20; Heb. 10:34,35 [cf. 24,25], 12:15.

XLV. Also such to whom God hath given gifts in the church, may and ought to prophecy [viz., teach] according to the proportion of faith, and to teach publicly the word of God, for the edification, exhortation, and comfort of the church.
1 Cor. 14:3, etc.; Rom 12:6; 1 Pet. 4:10, 11; 1 Cor. 12:7; 1 Thess. 5:19, etc.

XLVI. Thus being rightly gathered, and continuing in the obedience of the gospel of Christ, none are to separate for faults and corruptions (for as long as the church consists of men subject to failings, there will be difference in the true constituted church) until they have in due order, and tenderness, sought redress thereof.
Rev. 2, 3; Acts 15:12; 1 Cor. 1:10; Heb. 10:25; Jude 19; Rev. 2:20,21,27; Acts 15:1,2; Rom. 14:1; 15:1,2,3.

XLVII. And although the particular congregations be distinct, and several bodies, every one as a compact and knit city within itself; yet are they all to walk by one rule of truth; so also they (by all means convenient) are to have the counsel and help one of another, if necessity require it, as members of one body, in the common faith, under Christ their head.
1 Cor. 4:17, 14:33,36, 16:1; Ps. 122:3; Eph. 2:12,19; Rev. 21; 1 Tim. 3:15, 6:13,14; 1 Cor. 4:17; Acts 15:2,3; Song of Sol. 8:8,9; 2 Cor. 8:1,4, 13:14.

XLVIII. A civil magistracy is an ordinance of God, set up by Him for the punishment of evil doers, and for the praise of them that do well; and that in all lawful things, commanded by them, subjection ought to be given by us in the Lord, not only for wrath, but for conscience sake; and that we are to make supplications

and prayers for kings, and all that are in authority, that under them we may live a quiet and peaceable life, in all godliness and honesty.
Rom. 13:1,2, etc.; 1 Pet. 2:13,14; 1 Tim. 2:1,2,3.

Note: The supreme magistracy of this kingdom we acknowledge to be the king and parliament (now established) freely chosen by the kingdom, and that we are to maintain and defend all civil laws and civil officers made by them, which are for the good of the commonwealth. And we acknowledge with thankfulness, that God hath made this present king and parliament honorable in throwing down the prelatical hierarchy, because of their tyranny and oppression over us, under which this kingdom long groaned, for which we are ever engaged to bless God, and honor them for the same. And concerning the worship of God; there is but one lawgiver, which is able to save and destroy, James 4:12; which is Jesus Christ, who hath given laws and rules sufficient in His word for His worship; and for any to make more, were to charge Christ with want of wisdom, or faithfulness, or both, in not making laws enough, or not good enough for His house: Surely it is our wisdom, duty, and privilege, to observe Christ's laws only, Ps 2:6,9,10,12. So it is the magistrates duty to tender the liberty of mens' consciences, Eccles. 8:8 (which is the tenderest thing unto all conscientious men, and most dear unto them, and without which all other liberties will not be worth the naming, much less enjoying) and to protect all under them from all wrong, injury, oppression and molestation; so it is our duty not to be wanting in nothing which is for their honor and comfort, and whatsoever is for the wellbeing of the commonwealth wherein we live; it is our duty to do, and we believe it to be our express duty, especially in matters of religion, to be fully persuaded in our minds of the lawfulness of what we do, as knowing whatsoever is not of faith is sin. And as we cannot do anything contrary to our understandings and consciences, so neither can we forebear the doing of that which our understandings and consciences bind us to do. And if the magistrate should require us to do otherwise, we are to yield our persons in a passive way to their power, as the saints of old have done, James 5:4. And thrice happy shall he be, that shall lose his life for witnessing (though but for the least tittle) of the truth of the Lord Jesus Christ, 1 Pet. 5; Gal. 5.

XLIX. But in case we find not the magistrate [or governing authority] to favor us herein; yet we dare not suspend our practice, because we believe we ought to go in obedience to Christ, in professing the faith which was once delivered to the saints, which faith is declared in the holy Scriptures, and this our confession of faith a part of them, and that we are to witness to the truth of the Old and New Testaments unto the death, if necessity require, in the midst of all trials and afflictions, as His saints of old have done; not accounting our goods, lands, wives, children, fathers, mothers, brethren, sisters; yea and our own lives dear unto us, so we may finish our course with joy; remembering always, that we ought to obey God rather than men, who will when we have finished our course, and kept the faith, give us the crown of righteousness; to whom we must give an account of all our actions, and no man being able to discharge us of the same.

Acts 2:40,41, 4:19, 5:28,29, 20:23; 1 Thess. 3:3; Phil. 1:28,29; Dan. 3:16,17, 6:7,10,22,23; 1 Tim. 6:13,14; Rom. 12:1,8; 1 Cor. 14:37; Rev. 2:20; 2 Tim. 4:6,7,8; Rom. 14:10, 12; 2 Cor. 5:10; Ps. 49:7,50:22.

L. It is lawful for a Christian to be a magistrate or civil officer; and also it is lawful to take an oath, so it be in truth, and in judgment, and in righteousness, for confirmation of truth, and ending of all strife; and that by wrath and vain oaths the Lord is provoked and this land mourns.
Acts 8:38, 10:1,2,35; Rom. 16:23; Deut. 6:13; Rom. 1:9; 2 Cor. 10,11; Jer. 4:2; Heb. 6:16.

LI. We are to give unto all men whatsoever is their due, as their place, age, estate, requires; and that we defraud no man of anything, but to do unto all men, as we would they should do unto us.
1 Thess. 4:6; Rom. 13:5,6,7; Matt. 22:21; Titus 3; 1 Pet. 2:15,17, 5:5; Eph. 5:21,23, etc. , 6:1,9; Titus 3:1,2,3.

LII. There shall be a resurrection of the dead, both of the just and unjust, and everyone shall give an account of himself to God, that every one may receive the things done in his body, according to that he hath done, whether it be good or bad. Acts 24:15; 1 Cor. 5:10; Rom. 14:12. [Matt. 25; Rev. 22:11,12,13,14,15.]

The Conclusion.

Thus we desire to give unto Christ that which is His; and unto all lawful authority that which is their due; and to owe nothing to any man but love; to live quietly and peaceably, as it becometh saints, endeavoring in all things to keep a good conscience, and to do unto every man (of what judgment soever) as we would they should do unto us, that as our practice is, so it may prove us to be a conscionable [viz., reasonable], quiet, and harmless people (no ways dangerous or troublesome to human society) and to labor and work with our hands that we may not be chargeable to any, but to give to him that needeth, both friends and enemies, accounting it more excellent to give than to receive. Also we confess, that we know but in part, and that we are ignorant of many things which we desire and seek to know; and if any shall do us that friendly part to show us from the word of God that which we see not, we shall have cause to be thankful to God and them; but if any man shall impose upon us anything that we see not to be commanded by our Lord Jesus Christ, we should in His strength rather embrace all reproaches and tortures of men, to be stripped of all outward comforts, and if it were possible, to die a thousand deaths, rather than to do anything against the least tittle of the truth of God or against the light of our own consciences. And if any shall call what we have said heresy, then do we with the Apostle acknowledge, that after the way they call heresy, worship we the God of our fathers, disclaiming all heresies (rightly so called) because they are against Christ, and to be steadfast and unmovable, always abounding in obedience to Christ, as knowing our labor shall not be in vain in the Lord.

Psalm 74:21,22:

Arise, O God, plead thine own cause; remember how the foolish man blasphemeth Thee daily.
O let not the oppressed return ashamed, but let the poor and needy praise Thy name.

Come, Lord Jesus, come quickly.

Appendix 4: The Impact of Unexamined Presuppositions

This article below appeared on the Founders blog, and was last accessed on 21 April 2015 here: http://founders.org/fj36/an-ethical-manifesto-1-timothy-18-11-and-the-decalogue/

Founders is a Calvinistic ministry within the Southern Baptist Convention and has contributed much needed good teaching and influence to that association. But this article does not commend them. My comments are in **bold italics**, within parenthesis. My intention is to point out presuppositions and errors in Barcellos' perspective and why they matter. We must test all things in light of Scripture and cling to that which is true and good (1 Thessalonians 5:21).

AN ETHICAL MANIFESTO: 1 TIMOTHY 1:8-11 AND THE DECALOGUE

Richard Barcellos

In this essay we will reassess 1 Timothy 1:8-11 with the goal of determining whether or not Paul's list of vices reflects both the content and order of the Decalogue from the first through the ninth commandments *(If the Decalogue is a unit that cannot be broken, why is the 10th Word not included?)*. This thesis occurs in Dr. George W. Knight's *The Pastoral Epistles: A Commentary on the Greek Text*. The scope of Dr. Knight's commentary on 1 Timothy 1:8-11 was purposely suggestive due to space constraints. The goal of this essay is to build upon the seminal work of Dr. Knight and suggest that his basic thesis can be supported from the text itself and other considerations. *(George McKnight is a Presbyterian and his presuppositions lead him to no other conclusion. The Baptist view of the covenants in Scripture is not based on the equality and same identity of the nation of Israel and the church as is the paedobaptist view.)*

Assuming the validity of Dr. Knight's thesis *(a very poor beginning – we are to test everything man speaks, not assume his view is valid; all the more when he is building on a covenantal view that is built to defend infant baptism)*, we are supplied with a strong arguments for both the perpetuity of the Decalogue, including the fourth commandment *(why the need to highlight this commandment and none of the others? Is the over-arching goal to convince people of sabbatarianism?)*, under the New Covenant and the continuing function of the Decalogue as the basic, fundamental law of God which is applicable to all men. This has major implications for Christian ethics and is in full agreement with historic Baptist theology as represented in *The Baptist Confession of Faith of 1689 (considering the person's work on which this essay is built, it is more reasonable to conclude that we are reading an essay that is represented in the WCF, from which the 1689 LBC drew its language on the law of Moses).*

1 Timothy 1:8-11 states: *But we know that the law is good if one uses it lawfully, knowing this: that the law is not made for a righteous person, but for the lawless and insubordinate, for the ungodly and for sinners, for the unholy and profane, for murderers of fathers and murderers of mothers, for manslayers, for fornicators, for sodomites, for kidnappers, for liars, for perjurers, and if there is any other thing that is contrary to sound doctrine, according to the glorious gospel of the blessed God which was committed to my trust.*[1]

In considering this passage, three preliminary questions will be asked in order to set the stage for a more careful consideration of a fourth question. The exposition unfolds in the following order: Why does Paul bring up the issue of the law? What is said about the law? To whom is Paul referring when he says "the law is not made for a righteous person"? What law is Paul referring to in verses 8 through 10?

Why does Paul bring up the issue of the law?
In verses 5 through 7 Paul makes mention of some who have strayed and turned aside to idle talk (see verses 5, 6). These desire to be teachers of the law though they are ignorant of what they claim is their expertise (see verse 7). In verse 8 a contrast between the way those who have strayed use the law and the proper use of the law is begun and completed in verse 11. Why does Paul bring up the issue of the law? He does so to combat the wrong use of the law and to set forth its right use. The law was being used unlawfully by some and Paul aims to present its lawful use (see Titus 3:9 for another instance of an unlawful use of the law).

What is said about the law?
In verse 8 Paul says, "that the law is good if one uses it lawfully." The law is both good and can be used lawfully. There is obviously a lawful and unlawful use of the law. Those described in verses 5 through 7 used the good law unlawfully but Paul is going to show its lawful use. Commenting on that which "we know" about the law, New Testament scholar George Knight says: That which "we know" is "that the law is good" ... The statement has striking similarities with several in Romans 7 (Romans 7:14,16 ...). The point in 1 Timothy 1:8, as in Romans 7, is to affirm that the *nomos* (law) is intrinsically good because it is given by God (cf. Romans 2; 7:22; 8:4) and is not to be considered bad, though it can be mishandled, with bad results, as the *nomodidaskaloi* (law-teachers) have done.[2]

It is very clear that in this passage the law is viewed in its intrinsic goodness as it reveals proper God-defined moral behavior. ***(Nowhere in his introduction does Barcellos define what he thinks "the law" in this passage is. This short phrase has several meanings, and context will reveal what meaning we are to infer.)***

To whom is Paul referring?
In verse 9 Paul states, "the law is not made for a righteous person." To whom is he referring? Some understand "a righteous person" to refer to the justified, the

saved, the Christian without qualification. "This view acknowledges that the law functions to bring a person to Christ as a sinner, but then asserts that a saved person is not to be concerned with or directed by the law."[3] *(This is a straw man argument, ignoring the fact that many agree the law has use for the saint all his life, even though one maintains that, in this passage, the contrast is between the righteous and the depraved. This means the righteous or just in verse 9 is the redeemed person, not the self-righteous Pharisee who needs to broken. This is the view found in the Jamieson-Faucett-Brown commentary, which has the same view as Knight – that Paul is referring to the Decalogue in this passage.)* This common view is contradicted by many texts in Paul's writings (see for instance Romans 7:14, 16, 22, 23; 13:8-10; and especially 2 Timothy 3:16, 17), other texts in the New Testament (Matthew 5:17, 18; James 2:8-11), and does not fit the context as will become clear. It is simply and emphatically not true that the law has no place in the life of the Christian. *(I agree with Barcellos' point here – the law of Moses reveals God's view of morality, though clothed in ceremonial language relevant only to Israel, and has a prominent place in the life of everyone who names Christ, as does ALL of Scripture. He might have also mentioned Romans 7:1 - 8, which shows us the relationship Christians have to the Law of Moses. It is good, it does not bind us nor convict us as it does those under the Law of Moses.)*

What then does Paul mean? Knight offers the following explanation: The meaning of *dikaios* [righteous] here would seem to be determined in large measure by its place preceding and contrasting with a list of terms concerned with moral behavior. Therefore, the point of this section is to emphasize, against the would-be *nomodidaskaloi* [law-teachers], that the law is given to deal with moral questions and not for speculation. The would-be *nomodidaskaloi* [law-teachers] are not Judaizers like those of Galatians, since the P[astoral] E[pistles] give no evidence of that, but rather those who deal with God's law from the perspective of myths, genealogies, and disputes about it (v. 4; see Titus 3:9). Thus Paul is saying that the law is not given to apply in some mystical way to people who are already "righteous," i.e., those already seeking to conform to the law. It is, rather, given to deal with people who are specifically violating its sanctions and to warn them against their specific sins (as the list in vv. 9b-10 goes on to do).[4] *(Exactly – the law is given to the lawless, to bind them and convict them. It does not apply in this way to those who are righteous in Christ.)*

The Expositor's Greek Testament agrees with Knight's interpretation when it says, "*diakaios* [righteous] is used here in the popular sense, as in 'I came not to call the righteous'."[5] The "righteous person" is anyone in *external* conformity to the law whether Christian or non-Christian.[6] Patrick Fairbairn seems to agree when he says: By the latter expression [righteous] is to be understood, not one who in a worldly sense is just or upright (for the apostle is not here speaking of such), but who in the stricter sense is such--one who, whether by nature or by grace, has the position and character of a righteous man. Why is the law not made for such? It can only be because he is of himself inclined to act in conformity with its requirements.[7]

These "righteous" ones are those who "conform" to the law. The word "righteous" is used elsewhere in the New Testament to refer to both non-Christians and Christians. For instance, Paul uses a form of this word in Philippians 3:6 when he says, "concerning the righteousness [*dikaiosune*] which is in the law, blameless." This verse is Paul's own description of his relationship to the Mosaic law prior to his conversion (see Philippians 3:9; Luke 1:5, 6; and Acts 10:22). Thus a person can be "righteous" and not a Christian.

James 5:16 states, "The effective, fervent prayer of a righteous man [*dikaiou*] avails much." Here Elijah is viewed as a believer, "a righteous person" (see Matthew 25:37, 46; and Romans 5:19). Thus a person can be "righteous" and a Christian.

In 1 Timothy 1:9 Paul is not referring to the law in a *soteriological* sense as it would point to Christ, but in an *ethical* sense as it defines proper behavior for man. In this sense the law defines proper behavior and rebukes those not in conformity to it. Thus it is not for "a righteous person" because such a person is already conforming to the ethical standards of the law.[8] But what about the person who is not conforming to its standards? He is obviously not "a righteous person" in the sense intended by Paul. It is this person whom Paul has in mind as he writes of the ethical use of the law. *(This word study by the Presbyterian reminds me of the way Dispensationalists do word studies to prove their point, failing to take into account the context of the word as the primary means of determining its meaning. "Righteous" and "the Law" have more than one meaning and the biblical context – not a lexicon – must be the first and final rule for determining meaning. If Paul meant the self-righteous Jews in verse 9 as the just or righteous, then I doubt he would ever claim the law is not meant for them in the same way it's meant for the reprobate. Both need to have their mouths stopped and their hearts broken over their sin.)*

This understanding of the passage makes this use of the law applicable to believers and unbelievers alike. The law is the standard for proper conduct as defined by God for mankind in general, Christian and non-Christian. This lawful use of the law points out sin and defines that conduct which "is contrary to sound doctrine, according to the glorious gospel."[9]

Notice in verses 10 and 11 that living according to the sins listed in verses 9 and 10 "is contrary to sound doctrine, according to the glorious gospel." In other words, lawless living is antithetical to sound gospel doctrine.[10] "The sound doctrine demands that man *must* keep God's law."[11] The gospel does not replace the law; it *upholds* the law. John Stott says, It is particularly noteworthy that sins which contravene the law (as breaches of the Ten Commandments) are also contrary to the sound doctrine of the gospel. So the moral standards of the gospel do not differ from the moral standards of the law. We must not therefore imagine that, because we have embraced the gospel, we may now repudiate the law![12] *(No argument. Again, there is another position between the Sabbatarian and the antinomian. God's law (not restricted or defined by the Decalogue) applies to Christians – yet it does not bind us or convict us. The purpose and use and applicability of the law is different for the Christian than for the unregenerate.)*

Knight agrees: [T]he "sound teaching" [doctrine] of the Christian faith has the same ethical perspective as the law, and that teaching also points out sins that are contrary to it. By this Paul indicates that law and "sound teaching" [doctrine] are together in opposing these sins and therefore have a common ethical perspective.[13] Living according to the list of vices in First Timothy 1:9, 10 is sin for the Christian and non-Christian alike.[14]

To what law is Paul referring?

In verses 8-10 some commentators see Paul referring to law in general and not the Mosaic law. There are, however, indicators within and beyond this context which show this view to be inadequate. *First*, when Paul details for us the lawful use of the law he clearly refers to commands contained in the law of Moses (see verses 9 and 10 and the exposition below). *Second*, "The ethical list in vv. 9-10 is similar to the Decalogue and the application of it in Exodus 21."[15] *Third*, in verses 5 through 7 where Paul brings up the would-be law-teachers it seems clear that there is an assumed and well known law. *Fourth*, in Titus 3:9 when the law is mentioned Paul again assumes that it would be well known to his readers. *Fifth*, it would be very difficult not to read these statements on the law in light of the rest of Paul's letters which deal extensively with this very issue.

To what law is Paul referring? Consider the following observations. In verse 8 Paul uses an article before the word law. "But we know that *the* [emphasis added] law is good." This indicates that Paul is referring to an identifiable body of law.[16] It is clear from verses 9b and 10 that Paul had in mind at least the fifth through the ninth commandments of the Decalogue.[17] Knight states, "from 'strikers of father and mother' onward the order of the second part of the Decalogue is followed."[18] It is also clear that Paul summarizes violations of the fifth through the ninth commandments with single words in the Greek text. Again, Knight comments, "single words are used in the latter part of the list to refer to violators of a specific commandment".[19]

The terms "murderers of fathers" (*patroloais*) and "murderers of mothers" (*matroloais*) are single word summaries of the fifth commandment in terms of its violation. The term "manslayers" (*androphonois*) is a single word summary of the sixth commandment in terms of its violation. The terms "fornicators" (*pornois*) and "sodomites" (*arsenkoitais*) are single word summaries of the seventh commandment in terms of its violation. The term "kidnappers" (*andrapodistais*) is a single word summary of the eighth commandment in terms of its violation. The terms "liars" (*pheustais*) and "perjurers" (*epiorkois*) are single word summaries of the ninth commandment in terms of its violation.[20] Paul's list clearly reflects both the *content* and *order* of the second part of the Decalogue. *(Clearly, the breaking of the law is what is being presented here – convicting the lawless of their lawlessness. This passage does not present the Decalogue as a binding law for Christians. The moral or universal law of God is bigger, older, and more glorious than the Decalogue, which was given to Israel on tablets as a testimony of His covenant with them.)*

Our final observation concerning what law Paul is referring to is best put in the form of a question. What part of the Mosaic law do the sins listed before verse 9b reflect? If the sins in 9b and 10 reflect both the *content* and *order* of the Decalogue, should we expect the sins in 9a to do so as well? In other words, since verses 9b and 10 reflect the *content* and *order* of the second part of the Decalogue, does verse 9a reflect the *content* and *order* of the first part?[21] Homer Kent says, "the list of sins that appears in verses 9 and 10 seems clearly to follow the order of the Ten Commandments."[22] Consider Knight's observations once again: Once it is recognized that from "strikers of father and mother" onward the order of the second part of the Decalogue is followed, then the question naturally arises whether the preceding part of the list in v. 9 corresponds to the earlier part of the Decalogue. An interesting correlation may well exist, especially if it is borne in mind that single words are used in the latter part of the list to refer to violators of a specific commandment, and therefore single words could also be used in the former part to characterize violators of the earlier commandments.[23]

Commenting on all of the vices in verses 9 and 10 Fairbairn says, "they admit of being all ranged under the precepts of the two tables."[24] He goes on to say: In regard to those for whom, he says, the law *is* made,--those, that is, who need the check and restraint of its discipline,--the apostle gives first a general description. Then he branches out into particulars, the earlier portion of which have respect to offences against God, the latter to offences against one's fellow-men [25]

Alfred Plummer **(another Presbyterian)** adds: In rehearsing the various kinds of sinners for whom law exists **(not for the righteous in Christ)**, and who are found to be (he hints) among these false teachers, he goes roughly through the Decalogue. The four commandments of the First Table are indicated in general and comprehensive terms; the first five commandments of the Second Table are taken one by one, flagrant violators being specified in each case.[26]

Let's take a closer look at verse 9 going backward from Paul's reference to the fifth commandment at the end of the verse.[27] The first sin category going backward from "murderers of fathers and mothers" mentioned by Paul is the "profane". The noun form of "profane" is used of persons in the New Testament only twice; here in 1 Timothy 1:9 and in Hebrews 12:16. The verb form of "profane" is used of persons twice in the New Testament as well.[28] In Acts 24:6 it is used in the context of profaning the temple. In Matthew 12:5 it is used in the context of profaning the Sabbath. Concerning the verb form of the word "profane", the *Theological Dictionary of the New Testament* says, "To desecrate,":...Common in the LXX[29] I thus...of the *holy day* [emphasis added] of God in Nehemiah 13:17f. In the NT the only use is at Matthew 12:5 of the violation of the Sabbath and at Acts

24:6 of that of the temple, in both cases in the sense of the OT view of holiness.[30]

One Greek-English lexicon indicates that the Septuagint uses this word to refer to desecrating or profaning the Sabbath in Nehemiah 13:17; Ezekiel 20:13 and Isaiah 56:2.[31] Notice that the Septuagint uses a form of the word "profane" in Isaiah 56:2 (see Isaiah 56:6 as well) in the context of the Sabbath being defiled (verse 2) and kept (verse 4). This is especially instructive considering the fact that Isaiah's prophecy concerns the interadvental days of the New Covenant. The word "profane" then refers to breaking the fourth commandment.[32] This understanding is supported by several considerations. Paul was very familiar with the Septuagint. He was reducing other commands of the Decalogue to one word. He was following the *content* and *order* of other commands of the Decalogue. He was reducing other commands of the Decalogue to single words in a negative form.[33] Knight concludes, "Since the keynote of the sabbath is to keep it holy (Exodus 20:8) and since Paul's list is in negative terms, the single term [profane], might well characterize those who profane that day, putting the command negatively in terms of its violation "[34] This sin is a violation of the fourth commandment of the Decalogue.[35] *(Yet the Scriptures tell us many times in both Testaments not to profane the name of God. We cannot rely on "One Greek-English lexicon" referring to the Septuagint to be the only reference. Although I have no argument against the position that those under the Law of Moses are bound to keep it all, including the Sabbath commandment.)*

The second sin category going backward from "murderers of fathers and mothers" mentioned by Paul is "*the* unholy." Knight says, Likewise, those who take the Lord's name in vain (Exodus 20:7) might well be designated negatively by a single term as those who are "unholy"... This understanding is strengthened if the language associated with this command has been influenced by the petition of the Lord's Prayer that the Lord's name be hallowed or regarded as holy (Matthew 6:9; Luke 11:2).[36]

This sin is a violation of the third commandment of the Decalogue.

The third sin category going backward from "murderers of fathers and mothers" mentioned by Paul is "sinners". The Greek word for sinner is often used in the NT with the broad meaning "sinner," as it is in 1 Timothy 1:15, ... At times, however, it is used in the NT more specifically of those who fail to keep the Mosaic law, particularly Gentiles, especially because of their idolatry ... This usage is found also in Paul in Galatians 2:15 (cf. on idolatry Romans 2:22). Thus one who violates the prohibition of making and worshipping idols (Exodus 20:4-6) might well be designated a "sinner" in the specific sense (so Exodus 20:5 LXX ...).[37]

This sin is a violation of the second commandment of the Decalogue.

The fourth sin category going backward from "murderers of fathers and mothers" mentioned by Paul is "*the* ungodly." "[T]he first commandment of the Decalogue (Exodus 20:3) prohibits having other gods and abandoning God as the one and only true God...."[38]The New Testament uses a positive form of the word which Paul uses here in 1 Timothy 1:9, "ungodly," "of those who accepted the ethical monotheism of the OT (see Acts 13:43, 50; 16:14; 17:4, 17; 18:7)"[39] though they were not even Christians. In other words, those in the texts just cited were not violating the first commandment, at least externally, and those in 1 Timothy 1:9, "the ungodly", were. This sin is a violation of the first commandment of the Decalogue.

It seems quite clear that both the *content* and the *order* of the Decalogue from the first through the ninth commandment is followed by Paul in this list of sins which are "contrary to sound doctrine, according to the glorious gospel. Knight concludes, and rightly so, "The order of the Decalogue seems, then, to give a satisfactory explanation of Paul's list from ["*the* ungodly"] onward."[40]

One question still remains. What about the first two sins in Paul's list "*the* lawless and insubordinate?" These first pair of terms function as a general introduction to the more specific list that follows. "These two terms bring into perspective those for whom the law is given, namely, those who need its discipline and restraint in their propensity for lawlessness and disobedience."[41]

Knight's concluding comments serve as a fitting end to our study of this crucial text. Paul has shown how the law may be used lawfully in accordance with its purpose as an ethical guide to warn against sin. He has demonstrated this by presenting a list that shows that the Decalogue is so understood in the OT. He has concluded by stating that this is also the ethical perspective of the truly healthy teaching based on the gospel, so that both it and a proper use of the law concur in terms of their concern for a righteous life and in their teaching against sin. Thus when the law is rightly applied as an ethical restraint against sin, it is in full accordance with the ethical norm given in the gospel as the standard for the redeemed life. A different use of the law, for example, in a mythological or genealogical application to the righteous, is thereby shown to be out of accord with the law's given purpose and the gospel and its teaching.[42] *(Again, no argument. Law has a different role, in the church than in the world. We must take care to define "law" to know how and to whom it applies.)*

It now becomes obvious what law Paul was referring to in 1 Timothy 1:8-11. He was referring to the heart of the law of the Old and New Covenants. He was referring to the basic, fundamental law of the Bible. He was referring to the law common to believer and unbeliever. He was referring to the law whose work is written on the hearts of all men by creation. He was referring to the Decalogue in its function of revealing God-defined ethical norms for all men.[43] *(This is a complex assertion – that the Decalogue is "the heart of the law in Old and New Covenants." The application of the law in this passage is to the condemnation of sinners, not heralded as the rule of life for Christians.*

Where is it taught that what was written on the tablets is the heart of the New Covenant? The heart of the New Covenant must be the blood of Christ, not tablets of stone that sit in an ark that is to be forgotten IAW Jer 3:15 & 16. Further, the assertion that the Decalogue is the moral law written on the hearts of all men by creation does not square with Scripture. It was a consequence of the Fall that Adam had knowledge of good and evil, not creation (Gen 3:22). Paul clearly teaches that knowledge of the law is what brings knowledge of sin (Rom 7:7-9). One would have to conclude that Adam knew the goodness of God before the Fall, but not evil until he fell. Hence, the "moral law" of God was written on man's heart at the Fall.)

1 Timothy 1:8-11 now becomes for us a vital text in the whole question surrounding the utility of the Decalogue *(yet the opening sentence of this article admits the 10th Word is not included – contradicting the assertion that the Decalogue is a unit – a key part of the sabbatarian argument).* According to the exposition of this text, both Christian and non-Christian are held to an ethical standard which is reflected in the Decalogue.[44] It becomes quite clear that the utility of the Decalogue transcends the Old Covenant. The Decalogue is used by Paul as the basic, fundamental law or body of ethical divinity applicable to all men. *(In 1 Tim 1 the Law of Moses is only being held up as that which condemns sinners.)* It is clear that the Decalogue has more usefulness than a temporary law governing the life of Israel under the Old Covenant. The Decalogue is transcovenantal *(One should be careful to differentiate between the totality of words Moses spoke, captured in Ex 20, and the moral principles that transcend time and covenant.).* This point is supported by considering the fact that Paul was writing to Timothy who was ministering in Asia Minor (Ephesus) where Jews and Gentiles lived and after the Old Covenant had been abolished and replaced by the New Covenant. *(This is a correlation without meaning, like Walter Chantry's observation that the Sabbath is talked about in the NT in Jewish contexts (page 52 of Call the Sabbath a Delight), thereby proving the applicability of the Sabbath to Christians.)*

The goal of this essay was to reassess 1 Timothy 1:8-11 in light of Dr. George W. Knight's seminal work on this text. *(Again – the entire aim of this essay is based on proving the Paedobaptist view of covenant theology. No serious Christian thinks there is no moral law of God that operates on man. There is simply no biblical warrant for the Roman Catholic/Paedobaptist view that the Decalogue is that moral law and binds Christians and reprobates alike or in the same way.)* The attempt has been made to build upon his work and show that his basic thesis stands: Paul's list of vices reflects both the content and order of the Decalogue from the first through the ninth commandments. This text functions as an ethical manifesto of Paul's view of the utility of the Decalogue in Christian ethics. This interpretation is reflected in the Reformed and historic Baptist view of the utility of the Decalogue as articulated by *The Baptist Confession of Faith of 1689* which reads: The moral law [Decalogue] *(The 1689 LBC does not, in 19.5 include the identification of the Decalogue as the moral law.)*

doth for ever bind all, as well justified persons. *(And here the 1689 LBC runs afoul of Scripture, as Romans 7 describes how we who have been raised to new life in Christ have died to the law and are not bound to it, as is the man whose wife has died is not bound to her.)* as others, to the obedience thereof, and that not only in regard of the matter contained in it, but also in respect of the authority of God the Creator, who gave it; neither doth Christ in the gospel any way dissolve, but much strengthen this obligation (19:5).

It is hoped that this essay will not only contribute to our understanding of 1 Timothy 1:8-11 but call Baptists and all Christians back to the ethical paths of our theological forebears. *(Shame on Founders for failing to use historic Baptists and rest on Paedobaptists. This reveals a higher desire to cling to a confession that was built on the Westminster Confession of Faith than to reform to Scripture. And are the Paedobaptists, upon whom this entire article was constructed, "theological forebears" of us who are Baptists? I think not!)*

Appendix 5: A Biblical Defense of Predestination

When I was confronted about predestination by deacons in the church I served as pastor, I went to the Word of God to bring His Word to bear on this topic. One deacon said he would not be convinced of predestination by Scripture since he believed in man's free will and preferred the opinion of his favorite celebrity preachers to the Word of God. This broke my heart, not because they did not want me as pastor, but that professing Christians would purposely turn a deaf ear to God's Word. Nonetheless, what says the Scripture?

On Predestination:

Psalms 65:1-4

Praise is due to you, O God, in Zion,
to you shall vows be performed.
O you who hear prayer,
to you shall all flesh come.
When iniquities prevail against me,
you atone for our transgressions.
Blessed is the one you choose and bring near,
to dwell in your courts!
We shall be satisfied with the goodness of your house,
the holiness of your temple!

Psalm 139:13-16 (HCSB) *For it was You who created my inward parts; You knit me together in my mother's womb. I will praise You because I have been remarkably and wonderfully made. Your works are wonderful, and I know [this] very well. My bones were not hidden from You when I was made in secret, when I was formed in the depths of the earth. Your eyes saw me when I was formless; all [my] days were written in Your book and planned before a single one of them began.*

Matthew 25:31-34 *When the Son of Man comes in his glory, and all the angels with him, then he will sit on his glorious throne. Before him will be gathered all the nations, and he will separate people one from another as a shepherd separates the sheep from the goats. And he will place the sheep on his right, but the goats on the left. Then the King will say to those on his right, 'Come, you who are blessed by my Father, inherit the kingdom prepared for you from the foundation of the world.*

John 1:11-13 *He came to his own, and his own people did not receive him. But to all who did receive him, who believed in his name, he gave the right to become children of God, who were born, not of blood nor of the will of the flesh nor of the will of man, but of God.*

John 3:6-8 *That which is born of the flesh is flesh, and that which is born of the Spirit is spirit. Do not marvel that I said to you, 'You must be born again.' The wind blows where it wishes, and you hear its sound, but you do not know where it comes from or where it goes. So it is with everyone who is born of the Spirit."*

John 10:25-30 *Jesus answered them, "I told you, and you do not believe. The works that I do in my Father's name bear witness about me, but you do not believe because you are not among my sheep. My sheep hear my voice, and I know them, and they follow me. I give them eternal life, and they will never perish, and no one will snatch them out of my hand. My Father, who has given them to me, is greater than all, and no one is able to snatch them out of the Father's hand. I and the Father are one."*

John 15:15-17 *No longer do I call you servants, for the servant does not know what his master is doing; but I have called you friends, for all that I have heard from my Father I have made known to you. You did not choose me, but I chose you and appointed you that you should go and bear fruit and that your fruit should abide, so that whatever you ask the Father in my name, he may give it to you. These things I command you, so that you will love one another.*

Acts 13:44 - 48 (HSCB) *The following Sabbath almost the whole town assembled to hear the message of the Lord. But when the Jews saw the crowds, they were filled with jealousy and began to oppose what Paul was saying by insulting him. Then Paul and Barnabas boldly said: "It was necessary that God's message be spoken to you first. But since you reject it and consider yourselves unworthy of eternal life, we now turn to the Gentiles! For this is what the Lord has commanded us:*

I have made you
a light for the Gentiles
to bring salvation
to the ends of the earth."

When the Gentiles heard this, they rejoiced and glorified the message of the Lord, and all who had been appointed to eternal life believed.

Romans 8:28-30 *And we know that for those who love God all things work together for good, for those who are called according to his purpose. For those whom he foreknew he also predestined to be conformed to the image of his Son, in order that he might be the firstborn among many brothers. And those whom he predestined he also called, and those whom he called he also justified, and those whom he justified he also glorified.*

Romans 9:9-13 *For this is what the promise said: "About this time next year I will return, and Sarah shall have a son." And not only so, but also when Rebekah had conceived children by one man, our forefather Isaac, though they were not yet born and had done nothing either good or bad—in order that God's purpose of election might continue, not because of works but because of him who calls—she was told, "The older will serve the younger." As it is written, "Jacob I loved, but Esau I hated."*

Ephesians 1:3-6 *Blessed be the God and Father of our Lord Jesus Christ, who has blessed us in Christ with every spiritual blessing in the heavenly places, even as he chose us in him before the foundation of the world, that we should be holy and blameless before him. In love he predestined us for adoption as sons through Jesus Christ, according to the purpose of his will, to the praise of his glorious grace, with which he has blessed us in the Beloved.*

Ephesians 1:11-14 *In him we have obtained an inheritance, having been predestined according to the purpose of him who works all things according to the counsel of his will, so that we who were the first to hope in Christ might be to the praise of his glory. In him you also, when you heard the word of truth, the gospel of your salvation, and believed in him, were sealed with the promised Holy Spirit, who is the guarantee of our inheritance until we acquire possession of it, to the praise of his glory.*

2 Timothy 1:9 & 10 (HSCB) *He has saved us and called us with a holy calling, not according to our works, but according to His own purpose and grace, which was given to us in Christ Jesus before time began. This has now been made evident through the appearing of our Savior Christ Jesus, who has abolished death and has brought life and immortality to light through the gospel.*

Titus 1:1 – 4 *Paul, a servant of God and an apostle of Jesus Christ, for the sake of the faith of God's elect and their knowledge of the truth, which accords with godliness, in hope of eternal life, which God, who never lies, promised before the ages began and at the proper time manifested in his word through the preaching with which I have been entrusted by the command of God our Savior; To Titus, my true child in a common faith: Grace and peace from God the Father and Christ Jesus our Savior.*

Titus 3:4 – 7 *But when the goodness and loving kindness of God our Savior appeared, he saved us, not because of works done by us in righteousness, but according to his own mercy, by the washing of regeneration and renewal of the Holy Spirit, whom he poured out on us richly through Jesus Christ our Savior, so that being justified by his grace we might become heirs according to the hope of eternal life.*

James 1:16-18 *Do not be deceived, my beloved brothers. Every good gift and every perfect gift is from above, coming down from the Father of lights with whom there is no variation or shadow due to change. Of his own will he brought us forth by the word of truth, that we should be a kind of firstfruits of his creatures.*

Revelation 13:5-8 *And the beast was given a mouth uttering haughty and blasphemous words, and it was allowed to exercise authority for forty-two months. It opened its mouth to utter blasphemies against God, blaspheming his name and his dwelling, that is, those who dwell in heaven. Also it was allowed to make war on the saints and to conquer them. And authority was given it over every tribe and people and language and nation, and all who dwell on earth will worship it, everyone whose name has not been written before the foundation of the world in the book of life of the Lamb who was slain.*

Revelation 17:6-8 *And I saw the woman, drunk with the blood of the saints, the blood of the martyrs of Jesus. When I saw her, I marveled greatly. But the angel said to me, "Why do you marvel? I will tell you the mystery of the woman, and of the beast with seven heads and ten horns that carries her. The beast that you saw was, and is not, and is about to rise from the bottomless pit and go to destruction. And the dwellers on earth whose names have not been written* *in the book of life from the foundation of the world will marvel to see the beast, because it was and is not and is to come.*

On man's inability:

Ecclesiastes 7:20 *Surely there is not a righteous man on earth who does good and never sins.*

Isaiah 64:7 *There is no one who calls upon your name, who rouses himself to take hold of you; for you have hidden your face from us, and have made us melt in the hand of our iniquities.*

Jeremiah 10:23 *I know, O LORD, that the way of man is not in himself, that it is not in man who walks to direct his steps.*

Romans 3:9-12 *What then? Are we Jews any better off? No, not at all. For we have already charged that all, both Jews and Greeks, are under sin, as it is written: "None is righteous, no, not one; no one understands; no one seeks for God. All have turned aside; together they have become worthless; no one does good, not even one."*

Romans 9:19-24 *You will say to me then, "Why does he still find fault? For who can resist his will?" But who are you, O man, to answer back to God? Will what is molded say to its molder, "Why have you made me like this?" Has the potter no right over the clay, to make out of the same lump one vessel for honorable use and another for dishonorable use? What if God, desiring to show his wrath and to make known his power, has endured with much patience vessels of wrath prepared for destruction, in order to make known the riches of his glory for vessels of mercy, which he has prepared beforehand for glory — even us whom he has called, not from the Jews only but also from the Gentiles?*

Ephesians 2:1-3 *And you were dead in the trespasses and sins in which you once walked, following the course of this world, following the prince of the power of the air, the spirit that is now at work in the sons of disobedience — among whom we all once lived in the passions of our flesh, carrying out the desires of the body and the mind, and were by nature children of wrath, like the rest of mankind.*

Ephesians 2:8-9 *For by grace you have been saved through faith. And this is not your own doing; it is the gift of God, not a result of works, so that no one may boast.*

1 John 5:11-12 *And this is the testimony, that God gave us eternal life, and this life is in his Son. Whoever has the Son has life; whoever does not have the Son of God does not have life.*

God saves, not man:

John 6:36-40 *But I said to you that you have seen me and yet do not believe. All that the Father gives me will come to me, and whoever comes to me I will never cast out. For I have come down from heaven, not to do my own will but the will of him who sent me. And this is the will of him who sent me, that I should lose nothing of all that he has given me, but raise it up on the last day. For this is the will of my Father, that everyone who looks on the Son and believes in him should have eternal life, and I will raise him up on the last day."*

John 6:44 *"No one can come to me unless the Father who sent me draws him. And I will raise him up on the last day."*

John 17:1-2 *When Jesus had spoken these words, he lifted up his eyes to heaven, and said, "Father, the hour has come; glorify your Son that the Son may glorify you, since you have given him authority over all flesh, to give eternal life to all whom you have given him.*

John 17:25-26 *O righteous Father, even though the world does not know you, I know you, and these know that you have sent me. I made known to them your name, and I will continue to make it known, that the love with which you have loved me may be in them, and I in them."*

Titus 3:4-7 *But when the goodness and loving kindness of God our Savior appeared, he saved us, not because of works done by us in righteousness, but according to his own mercy, by the washing of regeneration and renewal of the Holy Spirit, whom he poured out on us richly through Jesus Christ our Savior, so that being justified by his grace we might become heirs according to the hope of eternal life.*

Romans 9:14-18 *What shall we say then? Is there injustice on God's part? By no means! For he says to Moses, "I will have mercy on whom I have mercy, and I will have compassion on whom I have compassion." So then it depends not on human will or exertion, but on God, who has mercy. For the Scripture says to Pharaoh, "For this very purpose I have raised you up, that I might show my power in you, and that my name might be proclaimed in all the earth." So then he has mercy on whomever he wills, and he hardens whomever he wills.*

1 Peter 1:18-21 *knowing that you were ransomed from the futile ways inherited from your forefathers, not with perishable things such as silver or gold, but with the precious blood of Christ, like that of a lamb without blemish or spot. He was foreknown before the foundation of the world but was made manifest in the last times for the sake of you who through him are believers in God, who raised him from the dead and gave him glory, so that your faith and hope are in God.*

This doctrine is so clearly taught in Scripture that we must bow to it and seek to understand passages less clear than seem to go against it. An honest examination of Scripture and self will expose our natural desire to bring God low and exalt self. Brothers, this should not be so with us!

Appendix 6: The Old Covenant Compared to the New Covenant

Throughout the Church Age, there have been many religious institutions and groups that have advocated the keeping of certain Old Testament laws. The two most popular O.T. laws today are tithing and sabbath keeping. Some groups take the concept so far as to wear fringes on their underwear! We realize that there is nothing wrong with someone setting aside money or time to the Lord, but there is something wrong with using Old Testament laws as the basis for doing so. Christians are to rely on the Holy Spirit for our direction and not the Mosaic Law. The following table shows conclusively that the Mosaic Law has ended and is no longer in effect, and that the Law of the Spirit is the present manifestation of God's direction for our lives.

Mosaic Covenant	New Covenant
Old covenant II Cor. 3:14	New covenant II Cor. 3:6
First covenant Heb. 8:7, 9:1	Second covenant Heb. 8:7, 10:1-9
Came by Moses John 1:17	Came by Christ Heb. 8:6, 9:15
Law of Moses Acts 13:38-39	Law of Christ Gal. 6:2
Law of sin Rom. 7:5-6	Law of righteousness Rom. 9:30-31
Law of the flesh Rom. 7:5-6	Law of the Spirit Rom. 8:2
Not of faith Gal. 3:2	Law of faith Rom. 3:27
Yoke of bondage Gal. 5:1	Law of liberty Jam. 1:25
Ended by Christ Rom. 10:4	Established by Christ Heb. 8:6, 10:9
Law of death II Cor. 3:7	Law of life Gal. 3:11, 6:8
Entangles Gal. 5:1	Makes free John 8:32, 36
A shadow Col. 2:14-17	The reality Heb. 10:1-18
Fulfilled Mat. 5:17-18	Now in force Heb. 8:6, 10:9

Leaves imperfect Heb. 7:19	Makes perfect Heb. 7:19
Glorious II Cor. 3:7	More glorious II Cor. 3:8-10
Powerless to save Heb. 9:9, 10:4	Saves to uttermost Heb. 7:25
Many sacrifices Heb. 9:12-13	One sacrifice for sin Heb. 10:12
Temporary priest Heb. 7:23	Eternal priest Heb. 7:17
Remembers sins Heb. 10:3	Forgets sins Heb. 8:12, 10:17
Yearly atonement Heb. 10:3	Eternal atonement Heb. 10:14
Priests have sin Heb. 5:1-4	Sinless priest Heb. 7:26
Aaronic priesthood >Heb. 7:11	Melchisedec priesthood Heb. 5:5-10, 7:21
Out of Levi Heb 7:11	Out of Judah Heb. 7:14
Animal sacrifices Heb. 9:12	Human sacrifice Heb. 9:14-28
Earthly tabernacle Heb. 9:2	Heavenly tabernacle Heb. 8:2
Imperfect mediator Gal. 3:19	Sinless mediator I Tim. 2:5
No inheritance Rom. 4:13	Eternal inheritance Heb. 9:15
Instituted upon animal blood Heb. 9:16-22	Instituted upon blood of Christ Mat. 26-28
Law of works Rom. 3:27	Law of grace and faith John 1:17
Works wrath Rom. 4:15	Saves from wrath Rom. 5:9
Non-redeeming Heb. 10:4	Redeems Gal. 3:13, Heb. 9:12-15
Non-pleasing Ps. 40:6	Pleasing to God Heb 10:5-18
Abolishment predicted Is. 51:6	Establishment predicted Heb. 8:7
Circumcision Ex. 12:48	No circumcision Rom. 4:9-12
Made to change Heb. 7:12, Gal. 3:25	Made eternal Heb. 13:20
Faulty Heb. 8:7	Perfect James 1:25

Weak Heb. 7:18	Strong Heb. 7:25
Unprofitable Heb. 7:18	Profitable Heb. 7:19,25
Natural program Heb. 9:10-14	Spiritual program II Cor. 3:6, 18
Daily program Heb. 7:27	Finished program Heb. 10:10-18
Infirm high priests Heb. 5:2, 7:28	Perfect high priest Heb. 7:26
Made priests by law Heb. 7:12, 28	Made priest by an oath Heb. 7:21, 28
No salvation Heb. 10:2-4	Eternal salvation Heb. 5:9, 10:10
Perfected nothing Heb. 7:19	Perfects believers Heb. 7:19, 10:14
Earthly priests Heb. 5:1-4	Heavenly priest Heb. 9:24, 10:12
Repeated inability Heb. 10:11	Glorious success Heb. 10:10-18
Many offerings Heb. 9:7	One offering Heb. 10:10-14
Good promises Dt. 28:1-14	Better promises Heb. 8:6
A good covenant Rom 7:12	A better covenant Heb. 7:22, 8:6
Many high priests Heb. 7:23	One high priest Heb. 7:24-28
Typical tabernacle Heb. 9	True tabernacle Heb. 8:2, 9:11
No mercy Heb. 10:28	Complete mercy Heb. 8:12
Handmade things Heb. 9:1-5, 24	Not handmade Heb. 9:23-24
An old way Heb. 8:13	New and living way Heb. 10:19-20
Unavailing ministers Heb. 7:18	Able ministers II Cor. 3:6
Carnal ministry Heb. 9:9-10	Spiritual ministry II Cor. 3:6
Ministration of condemnation II Cor. 3:9	Ministration of righteousness II Cor. 3:9
Glory covered II Cor. 3:13	Glory uncovered II Cor. 3:18
Brings bondage Gal. 4:24-25	Brings liberty II Cor. 3:17
Cannot justify Gal. 2:16	Does justify Acts 13:38-39

Brings a curse Gal. 3:10	Redeems from the curse Gal. 3:13
Live by works Gal 3:10	Live by faith Gal. 3:11
Cannot give life Gal. 3:21	Does give life John 6:63-68
Exposes sin Gal 3:19	Covers sin Rom. 4:1-8
Under law Rom 6:14-15	Under grace Gal. 3:22-25
Done away II Cor. 3:7-14	Not done away II Cor. 3:11
Abolished II Cor. 3:13	Continues glorious II Cor. 3:11
Ministry of death II Cor. 3:7	Reconciliation ministry II Cor. 5:18
For Israel only Dt. 4:7-8, 5:3	For all men Luke 22:20, Mark 14:24

Mixing the Old Covenant with the New is liking mixing the blood of bulls and goats with the blood of Christ. Foolish Christians, who has bewitched you?!
(Gal. 3:1)

Posted here: http://www.tentmaker.org/tracts/OldVsNewCovenant.html

Beware – site is based on "Christian Universalism" heresy

Notes

Chapter 1

1. Sam Storms, "Zwingli and Anabaptists," (2009) accessed 9 June 2016, http://www.samstorms.com/all-articles/post/zwingli-and-anabaptists/
2. Henry Clay Vedder, *Balthasar Hübmaier: the leader of the Anabaptists*, page 35.
3. Ibid, pages 35 – 37
4. Ibid, pages 37 – 39. Montanism was founded by a man named Montanus, who declared he was a prophet, speaking with the voice of the Paraclete, the "helper" that Christ had promised to send.
5. Ibid, pages 38 & 39
6. Ibid, page 40
7. For the sake of clarity, the adjectives General and Particular refer to the doctrine of atonement held by each group, as they declared their answer to the question, "For whom did Christ die?" Particular Baptists see the atonement being applied to the particular people God has chosen before time to redeem. General Baptists see the atonement being applied to people in general, with each person having opportunity to be saved.
8. Maxcey, Zachary S., Providence Theological Seminary Journal, Issue 1, Nov 2014, "Historical Forerunners of New Covenant Theology", citing Glenn H. Stassen, "Anabaptist Influence in the Origin of the Particular Baptist," *The Mennonite Quarterly* 36:4 (1962): 341-343
9. Goadby, Joseph Jackson, *Bye-paths in Baptist history**, page 72, Bracketed comments are from this author.
10. Vedder, Henry Clay, *A Short History of the Baptists**, Introduction
11. Ibid, pages 110-111

Chapter 2

1. Brunson, Hal, *The Rickety Bridge and the Broken Mirror*, pages xiii - xv
2. Such was the case with Constantine, who refused to be baptized until he was on his death bed. Eusebius, *Life of Constantine*, page 147
3. This theme is woven throughout much of Andrew Miller's *Short Papers on Church History**.
4. Adams, John Quincy, *Baptists, the Only Thorough Reformers*, page 92, Free Grace Publisher
5. Clark, John, *Defense of Credo-Baptism**, item 4
6. William R, Downing, *Believer's Baptism By Immersion**, page 4
7. Johnson, Jeffrey D. *The Fatal Flaw of the Theology Behind Infant Baptism*, Introduction, Free Grace Publisher
8. Brunson, Hal, *The Rickety Bridge and the Broken Mirror*, page 60
9. Ibid, page 63
10. Ibid, page 64
11. http://www.ewtn.com/library/THEOLOGY/PROBMASS.HTM accessed 30 March 2015
12. D'Aubigne, J.H. Merle, *History Of The Reformation Of The Sixteenth Century**, Volume 3, page 255, Sprinkle Publications, 2003)

13. Brunson, Hal, *The Rickety Bridge and the Broken Mirror,* page 71
14. Gill, John, Commentary on Matthew 26:23*
15. Meyer, http://biblehub.com/commentaries/matthew/26-26.htm accessed 9 June 2016
16. Ditzel, http://www.wordofhisgrace.org/lordssupperelements1.html accessed 7 Oct 2015
17. Johnson, Jeffrey D. email, 8 April 2015
18. Lyons, Louis, email, 5 April 2015
19. Gill, John, *A Body of Practical Divinity** - Book 3, chapter 2
20. Ibid
21. Ibid
22. Ibid
23. Quotes in the section above are taken from Gill, John, *A Body of Practical Divinity** - Book 3, chapter 2
24. O'Hare, Terrence D., *The Sabbath Complete,* pages 237 ff
25. Gibbs, Alfred, *The Lord's Supper*, page 186

Chapter 3
1. Schaff, Philip, *History of the Christian Church**, Volume II: Ante-Nicene Christianity. A.D. 100-325*, § 42. Clergy and Laity
2. Howell, Robert Boyt C., *The Deaconship**, Chapter 1
3. Witmer, Timothy Z., *The Shepherd Leader: Achieving Effective Shepherding in Your Church,*
4. Semper Reformanda Conference, October 2012, Houston, TX
5. Zanchius, Jerome, *Absolute Predestination**, page 59, Free Grace Press
6. Hobbs, http://www.brenthobbs.com/index_files/john_3_16.php accessed 25 May 2015
7. Lashua, http://www.freegracealliance.com/pdf/Some%20Insights%20on%20the%20Practical%20Implications%20of.pdf, accessed on 9 May 2014
8. Mbewe, http://www.conradmbewe.com/2015/04/the-new-birth-and-conversionwhat-comes.html accessed 9 June 2016

Part 2 – Introduction
1. http://www.wts.edu/lifelong/what_is_reformed_theology.html, accessed 7 Jan 2015

Chapter 4
1. Foxe, John, *The Acts and Monuments*, book 8, The Unabridged Acts and Monuments Online or TAMO (1583 edition) (HRI Online Publications, Sheffield, 2011). Available from: http//www.johnfoxe.org, accessed: 7 December 2014
2. Grudem, Wayne, *Systematic Theology*, Chapter 7
3. 21st century Gnosticism: http://magdalenecommunity.blogspot.com/ accessed 1 Jan 2015

4. Modern day Roman Catholicism: http://www.rosary-center.org/fatima.htm accessed 1 Jan 2015
5. Josh McDowell's book, *The New Evidence That Demands a Verdict*, is an excellent reference and great encouragement to the Christian. It is not a witnessing tool to be given to lost people.
6. Cyril of Jerusalem (A.D. 315-386) NPNF2, Vol. 7, Catechetical Lectures 4:17*
7. Martin, Robert, *Accuracy of Translation*, page 14
8. Ibid, page 20
9. Ibid, page 70
10. Hodge, Charles, *Systematic Theology*, Vol. 1, pages 113-114
11. Ibid, chapter 6, The Protestant Rule of Faith, pg 151 – 152): *Perspicuity of the Scriptures. The Right of Private Judgment.*
12. Ibid, page 187
13. O'Hare, Terrence D., *The Sabbath Complete*, pages 225 – 232
14. Ibid, page 230
15. Ibid, page 231
16. Patient, Thomas, *Discourse on Baptism and the Distinctiveness of the Covenants*
17. Spurgeon, C.H., "A Defense of Calvinism*," page 3
18. Custance, Arthur C. *The Sovereignty of Grace*, pages 363, 364
19. James M. Boice & Philip G. Ryken, *The Doctrines of Grace*, page 33

Chapter 5
1. http://www.arbca.com/arbca-constitution accessed 17 Feb 2015
2. http://www.arbca.com/frequently-asked-questions accessed 17 Feb 2015
3. Riddlebarger, http://kimriddlebarger.squarespace.com/ promoting a conference on the end times, to be held April 16, 2016; accessed 8 April 2016
4. I personally experienced this, having been trained and tested for eldership in a 1689 church. When I asked if I was qualified to serve, other than my inability to fully subscribe to the 1689 LBC, I was asked if I meant qualifications like Titus 3. When I answered in the affirmation, I was told that they hadn't thought of it in those terms.
5. D'Aubigne, J.H. Merle, *History Of The Reformation Of The Sixteenth Century*, Volume 3, page 30, Sprinkle Publications, 2003
6. C.H. Spurgeon, "The London Baptist Confession of Faith of 1689," accessed 10 Jun 2016, https://www.monergism.com/london-baptist-confession-faith-1689-ebook
7. Goadby, Joseph Jackson, *Bye-Paths in Baptist History* page 106, 1871
8. Renihan, http://www.reformedreader.org/ctf.htm accessed 9 June 2016
9. Ibid
10. Ibid
11. Ibid
12. Goadby, Joseph Jackson, *Bye-Paths in Baptist History* page 96, 1871
13. Ivey, Michael N. *A Welsh Succession of Primitive Baptist Faith and Practice*, pages 29 & 30

14. Ibid, pages 30 – 32

15. Copeland, Kenneth, *The Price of It All*, page 4

Chapter 6

1. Gonzales, http://drbobgonzales.com/2014/01/09/the-danger-of-reformed-traditionalism/ accessed 9 January 2014

2. Waters, Guy Prentiss, *EP Study Commentary on Acts*, page 9

3. D'Aubigne, J.H. Merle, *History Of The Reformation Of The Sixteenth Century**, Volume IV, page 89, Sprinkle Publications, 2003

4. C.H. Spurgeon, "The London Baptist Confession of Faith of 1689," accessed 10 Jun 2016, https://www.monergism.com/london-baptist-confession-faith-1689-ebook

5. Reisinger, John G. *Tablets of Stone & The History of Redemption*, New Covenant Media, 2004, page 142

6. Ibid, page 145

7. Barcellos, http://www.1689federalism.com/john-owen-and-new-covenant-theology/ accessed 9 Jun 2016

8. Chantry, Walter, *Call the Sabbath a Delight*, page 25

9. O'Hare, Terrence D. *The Sabbath Complete*, page 264

10. Schreiner, Thomas, *40 Questions About Christians and Biblical Law*, page 200

11. Lehrer, Steve, *New Covenant Theology*, page 159

12. Schaff, Philip, *History of the Christian Church**, vol.II, page 203

13. Ante-Nicene Fathers, *Dialogue With Trypho the Jew**, 150-165 AD, vol. 1, page 204

14. Gill, John, Commentary, Revelation 1:10*

15. O'Hare, Terrence D. *The Sabbath Complete*, pages 329 – 330

16. Ibid, page 330

17. Ibid, page 321

18. Ibid, page 321

19. Jamieson-Faucet-Brown Bible Commentary, Leviticus 23:3

20. O'Hare, Terrence D. *The Sabbath Complete*, page 289

21. D'Aubigne, J.H. Merle, *History Of The Reformation Of The Sixteenth Century**, Volume 2, page 33, Sprinkle Publications, 2003

22. McHugh, http://www.cnsnews.com/commentary/paul-mchugh/johns-hopkins-psychiatrist-it-starkly-nakedly-false-sex-change-possible accessed 19 Jun 2015

23. D'Aubigne, J.H. Merle, *History Of The Reformation Of The Sixteenth Century**, Volume 1, page 297, Sprinkle Publications, 2003

24. Ibid, Volume 2, page 119

25. Brewer, Jehoida (1752-1817), Hiding Place, as revised by Matthew Smith, 2014 http://matthewsmith.bandcamp.com/album/hiding-place

26. Zanchius, Jerome, *Absolute Predestination**, page 59, Free Grace Press

27. Hobbs, http://www.brenthobbs.com/index_files/john_3_16.php accessed 25 May 2015

28. Lashua, http://www.freegracealliance.com/pdf/Some%20Insights%20on%20the%20Practical%20Implications%20of.pdf, accessed on 9 May 2014

29. Mbewe, http://www.conradmbewe.com/2015/04/the-new-birth-and-conversionwhat-comes.html accessed 9 June 2016

30. Pendleton, James, *Formative and Corrective discipline**, chapter 6

31. Ibid

32. Ibid

33. Savage, Eleazer, *Formative and Corrective discipline**,

34. Keach, Benjamin, *The Glory of a True Church**, page 71

35. Long, Gary, *New Covenant Theology*, page 18

36. Atherstone, http://biblicalstudies.org.uk/pdf/anvil/26-1_031.pdf accessed 26 April 2015

Part 3 – Introduction

1. Spurgeon, C.H. Sermon 3326 – The Wondrous Covenant*

2. Reisinger, John G. *Abraham's Four Seeds*, page 57

3. Sproul, R.C. "Terms for the Covenant", http://www.ligonier.org/learn/articles/terms-covenant/, accessed 13 January, 2016

4. Reisinger, John G. *Abraham's Four Seeds*, page 28

Chapter 7

1. Keach, Benjamin, *The Display of Glorious Grace**, Sermon I,

2. Barnes, Albert, *Notes on the New Testament*,

3. Pink, A.W. *Divine Covenants**, page 12 – The Everlasting Covenant

Chapter 8

1. The view that God's redemptive plan preceded creation and, by extension, the Fall.

2. Whitefield, George, "Method of Grace," http://www.biblebb.com/files/whitefield/GW058.htm

3. Gentry and Wellum, *Kingdom Through Covenant*, page 156

4. Pink, A.W. *The Divine Covenants**, chapter 2

5. Owen, John Commentary on Hebrews 8:6,

6. Keach, Benjamin, *Display of Glorious Grace**, Sermon I,

7. Ibid

8. Bunyan, John, *The Doctrine of Law and Grace Unfolded**, page 66

9. Jamieson-Fausset-Brown, *A Commentary: Critical, Experimental, and Practical on the Old and New Testaments*. Galatians 3

10. Luther, Martin, *A Commentary on St. Paul's Epistle to the Galatians*

11. Lehrer, Steve, *New Covenant Theology*, page 85

12. Johnson, Jeffrey D. *The Fatal Flaw of the Theology Behind Infant Baptism*, page 210

13. Denault, Pascal, *The Distinctiveness of Baptist Covenant Theology*, pages 116 & 117

14. Reisinger, John G. *Abraham's Four Seeds*, page 61

15. Ibid, chapter 2

16. Ibid, page 35

17. Ibid, page 74

18. O'Hare, Terrence D. *The Sabbath Complete*, page 7

19. Denault, Pascal, *The Distinctiveness of Baptist Covenant Theology*, page 131

20. Gill, John, Commentary on Jeremiah 33, Introduction

21. Lehrer, Steve, *New Covenant Theology*, page 89

22. Maxcey, Zachary S. Questions Surrounding New Covenant Theology: Popular & Doctrinal, PTSJ Issue #4, Jan 2016

23. Section was taken from John G. Reisinger's *The Four Seeds of Abraham*, pages 40 – 43, with quoted remarks taken directly from that work.

24. Walvoord, John F. *Major Bible Themes*, Academic Books, page 145

25. Pitchford, Nathin, in an article entitled "Dispensationalism was destructive to my ability to grasp the unity and significance of the biblical story" describes how he found clarity in Scripture when he left John Darby behind, located at http://www.reformationtheology.com/2006/06/dispensationalism_and_the_ecli_1.php

26. Kelley, Joe W. The New and Better Covenant in Hebrews 7 & 8, PTSJ, Jan 2016

27. Coxe, Nehemiah, *Discourse on the Covenants**, pages 48 – 49

28. Hodge, Charles, *Systematic Theology* Vol III*, page 555

29. Keach, Benjamin, *Display of Glorious Grace**, Sermon I

30. Denault, Pascal, *The Distinctiveness of Baptist Covenant Theology*, page 141

31. O'Hare, Terrence D. *The Sabbath Complete*, page 46

32. Denault, Pascal, *The Distinctiveness of Baptist Covenant Theology*, pages 56 – 57

33. Spilsbery, John, *A Treatise Concerning the Lawful Subject of Baptism**, The Church Under the Old Covenant Contrasted with The Church Under the New Covenant, 1652

34. Patient, Thomas, *Doctrine of Baptism and the Distinctiveness of the Covenants**, opening of chapter 9

35. For a more complete review of this topic, see Pascal Denault's *The Distinctiveness of Baptist Covenant Theology*, chapter 2.

36. Coxe, Nehemiah, *Discourse on the Covenants**, page 91

37. Seiver, https://truthunchanging.wordpress.com/2011/11/15/the-sign-and-seal-of-the-new-covenant-luke-2220/ accessed 15 Jul 2015

38. Johnson, Jeffrey D. *The Fatal Flaw of the Theology Behind Infant Baptism*, page 164

39. gKeach, Benjamin, *The Display of Glorious Grace**, Sermon IX

40. Francis, Turretin, *Institutes of Elenctic Theology*, vol 2, page 232

41. Ibid

42. For more on this topic, see Pascal Denault's *The Distinctiveness of Baptist Covenant Theology*, chapter 4.

43. Schreiner, Thomas, *40 Questions about Christians and Biblical Law*, page 189

44. Ibid, page 204

45. Poythress, Vern S. *The Shadow of Christ in the Law*, unpublished manuscript, page 98

46. Denault, Pascal, *The Distinctiveness of Baptist Covenant Theology*, page 38

47. http://www.britannica.com/topic/antinomianism accessed 23 March 2016

48. http://www.theopedia.com/antinomianism, accessed 23 March 2016

49. http://bjorkbloggen.com/2013/11/20/gods-everlasting-or-eternal-covenant-with-israel-was-broken/ accessed 26 March 2016

50. Reisinger, John G. *Tablets of Stone & The History of Redemption*, New Covenant Media, 2004, page 48

51. Ibid, page 49

52. Reisinger, John G. *Abraham's Four Seeds*, Chapter 11

Chapter 10

1. http://hirr.hartsem.edu/research/fastfacts/fast_facts.html#sizecong accessed 24 April 2016

2. Cowan, Steven B. editor, *Who Runs the Church?: 4 Views on Church Government (Counterpoints: Church Life)*, page 216

3. Details available at http://www.drurywriting.com/keith/sunday.school.history.htm accessed 15 June 2016

4. Lifeway article available at http://www.lifeway.com/lwc/files/lwcF_pdf_VBS_2010_Assoc_Res_HISTORY_OF_VBS.pdf accessed 15 June 2016

Chapter 11

1. This practice was documented in a now out-of-print booklet published by Broadman, entitled, "How To Join A Baptist Church" and found on some Baptist church websites.

2. Johnson, Jeffrey D. *The Church - Why Bother?*, page 97

3. Ibid, pages 99 & 100

4. An example found here: http://www.independencebaptist.org/Online%20Books/The%20Church%20Covenant.pdf accessed 11 June 2016

5. O'Hare, Terrence D. *The Sabbath Complete*, page 235

6. Ibid

Chapter 12

1. Johnson, Jeffrey D. *The Church – Why Bother?*, page 23

2. Guide to the Stone Chapel, located on http://www.laniertheologicallibrary.net/ accessed 15 June 2013

3. Smith, T. Roger and Slater, John *Classic and Early Christian Architecture** ebook position 249.2

4. Hamlin, Talbot, *Architecture Through the Ages*, (New York: G.P. Putnam's Sons, 1953) page 187

5. Ibid, page 190

6. Smith, T. Roger and Slater, John *Classic and Early Christian Architecture** ebook position 262.6

7. After hurricane Katrina hit New Orleans in 2005, two of my personal friends who did not know each other attended a large gathering where plans were made on how Houston would help the refugees from New Orleans. Each of these men told me that they heard Ed Young, "senior pastor" of 2nd Baptist Church in Houston, declare during that meeting that Muslims and Christians worshipped the same God.

8. Dever, Mark, *The Deliberate Church*, page 81

9. Phillips, http://teampyro.blogspot.com/2009/03/bible-reading-in-church.html accessed 21 May 2016

10. David Murray, "Preacher's Checklist: Selecting a Text," (2016), accessed 21 May 2016, http://headhearthand.org/blog/2016/03/08/preachers-checklist-selecting-a-text/

11. David Murray, "Preacher's Checklist: Exegeting the Text," (2016), accessed 21 May 2016, http://headhearthand.org/blog/2016/03/10/preachers-checklist-exegeting-the-text/

12. Thomas, W.H. Griffin, *HOW WE GOT OUR BIBLE** chapter 3

Chapter 13

1. Chafer, Lewis Sperry, *True Evangelism**, epub, positions 38.6 & 40.4

2. D'Aubigne, J.H. Merle, *History Of The Reformation Of The Sixteenth Century**, Volume IV, page 187, Sprinkle Publications, 2003

3. Ibid, Volume IV, page 263

Bibliography

1. A.W. Pink, *Divine Covenants**, (Grand Rapids : Baker Book House, 1973), page 12
2. Albert Barnes, *Notes on the New Testament*, accessed 12 June 2016, http://biblehub.com/commentaries/barnes/matthew/1.htm
3. Alfred Gibbs, *The Lord's Supper*, (Kansas City, Walterick, 1963), page 186
4. Andrew Atherstone, "The Implications of Semper Reformanda," (2008), accessed 26 April 2015, http://biblicalstudies.org.uk/pdf/anvil/26-1_031.pdf
5. Annikalbjork, "God's EVERLASTING (or eternal) COVENANT with Israel was broken," accessed 26 March 2016, http://bjorkbloggen.com/2013/11/20/gods-everlasting-or-eternal-covenant-with-israel-was-broken/
6. Ante-Nicene Fathers, *Dialogue With Trypho the Jew**, 150-165 AD, vol. 1, page 204
7. Arthur C. Custance, *The Sovereignty of Grace*, (Phillipsburg, N.J.: Presbyterian and Reformed, 1979), pages 363, 364
8. Association of Reformed Baptist Churches of America, "Constitution of the Association of Reformed Baptist Churches of America" (2014) accessed 17 Feb 2015, http://www.arbca.com/arbca-constitution
9. Association of Reformed Baptist Churches of America, "Frequently Asked Questions," accessed 17 Feb 2015, http://www.arbca.com/frequently-asked-questions
10. Benjamin Keach, *The Display of Glorious Grace**, Sermon I, (London, S. Bridge, 1698)
11. Benjamin Keach, *The Glory of a True Church*, (Conway, AR, Free Grace Press, 2015) page 71
12. Bob Gonzales, "The Danger of Reformed Traditionalism,"* accessed 9 January 2014, http://drbobgonzales.com/2014/01/09/the-danger-of-reformed-traditionalism/
13. Brent Hobbs, "How Did God "So" Love the World?," (2010), accessed 25 May 2015, http://www.brenthobbs.com/index_files/john_3_16.php
14. C.H. Spurgeon, "A Defense of Calvinism,"* page 3
15. C.H. Spurgeon, "The London Baptist Confession of Faith of 1689," accessed 10 Jun 2016, https://www.monergism.com/london-baptist-confession-faith-1689-ebook
16. C.H. Spurgeon, Sermon 3326 – The Wondrous Covenant
17. Charles Hodge, *Systematic Theology**, (London, Wm. B. Eerdmans, 1968), Vol. 1, pages 113-114; Vol III page 555
18. Conrad Mbewe, "The new birth and conversion—what comes first?," (2015), accessed 9 June 2016, http://www.conradmbewe.com/2015/04/the-new-birth-and-conversionwhat-comes.html

19. Cyril of Jerusalem (A.D. 315-386) NPNF2, Vol. 7, Catechetical Lectures 4:17

20. Dan Phillips, "Bible Reading in Church," (2009), accessed 21 May 2016, http://teampyro.blogspot.com/2009/03/bible-reading-in-church.html

21. David Murray, "Preacher's Checklist: Exegeting the Text," (2016), accessed 21 May 2016, http://headhearthand.org/blog/2016/03/10/preachers-checklist-exegeting-the-text/

22. David Murray, "Preacher's Checklist: Selecting a Text," (2016), accessed 21 May 2016, http://headhearthand.org/blog/2016/03/08/preachers-checklist-selecting-a-text/

23. Dominican Fathers, "The Fatima Message," accessed 1 Jan 2015, http://www.rosary-center.org/fatima.htm

24. Eleazer Savage, *Formative and Corrective discipline**, (Rochester, N.Y., Sheldon & Company, 1863),

25. Encyclopædia Britannica, "Antinomianism," accessed 23 March 2016, http://www.britannica.com/topic/antinomianism

26. Ante-Nicene Fathers, Vol 1, Eusebius, *Life of Constantine*, page 147

27. Francis Turretin, *Institutes of Elenctic Theology*, vol 2, (Phillipsburg, New Jersey, P&R Publishing, 1994), page 232

28. Peter J. Gentry, Stephen J. Wellum, *Kingdom Through Covenant*, (Wheaton, IL, Crossway, 2012), page 156

29. George Whitefield, "Method of Grace," accessed 15 June 2016, http://www.biblebb.com/files/whitefield/GW058.htm

30. Guy Prentiss Waters, *EP Study Commentary on Acts*, (Holywell, UK, EP Books, 2015), page 9

31. Hal Brunson, *The Rickety Bridge and the Broken Mirror,* (New York, iUniverse, 2007), pages xiii - xv

32. Hartford Institute, "Fast Facts about American Religion," accessed 24 April 2016, http://hirr.hartsem.edu/research/fastfacts/fast_facts.html#sizecong

33. Heinrich August Wilhelm Meyer, "Meyer's NT Commentary," accessed 9 June 2016, http://biblehub.com/commentaries/matthew/26-26.htm

34. Henry Clay Vedder, *A Short History of the Baptists**, (New York: G. P. Putnam's Sons, 1907), Introduction

35. Henry Clay Vedder, *Balthasar Hübmaier: the leader of the Anabaptists**, (New York: G. P. Putnam's Sons, 1905), page 35.

36. J.H. Merle D'Aubigne, *History Of The Reformation Of The Sixteenth Century**, Sprinkle Publications, 2003)

37. James M. Boice & Philip G. Ryken, *The Doctrines of Grace*, (Wheaton, IL, Crossway, 2009),page 33

38. James M. Renihan, "Confessing The Faith In 1644 And 1689," accessed 9 June 2016, http://www.reformedreader.org/ctf.htm

39. James Pendleton, *Formative and Corrective discipline**, (Philadelphia, The Judson Press, 1867), chapter 6

40. Jamieson-Fausset-Brown, *A Commentary: Critical, Experimental, and Practical on the Old and New Testaments.*
41. Jeffrey D. Johnson, email, 8 April 2015
42. Jeffrey D. Johnson, *The Church - Why Bother?*, ((Birmingham, AL, Solid Ground Christian Books, 2012), page 97
43. Jeffrey D. Johnson, *The Fatal Flaw of the Theology Behind Infant Baptism*, (Conway, AR, Free Grace Press, 2010), Introduction, pages 164 & 210
44. Jehoida Brewer, (1752-1817), Hiding Place, as revised by Matthew Smith, 2014 http://matthewsmith.bandcamp.com/album/hiding-place
45. Jerome Zanchius, *Absolute Predestination*, (Conway, AR, Free Grace Press, 2012), page 59
46. Joe W. Kelley, "The New and Better Covenant in Hebrews 7 & 8", (Providence Theological Seminary Journal, Jan 2016)
47. John Bunyan, *The Doctrine of Law and Grace Unfolded**, (1659), page 66
48. John Clark, *Defense of Credo-Baptism**, item 4
49. Lewis S. Chafer and John F. Walvoord, *Major Bible Themes*, (Grand Rapids, MI, Zondervan, 1974), page 145
50. Lifeway, "VBS: An Historical Perspective," (1993), accessed 15 June 2016, http://www.lifeway.com/lwc/files/lwcF_pdf_VBS_2010_Assoc_Res_HISTORY_OF_VBS.pdf
51. John Foxe, *The Acts and Monuments*, book 8, The Unabridged Acts and Monuments Online or TAMO (1583 edition) (HRI Online Publications, Sheffield, 2011), accessed 7 December 2014, Available from: http//www.johnfoxe.org
52. John G. Reisinger, *Abraham's Four Seeds*, page 57
53. John G. Reisinger, *Tablets of Stone & The History of Redemption*, (New Covenant Media, 2004), page 142
54. John Gill, *A Body of Practical Divinity** - Book 3, chapter 2
55. John Gill, Commentary, Jeremiah 33, Introduction*
56. John Gill, Commentary, Revelation 1:10*
57. Gary Long, *New Covenant Theology*, (Scotts Valley, CA, Createspace, 2013), page 10
58. John Owen, Commentary on Hebrews 8:6
59. John Quincy Adams, *Baptists, the Only Thorough Reformers**, (Conway, AR, Free Grace Press, 2014), page 92
60. John Spilsbery, *A Treatise Concerning the Lawful Subject of Baptism**, The Church Under the Old Covenant Contrasted with The Church Under the New Covenant, 1652
61. Joseph Jackson Goadby, *Bye-paths in Baptist history**, page 72
62. Kenneth Copeland, "The Price of It All", (Believer's Voice of Victory, September 1991)page 4
63. Kim Riddlebarger, "the end times," (2016), accessed 8 April 2016, http://kimriddlebarger.squarespace.com/the-latest-post/2016/4/8/know-anyone-in-the-cincinnati-area-im-speaking-on-the-end-ti.html

64. Lanier Theological Library, "Guide to the Stone Chapel," accessed 15 June 2013, http://www.laniertheologicallibrary.net/

65. Lewis Sperry Chafer, *True Evangelism**, epub, positions 38.6 & 40.4

66. Louis Lyons, email, 5 April 2015

67. M. De La Taille, "THE PERIOD OF THE SCHOOLMEN: THE SACRIFICE," accessed 30 March 2015, http://www.ewtn.com/library/THEOLOGY/PROBMASS.HTM

68. MAGDALENE COMMUNITY, "Core Beliefs," accessed 1 Jan 2015, http://magdalenecommunity.blogspot.com/

69. Mark Dever & Paul Alexander, *The Deliberate Church*, (Wheaton, IL, Crossway, 2005), page 81

70. Martin Luther, *A Commentary on St. Paul's Epistle to the Galatians*

71. Michael N. Ivey, *A Welsh Succession of Primitive Baptist Faith and Practice**, pages 29 & 30

72. Nathin Pitchford, in an article entitled "Dispensationalism was destructive to my ability to grasp the unity and significance of the biblical story" describes how he found clarity in Scripture when he left John Darby behind, located at http://www.reformationtheology.com/2006/06/dispensationalism_and_the_ecli_1.php

73. Nehemiah Coxe, *Discourse on the Covenants**, page 91

74. Pascal Denault, *The Distinctiveness of Baptist Covenant Theology*, (Birmingham, AL, Solid Ground Christian Books, 2013), pages 116 & 117

75. Patient, Thomas, *Discourse on Baptism and the Distinctiveness of the Covenants**

76. Paul McHugh, "Johns Hopkins Psychiatrist: It Is Starkly, Nakedly False That Sex Change Is Possible," (2015), accessed 19 Jun 2015, http://www.cnsnews.com/commentary/paul-mchugh/johns-hopkins-psychiatrist-it-starkly-nakedly-false-sex-change-possible

77. Peter Ditzel, "What Kind of Bread and Fruit of the Vine Are We to Use?", (2009) accessed 7 Oct 2015, http://www.wordofhisgrace.org/lordssupperelements1.html

78. Philip Schaff, *History of the Christian Church**

79. R.A. Torrey, *The Divine Origin of the Bible*, New York: Fleming H. Revell, 1899, page 38

80. R.C. Sproul, "Terms for the Covenant", located at http://www.ligonier.org/learn/articles/terms-covenant/, accessed 13 January, 2016

81. Randy Seiver, "the sign and seal of the new covenant–luke 22:20," (2011), accessed 15 Jul 2015, https://truthunchanging.wordpress.com/2011/11/15/the-sign-and-seal-of-the-new-covenant-luke-2220/

82. Richard C. Barcellos, "JOHN OWEN AND NEW COVENANT THEOLOGY," accessed 9 Jun 2016, http://www.1689federalism.com/john-owen-and-new-covenant-theology/

83. Robby Lashua, "Some Insights on the Practical Implications of Teaching Teenagers from a Free Grace Perspective," accessed on 9 May 2014, http://www.freegracealliance.com/pdf/Some%20Insights%20on%20the%20Practical%20Implications%20of.pdf

84. Robert Boyt C. Howell, *The Deaconship**, Chapter 1

85. Robert Martin, *Accuracy of Translation*, (Carlisle, PA, Banner of Truth Trust, 1989), page 14

86. Sam Storms, "Zwingli and Anabaptists," (2009) accessed 9 June 2016, http://www.samstorms.com/all-articles/post/zwingli-and-anabaptists/

87. Smith, T. Roger and Slater, John *Classic and Early Christian Architecture** ebook position 249.2

88. Steve Lehrer, *New Covenant Theology*, page 159

89. Steven B. Cowan, editor, *Who Runs the Church?: 4 Views on Church Government (Counterpoints: Church Life)*, page 216

90. T. Roger Smith and John Slater, *Classic and Early Christian Architecture** ebook position 262.6

91. Talbot Hamlin, *Architecture Through the Ages*, (New York, G.P. Putnam's Sons, 1953) page 187

92. Terrence D. O'Hare, *The Sabbath Complete*, (Eugene, OR, Wipf & Stock, 2011), pages 237 ff

93. Theopedia, "Antinomianism," accessed 23 March 2016, http://www.theopedia.com/antinomianism

94. Thomas Patient, *Doctrine of Baptism and the Distinctiveness of the Covenants**, opening of chapter 9

95. Thomas Schreiner, *40 Questions About Christians and Biblical Law*, (Grand Rapids, MI, Kregal Publications, 2010), page 200

96. Timothy Z. Witmer, *The Shepherd Leader: Achieving Effective Shepherding in Your Church*, (Phillipsburg, NJ, R&R Publishing, 2010), page

97. Vern S. Poythress, *The Shadow of Christ in the Law*, unpublished manuscript, page 98

98. W.H. Griffin Thomas, *HOW WE GOT OUR BIBLE** chapter 3

99. Walter Chantry, *Call the Sabbath a Delight*, (Carlisle, PA, Banner of Truth Trust, 1991), page 25

100. Wayne Grudem, *Systematic Theology*, (Grand Rapids, MI, Zondervan, 2000), pages 77, 78, 106, 118, 127

101. Wesleyan University, "Short History of the Sunday School," accessed 15 June 2016, http://www.drurywriting.com/keith/sunday.school.history.htm

102. Westminster Theological Seminary, "What is Reformed Theology?" accessed 7 Jan 2015, http://www.wts.edu/lifelong/what_is_reformed_theology.html

103. William R. Downing, *Believer's Baptism By Immersion**, page 4

104. Zachary S. Maxcey, "Historical Forerunners of New Covenant Theology", citing Glenn H. Stassen, "Anabaptist Influence in the Origin of the Particular Baptist," *The Mennonite Quarterly* 36:4 (1962): 341-343, (Providence Theological Seminary Journal, Issue #1, Nov 2014)

105. Zachary S. Maxcey, "Questions Surrounding New Covenant Theology: Popular & Doctrinal," (Providence Theological Seminary Journal Issue #4, Jan 2016)

PUBLISHED *by* PARABLES
Earthly Stories with a Heavenly Meaning

CPSIA information can be obtained
at www.ICGtesting.com
Printed in the USA
FFOW01n1853020417
34112FF